Financial Management Practices

India Studies in Business and Economics

For further volumes:
http://www.springer.com/series/11234

P.K. Jain • Shveta Singh • Surendra Singh Yadav

Financial Management Practices

An Empirical Study of Indian Corporates

Springer

P.K. Jain
Department of Management Studies
Indian Institute of Technology
New Delhi, India

Shveta Singh
Department of Management Studies
Indian Institute of Technology
New Delhi, India

Surendra Singh Yadav
Department of Management Studies
Indian Institute of Technology
New Delhi, India

ISBN 978-81-322-0989-8 ISBN 978-81-322-0990-4 (eBook)
DOI 10.1007/978-81-322-0990-4
Springer New Delhi Heidelberg New York Dordrecht London

Library of Congress Control Number: 2013932645

Printed on acid-free paper

Springer is part of Springer Science+Business Media (www.springer.com)

To
The Almighty
and
Our Family Members

Preface

Practice without theory is blind.
Theory without practice is sterile.

(Marx, *Contribution to the Critique of Hegel's Philosophy of Law*, Jan. 1844, MECW, Vol. 3, p. 182)

Sound financial management practices followed by a corporate are likely to have a marked bearing on its profitability, competitiveness and survival. In other words, the financial performance of an industrial enterprise, inter alia, is influenced by its financial management policies and practices. The subject assumes greater significance now than ever before for the business enterprises in view of the present dynamic and turbulent business environment.

This book is an outcome of a research study. The study has examined financial management practices of the Indian corporate sector enterprises. The analysis examines virtually all the major financial decisions. The findings of the study would have policy implications for financial system regulators, financial institutions and finance managers of corporate sector. Above all, the study perhaps is the first attempt to present a comprehensive picture of management practices in recent times in India, especially in the period after global financial crisis of 2008.

Even though there is enough information available on corporates, most of it is essentially aggregative in nature. It does not reflect the decision-making that is behind the resulting figures. For instance, it does not indicate which method of investment decision (say, net present value, internal rate of return or payback method) is followed by different companies. What approaches are adopted to incorporate project risk by them? Which are the preferred sources of raising funds? What type of dividend policy is pursued by them? In the case of their international operations, what are their hedging strategies/techniques to manage various types of risks, namely, political risk, exchange rate risk and interest rate risk?

In brief, this study is a more comprehensive update on the studies carried out in the past.

Acknowledgements

At the outsct, we would like to thank the Almighty for His blessings to inspire us to accomplish this academic endeavour. This work has been possible because of the help, encouragement, cooperation and guidance of many people, and we convey our heartfelt thanks to all of them.

Special thanks to the Modi Chair Foundation for funding the research effort. We are grateful to Prof. R. K. Shevgaonkar, director, IIT Delhi, and Prof. Surendra Prasad, ex-director, IIT Delhi, for their encouragement and support. We express our gratitude towards Prof. M. Balakrishnan (ex-DDF) and Prof. Sushil, dean (faculty), for their unstinting support. Our thanks are also due to Prof. S. N. Singh (ex-dean, IRD), Prof. Sunil Tuli, Dean (IRD), V. K. Vashistha, AR (IRD), R. K. Gupta (ex-AR, IRD Accounts), Anup Kuksal, AR (IRD Accounts) and their staff for their support for our academic endeavour.

To thank the head of the department seems to be a ritual. But it has not been so in the case of Prof. Kanika T. Bhal, Head (DMS), and Prof. S. K. Jain (ex-head, DMS). They have kept us relatively free from administrative responsibilities, enabling us to concentrate on the present study. We thank Prof. Ravi Shankar for engaging discussions from time to time and all our colleagues in the Department of Management Studies (DMS) for their good wishes for this endeavour.

In addition, we sincerely acknowledge the cooperation of all the respondents of the survey who took out time from their busy schedules to provide data for this work. We are indebted to Amarjeet Singh of SEBI and Harjit Singh Sidhu and Yasmeen of DSE for helping us in contacting companies for the survey responses.

We are grateful to our students, Trapti Moolchandani, Kartik Goel and Shubhank Goswami, for their help with the primary data collection; our research scholars Sadaf Anwar, Vandana Bhama and Rajeev Pandey and our student Anshul Mittal for their help with data processing; our staff members Vimal Kumar for his help in formatting and Rajni for her help in typing.

Dr. Shveta Singh takes this opportunity to express her deepest gratitude to her *gurus* and co-authors, Prof. P. K. Jain and Prof. Surendra S. Yadav, for their valuable guidance, inspiration, motivation and untiring efforts in completion of this project.

Prof. P. K. Jain acknowledges his wife Uma for her patience, understanding, cooperation and encouragement.

Last but not the least, we are thankful to all those, not mentioned above, who helped in carrying out the study, our family members and loved ones for their continuous encouragement and support.

P.K. Jain
Shveta Singh
Surendra S. Yadav

Contents

Abbreviations

ANOVA	Analysis of variance
ARR	Average rate of return
ATR	Acid-test ratio
BB	Bank borrowings
BRIC	Brazil, the Russian Federation, India and China
BSE	Bombay Stock Exchange
C2C	Cash-to-cash
CA	Current assets
CAPM	Capital asset pricing model
CATR	Current assets turnover ratio
CEO	Chief executive officer
CFO	Chief financial officer
CG	Corporate governance
CGR	Corporate governance ratings
CL	Current liabilities
CPP	Creditors' payment period
CR	Current ratio
CRISIL	Credit Rating and Information Services of India Limited
CSO	Central Statistics Organization
CSR	Corporate social responsibility
D/A	Total debt to total assets ratio
DCF	Discounted cash flows
DCL	Degree of combined leverage
DCP	Debtors' collection period
D/E	Debt-to-equity ratio
DFL	Degree of financial leverage
DOL	Degree of operating leverage
D/P	Dividend payout ratio
DPS	Dividend per share
DSCR	Debt service coverage ratio
EBIT	Earnings before interest and taxes

EPS	Earnings per share
EU	European Union
FAPC	Fixed assets to permanent capital
FATR	Fixed assets turnover ratio
FDI	Foreign direct investment
FG	Finished goods
FMCG	Fast-moving consumer goods
FRA	Forward rate agreements
GDP	Gross domestic product
GP	General practitioners
GPM	Gross profit margin
GVC	Governance and value creation
GWCC	Gross working capital cycle
ICR	Interest coverage ratio
ICRA	Investment Information and Credit Rating Agency of India
ICT	Information and communications technologies
IMF–FSF	International Monetary Fund–Financial Stability Forum
INR	Indian rupee
IRR	Internal rate of return
LC	Letter of credit
LTD/E	Long-term debt-to-equity ratio
LTD/TA	Long-term debt to total assets ratio
MD	Managing director
MNC	Multinational company
MPS	Market price per share
NPM	Net profit margin
NPV	Net present value
NSE	National Stock Exchange
NWC	Net working capital
NWCC	Net working capital cycle
P/B	Price to book value ratio
PI	Profitability index
PSE	Public sector enterprise
PSU	Public sector undertaking
RBI	Reserve Bank of India
RMSP	Raw material and spare parts
RoR	Rate of return
ROTA	Return on total assets
ROCE	Return on capital employed
ROSE	Return on ordinary shareholders' equity
SEBI	Securities and Exchange Board of India
SL	Secured loans
SOX	Sarbanes–Oxley Act
SPSS	Statistical Package for Social Sciences
STO/E	Short-term obligations to equity

TATR	Total assets turnover ratio
TB	Total borrowings
TEOCR	Total external obligations coverage ratio
UNCTAD	United Nations Council for Trade and Development
USA	United States of America
WACC	Weighted average cost of capital
WCM	Working capital management
WIP	Work-in-process
WTO	World Trade Organisation
ZWC	Zero working capital

List of Appendices

List of Figures

List of Tables

Part I
Background

Chapter 1
Introduction

The survival and long-term success of firms is influenced by their sound financial management policies and decisions. The subject assumes greater significance now (than ever before) for the business enterprises in view of the present dynamic and turbulent business environment.

Given the importance of sound conceptual framework in decisions related to the finance function, it would be useful to know the present practices of Indian corporates in this regard. The important questions to be addressed include which method of investment decision (say, net present value, internal rate of return or payback) is followed by the companies, what approaches are adopted to incorporate project risk by them, which are the preferred sources of raising funds, how do they manage their working capital, what type of dividend policy is pursued by them, and in the case of their international operations, what are their hedging strategies/techniques to manage various kinds of risks, namely, political, exchange rate and interest rate?

Empirical studies (conducted so far to our knowledge) that address such questions have covered only one aspect or the other of the domain of financial management. For instance, Chandra (1973) as well as Porwal and Singhvi (1978) focused on capital budgeting practices; Rao (1985) dealt with working capital management. Even recent studies do not provide a comprehensive perspective. Allen (1991) studied the capital structure of listed Australian companies. Coates et al. (1992) assessed performance measurement systems of multinational companies. Ledgerwood (1999) built a perspective on microfinance companies. Borio (1990) studied leverage and financing decisions only. Hooghiemstra (2000) examined companies engaged in corporate social reporting. Jermakowicz (2004) explored the effect of adopting international financial reporting standards for Belgium companies. Jermakowicz and Gornik-Tomaszewski (2006) further examined the effect of adopting international financial reporting standards for the European Union (EU) publicly traded companies. Wahlen et al. (2010) undertook financial statement analysis from a strategic perspective. There are a few studies (Jain and Kumar 1997; Jain and Yadav 2000, 2005) which had covered all major domains of financial management practices in India. However, these studies are more than a decade old and need to be

P.K. Jain et al., *Financial Management Practices: An Empirical Study of Indian Corporates*, India Studies in Business and Economics,
DOI 10.1007/978-81-322-0990-4_1, © Springer India 2013

updated. Thus, the authors' modest aim is to fill this research gap and, amongst others, develop a comprehensive professional index by including all major financial parameters/decisions, having a bearing on profitability and financial soundness of corporate enterprises.

Objectives

The present study aims at covering virtually all the major aspects of financial management. It also aims at conducting an inter-sectoral study (amongst the sample companies) and developing an index of professionalism in financial management based on the sample companies' practices. The primary motivation is to make this research and its findings useful for practitioners and decision-makers. This research study would, perhaps, be the first of the type which would also provide normative framework for practitioners to execute their various finance functions.

In operational terms, the present study is a modest attempt to gain insight into the financial management practices, policies and techniques followed by the select corporate enterprises.

More specifically, the main objectives of the study are as follows:

1. To identify financial management practices followed in respect of all the major financial decisions (viz. capital budgeting, capital structure, dividend policies, working capital, corporate governance, global finance and risk management).
2. To examine and evaluate consistency of empirical practices with normative framework/requirements as per theory of financial management and to suggest guidelines for practitioners based on the findings.
3. To analyse the causes of deviations, if any, depending upon availability of data.
4. To ascertain whether there has been a major change in financial performance (measured in terms of profitability) and financial policies/decisions of the sample companies over the period (2000–2001 to 2010–2011) covered by the study. There would be a special focus on a pre- and post-recession analysis.
5. To develop an index of professionalism based on the financial management practices followed by the sample companies.
6. To delve deeper into current research areas like zero working capital, real options in capital budgeting, pecking order in capital structure and clause 49[1] in corporate governance, through the financial management decisions of the sample companies.

[1]Clause 49 (based on the Sarbanes–Oxley Act (enacted in the USA) of 2002) is the number of the clause in the Listing Agreement which deals with corporate governance. Corporate governance could be defined as 'the set of systems, processes and principles which ensure that a company is governed in the best interest of all stakeholders'. The Securities and Exchange Board of India (SEBI) had initially mandated the adherence of clause 49 (for all listed companies) from 1 April 2004. However, there were modifications made to clause 49, based on the recommendations of the Narayan Murthy committee on corporate governance. The modified clause 49 came into effect from 1 January 2006 and all listed companies were mandated to adhere to clause 49 with effect from 1 April 2006 (Source: SEBI website: http://www.sebi.org/).

This monograph is based on the research undertaken to respond to the above-listed objectives. The analysis is based primarily on the secondary data collected from Capitaline database and primary data collected through a questionnaire survey.

Rationale

The study has academic as well as practical significance. The study would indirectly be helpful in bringing forth the empirical evidence regarding the level of professionalism in financial decision-making of the sample companies. Above all, the study (being diagnostic in nature) is likely to unfold the causes for not practising all or some of the normative techniques. In the light of the findings, attempt would also be made to suggest concrete measures to blend finance theory with practice. Given that the objective/focus of management research and education is to improve existing practices, then this monograph is an important link in the chain. It is also believed that the monograph would add to the body of literature in finance in a significant way as it also addresses current and emerging areas of research in financial management.

Research Methodology

Research methodology adopted in the present study to analyse financial management practices of the sample companies has been delineated hereunder.

Scope

The BSE 200 index of the Bombay Stock Exchange (BSE) comprises of the top 200 companies listed with the Bombay Stock Exchange, based on their market capitalisation. The selected sample comprised 84.32% of the total market capitalisation on the Bombay Stock Exchange, as on 1 April 2010 (Source: Bombay Stock Exchange (BSE) website. http://www.bseindia.com/about/abindices/bse200.asp). Out of these 200 companies, 34 companies were engaged in the financial sector (as on 1 April 2010, the date of sample selection). Therefore, the scope of this study is limited to the 166 non-financial BSE 200 companies engaged in manufacturing and service-rendering businesses. The sample is *representative* in nature as the BSE 200 companies represent all industry groups (Refer to Appendix 1.1 for the complete list of BSE 200 companies and Appendix 1.2 for the 34 financial companies that have been excluded from the sample for the study). The period of the study is 2000–2001 to 2010–2011.

This universe was chosen for the convenience of access to the data required and on the assumption that it would be an accurate representation of the largest firms in India. Small businesses tend to use naïve methods rather than the ones prescribed by financial theory (Block 2005; Danielson and Scott 2006), hence the focus on large firms. Also, selecting the population as large firms with a similar sampling frame to previous studies facilitated comparison with these studies.

BSE 200 Index Background

Over the years, the number of companies listed on Bombay Stock Exchange (BSE) has continued to register a phenomenal increase. Rapid growth of the market necessitated compilation of a new broad-based index series (reflecting the market trends in a more effective manner) and provided a better representation of the increased equity stocks, market capitalisation and also the new industry groups. As such, BSE launched on 27 May 1994, two new index series, BSE 200 and Dollex 200 (Source: Bombay Stock Exchange (BSE) website. http://www.bseindia.com/about/abindices/bse200.asp).

The equity shares of 200 companies were considered for inclusion in 'BSE 200' primarily on the basis of the then (1994) market capitalisation of the listed scrips; moreover, the market activity of the companies as reflected by the volumes of turnover and certain fundamental factors were also considered for the final selection of the 200 companies.

Primary Data

The primary data consists of opinions/preferences of finance managers of the sample companies related to all the major financial decisions being studied (listed in objectives).

The research instrument for primary data consisted of a questionnaire (Appendix 1.3). Minor problems with language and interpretation in some questions were addressed in the pretest. Questions designed were simple and specific relating to objectives, policies and techniques relating to various aspects of financial management. Opinion-based and subjective information was kept to a minimum in order to keep the study more objective and scientific. The questionnaire (along with a covering letter) was sent by courier to the CFO/finance manager/director finance of each of the 166 companies. At the same time, an attachment file of the copy of the questionnaire was also emailed (along with the covering letter) so that in case the respondent had a problem in the physical delivery of the questionnaire, he/she could download the questionnaire from the file attached. Subsequently, the questionnaire was re-mailed to the non-responding companies for follow-up in order to maximise the response rate. It was indicated to the CFOs that the individual responses would be kept strictly confidential and only aggregate generalisations would be published.

The initial response was poor; only a few companies (eight) responded. Subsequently two reminders (both through post and email) were sent to the remaining (non-responding) companies. Personal contacts were also established with the

Table 1.1 Sector-wise classification of BSE 200 companies

Sl. No.	Sector	Number	Percentage of market capitalisation
	BSE 200	200	100.00
1	Finance	34	24.37
2	Oil and gas	16	12.34
3	Information technology	12	11.16
4	Metal, metal products and mining	18	8.46
5	Fast-moving consumer goods (FMCG)	10	8.02
6	Transport equipments	12	7.05
7	Capital goods	13	6.93
8	Power	14	4.81
9	Healthcare	14	4.70
10	Housing related	18	3.07
11	Telecom	6	2.81
12	Diversified	9	1.56
13	Transport services	6	0.94
14	Agriculture	6	0.67
15	Chemical and petrochemical	3	0.67
16	Textile	1	0.64
17	Media and publishing	3	0.57
18	Miscellaneous	2	0.49
19	Consumer durables	2	0.49
20	Tourism	1	0.26

companies located in and around Delhi.[2] This part of the analysis is based on 31 responses received out of 166 after 2 reminders (a response rate of 18.67%).

Prima facie, the response rate may be seen as low; however, the number of respondents and the response rate are similar to previous studies using a similar method (Jain and Kumar 1997; Jain and Yadav 2000, 2005). Also, considering that the survey was addressed to time-constrained CFOs, as well as the commercial sensitivity of some of the requested information, we had no option but to rely only on 31 responses for the present study; the findings of the present research should, therefore, be viewed in the light of this limitation of primary data.

Secondary Data and Analysis

The relevant data was collected from the Capitaline database, for 11 years (2001–2011). The other secondary data sources used to substantiate any missing data were the Bombay Stock Exchange's website and the company's annual reports. More importantly, the sample data of 166 companies can be considered representative of the universe as it adequately covers all industry groups (Table 1.1).

[2]Assistance was also sought through the Delhi Stock Exchange and Securities and Exchange Board of India, as a part of the primary data collection exercise.

Data Analysis

The entire set of data has been analysed using Microsoft Excel spreadsheets and the statistics software SPSS, namely, Statistical Package for the Social Sciences. The analysis is based on well-accepted tools and techniques used in financial management and statistics. Primarily, 'financial ratios' have been relied on for the purpose of the study and key financial ratios have been computed for all financial decisions.

For instance, percentage growth in gross fixed assets and relative share of net fixed assets to permanent capital have been some of the ratios computed in the case of capital budgeting decisions. Debt–equity ratio, total debt (total external obligations) to total assets ratio and interest coverage ratios are some of the important ratios computed to understand capital structure decisions. While dividend payout ratio has constituted the primary ratio for dividend decisions, a set of ratios, say, current ratio, acid-test ratio, debtors' collection period, inventories' holding period, etc., have been calculated to gain insight into working capital practices.

All the ratios were calculated on a year-to-year basis for the sample companies. To study the trend and its implications, descriptive statistical values/positional values, that is, mean, standard deviation, coefficient of variation, skewness, kurtosis, median and quartiles have been computed for each year. The sample size varies from year to year depending upon the availability of data. To do away with the influence of extreme values, they have been excluded from computing average values. However, where their inclusion has been considered important, say, for preparation of frequency distribution, extreme values are also considered.

The 11-year period of the study is divided into two subperiods/subphases to ascertain whether there has been any significant change in financial decision-making of the companies over the years. For the purpose of the analysis, the first 6 years, w.e.f. 1 April 2000 to 31 March 2006 (for brevity referred to as 2001–2006) are referred to as phase 1 and the next 5 years, w.e.f. 1 April 2006 to 31 March 2011 (for brevity referred to as 2007–2011) as phase 2. The rationale behind phase 2 beginning from 1 April 2006 is the Securities and Exchange Board of India (SEBI) regulation, mandating the adherence of clause 49 (on corporate governance) by all listed companies, from 1 April 2006. Phase 1 and phase 2 are considered two independent samples. The *t*-test as well as ANOVA (analysis of variance) have been administered to assess whether financial decisions relating to capital budgeting differed/changed during the second phase compared to the first phase, for the sample companies. A sectoral analysis has been conducted to understand whether variances (if any) could be attributable to one/many constituent industrial sectors of the sample companies.

For the purpose of the sectoral analysis, the 166 companies were regrouped into constituent sectors to reduce the number of sectors to 11 from 20, primarily for the sake of providing an adequate/good number of companies in each sector and for the sake of better statistical analysis (Table 1.2).

The period of the study is of particular importance because of the recession (originating due to the American financial crisis) that impacted the world economy

Table 1.2 Sector-wise reclassification of the sample companies

Sl. No.	Broad sector classification		Number of companies	Percentage of companies
1.	Capital goods		13	7.80
2.	Diversified		9	5.42
3.	Fast-moving consumer goods (FMCG)		12	7.22
	Fast-moving consumer goods	*9*		
	Retail	*1*		
	Consumer durables	*2*		
4.	Healthcare		14	8.43
5.	Housing		18	10.84
6.	Internet and communications technologies (ICT)		18	10.84
	Internet technologies	*12*		
	Telecom	*6*		
7.	Oil and gas		16	9.63
8.	Power		14	8.43
9.	Metals		18	10.84
10.	Transport		18	10.84
	Transport equipment	*12*		
	Transport services	*6*		
11.	Miscellaneous		16	9.63
	Media and publishing	*3*		
	Agriculture	*6*		
	Chemicals and petrochemicals	*3*		
	Tourism	*1*		
	Textiles	*1*		
	Miscellaneous	*2*		
	Total		166	100

towards the second half of 2008. According to the United Nations Council on Trade and Development (UNCTAD) investment brief (1 November 2009), the year 2008 marked the end of a growth cycle in global foreign direct investment (FDI) with worldwide flows down by more than 20%. Due to the global financial crisis, the capacity of companies to invest has been weakened by reduced access to financial resources, both internally and externally. The propensity to invest has also been severely affected by collapsed growth prospects and heightened risks. Developed countries suffered from a one-third contraction in total FDI inflows in 2008, being at the epicentre of the crisis. In India, total net capital flows fell from US$17.3 billion in April–June 2007 to US$13.2 billion in April–June 2008 (Source: UNCTAD investment briefs, investment issues analysis branch of UNCTAD 2009).

Consequently, phase 2 (2006–2007 to 2010–2011) of the study has been divided into two subphases to ascertain the impact of recession. The 2 years of 2006–2007 and 2007–2008 denote the pre-recession phase (phase 3), and the subsequent 3 years of 2008–2009, 2009–2010 and 2010–2011 denote the post-recession phase (phase 4) for the purpose of this study. It needs to be noted that though the impact of recession was assumed to be felt towards the second half of 2008 (June 2008, cited above), the entire year has been included in the post-recession phase primarily due to two reasons: first, data was available in a consolidated manner (in the balance sheets), and second, it was not feasible to separate it for a particular year (2008) on the basis of when recession actually started impacting a particular data variable. It is pertinent to note here that the year 2006–2007 indicates the Indian financial year beginning on 1 April 2006 and ending on 31 March 2007 and so on. The same holds true for all subsequent notations.

Finally, an attempt has been made to develop an index of professionalism related to financial management practices amongst the sample companies (professionalism in finance would indicate the extent of systematic use of sound techniques/principles of finance in practice).

It is pertinent to state here that the authors have conducted three more studies in the past (Jain and Kumar 1997; Jain and Yadav 2000, 2005), spanning from 1991 to 2003. An effort has been made to link the findings of these studies with the current one with the aim to establish trends (if any) in certain aspects of financial decision-making over the past two decades (to provide a broader perspective).

Plan of the Study

The monograph would be divided into four parts. Part I of the monograph would consist of a chapter highlighting the background of the study and the methodology followed.

The core of the study would be found in Parts II and III. Part II would focus on the major financial decisions, namely, capital budgeting practices, capital structure decisions, dividend policy and working capital management. An inter-sectoral analysis would also be undertaken as a part of each chapter. Part III of the study would focus on current and emerging issues of corporate governance, risk management and professionalism (through the creation of an index) of the sample companies. Part IV would contain a chapter on the profitability analysis of the sample companies (with emphasis on the impact of recession) and a chapter containing the summary, recommendations and concluding observations.

Summary

The present study aims to have an insight into the financial management practices of the 166 non-financial companies of the BSE 200 index of the Bombay Stock Exchange. The period of the study is 2001–2011. The study uses both primary and secondary data. The data analysis is based on well-accepted tools and techniques in financial management and statistics.

Financial ratios have been predominantly used for analysis. To lend credence to findings, statistical techniques like *t*-test, 'analysis of variance (ANOVA)' and correlations have also been used, where applicable.

The study also contains the results of a survey of opinions/preferences of corporate finance managers (from the sample companies) on various aspects of financial decision-making. The response came from only 31 companies. Prima facie, it appears to be on the lower side. However, this response level may be seen in the light of what is commonly perceived as sensitive nature of information sought for the purpose of the study and the much smaller response level for the past studies.

An index of professionalism has also been prepared/developed based on the practices being followed by the respondent companies. Finally, a normative framework (guidelines), perhaps for the first time, has also been suggested to make this research useful for practitioners.

Appendices

Appendix 1.1: Constituent companies and sectors of BSE 200 (as of 1 April 2010)

Company name	Sector
Aban Offshore Ltd.	Oil and gas
ABB Ltd.	Capital goods
ACC Ltd.	Housing related
Adani Enterprises Ltd.	Diversified
Adani Power Ltd.	Power
Aditya Birla Nuvo Limited	Diversified
Allahabad Bank	Finance
Ambuja Cements Ltd.	Housing related
Amtek Auto Ltd.	Transport equipments
Anant Raj Industries Ltd.	Housing related
Andhra Bank	Finance
Apollo Hospitals Enterprises Ltd.	Healthcare
Areva T&D India Ltd.	Capital goods
Ashok Leyland Ltd.	Transport equipments
Asian Paints Ltd.	Chemical and petrochemical
Aurobindo Pharma Ltd.	Healthcare
AXIS Bank Ltd.	Finance
Bajaj Auto Ltd.	Transport equipments
Bajaj Finserv Ltd.	Finance
Bajaj Hindustan Ltd.	Agriculture
Bajaj Holdings & Investment Ltd.	Finance
Balrampur Chini Mills Ltd.	Agriculture

(continued)

Appendix 1.1: (continued)

Company name	Sector
Bank of Baroda	Finance
Bank Of India	Finance
BEML Ltd.	Capital goods
Bharat Electronics Ltd.	Capital goods
Bharat Forge Ltd.	Transport equipments
Bharat Heavy Electricals Ltd.	Capital goods
Bharat Petroleum Corporation Ltd.	Oil and gas
Bharti Airtel Ltd.	Telecom
Bhushan Steel & Strips Ltd.	Metal, metal products and mining
Biocon Ltd.	Healthcare
Bombay Dyeing & Mfg Co Ltd.	Textile
Bosch Ltd.	Transport equipments
Cadila Healthcare Ltd.	Healthcare
Cairn India Ltd.	Oil and gas
Canara Bank	Finance
Castrol India ltd.	Oil and gas
Century Textiles	Diversified
CESC Ltd.	Power
Chambal Fertilisers & Chemical	Agriculture
Cipla Ltd.	Healthcare
Colgate-Palmolive (India) Ltd.	FMCG
Container Corporation of India	Transport services
Crompton Greaves Ltd.	Capital goods
Cummins India Ltd.	Transport equipments
Dabur India Ltd.	FMCG
Deccan Chronicle Holdings Ltd.	Media and publishing
Dena Bank	Finance
Divi's Laboratories Ltd.	Healthcare
DLF Ltd.	Housing related
Dr Reddy's Laboratories Ltd.	Healthcare
Educomp Solutions Ltd.	Information technology
Engineers India Ltd.	Miscellaneous
Essar Oil Ltd.	Oil and gas
Essar Shipping Ports & Logistics Ltd.	Transport services
Exide Industries Co. Ltd.	Transport equipments
Federal Bank Ltd.	Finance
Financial Technologies (India) Ltd	Information technology
Gail (India) Ltd.	Oil and gas
GlaxoSmithKline Pharmaceuticals Ltd.	Healthcare
Glenmark Pharmaceuticals Ltd.	Healthcare
GMR Infrastructure Ltd.	Diversified
Godrej Consumer Products Ltd.	FMCG
Godrej Industries Ltd.	Chemical and petrochemical
Grasim Industries Ltd.	Diversified
Great Eastern Shipping Co. Ltd.	Transport services

(continued)

Appendix 1.1: (continued)

Company name	Sector
Great Offshore Ltd.	Transport services
GTL Ltd.	Information technology
Gujarat Mineral Development Corporation	Metal, metal products and mining
Gujarat Nre Coke Ltd.	Metal, metal products and mining
Gujarat State Petronet Ltd.	Oil and gas
GVK Power & Infrastructure Ltd.	Diversified
Havells India Ltd.	Capital goods
HCL Technologies Ltd.	Information technology
HDFC	Finance
HDFC Bank Ltd.	Finance
Hero Honda Motors Ltd.	Transport equipments
Hindalco Industries Ltd.	Metal, metal products and mining
Hindustan Construction Co. Ltd.	Housing related
Hindustan Copper Ltd.	Metal, metal products and mining
Hindustan Oil Exploration Co. Ltd.	Oil and gas
Hindustan Petroleum Corp Ltd.	Oil and gas
Hindustan Unilever Ltd.	FMCG
Hindustan Zinc Ltd.	Metal, metal products and mining
Housing Development & Infrastructure Ltd.	Housing related
ICICI Bank Ltd.	Finance
Idea Cellular Ltd.	Telecom
IFCI Ltd.	Finance
India Cements Ltd.	Housing related
India Infoline Ltd.	Finance
Indiabulls Financial Services Ltd.	Finance
Indiabulls Power Ltd.	Power
Indiabulls Real Estate Ltd.	Housing related
Indian Bank	Finance
Indian Hotels Co Ltd.	Tourism
Indian Oil Corporation Ltd.	Oil and gas
Indian Overseas Bank	Finance
IndusInd Bank Ltd.	Finance
Industrial Dev Bank of India	Finance
Infosys Technologies Ltd.	Information technology
Infrastructure Development Finance Co. Ltd.	Finance
IRB Infrastructure Developers Ltd.	Housing related
Ispat Industries Ltd.	Metal, metal products and mining
ITC Ltd.	FMCG
IVRCL Infrastructures & Projects Ltd.	Housing related
Jai Corp Ltd.	Metal, metal products and mining
Jain Irrigation Systems Ltd.	Agriculture
Jaiprakash Associates Ltd.	Housing related
Jaiprakash Hydro-Power Ltd.	Power
Jindal Saw Ltd.	Metal, metal products and mining
Jindal Steel & Powers Ltd.	Metal, metal products and mining

(continued)

Appendix 1.1: (continued)

Company name	Sector
JSW Steel Ltd	Metal, metal products and mining
Jubilant Organosys Ltd.	Chemical and petrochemical
Kotak Mahindra Bank Ltd.	Finance
KSK Energy Ventures Ltd.	Power
Lanco Infratech Ltd.	Housing related
Larsen & Toubro Limited	Capital goods
LIC Housing Finance Ltd.	Finance
Lupin Ltd.	Healthcare
M M T C Ltd.	Miscellaneous
Madras Cements Ltd.	Housing related
Mahanagar Telephone Nigam Ltd.	Telecom
Mahindra & Mahindra Ltd.	Transport equipments
Mangalore Refinery & Petro Ltd.	Oil and gas
Maruti Suzuki India Ltd.	Transport equipments
Max India Ltd.	Diversified
MCLEOD RUSSE	FMCG
Mphasis Ltd.	Information technology
MRF Ltd.	Transport equipments
Mundra Port & Special Economic Zone	Transport services
Nagarjuna Construction Co. Ltd.	Housing related
National Aluminium Co. Ltd.	Metal, metal products and mining
Nestle India Ltd.	FMCG
Neyveli Lignite Corporation	Power
NHPC Ltd.	Power
NMDC Ltd.	Metal, metal products and mining
NTPC Ltd.	Power
Oil India Ltd.	Oil and gas
ONGC Ltd.	Oil and gas
Opto Circuits (India) Ltd.	Healthcare
Oracle Financial Services Software Ltd.	Information technology
Oriental Bank of Commerce	Finance
Pantaloon Retail (India) Ltd.	Miscellaneous
Patel Engineering Ltd.	Housing related
Patni Computer Systems Ltd.	Information technology
Petronet LNG Ltd.	Oil and gas
Piramal Healthcare Ltd.	Healthcare
Power Finance Corporation Ltd.	Finance
Power Grid Corporation of India Ltd.	Power
Praj Industries Ltd.	Capital goods
PTC India Ltd.	Power
Punj Lloyd Ltd	Capital goods
Punjab National Bank	Finance
Ranbaxy Laboratories Ltd.	Healthcare
Reliance Capital Ltd.	Finance
Reliance Communications Limited	Telecom

(continued)

Appendix 1.1: (continued)

Company name	Sector
Reliance Industries Ltd.	Oil and gas
Reliance Infrastructure Ltd.	Power
Reliance Natural Resources Limited	Oil and gas
Reliance Power Ltd.	Power
Rolta India Ltd.	Information technology
Rural Electrification Corp. Ltd.	Finance
Sesa Goa Ltd.	Metal, metal products and mining
Shipping Corporation Of India Ltd.	Transport services
Shree Renuka Sugars Ltd.	Agriculture
Shriram Transport Fin Co. Ltd.	Finance
Siemens Ltd.	Capital goods
Sintex Industries Ltd.	Housing related
State Bank of India	Finance
Steel Authority of India Ltd.	Metal, metal products and mining
Sterlite Industries Ltd.	Metal, metal products and mining
Sun Pharmaceutical Inds Ltd.	Healthcare
Sun TV Network Ltd.	Media and publishing
Suzlon Energy Limited	Capital goods
Tata Chemicals Ltd.	Diversified
Tata Communications Ltd.	Telecom
Tata Consultancy Services Ltd.	Information technology
Tata Motors Ltd.	Transport equipments
Tata Power Co. Ltd.	Power
Tata Steel Ltd.	Metal, metal products and mining
Tata Tea Ltd.	FMCG
Tata Teleservices (Maharashtra) Ltd.	Telecom
Tech Mahindra Ltd.	Information technology
Thermax Ltd.	Capital goods
Titan Industries Ltd.	Consumer durables
Torrent Power Ltd.	Power
UCO Bank	Finance
Ultratech Cement Limited	Housing related
Union Bank of India	Finance
Unitech Ltd.	Housing related
United Phosphorus Ltd.	Agriculture
United Spirits Ltd.	FMCG
Videocon Industries Ltd.	Consumer durables
Vijaya Bank	Finance
Voltas Ltd.	Diversified
Welspun Gujarat Stahl Rohren Ltd.	Metal, metal products and mining
Wipro Ltd.	Information technology
Yes Bank Ltd.	Finance
Zee Entertainment Enterprises Ltd.	Media and publishing

Appendix 1.2: Finance sector companies excluded from the sample

Name	Sector
Allahabad Bank	Finance
Andhra Bank	Finance
AXIS Bank Ltd.	Finance
Bajaj Finserv Ltd.	Finance
Bajaj Holdings & Investment Ltd.	Finance
Bank of Baroda	Finance
Bank Of India	Finance
Canara Bank	Finance
Dena Bank	Finance
Federal Bank Ltd.	Finance
HDFC	Finance
HDFC Bank Ltd.	Finance
ICICI Bank Ltd.	Finance
IFCI Ltd.	Finance
India Infoline Ltd.	Finance
Indiabulls Financial Services Ltd.	Finance
Indian Bank	Finance
Indian Overseas Bank	Finance
IndusInd Bank Ltd.	Finance
Industrial Dev Bank of India	Finance
Infrastructure Development Finance Co. Ltd.	Finance
Kotak Mahindra Bank Ltd.	Finance
LIC Housing Finance Ltd.	Finance
Oriental Bank of Commerce	Finance
Power Finance Corporation Ltd.	Finance
Punjab National Bank	Finance
Reliance Capital Ltd.	Finance
Rural Electrification Corp. Ltd.	Finance
Shriram Transport Fin Co. Ltd.	Finance
State Bank of India	Finance
UCO Bank	Finance
Union Bank of India	Finance
Vijaya Bank	Finance
Yes Bank Ltd.	Finance

Appendix 1.3: Questionnaire on financial management perspective of BSE 200 companies

Objective: This study is a part of a research project. The purpose of the study is to develop a comprehensive financial perspective of the BSE 200 companies for the past decade (2000–2010) and to derive useful conclusions therefrom. Your response will be extremely important to complete the present work. The information provided by you will be kept confidential and reported only in summary form.

Though we would appreciate your response to all questions, you may find a few questions of sensitive nature; we appreciate your constraints of nonresponse to such questions.

Flow of questions: Section A commences with the basic information about the company. Sections B, C and D relate to the corporate finance decisions of the company. Dividend policy for shareholders and the corporate governance decisions have been dealt in Sections E and F. Sections G and H conclude with aspects related to globalisation and its resultant impact on risk management for the company.

Section A: Basic Information

1. (a) Name of the company ________________________
   (b) Year of incorporation _______
   (c) Nature of industry (products manufactured/services rendered) ____________
   (d) In order of their importance, please rank the financial objectives of your organisation (e.g. 1 for most important, 2 for next important)

      (i) [ ] Maximise return on assets
      (ii) [ ] Achieve desired growth rate in earnings per share
      (iii) [ ] Maximise ordinary share prices
      (iv) [ ] Maximise aggregate earnings
      (v) [ ] Maximise return on capital employed
      (vi) [ ] Any other (please specify) ________________

Section B: Items Related to Capital Budgeting Decisions

2. In the past decade, the capital expenditure of your company has mainly constituted of outlays on

   (a) [ ] New investment in existing line of business (capacity build-up)
   (b) [ ] New investment in other areas (diversification)
   (c) [ ] Technology upgradation (modernisation)
   (d) [ ] Replacement of machinery
   (e) [ ] Any other (please specify) ___________________

3. During the course of capital expenditure projects, does your company opt for sound capital structure to ensure a low cost of capital for the project? Yes [ ] No [ ]
4. In your company, the new investment proposals originate
   (a) [ ] At central/head office level
   (b) [ ] At divisional/regional office level
   (c) [ ] At plant level
   (d) [ ] At any other level (please specify) ____________________
5. How many year(s) ahead do you plan for capital expenditure?
   (a) [ ] For next 1 year only
   (b) [ ] For next 5 years
   (c) [ ] For next 10 years
   (d) [ ] As and when the opportunity takes place
   (e) [ ] Any other (please specify) ____________________
6. Does your company ever forego any expected profitable investment opportunity because of paucity of financial resources? Yes [ ] No [ ]
7. (A) Please identify capital expenditure evaluation technique(s) used in your company
   (a) [ ] Accounting rate of return on investment
   (b) [ ] Payback period

   Discounted cash flow techniques
   (i) [ ] Net present value
   (ii) [ ] Internal rate of return
   (iii) [ ] Profitability index/Present value index
   (iv) [ ] Any other (please specify) ____________________

   (B)[3] Is your company using the following techniques?
   (a) [ ] Real options Yes [ ] No [ ]
   (b) [ ] Abandonment options Yes [ ] No [ ]
8. If your company is using payback period method, please state the reason(s)
   (a) [ ] Shortage of liquid funds
   (b) [ ] Obsolescence due to technological developments
   (c) [ ] Easy to explain to top management
   (d) [ ] Simplicity leading to less time and cost involved
   (e) [ ] Any other (please specify) ____________________

[3]Real options – have positive value when investment in a new project brings with it a potential increase in the firm's future opportunities. Evidently, such options are valuable and add to the project's profitability.

Abandonment options – relate to the flexibility of abandoning a project (prior to its projected full economic/useful life). Such embedded options lower project risk by limiting downside losses.

9. Please state method(s) followed to incorporate project risk into your investment decision

   (a) [ ] Shorter payback period for risky projects
   (b) [ ] Higher cut-off rate for risky projects
   (c) [ ] Sensitivity analysis
   (d) [ ] Any other (please specify) _______________

10. In the past decade, the reasons for failure of capital budgeting decisions (if any) have been (rank in order of impact: 1 for highest, 7 for lowest)

    (a) [ ] Higher cost of capital
    (b) [ ] Decrease in cash inflows due to decrease in expected sales
    (c) [ ] Unexpected increase in cost of production
    (d) [ ] Inefficiencies in terms of technology usage and revamp
    (e) [ ] Very high fixed cost component
    (f) [ ] Increased competition in the chosen area impacting sales
    (g) [ ] Any other (please specify) _______________

Section C: Items Related to Capital Structure Decisions

11. (A) Which method do you use to determine cost of capital?

    (a) [ ] Weighted average cost of long-term sources of finance
    (b) [ ] Marginal cost of additional funds raised to finance new asset
    (c) [ ] Decided by the top management
    (d) [ ] Any other (please specify) _________________

    (B) Weights used for average cost of capital are equivalent to

    (a) [ ] Market value weights
    (b) [ ] Book value weights
    (c) [ ] Target weights

12. (A) Have there been changes in the capital structure of your firm in the wake of liberalisation of the country's economy and globalisation?

    [ ] Yes [ ] Expected in near future [ ] No

    (B) If yes, it is moving towards [ ] More equity [ ] More debt
    (C) In the wake of opening up of the economy, your company's dependence on the capital market has [ ] Increased [ ] Remained unchanged [ ] Decreased

13. In your opinion

    (A) Debt should be tapped to the maximum extent possible. Yes [ ] No [ ]
    (B) The ratio of debt to equity should be maintained less than 1, 1:1, 2:1, 3:1 or greater than 3.
    (C) In general, the debt is preferred to equity as

        (a) [ ] Debt is cheaper than equity.
        (b) [ ] It is easier to raise debt as investors are risk averse and equity is risk capital.
        (c) [ ] Debt is more flexible than equity in terms of callability clause, repayment schedules, etc.
        (d) [ ] The perceived advantage of flexibility in payment of dividend is more illusory than real.
        (e) [ ] Any other (please specify) ______________

14. If your firm prefers to have predominantly more equity, the reason(s) could be

    (a) [ ] Firm is not under obligations to pay dividends.
    (b) [ ] There is flexibility in paying dividends.
    (c) [ ] Equity is easy to raise.
    (d) [ ] Any other (please specify) ________________

15. Cost of equity capital in your firm is equivalent to

    [ ] Primary rate of return available to investors on securities of balanced mutual funds
    [ ] Primary rate of return plus risk premium

    Absolute sum

    (i) [ ] >20%
    (ii) [ ] 15–20%
    (iii) [ ] 10–14%
    (iv) [ ] Any other (please specify) __________
    [ ] Dividend valuation model
    [ ] Capital Asset Pricing Model (CAPM)
    [ ] No cost is considered

16. Cost of retained earnings in your company is equivalent to

    (a) [ ] Cost of equity capital
    (b) [ ] Opportunity cost of using these funds by company
    (c) [ ] Opportunity cost of using these funds by equity-holders
    (d) [ ] No cost is considered
    (e) [ ] Any other (please specify) _______________

17. Do you use a pecking order approach in financing projects (i.e. order of preference is using retained earnings first followed by debt and issue of additional equity capital as a last resort)? Yes [ ] No [ ]
18. Please give your opinion regarding the importance of the following factors in the capital structure decision

	1	2	3	4
(a) Corporate control	[ ]	[ ]	[ ]	[ ]
(b) Stability in sales/profits	[ ]	[ ]	[ ]	[ ]
(c) State of the capital market	[ ]	[ ]	[ ]	[ ]
(d) Business/Operational risk	[ ]	[ ]	[ ]	[ ]
(e) Financial risk	[ ]	[ ]	[ ]	[ ]
(f) Restrictions imposed by lenders	[ ]	[ ]	[ ]	[ ]
(g) Regulatory framework	[ ]	[ ]	[ ]	[ ]
(h) Corporate tax	[ ]	[ ]	[ ]	[ ]

(i) Any other (please specify) ________________
(1. Very important, 2. Important, 3. Not so important, 4. Not at all important)

Section D: Items Related to Working Capital Management

19. Which of the following forms the basis for working capital determination?

(a) [ ] Percentage of budgeted production
(b) [ ] Percentage of budgeted sales
(c) [ ] Length of operating cycle
(d) [ ] Determination of individual components of current assets and current liabilities (based on raw material holding period, debtors collection period, creditors payment period and so on)
(e) [ ] Any other (please specify) _______________

20. Please state your company's policy regarding financing of working capital

(a) [ ] Mainly from long-term sources
(b) [ ] Mainly from short-term sources
(c) [ ] Temporary/seasonal needs from short-term sources and only for period needed
(d) [ ] Permanent needs from long-term sources and temporary/seasonal needs from short-term sources
(e) [ ] Any other (please specify) _________________

21. (A) Have you experienced working capital shortage? Yes [ ] No [ ]
(B) If yes, it occurs Very frequently [ ] Occasionally [ ]
(C) Main reason(s) of the shortage may be

(a) [ ] Excess inventory
(b) [ ] Less than expected sales
(c) [ ] Default from debtors
(d) [ ] Any other (please specify) ______________

22. (A) Were there any excess working capital situations? Yes [ ] No [ ]
(B) If yes, excess was

(a) [ ] Temporarily invested (say, in marketable securities)
(b) [ ] Invested in long-term securities
(c) [ ] Invested in fixed assets
(d) [ ] Utilised for repayment of debt
(e) [ ] Any other (please specify) ________________

23. How do you manage emergency requirements of cash?
(Arising due to unexpected events or to exploit an opportunity)

(a) [ ] Always maintain minimum cash balance over and above the required amount
(b) [ ] Bank overdraft
(c) [ ] Utilisation of cash credit limit from bank
(d) [ ] Discount bill receivables
(e) [ ] Have special arrangements with some lending agency for such purposes
(f) [ ] Sell marketable securities
(g) [ ] Raise loan against warehouse receipt
(h) [ ] Any other (please specify) ______________

24. In case your lending agency has given assurance to stand by you in emergency, the terms are

(a) [ ] At normal rate of interest
(b) [ ] At more than normal rate of interest
(c) [ ] Any other (please specify) ______________

25. (A) Please rank the objectives of your credit policy

(a) [ ] Growth in sales
(b) [ ] Match credit terms with that of competitors
(c) [ ] Better credit terms than those of competitors
(d) [ ] Any other (please specify) ______________

(B) Is risk analysis of customers made before granting credit? Yes [ ] No [ ]
(C) Is the ageing schedule of debtors prepared? Yes [ ] No [ ]

26. In general, payment from debtors is received

	Never	Infrequently	Frequently	Always
(a) Before due date	[ ]	[ ]	[ ]	[ ]
(b) On due date	[ ]	[ ]	[ ]	[ ]
(c) After due date	[ ]	[ ]	[ ]	[ ]

Section E: Items Related to Dividend Policy

27. (A) Does your company follow a stable dividend policy? Yes [ ] No [ ]
    (B) Does your company follow a constant payout ratio? Yes [ ] No [ ]
    (C) If yes, please specify the percentage of earnings paid out generally as dividends by your company

    (a) [ ] Less than 10%
    (b) [ ] 10–25%
    (c) [ ] 25–50%
    (d) [ ] Above 50%

28. What were the considerations that affected your dividend policy in the past decade?

    (a) [ ] Consideration of taxes
    (b) [ ] Consideration of returns
    (c) [ ] Contractual constraints
    (d) [ ] Legal constraints
    (e) [ ] Cash flow constraints
    (f) [ ] Any other (please specify) ______________

29. (A) Did your company issue bonus shares in the past decade? Yes [ ] No [ ]
    (B) If yes, what were the benefits of such a decision?

    (a) [ ] Made the stock more attractive to the investors
    (b) [ ] Eased the sale of new common stock
    (c) [ ] Sent a positive signal about the firm's future prospects
    (d) [ ] Helped conserve cash
    (e) [ ] Any other (please specify) ______________

30. (A) Did your company announce a stock split in the past decade?
    Yes [ ] No [ ]

    (B) If yes, what were the benefits of such a decision?

    (a) [ ] Brought the share price into a popular trading range
    (b) [ ] Increased the number of shareholders

(c) [ ] Made the stock more attractive to individual shareholders by lowering the share prices
(d) [ ] Sent a positive signal about the firm's future prospects
(e) [ ] Any other (please specify) ______________

Section F: Items Related to Corporate Governance

31. (A) Does your company have a corporate governance policy?
Yes [ ]   No [ ]

(B) If yes, your corporate governance policy focuses on

(a) [ ] Shareholders
(b) [ ] Management
(c) [ ] Board of Directors
(d) [ ] Customers
(e) [ ] Employees
(f) [ ] Creditors
(g) [ ] Regulatory authorities
(h) [ ] Suppliers
(i) [ ] Community at large
(j) [ ] Any other (please specify) ___________________

32. (A) Does your company have an internal team dedicated to corporate governance?
Yes [ ]   No [ ] If yes,

(B) The internal corporate governance policy includes

(a) [ ] Monitoring by Board of Directors
(b) [ ] Balance of power
(c) [ ] Remuneration

(C) The external corporate governance policy includes

(a) [ ] Competition
(b) [ ] Debt covenants
(c) [ ] Demand for and assessment of performance information (especially financial statements)
(d) [ ] Government regulations
(e) [ ] Managerial labour market
(f) [ ] Media pressure
(g) [ ] Takeovers

33. (A) Has the company been assessed for its corporate governance practices by any rating agency like CRISIL or ICRA? Yes [ ] No [ ]
    (B) If yes, kindly state the corporate governance rating of the company by rating agency

GVC level 1 by CRISIL [ ]	CGR1 By ICRA [ ]
GVC level 2 by CRISIL [ ]	CGR2 By ICRA [ ]
GVC level 3 by CRISIL [ ]	CGR3 By ICRA [ ]
GVC level 4 by CRISIL [ ]	CGR4 By ICRA [ ]
GVC level 5 by CRISIL [ ]	CGR5 By ICRA [ ]
GVC level 6 by CRISIL [ ]	CGR6 By ICRA [ ]
GVC level 7 by CRISIL [ ]	
GVC level 8 by CRISIL [ ]	

34. Is senior management incentivised to work towards a higher share price for the company through ESOPs, share in profits etc.? Yes [ ] No [ ]
35. Please state the percentage of equity holding of CEO/MD in the company's equity?

    (a) [ ] Below 10%
    (b) [ ] 10–25%
    (c) [ ] 25–50%
    (d) [ ] Above 50%

36. (A) Does the company publish its annual report within stipulated time (6 months) of the end of the financial year?

    Always [ ] Mostly [ ] Occasionally [ ] Sometimes [ ] Never [ ]

    (B) Does the company publish/announce semi-annual reports within 1 month of the end of the half-year?

    Always [ ] Mostly [ ] Occasionally [ ] Sometimes [ ] Never [ ]

    (C) Does the company publish/announce quarterly reports within 1 month of the end of the quarter?

    Always [ ] Mostly [ ] Occasionally [ ] Sometimes [ ] Never [ ]

37. Does the company consistently disclose material-sensitive information to stakeholders?

    Always [ ] Sometimes [ ] Never [ ]

38. Are the Board Members and members of the executive/management committee separate individuals? Yes [ ] No [ ]
39. Are the statutory auditors of the company unrelated to the top management of company? Yes [ ] No [ ]

40. Does the Board include direct representatives of banks, financial/strategic investor and other large creditors of the company? Yes [ ] No [ ]
41. (A) Is there a whistle-blower policy in your company? Yes [ ] No [ ]
    (B) Is there an investors' grievance cell in your company?
    Yes [ ] No [ ]
42. (A) Is your company listed on any exchange abroad? Yes [ ] No [ ]
    (B) If yes, on which ones? ________________ ________________
    ____

43. [4]Is your company required to comply with Sarbanes–Oxley Act (SOX)?
    Yes [ ] No [ ]

44. (A) Does your company have an executive chairman?
    Yes [ ] No [ ]
    (B) Does your company have more than 50% independent directors on your Board? Yes [ ] No [ ]
    (C) Does your company have more than 33% independent directors on your Board? Yes [ ] No [ ]

45. Do the CEO and CFO of your company establish and maintain internal controls and implement remediation and risk mitigation towards deficiencies in internal controls?
    Yes [ ] No [ ]

46. Does your company submit a quarterly compliance report on corporate governance to the stock exchange (where it is listed) in the prescribed form? Yes [ ] No [ ]
47. Does your annual report contain a separate section on corporate governance with a detailed compliance report? Yes [ ] No [ ]
48. Does your company obtain a certificate either from auditors or practising company secretaries regarding compliance of conditions as stipulated in clause 49 and annex the same to the director's report? Yes [ ] No [ ]
49. (A) Does your company have the mandatory committee on corporate governance as per clause 49? Yes [ ] No [ ]
    (B) Does your company have the mandatory audit committee as per clause 49? Yes [ ] No [ ]
    (C) Does your company have the remunerations committee as per clause 49? Yes [ ] No [ ]

[4]Sarbanes–Oxley Act (SOX) – enacted in 2002 in the United States of America, is also known as the 'Public Company Accounting Reform and Investor Protection Act'. Akin to Clause 49 of SEBI, an Indian company is required to comply with SOX only if it is seeking or has already secured a listing on any US stock exchange.

50. (A) Does your company disclose contingent liabilities as per clause 49?
Yes [ ] No [ ]
(B) Does your company disclose the utilisation of the proceeds from an IPO to the audit committee on a quarterly basis as per clause 49?
Yes [ ] No [ ]

Section G: Items Related to Global Finance

51. (A) Does your company have international transactions also?
Yes [ ] No [ ]
(B) If yes, the transactions are in the form of

(a) [ ] Exports
(b) [ ] Imports
(c) [ ] Borrowing from abroad
(d) [ ] Receiving capital from abroad
(e) [ ] Subsidiary abroad
(f) [ ] Investing capital abroad
(g) [ ] Investing in foreign securities

52. What is the size of your yearly foreign exchange transactions?

(a) [ ] Less than Rs. 10 million
(b) [ ] Between Rs. 10 million and Rs. 50 million
(c) [ ] Between Rs. 50 million and Rs. 100 million
(d) [ ] Between Rs. 100 million and Rs. 500 million
(e) [ ] Between Rs. 500 million and Rs. 1 billion
(f) [ ] Above Rs. 1 billion

53. (A) The holding pattern of your company in percentage terms

	In 2000	In 2010
Domestic holding	_______	_______
Foreign holding	_______	_______

(B) The investment pattern of your company in percentage terms

	In 2000	In 2010
Foreign portfolio investment vis-à-vis total investment	_______	_______
Foreign direct investment vis-à-vis total investment	_______	_______

54. Please rank your sources of foreign currency in order of preference (1 being the most important, 2 for the next important and so on)

(a) [ ] Development financial institutions (DFIs)
(b) [ ] GDRs/ADRs/Euro issues, etc.

(c) [ ] Private banks
(d) [ ] Foreign banks
(e) [ ] Foreign collaborations/joint ventures
(f) [ ] Any other (please specify) ________________

55. (A) Do you project (forecast) exchange rates for future dates?

Yes [ ] No [ ]

(B) Your exchange rate forecasts are done for

(a) [ ] 1 week
(b) [ ] One fortnight
(c) [ ] 1 month
(d) [ ] 2 months
(e) [ ] 3 months
(f) [ ] Any other period (please specify) ____________

(C) Which of the following techniques/analyses are used for exchange rate forecast?

(a) [ ] Fundamental analysis
(b) [ ] Technical analysis
(c) [ ] Any other technique/model (please specify) ______________

(D) While using fundamental analysis for exchange rate forecasts, you consider

(a) [ ] Structure of balance of payment
(b) [ ] Foreign exchange reserves
(c) [ ] Interest rates
(d) [ ] Inflation rates
(e) [ ] Any other (please specify) ___________

(E) In technical analysis, your organisation uses

(a) [ ] Bar charts
(b) [ ] Graphs
(c) [ ] Any other (please specify) ____________

Section H: Items Related to Risk Management

56. How would you summarise the attitude of your company towards overall risk management and internal controls?

(a) [ ] Risk is understood in its entirety and measures are taken to mitigate it.
(b) [ ] The Board thinks that risk management is 'not its problem'.
(c) [ ] The company is focused only on internal financial control rather than the wider scope of internal control.

(d) [ ] Risk management is seen as the responsibility of one function, such as audit or insurance.
(e) [ ] No key risk indicators have been determined.
(f) [ ] Employees have no training or experience in risk management.
(g) [ ] Any other (please specify) ______________

57. What kind of risks does the company specify under risk management?

(a) [ ] Financial risk
(b) [ ] Business/Operational risk
(c) [ ] Market risk
(d) [ ] Any other (please specify) ______________

58. What kind of risks does your company face?

Financial risk

(a) [ ] Credit risk
(b) [ ] Interest risk
(c) [ ] Currency risk
(d) [ ] Liquidity risk
(e) [ ] High cost of capital

Business/Operational risk

(f) [ ] Missed or ignored business opportunities
(g) [ ] Stock-out of raw materials
(h) [ ] Physical disasters (e.g. fire and explosion)
(i) [ ] Failure to create and exploit intangible assets
(j) [ ] Inability to reduce cost base

Market risk

(k) [ ] Over-reliance on key suppliers or customers
(l) [ ] Failure of new products or services
(m) [ ] Poor service levels
(n) [ ] Any other (please specify) _____________

59. What are some of the steps your company takes to mitigate its financial risk?

(a) [ ] Keep the debt/equity ratio close to the industrial benchmark.
(b) [ ] Make conscious efforts to keep the financial leverage as low as possible by reducing debt in the capital structure.
(c) [ ] Have internal control ratios like cash flow return on investment.
(d) [ ] Make conscious efforts to keep the interest coverage ratio as high as possible.
(e) [ ] Make extensive use of financial derivatives.
(f) [ ] Examine tax consequences of cross border activities and incorporate it in financial planning.
(g) [ ] Any other (please specify) _____________

60. What are some of the steps your company takes to mitigate its business/operational risk?

    (a) [ ] Use adequate insurance coverage against fixed asset loss.
    (b) [ ] Use leasing/hire-purchase arrangements to keep long-term investment as low as possible.
    (c) [ ] Examine components like transfer pricing, excise duties, etc., as consequences of cross border activities and incorporate it in operational planning.
    (d) [ ] Review acquisitions and handle disposal/liquidation of business components/joint ventures.
    (e) [ ] Budgets are regularly monitored and reallocated in line with revised risk/resource needs.
    (f) [ ] There is a strong and conscious effort to focus on variable-costs-dominated ventures and strategies.
    (g) [ ] Any other (please specify) ____________

61. If operating risk is high, does your company make a strong effort to reduce financial risk (or vice versa) in order to keep the overall risk low? Yes [ ] No [ ]
62. (A) Do you think with the advent of liberalisation process, volatility in the market has increased in the past decade? Yes [ ] No [ ]
    (B) If yes, how is volatility getting manifested in your company?

    (a) [ ] Fluctuations in input cost
    (b) [ ] Uncertainty about the product prices
    (c) [ ] Fluctuations in investments
    (d) [ ] Fluctuations in exchange rates
    (e) [ ] Increased uncertainty about receivables
    (f) [ ] Any other (please specify) ____________

63. (A) Do you think with the advent of liberalisation process, opportunity in the market has increased in the past decade? Yes [ ] No [ ]
    (B) If yes, how has your company been benefitted in the past decade due to increased opportunities?

    (a) [ ] Lower input cost
    (b) [ ] More lucrative investment opportunities
    (c) [ ] Hedging of risk by diversification of investments
    (d) [ ] Economies of scale
    (e) [ ] Any other (please specify) ____________

64. Indicate the order of preference as to which of the following precautions could help in minimising the political risk in international operations. (1 for most important, 2 for next preference and so on)

    (a) [ ] Incorporating a risk premium in the cost of capital
    (b) [ ] Integrating products of the host country in your business

(c) [ ] Taking loans from the financial institutions of the host country
(d) [ ] Increasing the number of the host country employees
(e) [ ] Creating joint ventures with an enterprise of the host country
(f) [ ] Any other (please specify) _______________

65. (A)[5] For managing exchange rate risk, do you use the following technique(s)?

	Yes	No
Leads and lags	[ ]	[ ]
Netting	[ ]	[ ]
Back-to-back swap	[ ]	[ ]
Re-invoicing through a centralised system	[ ]	[ ]
Risk sharing	[ ]	[ ]

Any other (please specify) ______________

(B) In case of anticipated depreciation of local currency, which of the basic hedging strategies are used by your company? (Please tick mark)

(a) [ ] Buy foreign currency forward.
(b) [ ] Reduce levels of local currency cash and marketable securities.
(c) [ ] Reduce local currency receivables.
(d) [ ] Delay collection of hard currency (appreciating currency) receivables.
(e) [ ] Borrow locally.
(f) [ ] Delay payments of local currency payable.
(g) [ ] Speed up dividend and other remittances to parent.
(h) [ ] Invoice exports in foreign currency and imports in loc.l currency.

(C) In case of anticipated appreciation of local currency which of the basic hedging strategies used by your company? (Please tick mark)

(a) [ ] Sell foreign currency forward.
(b) [ ] Increase levels of local currency cash and marketable securities.
(c) [ ] Relax local currency credit terms (i.e. increase local currency receivables)
(d) [ ] Speed up collection of soft currency (depreciating currency) receivables.
(e) [ ] Reduce local borrowing.
(f) [ ] Speed up payments of local currency payable.

[5] 'Leads and lags' consists of accelerating or delaying receipt or payment in foreign currency as warranted by the anticipated depreciation/appreciation of that currency.

'Netting' refers to matching the receivables and payables between two affiliates and making payment of the balance amount.

'Back-to-back swap' is simply exchange of equivalent sums of two different currencies between two companies.

'Re-invoicing' is a system where the payments and receipts between different affiliates are routed through a central treasury so as to centralise exchange risk management.

(g) [ ] Delay dividend and other remittances to parent.
(h) [ ] Invoice exports in local currency and imports in foreign currency.

66. What percentage of foreign exchange exposures does your company cover?

(a) [ ] 100%
(b) [ ] 90%
(c) [ ] 80%
(d) [ ] 70%
(e) [ ] 60%
(f) [ ] 50%
(g) [ ] Any other percentage (please specify) ______

67. Which of the following instruments are used by your company to hedge exchange rate risk? (Give order of preference, 1 for most important and so on)

(a) [ ] Currency forward contract
(b) [ ] Money market hedge
(c) [ ] Currency futures
(d) [ ] Currency options

68. Interest rate risk manifests in the form of

(a) [ ] Decrease in the value of credit
(b) [ ] Increase in the value of debts
(c) [ ] Decrease in financial income
(d) [ ] Increase in financial charges
(e) [ ] Any other (please specify) ______________

69. Indicate the order of preference for the use of following instruments when available to cover interest rate risk. (1 for highest preference, 2 for next and so on)

(a) [ ] Forward interest rate agreements (FRA)
(b) [ ] Forward contracts
(c) [ ] Interest rate futures
(d) [ ] Interest rate options
(e) [ ] Interest rate caps
(f) [ ] Interest rate floors
(g) [ ] Interest rate collar
(h) [ ] Interest rate swaps

70. From where do you get advice for foreign risk management?

(a) [ ] Outside individual consultants
(b) [ ] Outside institutional consultancy services
(c) [ ] Internal team
(d) [ ] Any other (please specify) ________________

Any other information which you feel may be useful for the study (please mention) ____

____

____

____

____

____

____

____

Thank you for your time and cooperation

References

Allen DE (1991) The determinants of the capital structure of listed Australian companies: the financial manager's perspective. Aust J Manage 16(2):103–128

Block S (2005) Are there differences in capital budgeting procedures between industries? Eng Econ 50(1):55–67

Bombay Stock Exchange (BSE) website. http://www.bseindia.com/about/abindices/bse200.asp. Accessed 1 Apr 2010

Borio CEV (1990) Leverage and financing of non-financial companies: an international perspective. BIS Economic Papers, No. 27

Chandra P (1973) Capital budgeting in Indian industries. Indian Management, New Delhi

Coates JB, Davis EW, Emmanuel CR, Longden SG, Stacey RJ (1992) Multinational companies performance measurement systems: international perspectives. Manage Acc Res 3(2):133–150

Danielson MG, Scott JA (2006) The capital budgeting decisions of small businesses. J Appl Finance (Fall/Winter) 16(2):45–56

Hooghiemstra R (2000) Corporate communication and impression management – new perspectives why companies engage in corporate social reporting. J Bus Ethics 27(1–2):55–68

Jain PK, Kumar M (1997) Comparative financial management: practices of India and South East Asia. Hindustan Publishing Corporation (India), New Delhi

Jain PK, Yadav SS (2000) Financial management practices in select private corporate enterprises – a comparative study of India, Thailand and Singapore. Hindustan Publishing Corporation (India), New Delhi

Jain PK, Yadav SS (2005) Financial management practices – a study of public sector enterprises in India. Hindustan Publishing Corporation (India), New Delhi

Jermakowicz EK (2004) Effects of adoption of international financial reporting standards in Belgium: the evidence from BEL-20 companies. Acc Eur 1(1):51–70

Jermakowicz EK, Gornik-Tomaszewski S (2006) Implementing IFRS from the perspective of EU publicly traded companies. J Int Acc Audit Tax 15(2):170–196

Ledgerwood J (1999) Microfinance handbook: an institutional and financial perspective. World Bank Publications, Washington, DC

Porwal LS, Singhvi SS (1978) A comparative study of capital expenditure evaluation techniques. Long Range Plann 11(5):25–31

Rao G (1985) Lending trends in the sugarcane sector. Fijian Stud 1(2):301–314

Securities and Exchange Board of India website. http://www.sebi.gov.in/informalguide/firstsource.pdf. Accessed 25 May 2011

United Nations Council on Trade and Development (UNCTAD) website. http://www.unctad.org/en/docs/webdiaeia20095_en.pdf. Accessed 17 Nov 2011

Wahlen JM, Stickney CP, Brown P, Baginski SP, Bradshaw M (2010) Financial reporting, financial statement analysis and valuation: a strategic perspective, 7th edn. South Western Publications, CENGAGE Learning

Part II
Financial Decisions

Chapter 2
Capital Budgeting Decisions

Introduction

Sound capital investment decisions are critical to the long-term success of firms. There are at least two major reasons for such an affirmation. The first is that fixed (long-term) assets are the real earning assets of a business enterprise; these assets enable the firm to generate products/services which result in sales/revenues, which in turn yield profits. The second is that an opportune investment decision can yield spectacular results in terms of profits but an ill-advised and incorrect decision can endanger the very survival of the business.

The capital budgeting process consists of four stages: identification, development, selection and control. Although all four stages are critical to the overall process, the selection stage is arguably the most vital since it includes the choices of analytical methods/techniques used, procedure followed to compute the cost of capital, the modus operandi followed to assess project risks and how capital rationing situations have been dealt with. The selection stage has also been the most investigated by survey researchers (particularly with respect to selection techniques) resulting in a relative neglect of the other stages.

The objective of this chapter is to delve into aspects relating to capital budgeting, for the sample companies, in detail. Based on the findings and the literature reviewed, an attempt has also been made to provide sound advice for practitioners (through a normative framework) enabling them to have better/effective investment decisions.

Further, in the post-liberalisation (1991) era, no major studies, except that by Jain and Kumar (1997), Anand (2002) and Jain and Yadav (2005) have been conducted on capital budgeting practices in India. The year 2008 was turbulent and unstable for the Indian corporate sector due to the impact of the global recession. Thus, there is a need to re-examine the corporate practices regarding capital budgeting decisions, particularly since a number of changes have taken place in the economic environment both domestically and internationally.

P.K. Jain et al., *Financial Management Practices: An Empirical Study of Indian Corporates*, India Studies in Business and Economics,
DOI 10.1007/978-81-322-0990-4_2, © Springer India 2013

According to the *World Investment Prospects Survey* undertaken by the United Nations Council on Trade and Development (UNCTAD) in 2009, four of the top five destinations preferred by the world's largest multinational companies are Brazil, the Russian Federation, India and China (the so-called BRIC economies). Interestingly, all these economies are estimated to have experienced a rise in inward foreign direct investment (FDI) in 2008 over 2007. However, the difficulties and uncertainties in their economies have increased substantially after the sudden worsening of the global financial crisis in September and October 2008. Coupled with the reduced availability of capital worldwide, this has led to a reversal of a growth cycle of inflows to these economies at year's (2008) end (source: UNCTAD website. http://www.unctad.org/en/docs/webdiaeia20095_en.pdf. Accessed 17 Nov 2011).

For better exposition, this chapter has been divided into thirteen sections. Section I lays down the scope and methodology. Section II contains the literature review on capital budgeting practices. (A brief literature review on the recent global financial crisis and its effect (if any) on India, has also been provided as Appendix 2.1.) Section III analyzes the level of investment activity undertaken by the sample companies. Section IV delves into their financing patterns. Section V contains the sectoral analysis based on the investment activity and its financing pattern. The level at which capital budgeting proposals originate in the sample companies constitutes the subject matter of section VI. Section VII examines evaluation techniques used by the companies for capital budgeting. Cost of capital and its determinants are discussed in section VIII. Risk considerations and related measures constitute the subject matter of section IX. Utilization of recent managerial strategic options like real options and abandonment options are also discussed in this section. Section X examines the investment patterns for the sample companies. Capital rationing forms the subject matter of Section XI. Section XII highlights the possible reasons for the failure of capital budgeting decisions (if any). Concluding observations are listed in section XIII. Finally, a normative framework is designed at the end of the chapter (based on teaching experience (to practitioners) of authors in India and abroad, literature reviewed and the present study's findings) for the possible benefit of and utilization by practitioners.

Section I Scope and Methodology

The BSE 200 index of the Bombay Stock Exchange (BSE) comprises of the top 200 companies listed with the Bombay Stock Exchange, based on their market capitalisation. Out of these 200 companies, 34 companies were engaged in the financial sector (as on 1 April 2010, the date of sample selection); therefore, the scope of this study is limited to the 166 nonfinancial BSE 200 companies engaged in manufacturing and service rendering businesses. The sample is representative in nature as the BSE 200 companies represent all industry groups (for details, refer to

Appendix 1.1, Chap. 1). This apart, the selected sample comprised 84.32% of the total market capitalisation on the Bombay Stock Exchange, as on 1 April 2010 (source: Bombay Stock Exchange (BSE) website. http://www.bseindia.com/about/abindices/bse200.asp). Clearly, the sample is representative of corporate sector enterprises in India.

The analysis in respect of the sample companies has been carried out on the basis of the two broad parameters: (1) the investment and financing activities of the sample companies and (2) the capital budgeting practices followed by such enterprises.

The relevant data (secondary) on the first aspect was collected from the Capitaline database, for 11 years (2001–2011). The other secondary data sources used to substantiate any missing data were the Bombay Stock Exchange's website and the company's annual reports. The 11-year period of the study is bifurcated into two subperiods/phases to ascertain whether there has been any significant change in investment and financing pattern of the companies over the years. For the purpose of the analysis, the first 6 years, w.e.f. 1 April 2000, to 31 March 2006 (for brevity referred to as 2000–2001 to 2005–2006), are referred to as phase 1 and the next 5 years, w.e.f. 1 April 2006, to 31 March 2011 (for brevity referred to as 2006–2007 to 2010–2011), as phase 2 (for detailed methodology, refer to Chap. 1). Phase 1 and phase 2 are considered two independent samples. The *t*-test as well as ANOVA (analysis of variance) has been administered to assess whether financial decisions relating to capital budgeting differed/changed during the second phase compared to the first phase, for the sample companies. A sectoral analysis has been conducted (for the level of investment and the financing pattern) to understand whether variances (if any) could be attributable to one/many constituent industrial sectors of our sample companies.

The period of the study is of particular importance because of the recession (originating due to the American financial crisis) that impacted the world economy towards the second half of 2008. Consequently, phase 2 (2007–2011) of the study has been divided into two sub-phases to ascertain the impact of recession. The first 2 years 2006–2007 and 2007–2008 denote the pre-recession phase (phase 3), and the subsequent 3 years 2008–2009, 2009–2010 and 2010–2011 denote the post-recession phase (phase 4) for the purpose of this study. It needs to be mentioned that though the impact of recession was assumed to be felt towards the second half of 2008 (June 2008, cited above), the entire year has been included in the post-recession phase primarily due to two reasons: data was available in a consolidated manner (in the balance sheets) and it was not feasible to separate it for a particular year (2008) on the basis of when recession actually started impacting a particular data variable.

Also, capital budgeting and other long-term financial decisions are based on 'stock' concepts (e.g. dividend payments and debt repayments are typically made at the end of the period; similarly, most of the capital investments do not normally take place in the beginning of the period), and changes (if any) in such decisions were expected to be made apparent only in the subsequent years, namely, 2009 onwards. It is also important to note here that the impact of recession ('…the worst is yet to come'; UNCTAD investment brief, 2009) would perhaps be felt for a longer period than the period covered by the study. However, the objective was to keep the study as contemporary and useful as possible, and this then constitutes the rationale for pre- and post-recession analysis.

To study the trend and its implications, descriptive statistical values/positional values, that is, mean, standard deviation, coefficient of variation, skewness, kurtosis, median and quartiles, have been computed for each year. The sample size varies from year to year depending upon the availability of data. To do away with the influence of extreme values, they have been excluded from computing average values. However, where their inclusion has been considered important, say, for preparation of frequency distribution, the extreme values are also considered.

The research instrument for primary data consisted of a questionnaire (Appendix 1.3, Chap. 1). Minor problems with language and interpretation in some questions were addressed in the pretest. Questions designed were simple and specific relating to objectives, policies and techniques relating to capital budgeting and other aspects of financial management as stated in Chap. 1 (Objectives). Opinion-based and subjective information was kept to a minimum in order to keep the study more objective and scientific.

The initial response was very poor; only a few companies (eight) responded. Subsequently, two reminders (both through post and email) were sent to the remaining (non-responding) companies. Personal contacts were also established with the companies located in and around Delhi. This part of the analysis is based on 31 responses received out of 166 after 2 reminders (a response rate of 18.67%).

The 31 respondent companies have not responded to all the questions contained in the questionnaire. Further, it is worth stating that the company response stating 'any other' is reckoned as a response and forms part of the analysis. The entire set of data has been analysed using Microsoft Excel spreadsheets and the statistics software SPSS, namely, Statistical Package for the Social Sciences.

Section II Literature Review

Literature is rife with varying aspects of capital budgeting decisions. The objective of this section is to enumerate the major findings of the select studies on the subject.

Kolb (1968) reviewed the state of development of the theory of capital budgeting, the progress made, the factors obscured and the problems that remained. Klammer (1973) observed that the success of capital budgeting depended on numerous factors including the generation of investment ideas, the availability of good analytical techniques, the proper use of these techniques and good estimates of the cash flows of proposed investments. Pike (1986) viewed capital budgeting within the broad framework of its structure and setting rather than with a focus on the technical apparatus involved. The study provided evidence of the continuing trend towards greater formalisation and sophistication in capital budgeting methods.

Mukherjee and Henderson (1987) carried out a survey with a four-stage framework for the capital budgeting process which revealed that many capital budgeting practices differed from what the relevant theory prescribed. Much of the gap, however, could be explained by deficiencies in the theory itself.

Lazaridis (2004) brought to surface some problems that small- and medium-sized companies in Cyprus encountered while implementing their investment policy. Block (2005) studied the use of capital budgeting procedures amongst industries.

Capital Budgeting Techniques

In the 1970s, the capital budgeting studies (Mao 1970) observed an increasing preference for nondiscounted capital budgeting techniques, in particular, the payback period. The studies (Petty et al. 1975; Chandra 1973; Porwal and Singhvi 1978) observed an inclination towards the use of discounted cash flow methods, in particular, the internal rate of return (IRR) method.

Gitman and Forrester (1977) surveyed the level of sophistication used in capital budgeting by leading firms and found that sophisticated techniques (for primary analysis) were most popular, particularly, the IRR. Taggart (1977) examined the capital budgeting decisions as a valuation problem; he observed that three capital budgeting procedures (the net present value, adjusted present value and flows-to-equity methods) corresponded to three different ways of approaching firm valuation. However, the studies of 1980s (Pandey 1985) noted that payback method was most popular followed by IRR method.

Velez and Nieto (1986) indicated the extent to which capital budgeting tools used were higher for large firms than for small firms. More than one-half of the large firms used discounted methods compared to the small firms covered in the survey made in the United States.

Bierman (1993) conducted a survey of capital budgeting techniques of the largest 100 firms in the Fortune 500 industrial firms listing. All the responding firms used time discounting in some form, and 99% of the firms (all except one) used IRR or NPV as either the primary or secondary method. Cherukuri (1996) selected top 300 nongovernment companies and compared their capital budgeting practices with those of Hong Kong, Malaysia and Singapore. The study revealed that 51% of the respondent companies used IRR, 30% used NPV and 38% and 19% respondents used, respectively, payback period and average rate of return (ARR) methods. Further, Cherukuri (1996) in his survey of 74 Indian companies found that a majority of these (51%) used IRR as investment evaluation criteria.

Graham and Harvey (2001) surveyed 392 chief financial officers (CFOs) to ascertain practices related to the cost of capital, capital budgeting and capital structure. The survey indicated that the large firms relied heavily on present value techniques and the capital asset pricing model; in contrast, small firms relied more on the payback criterion. Sandahl and Sjogren (2003) showed that the public sector companies were most frequent users of discounted cash flows (DCF) methods. In general, the companies seemed unconcerned with the tax consequences of capital budgeting decisions.

Berkovitch and Israel (2004) examined the use of NPV as an investment criterion and how this criterion could be dominated by other capital budgeting criteria like the IRR and the profitability index (PI). Their proposition of capital allocation showed that there were plausible scenarios where the well-known and often criticised capital budgeting criteria like IRR and PI would perform better than the NPV criterion in implementing a value-maximising project selection process. Jain and Yadav (2005) in their study of public enterprises in India observed that the most popular method used was the IRR followed by payback and ARR. Notably, NPV and the PI were the least preferred methods in this regard.

Lam et al. (2007) analysed results related to capital budgeting evaluation practices relevant amongst Hong Kong building contractors and revealed that 'formal financial evaluation' (usage of both DCF and non-DCF techniques) was the most popular technique for capital budget evaluation. Hermes et al. (2007) compared the use of capital budgeting techniques by Dutch and Chinese firms. The empirical analysis provided evidence that Dutch CFOs, on an average, used more sophisticated capital budgeting techniques than Chinese CFOs. At the same time, it was also observed that the difference between the techniques of the Dutch and Chinese firms was smaller than expected (based upon the differences in the level of economic development).

Chen (2008) empirically examined capital budgeting methods. Amongst other findings, firms with high product standardisation were observed to place more emphasis on DCF analysis while firms with low standardisation were more likely to focus on nonfinancial measures. Osborne (2010) evaluated the two important criteria for choosing between capital investment projects, namely, NPV and IRR against each other. Kester and Robbins (2011) have conducted a survey of investment appraisal techniques, used by Irish-listed companies, and observe that the capital budgeting practices have improved over the past decade and increasing number of companies use more sophisticated DCF techniques.

Cost of Capital

Beranek (1978) propounded that a NPV decision rule (to accept/reject investment opportunities) using weighted average cost of capital (WACC) as a discount rate was derived to conform to the objective of maximisation of shareholders' wealth. Pinches (1982) found that progress had been made in capital budgeting in both theory and practice in recent years. More concern was given to the cash flows. Firms were also willing to recognise that different projects, classes of projects or divisions were exposed to different degrees of risk, and hence, adjustments were needed (in the discount rate) to account for these differences.

Risk Management

Salazar and Sen (1968) described a simulation model of capital budgeting under uncertainty. Techniques of simulation and stochastic linear programming were employed to compute the expected returns of different portfolios of projects. Fogler (1972) observed that mathematical programming models could be the most important and extremely efficient for implementation of tactical capital budgeting procedures especially where there were, in effect, only one or two constraints and the impact of risk diversification was manageable. Schall and Sundem (1980) enquired about the capital budgeting techniques employed, the computation of the discount rate and of cash flows and the method of estimating and adjusting for project risk.

A trend towards incorporation of risk was also indicated by these studies.

Schall et al. (1978) assessed that the firms in highly uncertain environments were more prone to using sophisticated capital budgeting methods. Antle and Eppen (1985) studied three aspects of capital budgeting (existence of organisational slack, rationing of resources and cut-off rate) in firms and showed that they were linked/related to the presence of asymmetric information amongst the stakeholders of the firm. Kulatilaka (1985) suggested financial-economic decision process for investments in flexible manufacturing systems (FMS). Kwan and Yuan (1988) solved a capital budgeting problem involving sequential decisions amongst mutually exclusive independent projects and provided considerable computational and analytical simplification over the commonly used decision-tree approach. Kim (1992) examined participative budgeting in the context of the psychology of risk and noted that risk-averse workers created more budgetary slack than risk-neutral ones.

About 90% of respondent firms used shortening of the payback period method and 59% used sensitivity analysis for incorporating risk (Cherukuri 1996). Cornell (1999) recognised that relation between risk and duration depends on the genesis of the systematic risk. Collier and Berry (2002) suggested that organisational participants used four domains of risk, namely, financial, operational, political and personal in assessing their capital budgeting decisions. Verbeeten (2006) examined the impact of uncertainty on the sophistication of capital budgeting practices. An increase in financial uncertainty was associated with the use and importance of sophisticated capital budgeting practices. Bennouna et al. (2010) evaluated current techniques (including real options) in capital budgeting decision-making in Canada.

Bierman (1993) in a survey of 74 Fortune-100 firms reported that sensitivity analysis was noted to be the most widely used project risk analysis technique. The use of sophisticated risk analysis techniques like capital asset pricing model (CAPM) or Monte Carlo simulation was very limited due to lack of understanding.

Capital Rationing

Lee Sang and Lerro (1974) formalised goal programming solutions to the problem of capital budgeting and investment planning under capital rationing. They asserted that financial management can be effective only if it is based on well-formulated goals and objectives. Kira and Kusy (1990) suggested optimal project selection for capital expenditures assuming uncertain budgetary allocations.

In spite of a large number of studies (documented above), there are few studies only which have dealt with primary data as well as secondary data. The present study is a modest attempt to fill this void.

Section III Level of Investment Activity

The objective of this section is to examine the size and rate of investments made by the sample of 166 nonfinancial BSE 200 companies. Size of investment made each year is measured in terms of change (in percentage) in gross fixed assets (defined to include land and building, plant and machinery, capital work-in-progress and other fixed assets) at the end of the year, vis-à-vis, the gross fixed assets at the beginning of the year, that is, by taking the ratio of gross fixed assets at the end of the year to the gross fixed assets at the beginning of the year.

It represents the true figure of additional investments in fixed/long-term assets provided no revaluation and no sale or writing-off of fixed assets took place during the period under reference. Since data related to revaluation of fixed assets was available, the change during the period has been taken net of revaluation. However, owing to non-availability of data for sale or writing-off of such assets, the percentage change in gross fixed assets should/would be lower. This point should be borne in mind while interpreting the findings of this part of the analysis. Pre- and post-recession analysis (on investment volume) has also been undertaken in the section.

The sample of 166 nonfinancial BSE 200 companies has undertaken impressive investments in gross fixed assets during the period under study. For instance, the gross fixed assets increased nearly fourfold during 2001–2010, the respective figures being Indian Rupees (INR) 2,112.60 billion in 2001 and INR 7,954.98 billion in 2010 (source: Bombay Stock Exchange (BSE) website. http://www.bseindia.com/about/abindices/bse200.asp. Accessed 1 Apr 2010).

The percentage growth in gross fixed assets for year 2002, for example, has been calculated dividing gross block of assets in year 2002 less gross block of assets in year 2001(*100) by gross block of assets in year 2001.

The rate of growth in gross fixed assets has been equally impressive when it has been measured on year-to-year basis. The relevant data presented in Table 2.1 shows that the gross fixed assets of the sample of 166 nonfinancial BSE 200 companies have increased at an average rate of 18.06% during the 11-year period of the study (2001–2011), a commendable growth of nearly three times when compared to the mean of 6.90% (for the period of 1991–2003) reported by the public sector enterprises (Jain and Yadav 2005). A paired samples t-test of percentage growth in gross fixed assets pertaining to the sample companies has also been given as a part of Table 2.1.

The sample companies recorded an increase in the growth of fixed assets in phase 3 (20.52%) which decelerated to 17.66% in phase 4 (statistically significant).

Table 2.1 Mean, standard deviation, coefficient of variation, skewness, kurtosis, median and quartile values of percentage growth in gross fixed assets of the sample companies, 2001–2011 (Figures are in percentages)

Year ending[a]	Number	Mean	Standard deviation	Coefficient of variation (%)	Skewness	Kurtosis	Median	Quartile 1	Quartile 3
2002	117	15.11	18.62	123.28	2.31	5.90	8.41	3.97	16.01
2003	121	14.83	15.65	105.49	1.64	2.82	8.66	3.24	23.48
2004	125	17.53	20.48	116.82	1.94	3.70	9.59	3.94	23.47
2005	134	18.08	19.47	107.65	1.78	3.31	10.28	4.84	23.85
2006	138	21.00	21.24	101.12	1.61	2.39	13.39	5.68	28.67
2007	137	21.88	21.34	97.53	1.57	2.25	14.74	6.81	29.23
2008	144	19.17	18.15	94.72	1.70	3.37	13.33	6.84	25.25
2009	153	20.55	17.96	87.38	1.59	3.11	15.91	7.84	28.39
2010	142	17.29	17.35	100.33	2.16	5.02	11.36	6.53	22.29
2011	143	15.14	12.94	85.49	1.28	1.33	10.91	5.32	22.21
2001–2011	135	18.06	18.32	101.98	1.76	3.32	11.66	5.50	24.29
Phase 1 (2000–2001 to 2005–2006)	128	17.31	19.09	110.87	1.86	3.62	10.07	4.33	23.10
Phase 2 (2006–2007 to 2010–2011)	145	18.81	17.55	93.09	1.66	3.02	13.25	6.67	25.47
Phase 3 (2006–2007 to 2007–2008)	141	20.52	19.75	96.13	1.63	2.81	14.03	6.82	27.24
Phase 4 (2008–2009 to 2010–2011)	148	17.66	16.08	91.07	1.68	3.15	12.73	6.56	24.30

[a]The Indian financial year begins on April 1 and ends on March 31 of the following year. The same holds true for all subsequent tables and notations

	Paired differences							
				95% Confidence interval of the difference				
	Mean	Standard deviation	Standard error mean	Lower	Upper	t	df	Significance (2-tailed)
Phase 1–Phase 2	−1.46112	14.13846	1.13563	−3.70454	0.78230	−1.287	154	0.200
Phase 3–Phase 4	3.65629	17.37289	1.39995	0.89057	6.42201	2.612	153	0.010

In the paired t-test and ANOVA, in case the value of significance (2-tailed) is 0.05 or less, the alternate hypothesis that there is significant difference in two phases is accepted; when its value exceeds 0.05, the alternate hypothesis is rejected implying that there is no significant difference in the two phases

Though this may seem as a matter of concern, it is encouraging to note that in spite of the recession, the average growth remained close to the entire period average (18.06%). This could perhaps be due to the inherent fundamental strength of the sample companies, the Indian economy's resilience and risk management measures undertaken by the Reserve Bank of India (e.g. prudential norms governing the financial sector and domestic financing of investments) as mentioned in the literature cited.

It is interesting to note here that the median value for the sample companies (11.66%) for the entire period of the study is lower than the median value (12.80%) reported by the study on private sector enterprises for the period 1986–1995 (Jain and Kumar 1997). However, more encouragingly, the mean value reported by them (16.10%) was considerably lower than the mean of 18.06 reported by the sample.

It is encouraging to note that the investment rate in acquisition of new fixed assets (say, plant and machinery, new technology, communication infrastructure, etc.) has shown an increase in phase 2 compared to phase 1. There was a higher average annual rate of investment (18.81%) during phase 2 (2006–2007 to 2010–2011) vis-à-vis 17.31% during phase 1 (2002–2006). However, the paired t-test result indicates that there is no statistically significant difference between the mean values of the two subperiods (phases 1 and 2). This is also supported by the trend (Fig. 2.1) which denotes a decline in 2008 (the year when the impact of recession was observed in the Indian economy) which continued till 2010, with indications perhaps of recovery in 2011.

The median related to growth rate of average annual investment is at a much lower figure of 11.66% for the period of the study. The quartile one value is low at 5.50% which indicates that one-fourth of the sample companies could invest only at a rate of around five and a half per cent per year in their fixed assets. Only one-fourth of the sample companies invested at a rate of about/less than 25% (quartile 3 value is 24.29%) per year.

Similar conclusions could be drawn on the basis of frequency distribution data (Table 2.2). The vast majority of the sample companies had growth rates of higher than 5% during 2001–2011. In phase 2, there was a decline in the negative growth trend of the sample companies (implying lesser sale or writing-off of fixed assets). The growth rate of 10% or more was observed in more than half of the sample enterprises during the second phase of the study (2006–2007 to 2010–2011). Data of 2011, however, indicates the presence of extreme values with 23.78% companies recording a negative growth in fixed assets; at the same time, more than four-tenth of the sample companies posted a growth in fixed assets of more than 100%.

The above findings of the high rate of capital investment and a marked increase in the investment rate over the years by the sample companies may be attributed to the economic liberalisation of the Indian economy in the year 1991 and the period of consolidation that followed. The Indian gross domestic product (GDP), at market prices, has increased more than 12 times from INR 6,547.29 billion in 1991–1992 to INR 78,756.27 billion in 2010–2011 (Source: Table 1 from Reserve Bank of India's Database on Indian Economy. http://dbie.rbi.org.in/InfoViewApp/listing/main.do?ap

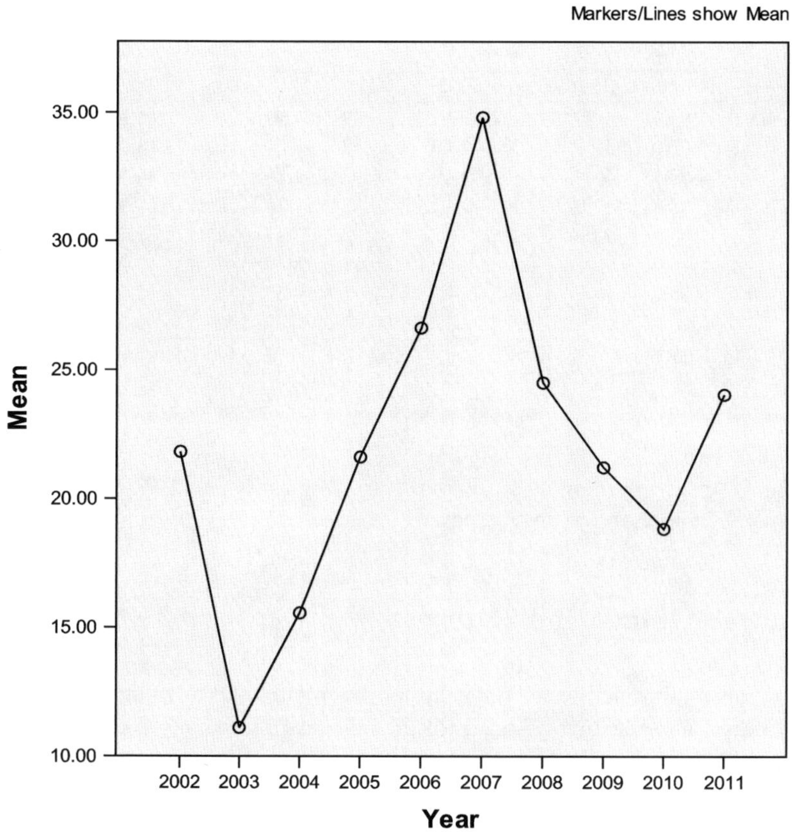

Fig. 2.1 Mean values of percentage growth in gross fixed assets of the sample companies, 2002–2011

pKind=InfoView&service=%2FInfoViewApp%2Fcommon%2FappService.do. Accessed 19 Oct 2011). It is also worth mentioning that the sample companies have a continual track record of profitability and good performance. Another aspect of increased level of investment in fixed assets by these companies is perhaps the encouraging environment for raising corporate finance because of the increasing robustness of the capital markets in the country over the same period. The market capitalisation at the Bombay Stock Exchange recorded a growth of a rather remarkable 21 times from INR 3,233.63 billion in 1991–1992 to INR 68,368.78 billion in 2010–2011(source: Table 99 from Reserve Bank of India's Database on Indian Economy. http://dbie.rbi.org.in/InfoViewApp/listing/main.do?appKind=InfoView&service=%2FInfoViewApp%2Fcommon%2FappService.do. Accessed 19 Oct 2011). Also, the assets under management of mutual funds grew nearly seven times from INR 858.22 billion in 1997 to INR 5,922.50 billion in 2011 (Source: Table 85

Table 2.2 Frequency distribution of the percentage growth in gross fixed assets of the sample companies, 2001–2011 (Figures are in percentages)

Growth in gross fixed assets (%)	2002	2003	2004	2005	2006	2007	2008	2009	2010	2011
Less than 0	8.33	14.29	13.10	7.10	8.28	4.97	4.27	4.24	7.32	23.78
0–5	36.90	35.71	31.55	23.87	20.38	18.01	19.51	13.94	14.02	1.22
5–10	18.45	16.07	14.88	19.35	15.92	11.80	14.02	16.36	27.44	1.22
10–20	14.88	11.90	14.88	16.13	19.75	21.74	22.56	27.88	20.73	0.61
20–50	10.71	17.86	15.48	21.29	22.93	25.47	26.83	29.70	20.73	9.76
50–100	4.76	2.98	7.74	7.74	10.19	8.70	5.49	5.45	4.88	22.56
Above 100	5.95	1.19	2.38	4.52	2.55	9.32	7.32	2.42	4.88	40.85
Total	100	100	100	100	100	100	100	100	100	100

Total (100) may not tally due to rounding off. The same holds true for other frequency distribution tables

from Reserve Bank of India's Database on Indian Economy. http://dbie.rbi.org.in/InfoViewApp/listing/main.do?appKind=InfoView&service=%2FInfoViewApp%2Fcommon%2FappService.do. Accessed 19 Oct 2011).

Section IV Financing Pattern

As per the sound principles of financial management, long-term investment/capital expenditure/capital budgeting needs of the business enterprises should be financed from permanent/long-term sources of finance. The subject matter of this section examines the financing practices of the sample companies in this regard.

The data pertaining to the relative share of net fixed assets to the total permanent capital employed in respect of the sample companies have been presented in Table 2.3 and Fig. 2.2. From the data contained in Table 2.3, it is gratifying to note that long-term investment needs (measured in terms of fixed assets, net of depreciation) have been financed by long-term sources/permanent capital (defined as equity capital + preference capital + reserves and surplus + long-term borrowings – revaluation reserves – miscellaneous expenses not written off).

In all the years of the study (2001–2011), the fixed assets (net)/permanent capital ratio was considerably lower than 100 (the range being 32–48%), signifying that long-term funds have been the main source of financing fixed/long-term assets. The relevant mean and median figures are 40 and 39% respectively for the sample companies for the period 2001–2011 as per Table 2.3. The skewness of the sample also varied considerably through the period of the study. From the fourth year (of the study) onwards, lesser and lesser companies recorded a large FAPC; this supports the trend. The negative kurtosis also indicates the dominance of low FAPC ratios. This is also in sharp contrast to the average FAPC of 68% reported by Jain and Kumar (1997) for private sector enterprises and the average of 69.06% reported by Jain and Yadav (2005) for public sector enterprises in India, indicative of a continual reduction in FAPC over a much larger time span than covered by the present study.

Table 2.3 Mean, standard deviation, coefficient of variation, skewness, kurtosis, median and quartile values related to percentage share of fixed assets (net) to permanent capital employed (FAPC) of the sample companies, 2001–2011 (Figures are in percentages)

Year ending	Number	Mean	Standard deviation	Coefficient of variation (%)	Skewness	Kurtosis	Median	Quartile 1	Quartile 3
2001	135	44.00	23.00	52.76	−12.00	−61.00	45.00	28.00	61.00
2002	141	48.00	26.00	55.11	−5.00	−74.00	47.00	30.00	67.00
2003	145	46.00	26.00	56.76	−7.00	−78.00	47.00	27.00	65.00
2004	145	44.00	27.00	60.28	8.00	−87.00	45.00	26.00	63.00
2005	149	42.00	27.00	63.62	32.00	−72.00	40.00	24.00	59.00
2006	153	39.00	25.00	64.49	40.00	−59.00	37.00	19.00	54.00
2007	157	39.00	26.00	66.18	46.00	−64.00	37.00	18.00	55.00
2008	160	36.00	24.00	67.73	43.00	−62.00	33.00	17.00	52.00
2009	162	37.00	25.00	69.02	43.00	−65.00	34.00	16.00	53.00
2010	158	34.00	25.00	72.67	54.00	−57.00	32.00	13.00	50.00
2011	159	32.00	25.00	77.90	67.00	−37.00	29.00	10.00	48.00
2001–2011	149	40.00	25.00	64.23	28.00	−65.00	39.00	21.00	57.00
Phase 1 (2000–2001 to 2005–2006)	144	44.00	26.00	58.84	9.00	−72.00	43.00	26.00	62.00
Phase 2 (2006–2007 to 2010–2011)	160	36.00	25.00	70.70	51.00	−57.00	33.00	15.00	52.00
Phase 3 (2006–2007 to 2007–2008)	159	37.50	25.00	66.96	44.00	−63.00	35.00	18.00	54.00
Phase 4 (2008–2009 to 2010–2011)	160	34.33	25.00	73.20	55.00	−53.00	32.00	13.00	50.00

	Paired differences							
				95% Confidence interval of the difference				
	Mean	Standard deviation	Standard error mean	Lower	Upper	*t*	*df*	Significance (2-tailed)
Phase 1–Phase 2	0.07699	0.19607	0.01550	0.04638	0.10761	4.967	159	0.000
Phase 3–Phase 4	0.02733	0.13411	0.01057	0.00645	0.04820	2.585	160	0.011

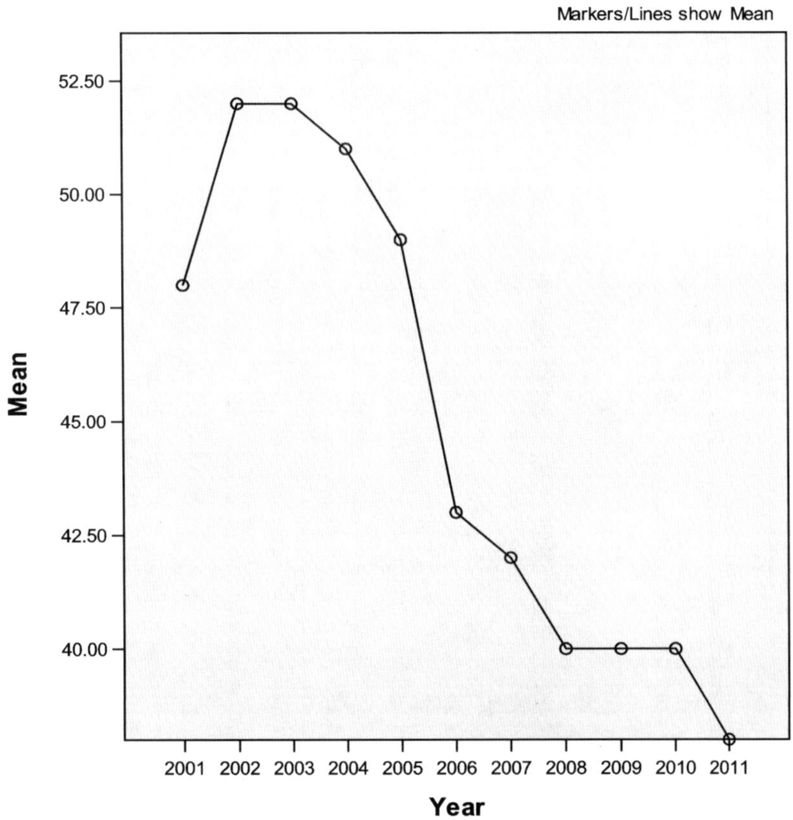

Fig. 2.2 Mean values of percentage share of fixed assets (net) to permanent capital employed (FAPC) of the sample companies, 2001–2011

The paired samples t-test indicates a significant difference in the mean values over the four phases under consideration, indicating that the financing pattern changed significantly; in fact, the ratio declined throughout the period of the study. This sound financing pattern of having long-term funds, as a primary source of financing fixed assets, seems to have facilitated (to a marked extent) to withstand better the adversities of post-recession period (2009–2011). Similar soundness in financing patterns was observed in the study of private enterprises of India, Singapore and Thailand (Jain and Yadav 2000).

The frequency distribution data (Table 2.4) is more revealing on the subject. Data of the year 2011 shows that on average, only about 3.64% of the sample companies do not have the required long-term funds even to meet their capital investment needs as the FAPC exceeds 100%.

It is important to emphasise that the long-term capital is also preferred/desired to meet core/permanent working capital needs of an enterprise. Therefore, the

Table 2.4 Frequency distribution of relative share of fixed assets (net) to permanent capital employed of the sample companies, 2001–2011 (Figures are in percentages)

FAPC ratio (%)	2001	2002	2003	2004	2005	2006	2007	2008	2009	2010	2011
Less than 20	15.60	15.44	15.69	18.83	20.75	24.22	27.61	27.71	28.31	34.94	38.18
20–40	22.70	20.81	26.14	24.03	25.79	26.71	26.99	30.72	25.30	22.89	26.67
40–60	27.66	24.83	24.18	24.03	25.16	24.22	22.70	19.88	25.30	22.29	18.18
60–80	25.53	22.15	19.61	17.53	10.69	13.04	10.43	13.86	12.05	7.23	6.06
80–100	4.26	11.41	9.15	9.74	11.32	6.83	8.59	4.22	6.63	7.83	7.27
Above 100	4.26	5.37	3.92	5.84	6.29	4.35	3.07	3.61	2.41	4.82	3.64
Total	100	100	100	100	100	100	100	100	100	100	100

fixed assets to permanent capital (FAPC) ratio should also be viewed in conjunction with finances available to meet working capital needs of a business enterprise. The FAPC ratio can be used to know the extent of long-term funds available to meet working capital needs; the difference between 100 and FAPC ratio, expressed in percentage, indicates funds available to meet working capital needs. The FAPC ratio of the sample companies indicates that more than half of the long-term funds are available to finance working capital needs of these enterprises. This aspect, prima facie, is a clear indicator of the sample firms banking, to a marked extent, on long-term sources to finance their working capital needs. Viewed from another perspective, it is a matter of concern also as it is indicative of surplus funds available which could be used for long-term investment or to refund the long-term borrowings.

In operational terms, the low FAPC ratio may be indicative of the mismatch (in terms of surplus funds) between the long-term avenues of finance and long-term financial requirements of the business enterprises.

To provide greater insight into the employment of permanent capital by the sample companies, to cater to its long-term needs, net working capital for the sample companies was computed as current assets less operational current liabilities (excluding short-term financial obligations like bank overdraft, short-term bank loans, etc.). This figure was then added to the fixed assets (net), and the resultant ratio of fixed assets (net) + net working capital was computed and tabulated in Table 2.5. Value of 100 or less for this ratio is indicative of the companies financing their fixed assets as well as net working capital through their permanent capital, an example of extremely sound financial management (Fig. 2.3 and Table 2.6).

By and large, the sample companies are financing their fixed assets and net working capital through permanent capital, indicative of sound financial management practice. However, on the other hand, an average of 61% indicates that more than one-third of the funds are lying idle which could perhaps be utilised to finance additional fixed assets and/or paying off/redeeming debt. The sample companies would perhaps do well to consider deployment of excess funds.

Table 2.5 Mean, median and quartile values related to percentage share of fixed assets (net) + net working capital to permanent capital employed of the sample companies, 2001–2011 (Figures are in percentages)

Year ending	Number	Mean	Standard deviation	Coefficient of variation (%)	Skewness	Kurtosis	Median	Quartile 1	Quartile 3
2001	99	68.00	25.00	36.95	−78.00	−0.21	75.00	51.00	88.00
2002	124	44.00	32.00	71.92	10.00	−1.31	43.00	13.00	73.00
2003	102	68.00	27.00	39.14	−87.00	−0.15	74.00	52.00	89.00
2004	104	67.00	26.00	39.14	−74.00	−0.29	71.00	50.00	91.00
2005	104	62.00	28.00	45.00	−71.00	−0.53	68.00	45.00	87.00
2006	115	60.00	28.00	46.79	−55.00	−0.72	63.00	40.00	84.00
2007	119	61.00	27.00	43.88	−44.00	−0.81	64.00	43.00	85.00
2008	117	58.00	26.00	45.36	−41.00	−0.74	58.00	41.00	80.00
2009	125	61.00	26.00	41.88	−56.00	−0.68	66.00	43.00	82.00
2010	127	58.00	26.00	44.50	−24.00	−0.98	57.00	38.00	82.00
2011	148	62.00	25.00	40.47	−49.00	−0.59	67.00	42.00	82.00
2001–2011	124	61.00	27.00	45.00	−52.00	−0.64	64.00	42.00	84.00
Phase 1 (2000–2001 to 2005–2006)	112	62.00	28.00	46.49	−59.00	−0.54	65.00	42.00	85.00
Phase 2 (2006–2007 to 2010–2011)	134	60.00	26.00	43.22	−43.00	−0.76	62.00	41.0	82.00
Phase 3 (2006–2007 to 2007–2008)	118	60.00	27.00	44.62	−43.00	−0.78	61.00	42.00	82.00
Phase 4 (2008–2009 to 2010–2011)	137	60.00	25.00	42.28	−43.00	−0.75	63.00	41.00	82.00

	Paired differences							
				95% Confidence interval of the difference				
	Mean	Standard deviation	Standard error mean	Lower	Upper	t	df	Significance (2-tailed)
Phase 1–Phase 2	−0.02140	0.23977	0.01971	−0.06035	0.01755	−1.086	147	0.279
Phase 3–Phase 4	0.01064	0.18818	0.01650	−0.02201	0.04329	0.645	129	0.520

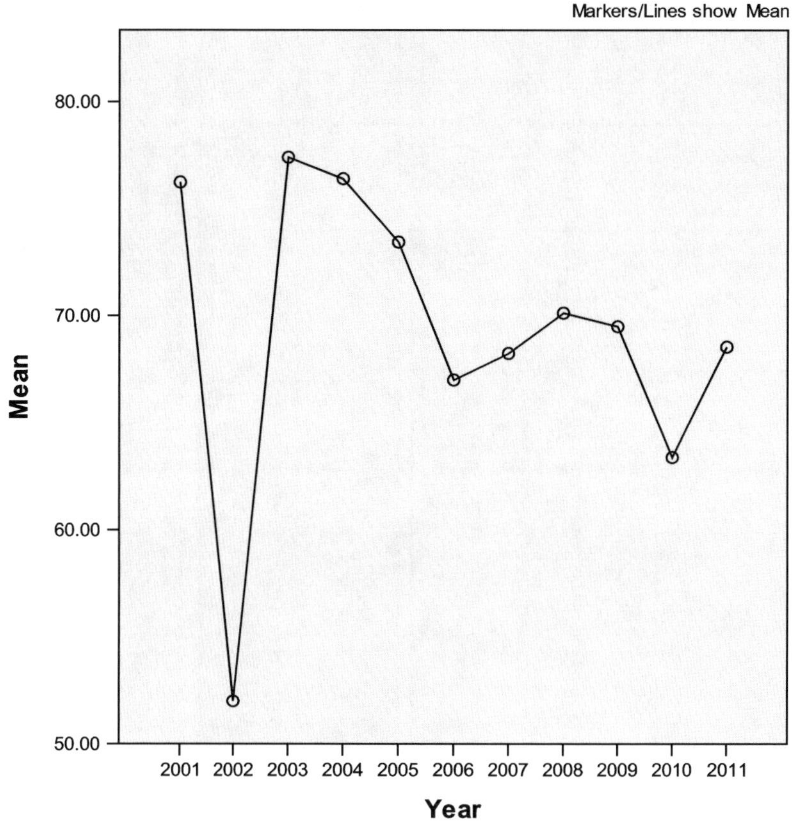

Fig. 2.3 Mean values of percentage of fixed assets (net) + net working capital to permanent capital employed of the sample companies, 2001–2011

Section V Sectoral Analysis

Investment Activity

The constituent sectors (Table 1.2, Chap. 1) of the sample companies maintained growth throughout the period of the study. The diversified sector companies (probably due to their diversified nature) were not only able to sustain recession (towards the second half of the study) but posted a substantial increase (nearly twofold) in the growth of gross fixed assets in phase 2 when compared with phase 1. ICT and metals sector also recorded statistically significant increase in their assets-building (Appendix 2.2).

It is rather commendable that none of the sectors appear to have a negative impact on their assets-building due to the recession (Appendix 2.3). The diversified sector companies posted a substantial increase (nearly four times) in the growth of gross fixed assets in the post-recession period vis-à-vis the pre-recession period.

Table 2.6 Frequency distribution of relative share of fixed assets (net) + net working capital to permanent capital employed of the sample companies, 2001–2011 (Figures are in percentages)

Fixed assets + net working capital/ permanent capital employed (%)	2001	2002	2003	2004	2005	2006	2007	2008	2009	2010	2011
Less than 50	16.31	44.45	21.42	21.93	22.65	27.95	27.61	27.10	24.69	31.32	28.49
50–80	26.24	20.37	24.02	23.87	25.16	24.47	25.15	28.31	29.25	27.11	38.79
80–100	29.08	14.81	25.97	27.10	20.13	21.74	23.31	17.47	22.29	21.08	24.24
100–120	11.35	6.17	14.94	9.03	11.32	6.21	6.75	10.24	7.83	5.42	3.64
120–150	4.97	3.09	3.25	6.45	6.92	3.73	3.68	7.23	4.82	3.01	3.64
Above 150	12.06	11.11	10.39	11.61	13.84	14.91	13.50	9.64	10.85	12.05	1.21
Total	100	100	100	100	100	100	100	100	100	100	100

The sample underwent statistically significant changes in the variances in a consolidated form (through the ANOVA test), for the entire period of the study, whereas the housing sector did the same for phases 1 and 2 (Appendix 2.4).

Financing Pattern

Transport sector recorded the highest FAPC at 56.60% in phase 1 which reduced to 44.20% (statistically significant) in phase 2 (Appendix 2.5); it further declined to 41.50% in phase 4 from 48.20% in phase 3 (Appendix 2.6). The other sectors that noted a statistically significant decline were diversified, healthcare, housing and oil and gas in phase 2 over phase 1.

ANOVA statistics were significant for the consolidated sample as a whole throughout the period of the study and for the healthcare and transport sectors during phases 1 and 2 (Appendix 2.7).

In terms of the fixed assets + net working capital to permanent capital employed, the capital goods sector (expectedly) recorded the highest percentage at 71.20% in phase 1 which increased to 72.70% in phase 2 (Appendix 2.8). The FMCG sector reported the lowest percentage at 40% which increased to 45.30% in phase 2 (indicative of more than half of funds lying idle, which could be a matter of concern).

The sectors that reported a decrease in the above ratio in phase 4 over phase 3 were capital goods, ICT, metals, oil and gas, transport and miscellaneous (Appendix 2.9). None of these changes were statistically significant. The ANOVA was statistically significant only for the consolidated sample in phases 3 and 4 (Appendix 2.10).

By and large, the constituent sectors appear to have withstood the recession, without substantial changes in their asset building and financing activities.

In view of the significant value of investments made by the sample companies, it is imperative for them to follow sound/prudent capital budgeting practices rather than rule-of-thumb or ad hoc approach. What have been the actual practices in this regard amongst the sample corporate enterprises constitute the subject matter of the subsequent sections.

Section VI Origination and Planning of Capital Budgeting Proposals

The level of origination of new investment proposals in the sample companies would provide an insight into the management hierarchy followed by the companies while making long-term investment decisions. From Table 2.7, it is evident that majority of the sample companies (72.41%) have the origination of new investment proposals at central/head office level indicating control by the top management on such decisions. In fact, in nearly half (48.27%) of the sample companies, new investment proposals originate at the highest level exclusively. This aspect has

Table 2.7 Origination of new investment proposals for the sample companies

Origination of new investment proposals	Percentage
At central/head office level	72.41 (48.27)
At plant level	31.03 (10.34)
At divisional/regional office level	27.58 (6.89)
At any other level[a]	3.44 (3.44)

Figures in brackets indicate that the new investment proposals have originated exclusively at the level stated. (–) indicates not even one BSE 200 company uses the technique exclusively

These notes are applicable to all other tables prepared on the basis of survey

[a]There was no specific level mentioned as a part of this response

Table 2.8 Planning horizon for capital expenditure for the sample companies

Planning horizon for capital expenditure	Percentage
For next 5 years	68.96 (62.06)
For next 1 year only	17.24 (6.89)
For next 10 years	6.89 (6.89)
As and when the opportunity takes place	6.89 (3.44)
Any other[a]	17.24 (6.89)

[a]Included 'period of 1–2 years', '3 years', '3 years view on product and capacities' and 'depends on the industry segment targeting'

shown an increase from the 67% reported by Jain and Kumar (1997) from a study of private sector enterprises in India over 1986–1995. More than one-fourth (27.58%) of the sample companies indicate that the new investment proposals originate at divisional/regional office level as well, pointing towards decision-making at regional levels. A revealing finding of our survey is an indication of participative style of management; it is evidenced by the fact that nearly one-third of the sample companies report that new investment proposals originate at plant level (with nearly one-tenth companies stating this exclusively).

On a priori basis, the investment planning horizon is directly related to the level at which proposals generally originate; in general, the higher the level, the longer is the planning horizon time span.

Data contained in Table 2.8 indicates that more than half of the responding companies (68.96%) have been planning their capital budgets for the next 5 years; in contrast, less than one-fifth (17.24%) of the sample companies are planning 1 year in advance. Further, it is satisfying to note that only a few companies use ad hoc approach (as and when opportunity takes place) to plan their long-term investments.

Table 2.9 Capital budgeting decision technique(s) used by the sample companies in India

Capital expenditure evaluation technique	Percentage
Companies using DCF as well as non-DCF techniques	**100.00**
Internal rate of return	78.57
Payback period	64.28
Net present value	50.00
Accounting rate of return on investment	39.28
Profitability index/present value index	21.42
Any other technique[a]	7.14

[a]Specific responses stated 'economic profit'

Likewise, planning for capital projects in advance is a rare phenomenon; the probable reason is that it is difficult to forecast revenues and costs for such a distant future in this highly turbulent business world.

Section VII Evaluation Techniques

Previous researches show that conceptually sound techniques (as per scholarly literature) are well accepted. However, they are not universally observed in management practice (Bennouna et al. 2010). Given the strategic nature of the capital budgeting decisions and their implication for growth, profitability and, above all, survival of the firms, the adoption of theoretically correct and sound evaluation techniques (naturally) assumes paramount significance.

The objective of this section is to have insight regarding the state of current practices on the subject and assess whether the responding sample companies are following appropriate and sound evaluation techniques or not. The survey data related to the use of capital expenditure techniques are contained in Table 2.9.

It is encouraging to note that all the respondent companies used both discounted and nondiscounted cash flow techniques to evaluate capital expenditure. This is in sharp contrast to findings of the Bennouna et al. (2010) study of large Canadian firms and Jain and Yadav (2005) study of public sector enterprises in India, where 17% did not use discounted cash flows (DCF). Amongst DCF techniques, the majority favoured net present value (NPV) and internal rate of return (IRR). These findings are in contrast also to the findings of Jain and Kumar (1997) where nearly one-fifth of the sample companies used only traditional methods.

The traditional nondiscounted techniques, though used rigorously initially, are today mostly applied as a supplementary method in combination with the DCF techniques. Similar findings are observable in our survey. A sizable number of responding companies although continue to follow traditional methods, namely, payback period (64.28%) and accounting rate of return (39.28%), it is pertinent to note that the sample companies are using these methods in conjunction with the discounted cash flow (DCF) techniques (Table 2.9).

Table 2.10 Reasons behind the usage of payback period method for the sample companies

Reasons for using the payback period method	Percentage
Easy to explain to top management	31.25 (12.50)
Simplicity leading to less time and cost involved	31.25 (18.75)
Shortage of liquid funds	12.50 (12.50)
Obsolescence due to technological developments	12.50 (12.50)
Any other[a]	50.00 (43.75)

[a]Includes 'helps in optimal resource allocation', 'suitable for small projects', 'determines timely return on assets', 'relates to period of investments getting returned', 'useful as a tool for cash management' and 'gives quick view of cash flows'

Another notable finding of the survey is that the conceptually sound method of NPV is followed only by one-half of the companies; IRR (relatively deficient compared to NPV) has been observed to be practised most (more than three-fourths) by the respondent companies. Firms in Canada also prefer to use IRR. The accounting rate of return (ARR) and the profitability index (21.42%) are the least preferred methods in this regard. Studies in the past 50 years show the increase in DCF techniques have come at the expense of naïve methods, particularly the ARR (Bennouna et al. 2010).

The payback period continues to be a popular method amongst the nondiscounted cash flow (non-DCF) techniques used in evaluating capital budgeting proposals due to its simple calculation and ease of understanding (Table 2.10).

Also, a number of other varied reasons have also emerged (cited above as a part of the 'any other' response category) that would perhaps ensure its longevity in Indian capital budgeting evaluation techniques.

Section VIII Cost of Capital

Cost of capital forms an integral part of capital budgeting in that it provides a yardstick to measure the worth of investment proposals and thus performs the role of accept–reject criterion. The accept–reject rule requires that a business enterprise should avail of only such investment opportunities that promise a rate of return higher than cost of capital. Conversely, the enterprise would do well to reject proposals whose rates of return are less than the cost of capital. The cost of capital, thus, provides a rational mechanism for making optimum investment decisions.

The preceding discussion clearly underlines the crucial significance of the correct computation of cost of capital. Despite the vital importance of cost of capital as the minimum required rate of return/target rate, the basis of its computation has been a source of considerable controversy amongst both theoreticians and practitioners.

Table 2.11 Method(s) used to determine cost of capital by the sample companies

Method used to determine cost of capital	Percentage
Weighted average cost of long-term sources of finance	67.85 (53.57)
Marginal cost of additional funds raised to finance new asset	28.57 (14.28)
Decided by the top management	14.28 (10.71)
Any other[a]	7.14 (3.57)

[a]Includes 'cost of equity' and 'capital asset pricing method (CAPM) being used exclusively'

The methods followed, in practice, by the sample companies to determine the cost of capital form the subject matter of this section.

It is evident from the data contained in Table 2.11 that more than that two-thirds (67.85%) of the sample companies adopt theoretically sound and conceptually correct basis for determining cost of capital, that is, weighted average cost (WACC) of long-term sources of finance. In fact, more than half (53.57%) adopt this method exclusively. This is a heartening finding as it shows that the sample companies are following sound financial tenets in determining cost of capital. This is similar to the finding of Jain and Kumar (1997) where 67% of the respondent companies (related to private sector corporate enterprises) utilised WACC and in contrast to the findings of Jain and Yadav (2005) where less than half of the sample companies (central public sector enterprises) adopted WACC.

Theory suggests that in order to use the WACC as the discount rate for all proposed capital investments, the proposed investments must have the same risk level as the average risk of the firm. If the risk of a proposed investment differs substantially from that of the overall firm, then it is necessary to determine a specific minimum acceptable return for that investment. In other words, if proposed capital investments vary with respect to risk, a multiple risk-adjusted discount (hurdle) rate system should be employed, with riskier investments requiring higher minimum rates of return. Otherwise, accept/reject decisions will be biased in favour of high-risk investments and against low-risk investments (Kester and Robbins 2011). To the extent that divisions in a corporate have degrees of risk and financial characteristics that are different from the parent corporate, using the overall corporate hurdle rate leads to incorrect decisions and failure to maximise stockholder wealth (Block 2005).

However, at the same time, it is ironical to note that one-tenth of the sample companies use cost of capital which is exclusively determined by the top management. 'Marginal cost of additional funds raised to finance new asset' method of computing cost of capital is followed by nearly one-third of the sample companies (28.57%).

One revealing finding of the survey is that capital asset pricing model (CAPM) is yet to have its foothold as a measure of determination of cost of equity amongst Indian corporates.

Table 2.12 Weights used for average cost of capital for the sample companies

Weights used for average cost of capital	Percentage
Market value weights	45.45
Target weights	31.81
Book value weights	18.18

Table 2.13 Sample companies opting for sound capital structure in the course of capital expenditure projects to ensure a low cost of capital

Opting for sound capital structure to ensure low cost of capital	Percentage
Yes	100.00
No	–

It was of interest to enquire about the 'type of weights' used in computing the cost of capital. The survey data (contained in Table 2.12) indicate that a sizeable number of the sample companies (45.45%) use market value weights and target weights (31.81%) which are sound as per financial theory. The book value weights which are operationally convenient to be used are the least preferred (less than one-fifth of the companies).

Given the fact that the vast majority of the sample companies use appropriate weights, it is reasonable to conclude that the sample companies seem to follow the sound methods of determining cost of capital.

Sound capital structure ensures the lowest plausible weighted average cost of capital; it is expected that the sample companies would make a conscious effort towards designing and maintaining such a capital structure. It is overwhelming to note (from the survey) that all the respondent companies (100%) opt for sound capital structure to ensure a low cost of capital (Table 2.13). It is thus encouraging to note the sample companies have knowledge of sound financial theories related to capital structure and cost of capital, as well as they seem to be practising them.

Section IX Risk Considerations

The term risk with reference to capital budgeting/investment decision may be defined as the variability in actual returns emanating from a project, over its working life, in relation to the estimated return as forecasted at the time of the initial capital budgeting decision.

The effective handling of risk is an important but complex task in capital budgeting process. Since the element of uncertainty in estimates of future cash flows, economic life of project and cost of capital cannot be completely eliminated, each firm is expected to recognise and explicitly deal with it. Hence, the sample companies were asked to specify the technique/approach used to deal with project risk.

Table 2.14 Approaches to incorporate project risk in investment decision process of the sample companies

Approaches to incorporate project risk	Percentage
Sensitivity analysis	96.15 (69.23)
Shorter payback period for risky projects	11.53 (3.84)
Higher cut-off rate for risky projects	11.53 (–)
Any other[a]	7.69 (–)

[a]Includes 'higher hurdle rate 'and 'scenario analysis'

As depicted in Table 2.14, the survey reveals that almost all respondent companies use sensitivity analysis as an approach to incorporate project risk in investment decisions (96.15%). In fact, 69.23% companies use this method exclusively.

It appears that the advent of computer technologies and software is perhaps enabling and encouraging the sample companies to carry out complex sensitivity analysis (by incorporating numerous economic and financial scenarios).

Sensitivity analysis is followed by 'shorter payback period for risky projects' and 'higher cut-off rate for risky projects' methods; each of these methods is used by more than one-tenth (11.53%) of the companies. The low-risk projects are assigned the minimum discount rate and the high-risk projects the maximum rate.

Real Options and Abandonment Options

In making capital budgeting decisions, opportunities available to respond to changing circumstances (influencing the outcome of a project) are called managerial strategic options; in practice, they are more popularly known as real options as they are associated with real assets. In operational terms, a project having negative NPV may turn out eventually worth accepting, keeping in mind the options such a project creates in terms of opportunities to expand in the future.

Like real options, abandonment options assume equal significance in capital projects. An abandonment option is an option to abandon/shut down/terminate a project prior to its expected useful life. Such an embedded option enables the management to minimise a firm's losses, in case the project turns out to be bad/unsuccessful. In other words, the projects having abandonment value, in many cases, can lower the project's risk by limiting downside losses and enhancing its expected profitability (NPV).

Since these are relatively new options/techniques used to address risk in capital budgeting decisions, it has been desired to explore whether the sample companies are knowledgeable about such techniques and better still, if these new techniques are already being practised by the sample companies.

It is encouraging to note that half of the sample companies are using real options as a viable technique in making capital budgeting decisions (Table 2.15). It is also revealing to note that all companies using the abandonment option are necessarily using the real option too, in combination, while making their capital budgeting decisions. This is in sharp contrast to findings of the Bennouna et al. (2010) study of large Canadian firms, where, even in large firms, only 8% use real options.

Table 2.15 Utilisation of techniques of real options and abandonment options by the sample companies

Utilisation of techniques	Percentage
Real options	50.00 (35.00)
Abandonment options	17.64

All companies that use the abandonment option use the real option too

Table 2.16 Constituents of capital expenditure outlays for the sample companies

Constituents of capital expenditure outlays	Percentage
New investment in existing line of business (capacity build-up)	86.24 (31.03)
Technology upgradation (modernisation)	44.82 (–)
New investment in other areas (diversification)	27.58 (6.89)
Replacement of machinery	20.68 (–)
Any other[a]	10.34 (–)

[a]Includes 'mergers and acquisitions' and 'joint ventures in allied areas (backward, forward and integral)'

Section X Investment Pattern

The investment options available to companies and the path they take would ultimately impact their future strategy. The study of investment pattern of the sample companies would give us an insight into the strategic direction of these companies. It is to gain an understanding of the same, that the sample companies have been requested to list the constituents of their capital expenditure/outlays, the results of which are enumerated in Table 2.16.

An overwhelming majority of companies (86.24%) focus on capacity build-up by investing in the existing line of business. This is perhaps an indication of the growing markets for such companies encouraging them to increase production. Another encouraging aspect is the outlay on modernisation/technology upgradation as the second most important constituent for capital expenditure outlay (44.82%). This could be indicative of the sample companies laying importance on working with the latest technologies in the business to enable them to compete globally. 'New investment in other areas (diversification)' is the third important constituent for capital expenditure outlays, hinting towards aggressive expansion into other areas by more than one-fourth (27.58%) of the sample companies.

From the above, it can be deduced comfortably that companies are aggressively looking at increasing capacity and technology upgradation as the means to increasing profitability and growth.

Table 2.17 Sample companies foregoing expected profitable investment opportunity due to paucity of financial resources

Foregoing investment opportunities	Percentage
No	78.57
Yes	21.42

Section XI Capital Rationing

Capital rationing situation refers to the choice of investment proposals under financial constraints in terms of a given size of capital expenditure budget. The firm may impose such a limit primarily for two reasons: (1) there may be a paucity of funds and (2) corporate managers/owners may be conservative and may not like to invest more than a specified/stated sum in capital projects at one point of time; they may like to accept projects with a greater margin of safety, measured by NPV, later.

Further, given the fact that capital projects involve large volume of funds, it is hypothesised that many profitable investment proposals may be foregone by the sample companies due to paucity of funds. Hence, the sample companies were asked whether they would forego profitable investment opportunities due to paucity of financial resources.

It is encouraging to note that capital rationing does not seem to be a relevant factor for the sample companies as a vast majority of them (78.57%) denied that they forego profitable investment opportunities due to paucity of funds (Table 2.17). These findings are similar to the findings of Jain and Yadav (1999) of private sector corporate enterprises. Further, financial resources are not a constraint for these companies perhaps because the capital markets are readily available to provide funds for these listed companies. The finding is also in tune with the comfortable financial position of long-term funds in earlier section.

Section XII Reasons for Failures in Capital Budgeting Decisions

The reasons for failures in capital budgeting decisions, if any, would provide a glimpse into the challenges facing the sample companies and the threats that pose a roadblock to the success of the decision. This was the question posed in the survey; the responses are tabulated in Table 2.18.

It can be a safe deduction from the responses contained in Table 2.18 that the peculiarities of the market in terms of competition, sales and high fixed costs appear to be the important factors leading to failures of capital budgeting decisions amongst the sample companies. It is revealing to note that higher cost of capital and inefficiency in technology usage are not the important factors (responsible for failure of capital projects).

Table 2.18 Reasons for failure of capital budgeting decisions (if any), with rankings in order of impact (1 for highest, 7 for lowest) for the sample companies

Reasons for failure of capital budgeting decisions	1	2	3	4	5	6	7
Very high fixed-cost component	45.45 (9.09)	27.27	9.09	9.09	0.00	9.09	0.00
Increased competition in the chosen area impacting sales	45.45 (9.09)	9.09	0.00	18.18	9.09	18.18	0.00
Decrease in cash inflows due to decrease in expected sales	40.00(20.00)	20.00	20.00	10.00	10.00	0.00	0.00
Unexpected increase in cost of production	33.33 (–)	11.11	33.33	11.11	11.11	0.00	0.00
Higher cost of capital	25.00(12.50)	25.00	12.50	12.50	12.50	12.50	0.00
Inefficiencies in terms of technology usage and revamp	12.50(12.50)	0.00	0.00	12.50	37.50	37.50	0.00
Any other[a]	67.67(67.67)	0.00	0.00	0.00	0.00	0.00	33.00

[a]Includes 'market down cycle' and 'changes in business scenario' ranked number 1

Section XIII Concluding Observations

Capital budgeting decisions, being strategic in nature, are likely to have a marked bearing in shaping the future of the sample companies in India. The major findings of the study are summarised in this section.

Capital budgeting practices in India, at least amongst the top 166 listed nonfinancial companies of BSE 200, appear to have improved over the past decade or so with an increasing number of companies using more sophisticated DCF techniques. To assess risk, sensitivity analysis is perceived to be the most important technique.

It is a matter of encouragement to note that all the respondent sample companies used DCF techniques in conjunction with non-DCF techniques. There was a strong preference for DCF with 50% using NPV and 78.57% using IRR. The results also indicated that firms still relied on simple capital budgeting techniques such as the payback period and the ARR.

The theory–practice gap is a recurrent theme in the capital budgeting literature, in particular with regard to NPV. Despite the recommendations of the financial literature on using NPV as the primary technique, this research too found that respondent firms indicated a preference for IRR compared to NPV.

It is further encouraging noting that the vast majority of the sample companies follow theoretically sound and conceptually correct basis of computing cost of capital, that is, weighted average cost (WACC) of long-term sources of finance. More than two-thirds (67.85%) of the firms correctly employed the WACC compared to other methods suggesting a reduction in the theory–practice gap compared to past studies. The preference for the use of market weights over book value weights by a vast majority of the sample companies is perhaps a natural indication of the fact that the sample companies are all listed entities with the Bombay Stock Exchange.

Consistent with financial theory, the survey reveals that the sample companies are risk-averse. The majority of Indian firms use risk analysis tools; sensitivity analysis (96.15%) is the most widely used method. Sensitivity analysis is followed by shorter payback period and higher cut-off rate for more risky projects.

Another notable finding is the emergence of new techniques of real options and abandonment options as a part of practice by the sample companies, while evaluating capital budgeting proposals. This perhaps signals the adoption of emerging techniques by our sample companies, an encouraging indication of growing professionalism amongst the sample companies. Half of the respondent firms (50%) used real options when deciding on investment projects. The results are in sharp contrast with Graham and Harvey (2001) and Block (2005) who found a low usage of real options (11.4 and 14.3%, respectively).

It is evident from statistics related to investments in gross fixed assets of the sample companies that massive capital expenditure has been made by them during the period of the study. It is evident that the reform process initiated in 1991 has had a salutary effect on their investment activity with significant improvements being witnessed during the last decade (2001–2011).

As far as the financing pattern of long-term investment projects is concerned, the sample companies seem to be following sound tenets of financial management in this regard in that their fixed assets requirements have been financed from long-term sources. Further probing has yielded a profound finding that the sample companies are also financing their net working capital (current assets minus operating current liabilities) requirements through long-term sources. However, the sample companies would perhaps do well to consider the effective deployment of funds lying idle; these could be better utilised in either building up more assets or repaying external debt, as the case may be.

Very high fixed-cost components of capital projects and the irregularities in prediction of future cash flows due to decrease in sales and increased competition seem to be the major factors leading to failures of capital budgeting decisions for the sample companies. This is perhaps a reflection of the growing challenges of a volatile global marketplace.

Above all, the global recession has not impacted the sample companies (representing vital segment of Indian economy) significantly. The survey also reveals that paucity of funds is not a major hurdle for exploring profitable capital investment projects for a large majority of the sample companies. As far as industry-wise analysis is concerned, most of the sectors are not affected by recession (perhaps due to surplus funds).

There are several areas where more emphasis in training and practice could further enhance investment decision-making. Nonetheless, this research adds to the body of knowledge on capital investment decisions by showing where India fits in this decade and identifying specific areas for improvement. Pike (1996) indicates that capital budgeting has received considerable research attention and is unlikely to turn up surprising new findings, and this has partially proven to be the case here.

However, there are surprising (rather positive) findings like use of WACC, use of DCF methods, prevalence of use real options and sound financing of assets, which indicate the growing sophistication in the Indian capital budgeting practices.

Normative Framework

Guidelines for Practitioners

Given the experience of teaching at national and international levels by the authors, interactions with managers and based on the deficiencies pointed out by the literature survey, the following guidelines have been suggested for business executives, so that they can make better and sound capital budgeting decisions.

- *Capital budgeting evaluation techniques* – NPV is the best method as it is consistent with the objective of maximising shareholders' wealth and it has a uniform reinvestment rate which can be applied consistently to all capital projects. Literature as well as present survey still indicates wider acceptance of IRR. In general, both methods provide the same results. However, in the case of conflict, there is a risk of accepting a proposal based on IRR. When project cash flows are abnormal, this may lead to multiple IRR calculations, affecting both independent and mutually exclusive projects. When investment projects are mutually exclusive, scale and time differences may lead to incorrect investment decisions, and this is another problem associated with the reinvestment rate assumption of IRR (Brigham and Ehrhardt 2002; Bennouna et al. 2010). In operational terms, it implies rejection of better proposals (based on NPV) thereby adversely affecting shareholders' wealth.
- *Misinterpretation and misapplication of cash flow estimations* – Investment decisions require data pertaining to their costs and benefits which can be conveniently, wholly and exclusively indentified with proposed investment. Aspects commonly misapplied are determination of incremental sales revenue and incremental depreciation in replacement projects, deducting an allocation of existing fixed overhead costs, not deducting income tax, treatment of interest expense as well as other financial costs and ignoring inflation (Bierman 1993; Brigham and Ehrhardt 2002).
- *Discount rate* – Firms are expected to use the weighted average cost of funds from various sources, including debt, preferred stock and common equity (Brigham and Ehrhardt 2002). The weights used in calculating the cost of capital should preferably be based on the firm's capital structure target or market values, rather than book values. Also, using a single weighted average cost of capital (WACC) for all investment proposals is not advisable. It should be adjusted higher or lower, depending on the type of project (e.g. replacement projects are lower risk, whereas expansion or new ones are higher risk) or for different organisational units of the firm (Ross et al. 2005).
- *Risk analysis methods* – Sophisticated methods that should be employed consist of probabilistic risk analysis such as sensitivity analysis, decision-tree analysis and Monte Carlo simulation.

- *Emerging approaches like real options* – Conventional DCF analysis should be complemented by real options analysis in order to determine the true NPV. Previous empirical literature found that a relatively small number of firms employed real options (Block 2005; Brounen et al. 2004; Graham and Harvey 2001; Jog and Srivastava 1995).
- *Administrative procedures* – Preferably, there should be a capital investment manual (Pike 1986), full time capital budgeting staff (Pike 1986), use of standard model for deriving the NPV or IRR (e.g. a Microsoft Excel model), supportive information systems and post-investment audits (Pike 1996).

Appendices

Appendix 2.1: Impact of recent financial crisis on India

According to the remarks prepared for the International Monetary Fund (IMF)–Financial Stability Forum (FSF) high-level meeting, on the recent financial turmoil and policy responses for India, Reserve Bank of India (RBI, India's central bank) in October 2008 stated that India had (at that time) not been seriously affected by the recent financial crisis. The reasons for the relative resilience shown by the Indian economy, the impact and likely implications have been summarised below (source: RBI website. http://rbidocs.rbi.org.in/rdocs/Speeches/PDFs/87784.pdf; Economic Surveys of India).

India has been following a rather calibrated approach to the opening up of the capital account and the financial sector. Evidence suggests that the greatest gains are obtained from the opening to foreign direct investment, followed by portfolio equity investment. The benefits emanating from external debt flows have been found to be more questionable until greater domestic financial market development has taken place.

Accordingly, while encouraging foreign investment flows (in particular, direct investment flows), a cautious approach has been adopted related to debt flows. Debt flows in the form of external commercial borrowings are subject to ceilings and some end-use restrictions, which are modulated from time to time, taking into account evolving macroeconomic and monetary conditions. Similarly, portfolio investment in government securities and corporate bonds are also subject to macro ceilings, which are also modulated from time to time.

These prudential policies have attempted to prevent excessive recourse to borrowings and dollarisation of the economy. As far as capital outflows are concerned, the policy framework has been progressively liberalised to enable the nonfinancial corporate sector to invest abroad and to acquire companies in the overseas market.

As a result of conservative/cautious policy of the Government related to financial capital inflows, investments have been predominantly financed by domestic savings in India – the current account deficit has averaged between 1 and 2% of GDP since the early 1990s. The Government's fiscal deficit has been high by international standards but is also largely internally financed through a vibrant and well developed government securities market, and thus, despite large fiscal deficits, macroeconomic and financial stability has been maintained.

The financial sector, in particular banks, is subject to prudential regulations, both in regard to capital and liquidity (Mohan 2007). As the current global financial crisis has shown, liquidity risks could rise manifold during a crisis and can pose serious downside risks to macroeconomic and financial stability. The Reserve Bank of India has already put in place steps to mitigate liquidity risks at the very short end, risks at the systemic level as well as at the institutional level.

In addition to the exercise of normal prudential norms on the financial sector, RBI has also successively imposed additional prudential measures in respect of exposures to particular sectors, akin to a policy of dynamic provisioning. For example, in view of the accelerated exposure to the real estate sector, banks were advised to put in place a proper risk management system to contain the risks involved.

While the overall policy approach has been able to mitigate the potential impact of the turmoil on domestic financial markets and the economy, with the increasing integration of the Indian economy and its financial markets with the rest of the world, there is recognition that the country does face some downside risks from these international developments. The risks arise mainly from the potential reversal of capital flows on a sustained medium-term basis from the projected slowdown of the global economy, particularly in the advanced economies. As might be expected, the main impact of the global financial turmoil in India has emanated from the significant change experienced in the capital account. Total net capital flows fell from US$17.3 billion in April–June 2007 to US$13.2 billion in April–June 2008. Nonetheless, capital flows are expected to be more than sufficient to cover the current account deficit.

These characteristics of India's external and financial sector management coupled with ample foreign exchange reserves (INR 15,790 billion as on 25 November 2011, up from INR 2,466.66 billion in December 2010) coverage and the growing underlying strength of the Indian economy reduce the susceptibility of the Indian economy to global turbulence (source: Reserve Bank of India website. http://www.rbi.org.in/scripts/WSSViewDetail.aspx?TYPE=Section&PARAM1=2. Accessed 4 December 2011).

However, the financial crisis in the advanced economies and the likely slowdown in these economies could have some impact on the IT sector. According to the latest assessment by the NASSCOM (the software trade association), the current developments with respect to the US financial markets are very eventful; these developments may have a direct impact on the IT industry and are likely to create a downstream impact on other sectors of the US economy and worldwide markets. About 15–18% of the business coming to Indian outsourcers includes projects from banking, insurance and the financial services sector which is now uncertain. (source: Reserve Bank of India website. http://rbidocs.rbi.org.in/rdocs/Speeches/PDFs/87784.pdf).

According to the Economic Survey of India of 2010–2011, the Indian economy has emerged with remarkable rapidity from the slowdown caused by the global financial crisis of 2007–2009. With the growth in 2009–2010 estimated at 8% by the Quick Estimates released on 31 January 2011 and 8.6% in 2010–2011 as per the Advance Estimates of the Central Statistics Office (CSO) released on 7 February

2011 the turnaround has been fast and strong. Much of the economic stress (if any) in the current year (2011) can be attributed to continued food inflation and a temporary slowdown in industrial growth (source: http://indiabudget.nic.in/. Accessed 17 November 2011).

Appendix 2.2: Mean, median and quartile values of percentage growth in gross fixed assets of constituent sectors of the sample companies over phase 1 (2001–2006) and phase 2 (2007–2011) (figures are in percentages)

	Phase 1 (2001–2006)				Phase 2 (2007–2011)			
Sector	Mean	Median	Quartile 1	Quartile 3	Mean	Median	Quartile 1	Quartile 3
Internet and communications technology (ICT)	25.50	24.55	9.63	33.38	40.91	39.51	24.78	51.02
Healthcare	23.22	20.14	12.29	30.38	29.51	29.63	21.52	36.74
Housing	18.43	12.43	4.60	27.13	29.42	23.76	13.39	39.67
Miscellaneous[a]	18.29	10.23	4.34	23.52	27.75	20.93	13.70	38.08
Metals	17.40	10.89	4.64	24.42	26.11	24.01	15.97	31.61
Capital goods	17.13	7.55	2.92	21.45	26.59	23.33	15.69	35.20
Transport	15.12	10.83	5.08	19.83	26.60	23.91	15.26	33.87
Oil and gas	14.14	8.18	4.41	12.63	23.88	21.10	12.32	28.90
Diversified	12.78	3.53	1.71	12.40	24.92	23.29	19.54	27.61
Fast moving consumer goods (FMCG)	12.50	7.61	3.49	17.32	21.94	21.87	13.22	29.07
Power	10.97	7.33	3.99	15.42	18.00	13.17	8.57	21.79

[a]Miscellaneous sectors comprises of the media and publishing sector; agriculture, chemicals and petrochemicals; and tourism, textiles and miscellaneous sectors

	Phase 1 and Phase 2		
Sector	*t*	*df*	Significance (2-tailed)
ICT	−2.144	16	0.048
Housing	−1.696	14	0.112
Capital goods	−1.700	12	0.115
Transport	−1.601	15	0.130
Power	−1.426	10	0.184
Oil and gas	−1.332	13	0.206
Miscellaneous	−1.302	14	0.214
Healthcare	−1.038	13	0.318
FMCG	−0.886	11	0.395
Diversified	−0.357	8	0.731
Metals	−0.141	17	0.890

Appendix 2.3: Mean, median and quartile values of percentage growth in gross fixed assets of constituent sectors of the sample companies over phase 3 (2007–2008) and phase 4 (2009–2011) (figures are in percentages)

	Phase 3 (2007–2008)				Phase 4 (2009–2011)			
Sector	Mean	Median	Quartile 1	Quartile 3	Mean	Median	Quartile 1	Quartile 3
ICT	32.75	29.16	12.06	43.49	46.36	46.41	33.26	56.03
Housing	28.41	22.11	13.49	32.76	30.09	24.87	13.32	44.27
Miscellaneous	25.63	19.19	11.12	36.21	29.16	22.09	15.43	39.32
Capital goods	25.23	21.21	10.82	36.37	27.50	24.74	18.93	34.43
Transport	20.36	17.32	10.61	24.01	30.76	28.30	18.36	40.45
Healthcare	20.19	19.08	11.30	27.76	35.71	36.67	28.34	42.72
FMCG	16.09	11.44	6.26	16.59	25.84	28.82	17.86	37.40
Metals	15.31	10.96	3.27	19.98	33.30	32.71	24.43	39.37
Oil and gas	14.34	6.79	4.90	13.80	30.24	30.63	17.27	38.96
Power	12.20	4.68	2.94	15.02	21.87	18.83	12.33	26.29
Diversified	9.70	8.56	5.51	12.71	35.07	33.10	28.89	37.54

	Phase 3 and Phase 4		
Sector	*t*	*df*	Significance (2-tailed)
Metals	−2.257	17	0.037
Diversified	−1.743	7	0.125
Healthcare	−1.324	13	0.208
Oil and gas	−1.28	13	0.223
Power	−1.272	10	0.232
Capital goods	0.919	12	0.376
Transport	−0.806	16	0.432
Miscellaneous	0.321	15	0.753
ICT	0.259	16	0.799
Housing	0.132	12	0.897
FMCG	−0.044	11	0.966

Appendix 2.4: ANOVA of the consolidated sample and the constituent sectors of the sample companies based on growth in gross fixed assets over phase 1 (2001–2006) and phase 2 (2007–2011) and phase 3 (2007–2008) and phase 4 (2009–2011)

	Phase 1 and Phase 2		Phase 3 and Phase 4	
Sector	*F*	Significance	*F*	Significance
Consolidated	3.364	0.000	3.684	0.000
Housing	4.714	0.038	0.093	0.762
ICT	3.137	0.086	0.077	0.783
Transport	2.769	0.106	1.059	0.311
Capital goods	1.281	0.269	.363	0.553
Power	1.135	0.298	0.000	0.998
Miscellaneous	0.932	0.342	0.086	0.772
FMCG	0.581	0.454	0.001	0.971
Oil and gas	0.436	0.515	0.785	0.383
Healthcare	0.391	0.537	1.518	0.229
Diversified	0.175	0.681	4.068	0.062
Metals	0.015	0.903	2.594	0.117

Appendix 2.5: Mean, median and quartile values of fixed assets (net) to permanent capital employed of constituent sectors of the sample companies over phase 1 (2001–2006) and phase 2 (2007–2011) (figures are in percentages)

	Phase 1 (2001–2006)				Phase 2 (2007–2011)			
Sector	Mean	Median	Quartile 1	Quartile 3	Mean	Median	Quartile 1	Quartile 3
Transport	56.60	57.50	44.20	72.80	44.20	46.80	32.90	53.90
Miscellaneous	50.90	49.60	35.90	70.40	44.00	44.60	32.60	55.20
Oil and gas	49.20	49.90	37.20	69.70	38.50	29.80	12.70	65.00
Metals	47.60	48.10	33.90	61.80	39.10	33.33	22.00	53.70
Housing	46.50	45.60	27.50	65.00	35.90	36.30	7.80	59.60
Healthcare	42.50	41.20	30.00	55.40	28.10	26.60	16.00	39.90
Power	41.50	46.90	30.90	53.20	27.60	25.50	11.60	40.30
FMCG	36.20	35.10	5.92	49.20	40.40	44.30	6.14	58.70
ICT	35.30	32.80	20.60	45.70	35.30	31.50	17.40	46.70
Diversified	35.00	43.50	31.00	61.50	23.90	21.10	4.20	35.60
Capital goods	31.00	28.39	21.08	37.10	29.22	22.18	10.90	38.35

	Phase 1 and Phase 2		
Sector	t	df	Significance (2-tailed)
Healthcare	4.412	13	0.001
Transport	3.500	16	0.003
Housing	3.369	16	0.004
Diversified	2.584	8	0.032
Oil and gas	2.235	14	0.042
Miscellaneous	1.850	15	0.084
Metals	1.679	17	0.111
Power	1.071	10	0.310
ICT	−0.281	17	0.782
Capital goods	0.162	12	0.874
FMCG	−0.142	11	0.889

Appendix 2.6: Mean, median and quartile values of fixed assets (net) to permanent capital employed of constituent sectors of the sample companies over phase 3 (2007–2008) and phase 4 (2009–2011) (figures are in percentages)

	Phase 3 (2007–2008)				Phase 4 (2009–2011)			
Sector	Mean	Median	Quartile 1	Quartile 3	Mean	Median	Quartile 1	Quartile 3
Transport	48.20	49.50	39.90	57.80	41.50	45.10	28.20	51.30
Miscellaneous	44.90	46.30	36.10	54.30	43.40	43.50	30.30	55.80
Metals	41.80	35.00	24.70	55.70	37.20	32.10	20.20	52.40
Oil and gas	40.60	30.40	18.80	70.10	37.10	29.40	8.70	61.60
FMCG	39.90	47.10	5.83	55.60	40.70	42.30	6.34	60.80
ICT	36.50	32.70	19.90	43.20	34.50	30.70	15.80	49.10
Housing	35.60	36.40	8.00	60.00	36.20	36.30	7.70	59.40
Capital goods	31.20	23.90	12.30	43.20	27.90	21.00	10.00	35.10
Healthcare	30.90	27.40	19.20	43.20	26.20	26.00	13.80	37.70
Power	26.50	28.60	15.30	36.50	28.30	23.50	9.20	42.90
Diversified	25.70	23.20	4.90	38.30	22.60	19.70	3.70	33.70

(continued)

Appendix 2.6: (continued)

Sector	Phase 3 and Phase 4		
	t	*df*	Significance (2-tailed)
Healthcare	2.362	13	0.034
Diversified	2.085	8	0.071
Transport	1.732	15	0.104
Metals	1.304	17	0.210
ICT	0.937	17	0.362
Capital goods	0.632	12	0.539
Oil and gas	0.541	15	0.596
FMCG	0.479	11	0.641
Power	−0.394	11	0.701
Housing	0.315	17	0.756
Miscellaneous	0.202	14	0.843

Appendix 2.7: ANOVA of the consolidated sample and the constituent sectors of the sample companies based on fixed assets to permanent capital employed over phase 1 (2001–2006) and phase 2 (2007–2011) and phase 3 (2007–2008) and phase 4 (2009–2011)

Sector	Phase 1 and Phase 2		Phase 3 and Phase 4	
	F	Significance	*F*	Significance
Consolidated	2.743	0.003	2.285	0.013
Healthcare	6.343	0.018	0.567	0.458
Transport	4.483	0.042	1.089	0.304
Metals	1.621	0.212	0.129	0.721
Miscellaneous	1.087	0.306	0.189	0.667
Housing	1.065	0.310	0.014	0.908
Oil and gas	1.036	0.317	0.082	0.777
Diversified	0.675	0.423	0.070	0.794
Power	0.206	0.654	0.532	0.473
ICT	0.036	0.851	0.094	0.762
Capital goods	0.022	0.885	0.102	0.752
FMCG	0.011	0.919	0.066	0.800

Appendix 2.8: Mean, median and quartile values of fixed assets (net) + net working capital to permanent capital employed of constituent sectors of the sample companies over phase 1 (2001–2006) and phase 2 (2007–2011) (figures are in percentages)

Sector	Phase 1 (2001–2006)				Phase 2 (2007–2011)			
	Mean	Median	Quartile 1	Quartile 3	Mean	Median	Quartile 1	Quartile 3
Capital goods	71.20	78.50	58.60	87.80	72.70	80.10	64.80	92.60
Housing	70.80	77.90	54.60	87.10	68.40	70.30	59.10	84.40
Miscellaneous	70.60	73.50	61.30	84.40	66.80	70.50	49.10	83.30
Transport	67.30	67.80	51.50	85.90	62.50	63.20	50.90	81.20
Healthcare	66.90	68.80	49.50	84.30	64.40	69.60	48.00	85.20
ICT	66.60	66.60	35.30	78.30	58.80	62.30	45.40	75.90
Oil and gas	62.40	67.80	42.30	84.20	62.70	72.90	46.80	85.70

(continued)

Appendix 2.8: (continued)

	Phase 1 (2001–2006)				Phase 2 (2007–2011)			
Sector	Mean	Median	Quartile 1	Quartile 3	Mean	Median	Quartile 1	Quartile 3
Metals	59.40	59.60	44.00	80.30	57.20	56.70	42.70	71.70
Diversified	55.40	59.00	40.40	80.00	43.50	41.00	29.50	51.80
Power	46.80	49.00	36.50	61.10	46.50	48.20	35.30	54.50
FMCG	40.00	35.20	16.60	60.70	45.30	47.50	18.30	68.20

	Phase 1 and Phase 2		
Sector	*t*	d*f*	Significance (2-tailed)
Diversified	2.153	8	0.063
Housing	−1.348	16	0.197
ICT	0.916	15	0.374
Oil and gas	−0.751	13	0.466
Miscellaneous	0.711	13	0.490
FMCG	−0.450	11	0.662
Capital goods	−0.349	12	0.733
Metals	−0.251	14	0.805
Transport	0.215	15	0.833
Power	−0.201	10	0.845
Healthcare	−0.168	12	0.869

Appendix 2.9: Mean, median and quartile values of fixed assets (net) + net working capital to permanent capital employed of constituent sectors of the sample companies over phase 3 (2007–2008) and phase 4 (2009–2011) (figures are in percentages)

	Phase 3 (2007–2008)				Phase 4 (2009–2011)			
Sector	Mean	Median	Quartile 1	Quartile 3	Mean	Median	Quartile 1	Quartile 3
Capital goods	74.30	81.60	69.90	91.30	71.60	79.10	61.50	93.60
Miscellaneous	69.30	68.50	54.30	82.00	65.20	71.90	45.60	84.10
Oil and gas	67.70	80.90	53.80	93.00	59.40	67.60	42.10	80.90
Transport	66.80	69.90	54.90	82.80	59.60	58.70	48.30	80.20
Housing	65.00	67.30	55.10	80.20	70.80	72.40	61.80	87.20
Healthcare	60.70	67.40	38.20	87.30	67.00	71.20	54.60	83.80
ICT	59.90	63.60	40.20	81.80	58.10	61.40	48.90	72.00
Metals	59.10	59.90	46.10	71.40	55.90	54.60	40.50	71.80
Power	44.00	45.70	32.80	50.60	48.30	49.90	37.00	57.00
Diversified	36.50	40.50	24.40	44.30	48.10	41.30	32.90	56.80
FMCG	35.80	33.60	7.60	60.50	51.60	56.70	25.40	73.40

	Phase 3 and Phase 4		
Sector	*t*	d*f*	Significance (2-tailed)
Transport	2.177	13	0.049
FMCG	−1.796	9	0.106
Oil and gas	1.687	11	0.12

(continued)

Appendix 2.9: (continued)

	Phase 3 and Phase 4		
Sector	*t*	*df*	Significance (2-tailed)
Metals	1.088	13	0.296
Miscellaneous	0.863	12	0.405
Healthcare	–0.829	11	0.425
Diversified	–0.686	7	0.515
Capital goods	0.672	10	0.517
Power	–0.598	7	0.568
ICT	0.582	12	0.571
Housing	–0.567	14	0.579

Appendix 2.10: ANOVA of the consolidated sample and the constituent sectors of the sample companies based on fixed assets and net working capital to permanent capital employed over phase 1 (2001–2006) and phase 2 (2007–2011) and phase 3 (2007–2008) and phase 4 (2009–2011)

	Phase 1 and Phase 2		Phase 3 and Phase 4	
Sector	*F*	Significance	*F*	Significance
Consolidated	1.304	0.227	4.669	0.000
Diversified	1.544	0.232	0.811	0.382
Capital goods	0.899	0.353	2.691	0.115
ICT	0.857	0.361	0.017	0.897
Housing	0.657	0.423	0.391	0.536
Metals	0.268	0.608	0.357	0.555
Oil and gas	0.219	0.644	1.053	0.315
FMCG	0.109	0.744	1.900	0.183
Miscellaneous	0.067	0.797	0.001	0.982
Transport	0.031	0.860	0.854	0.363
Power	0.018	0.894	0.060	0.809
Healthcare	0.011	0.916	0.564	0.460

References

Anand M (2002) Corporate finance practices in India: a survey. Vikalpa 27(4):29–56

Antle R, Eppen GD (1985) Capital rationing and organizational slack in capital budgeting. Manage Sci 31(2):163–174

Bennouna K, Meredith GG, Marchant T (2010) Improved capital budgeting decision making: evidence from Canada. Manage Decis 48(2):225–247

Beranek W (1978) Some new capital budgeting theorems. J Finance Quant Anal 13(5):809–823

Berkovitch E, Israel R (2004) Why the NPV criterion does not maximize NPV. Rev Finance Stud 17(1):239–255

Bierman H (1993) Capital budgeting in 1992: a survey. Finance Manage 22(3):24

Block S (2005) Are there differences in capital budgeting procedures between industries? Eng Econ 50:55–67

Bombay Stock Exchange (BSE) website. http://www.bseindia.com/about/abindices/bse200.asp, Accessed 1 Apr 2010

Brigham EF, Ehrhardt MC (2002) Financial management: theory and practice, 10th edn. Thompson Learning, Inc., Mason

Brounen D, Jong AD, Koedijk CG (2004) Corporate finance in Europe: confronting theory with practice. Finance Manage 33:71–101

Chandra P (1973) Capital budgeting in Indian industries. Indian Manage 12(2):11–15

Chen S (2008) DCF techniques and nonfinancial measures in capital budgeting: a contingency approach analysis. Behav Res Acc 20(1):13–29

Cherukuri UR (1996) Capital budgeting practices: a comparative study of India and select South East Asian countries. ASCI J Manage 25(2):30–46

Collier PM, Berry AJ (2002) Risk in the process of budgeting. Manage Acc Res 13:273–297

Cornell B (1999) Risk, duration and capital budgeting: new evidence on some old questions. J Bus 72(2):183–200

Economic Surveys of India. http://indiabudget.nic.in/. Accessed 17 Nov 2011

Fogler HR (1972) Ranking techniques and capital budgeting. Acc Rev 47(1):134–143

Gitman LJ, Forrester JR (1977) A survey of capital budgeting techniques used by major U. S. firms. Finance Manage 6(3):66–71

Graham JR, Harvey CR (2001) The theory and practice of corporate finance: evidence from the field. J Finance Econ 60(2–3):187–243

Hermes N, Smid P, Yao L (2007) Capital budgeting practices: a comparative study of the Netherlands and China. Int Bus Rev 16:630–654

Jain PK, Kumar M (1997) Comparative financial management: practices of India and South East Asia. Hindustan Publishing Corporation, New Delhi

Jain PK, Yadav SS (2000) Financial management practices in select private corporate enterprises – a comparative study of India, Thailand and Singapore. Hindustan Publishing Corporation, New Delhi

Jain PK, Yadav SS (2005) Financial management practices – a study of public sector enterprises in India. Hindustan Publishing Corporation, New Delhi

Jog V, Srivastava AK (1995) Capital budgeting practices in corporate Canada. Finance Pract Educ 5(3):387–397

Kester G, Robbins G (2011) The capital budgeting practices of listed Irish companies – insights from CFOs on their investment appraisal techniques. Acc Ireland 43(3):38

Kim DC (1992) Risk preferences in participative budgeting. Acc Rev 67(2):303–318

Kira DS, Kusy MI (1990) A stochastic capital rationing model. J Oper Res Soc 41(9):853–863

Klammer T (1973) The association of capital budgeting techniques with firm performance. Acc Rev 48(2):353–364

Kolb BA (1968) Problems and pitfalls in capital budgeting. Finance Anal J 24(6):170–174

Kulatilaka N (1985) Capital budgeting and optimal timing of investments in flexible manufacturing systems. Ann Oper Res 3:35–57

Kwan CCY, Yuan Y (1988) Optimal sequential selection in capital budgeting: a shortcut. Finance Manage 17(1):54–59

Lam KC, Wang D, Lam MCK (2007) The capital budgeting evaluation practices of building contractors in Hong Kong. Int J Proj Manage 25:824–834

Lazaridis IT (2004) Capital budgeting practices: a survey of the firms in Cyprus. J Small Bus Manage 42(4):427–433

Lee Sang M, Lerro AJ (1974) Capital budgeting for multiple objectives. Finance Manage 3(1):58–66

Mao JCT (1970) Survey of capital budgeting: theory and practice. J Finance 25(2):349–360

Mohan R (2007) Coping with liquidity management in India: a practitioner's view. Reserve Bank of India Bulletin. http:www.rbidocs.rbi.org.in/rdocs/Speeches/PDFs/69613.pdf. Accessed 19 Oct 2011

Mukherjee TK, Henderson GV (1987) The capital budgeting process: theory and practice. Interfaces 17(2):78–90

Osborne MJ (2010) A resolution to the NPV–IRR debate? Q Rev Econ Finance 50:234–239

Pandey IM (1985) The financial leverage in India – a study. Indian Manage 23(3):21–34

Petty JW, Scott DF Jr, Bird MM (1975) The capital expenditure decision making process of the large corporations. Eng Econ 20(3):159–172
Pike RH (1986) The design of capital budgeting processes and the corporate context. Manage Decis Econ 7(3):187–195
Pike RH (1996) A longitudinal survey on capital budgeting practices. J Bus Finance Acc 23(1):79–92
Pinches GE (1982) Myopia, capital budgeting and decision making. Finance Manage 11(3):6–19
Porwal LS, Singhvi SS (1978) A comparative study of capital expenditure evaluation techniques. Long Range Plann 11(5):25–31
Reserve Bank of India's Database on Indian Economy. http://dbie.rbi.org.in/InfoViewApp/listing/main.do?appKind=InfoView&service=%2FInfoViewApp%2Fcommon%2FappService.do. Accessed 19 Oct 2011
Reserve Bank of India's website. http://rbidocs.rbi.org.in/rdocs/Speeches/PDFs/87784.pdf. Accessed 17 Nov 2011
Ross SA, Westerfield RW, Jaffe JF (2005) Corporate finance, 7th edn. McGraw-Hill Irwin, New York
Salazar RC, Sen SK (1968) A simulation model of capital budgeting under uncertainty. Manage Sci 15(4):B161–B179
Sandahl G, Sjogren S (2003) Capital budgeting methods among Sweden's largest groups of companies. The state of the art and a comparison with earlier studies. Int J Prod Econ 84:51–69
Schall LD, Sundem GL (1980) Capital budgeting methods and risk: a further analysis. Finance Manage 9(1):7–11
Schall LD, Sundem GL, William RG Jr (1978) Survey and analysis of capital budgeting methods. J Finance 33(1):281–287
Taggart RA (1977) Capital budgeting and the financing decision: an exposition. Finance Manage 6(2):59–64
United Nations Council on Trade and Development (UNCTAD) website. http://www.unctad.org/en/docs/webdiaeia20095_en.pdf. Accessed 17 Nov 2011
Velez I, Nieto G (1986) Investment decision-making practices in Colombia: a survey. Interfaces 16(4):60–65
Verbeeten FHM (2006) Do organizations adopt sophisticated capital budgeting practices to deal with uncertainty in the investment decision? Manage Acc Res 17:106–120

Chapter 3
Capital Structure Decisions

Introduction

Capital structure practices/decisions assume vital significance in corporate financial management as they influence both return and risk of equity owners of corporate enterprises. Whereas excessive use of debt may endanger their very survival, a conservative policy deprives them of its advantages to magnify the equity rates of return. The objective of this chapter is to have an in-depth examination of the capital structure/financing decision practices pursued by the 166 nonfinancial companies (constituting the BSE 200 index of the Bombay Stock Exchange (BSE); the selected sample represented 84.32% of the total market capitalisation on the BSE, as of 1 April 2010 (Source: Bombay Stock Exchange (BSE) website)). Based on the findings, suggestions have been made for practitioners to enable/facilitate them to have better financing decisions.

For better exposition, this chapter is divided into eleven sections. Section I outlines the scope and methodology. Section II contains a detailed literature review related to capital structure decisions. Section III describes the capital structure practices in terms of major capital structure ratios, namely, debt-equity (D/E) ratio, total debt (*total external obligations*) – total equity ratio and total debt to total assets (D/A) ratio. Composition of debt based on long-term debt to total assets ratio, relative share of secured loans to total borrowings and borrowings from banks and financial institutions to total borrowings, are explained in section IV. The other equally important aspects to examine capital structure practices are: (i) whether practicing managers in the sample companies have preference for debt over equity dominated capital structure; (ii) what level of debt is regarded as desirable? These and other capital structure related aspects (judged on the basis of 31 respondent companies) also constitute the subject matter of these two sections (III and IV). Preferred hierarchy of using various sources of long-term finance is discussed in section V. The risk considerations reckoned by the sample companies in designing

P.K. Jain et al., *Financial Management Practices: An Empirical Study of Indian Corporates*, India Studies in Business and Economics,
DOI 10.1007/978-81-322-0990-4_3,

their capital structure are examined in section VI. The capacity to service debt by the sample companies has been analyzed in section VII. A detailed sectoral analysis is provided in Section VIII. The procedure to determine cost of capital is described in Section IX. The major factors affecting capital structure choices are listed in Section X. Section XI contains concluding observations.

Section I Scope and Methodology

The Bombay Stock Exchange BSE 200 index comprises of the top 200 companies listed with the Bombay Stock Exchange, based on their market capitalisation. Out of these 200 companies, 34 companies were affiliated to the financial sector (as of 1 April 2010, the date of sample selection); the scope of this study is limited to the 166 nonfinancial BSE 200 companies engaged in manufacturing and service rendering businesses. The sample is representative in nature as the BSE 200 companies represent all industry groups as shown in Table 1.1 of Chap. 1.

Annual financial statements (balance sheet, profit and loss account and cash flows statement) of the BSE 200 companies have been the source of secondary data. It may be noted that the sample size varies on year-to-year basis primarily on account of the year of incorporation of the sample companies.

The relevant data (secondary) on the first aspect were collected from the Capitaline database, for 11 years (2001–2011). The other secondary data sources used to substantiate any missing data were the Bombay Stock Exchange's website and the company's annual reports. The 11 years period of the study is divided into two subperiods/phases to ascertain whether there has been any significant change in financing pattern of the companies over the years. For the purpose of the analysis, the first 6 years, w.e.f. 1 April 2000 to 31 March 2006 (for brevity referred to as 2000–20011 to 2005–2006), are referred to as phase 1 and the next 5 years, w.e.f. 1 April 2006 to 31 March 2011 (referred to as 2006–2007 to 2010–2011), as phase 2.

The rationale behind phase 2 beginning from 1 April 2006 is the Securities and Exchange Board of India (SEBI) regulation mandating the adherence of clause 49 (on corporate governance) by all listed companies, from 1 April 2006 (for detailed methodology, refer to Chap. 1). Phase 1 and phase 2 are considered two independent samples. The *t*-test as well as ANOVA (analysis of variance) has been administered to assess whether financing pattern changed during the second phase compared to the first phase, for the sample companies. Correlation coefficients have been computed to test the pecking order hypothesis on the sample companies in section 'Preferred Order of Long-Term Source of Funds'.

The period of the study is of particular importance because of the recession (originating due to the US financial crisis) that impacted the world economy towards the second half of 2008. Consequently, the last 5 years of the study (2005–2006 to 2010–2011) have been divided into two subphases to ascertain the impact of recession. The 2 years from 2005–2006 to 2007–2008 denote the pre-recession phase (phase 3), and the subsequent 3 years (2008–2009 to 2010–2011) denote the post-recession phase (phase 4) for the purpose of this study. It is useful to mention that though the impact of recession has been assumed to be felt towards the second half of 2008 (June 2008, cited above), the entire year has been included in the post-recession phase primarily due to two reasons; data was available in a consolidated manner (in the balance sheets), and it was not feasible to separate it for a particular year (2008) on the basis of when recession actually started impacting a particular data variable.

To study trends and its implications, the descriptive statistical values/positional values, that is, mean, standard deviation, coefficient of variation, skewness, kurtosis, median, quartile 1 and quartile 3, have been computed for each year. To do away with the influence of extreme values, they have been excluded from computing average values. However, where their inclusion has been considered important, say, for preparation of frequency distribution, these values have also been considered.

The research instrument for primary data consisted of a questionnaire (Appendix 1.3, Chap. 1). It appears that mailed questionnaires yield a higher return rate (Paolo et al. 2009). However, the initial response (in our case) was very poor; only eight companies responded. It is believed that follow-ups increase the response rate (Fox et al. 1988). Subsequently two reminders, one through post and other through email, were sent to the remaining companies. Personal contacts were also established with the companies located in and around Delhi. This part of the analysis is based on 31 responses received out of 166 after 2 reminders (a response rate of 18.67%).

Prima facie, the response rate may be seen as low; however, the number of respondents and the response rate are similar to previous studies using a similar method (Jain and Kumar 1997; Jain and Yadav 2000, 2005). There is also evidence to suggest that it is becoming more difficult to encourage GPs (general practitioners) to participate in surveys (Templeton et al. 1997). Also, considering that the survey was addressed to time-constrained CFOs, as well as the commercial sensitivity of some of the requested information, perhaps, this may be considered a good and adequate response.

The entire set of data has been analysed using Microsoft Excel spreadsheets and the statistics software SPSS, namely, Statistical Package for the Social Sciences.

Section II Literature Review

Since the seminal work of Modigliani and Miller (MM) in 1958 stating that the impact of financing on the value of the firm (under certain assumptions) is irrelevant, the literature has been expanded by many theoretical and empirical contributions. Much of the emphasis has been placed on releasing the assumptions made by MM, in particular, by taking into account corporate taxes, personal taxes (Miller 1977), bankruptcy costs (Titman 1984), agency costs and informational asymmetries (Myers 1984). According to Weston and Brigham (1992), the optimal capital structure was the one that maximised the market value of the firm's outstanding shares.

Preference of Equity over Debt

Gaud et al. (2005), in their study of Swiss companies, observed a positive relationship between the company size and tangible assets with the leverage of the firm and a negative relationship between growth and profitability with the leverage of the firm. Ebaid (2009) concluded that short-term debt to assets ratio and total debt to assets ratio had negative relationships with the firm's performance (measured in terms of return on assets ratio).

Preference of Debt over Equity

Donaldson (1961) was perhaps the first to have described firms' preferences for internal funds over external funds and firms' preferences for issuing debt over issuing equity. Chang et al. (2009) concluded that long-term debt was the most important source of capital in comparison to short-term and/or convertible debt. Margaritis and Psillaki (2010) indicated that leverage had significant impact on the performance of the firms. Afza and Hussain (2011) observed that large firms with good assets structure preferred debt financing over equity financing in financing new projects.

Relevant Factors in Making Choice of Equity vis-a-vis Debt

Jung et al. (1996) showed that firms used equity to finance their growth as such financing reduced agency costs between shareholders and managers, whereas firms with less growth opportunities used debt as it instilled financial discipline (Jensen 1986; Stulz 1990).

Faulkender and Petersen (2006) found that the desired level of leverage was low in firms due to the monitoring costs. Vasiliou and Daskalakis (2009) investigated differences in institutional characteristics and the resultant debt–equity choice of firms. Korteweg (2010) analysed that the net benefits to the firms increased with low debt-leverage firms, but the benefits subsequently decreased as the leverage increased. Haque et al. (2011) surveyed that better corporate governance in firms resulted in lower agency costs. Kayo and Kimura (2011) assessed the importance of characteristics of a firm, industry and country on the variance of firm leverage.

Determinants of Capital Structure

Empirical studies reported a positive relationship between size and leverage (Rajan and Zingales 1995; Booth et al. 2001; Frank and Goyal 2003). Less conclusive results were reported by other authors (Kremp et al. 1999).

Profitable firms had more internal financing and therefore a negative relationship existed between leverage and profitability (Rajan and Zingales 1995; Booth et al. 2001).

Most empirical studies observed positive relationship between collaterals and the level of debt (Rajan and Zingales 1995; Kremp et al. 1999; Frank and Goyal 2003). Inconclusive results were reported by Titman and Wessels (1988).

Many authors included a measure of risk as an explanatory variable at the debt level (Titman and Wessels 1988; Kremp et al. 1999; Booth et al. 2001). Firms that had high operating risk lowered the volatility of net profit by reducing the level of debt.

Bancel and Mittoo (2004) in their survey of European firms concluded that there were differences in capital structures based on dimensions like legal system and cost of capital. Brounen et al. (2004) examined the capital structure practices amongst four European countries and compared results with those of Graham and Harvey (2001) for US firms and Bancel and Mittoo (2004) for large European publicly listed firms. Chang et al. (2009) concluded that growth was the most important factor in the choice of capital structure.

Pecking Order Theory

According to pecking order theory, firms have no well-defined optimal debt ratios (Myers 1984). Instead, firms adopt a hierarchical order of financing preferences; internal financing was preferred to external financing. In the case of external financing, debt is the first option and equity the last. Shyam-Sunder and Myers (1999) stated that following the pecking order, firms issued or retired an amount of debt equal to the funds flow deficit or surplus; the slope coefficient provided information on the proportion financed by debt of a one dollar increase in deficits and the coefficient was close to unity. A linear specification to account for debt capacity was a popular methodology in this regard (Agca and Mozumdar 2007; Lemmon and Zender 2010). Larger firms exhibited greater pecking order behaviour than smaller firms (Fama and French 2002).

Section III Capital Structure Ratios

The objective of this section is to examine the financing pattern/policies of the sample of 166 nonfinancial BSE 200 companies. These have been addressed using well-accepted capital structure ratios (based on the relationship between borrowed funds and owners' funds). The major ratios used for the purpose of analysis are debt–equity ratio and total debt to total assets (net of depreciation and other intangible and fictitious assets) ratio. Total shareholders' funds are equal to equity capital + preference capital + reserves and surplus – revaluation reserves – miscellaneous expenses not written off – accumulated losses (if any). In the context of these ratios, current liabilities were also included in computing total external obligations/debt.

A related deficiency of the Indian financial system was the prevalence of financial practices of questionable prudence in financing of industrial enterprises. Since the development banks provided most of the funds in the form of term loans, there was a preponderance of debt in the financial structure of industrial enterprises, and the share of equity/risk capital was both low and declining. The corporate enterprises had debt-dominated/lop-sided capital structures which on consideration of the canons of corporate financing were highly imprudent (Khan 2011).

While there is no doubt that current liabilities are short term and the ability of a firm to meet such obligations is reflected in the liquidity ratios, they should form part of the total external liabilities to determine the ability of the firm to meet its long-term obligations for a number of reasons. For one thing, individual items of current liabilities are certainly short term and may fluctuate widely, but, as a whole, a fixed amount of them is always in use so that they are available more or less on a long-term footing. Moreover, some current liabilities like bank credit in India, which are ostensibly short term, are renewed year after year and remain, by and large, permanently in the business. In India, it has been a common practice to use short-term debt instruments like bank cash credit practically as long-term debt (Sen 1979). Also, current liabilities have, like the long-term creditors, a prior right on the assets of the business and are paid along with long-term lenders at the time of liquidation of the firm. Finally, the short-term creditors exercise as much, if not more, pressure on management. The omission of current liabilities in calculating the D/E ratio, therefore, would lead to misleading results. Therefore, the *total external obligations* (in the authors' perceptions) should form the basis of determining credible debt–equity (D/E) ratio.

For the purpose of analysis, book values (as shown in the balance sheet) have been employed. Apart from convenience, book values have been preferred over market values in view of the fact that debt–equity ratio based on market value creates systematic bias in financial risk measures (Chakraborty 1977). Finally, book values have been used with greater confidence than market value where extraneous influences would be many more and largely of unknown magnitude.

Gross Debt–Equity (D/E) Ratio (Based on Total External Obligations)

Relevant data in terms of mean, standard deviation, coefficient of variation, skewness, kurtosis, median and quartiles (1 and 3) for 2001–2011 are presented in Table 3.1. To present more representative and equitable picture, it has been desired to exclude extreme cases (D/E ratio less than zero and more than 5) in computing debt–equity ratio. The D/E ratio of the sample companies lies in the range of 1.07–1.37 during 2001–2011. The mean value of greater than 1 (1.24) for the 11-year period covered by the study signifies that debt has been a major source of financing

Table 3.1 Mean, standard deviation, coefficient of variation, skewness, kurtosis, median and quartile values of debt–equity ratio of the sample companies, 2001–2011

Year ending[a]	Number	Mean	Standard deviation	Coefficient of variation (%)	Skewness	Kurtosis	Median	Quartile 1	Quartile 3
2001	128	1.18	0.95	80.36	1.38	2.29	1.01	0.49	1.63
2002	137	1.37	1.09	79.60	1.00	0.59	1.08	0.56	2.07
2003	135	1.27	0.98	77.16	0.98	0.63	1.13	0.47	1.84
2004	140	1.34	1.07	79.48	1.07	0.71	1.19	0.52	1.86
2005	150	1.33	1.03	77.09	1.11	0.90	1.12	0.49	1.84
2006	154	1.30	0.92	70.79	0.80	0.05	1.11	0.57	1.82
2007	158	1.27	0.91	72.13	1.10	1.31	1.12	0.54	1.77
2008	159	1.13	0.86	76.11	1.29	1.98	0.93	0.52	1.53
2009	160	1.23	1.00	81.35	1.41	2.49	0.97	0.47	1.67
2010	156	1.07	0.80	74.92	0.87	0.13	0.86	0.45	1.55
2011	164	1.15	0.97	84.05	1.36	1.80	0.87	0.44	1.63
2001–2011	149	1.24	0.96	77.55	1.13	1.17	1.04	0.50	1.75
Phase 1 (2000–2001 to 2005–2006)	141	1.30	1.01	77.41	1.06	0.86	1.11	0.52	1.85
Phase 2 (2006–2007 to 2010–2011)	159	1.17	0.91	77.71	1.21	1.54	0.95	0.48	1.63
Phase 3 (2006–2007 to 2007–2008)	159	1.20	0.89	74.12	1.19	1.65	1.03	0.53	1.65
Phase 4 (2008–2009 to 2010–2011)	160	1.15	0.92	80.11	1.21	1.47	0.90	0.45	1.62

	Paired differences							
	Mean	Standard deviation	Standard error mean	Lower	Upper	t	*df*	Significance (2-tailed)
Phase 1–Phase 2	0.12800	0.15057	0.06733	−0.05895	0.31495	1.901	160	0.130
Phase 3–Phase 4	0.28163	3.63167	0.28187	−0.27491	0.83818	0.999	165	0.319

[a]The Indian financial year begins on April 1 and ends on March 31 of the following year. The same holds true for all subsequent tables and notations

In the paired t-test and ANOVA, in case the value of significance (2-tailed) is 0.05 or less, the alternate hypothesis that there is significant difference in two phases is accepted; when its value exceeds 0.05, the alternate hypothesis is rejected implying that there is no significant difference in the two phases

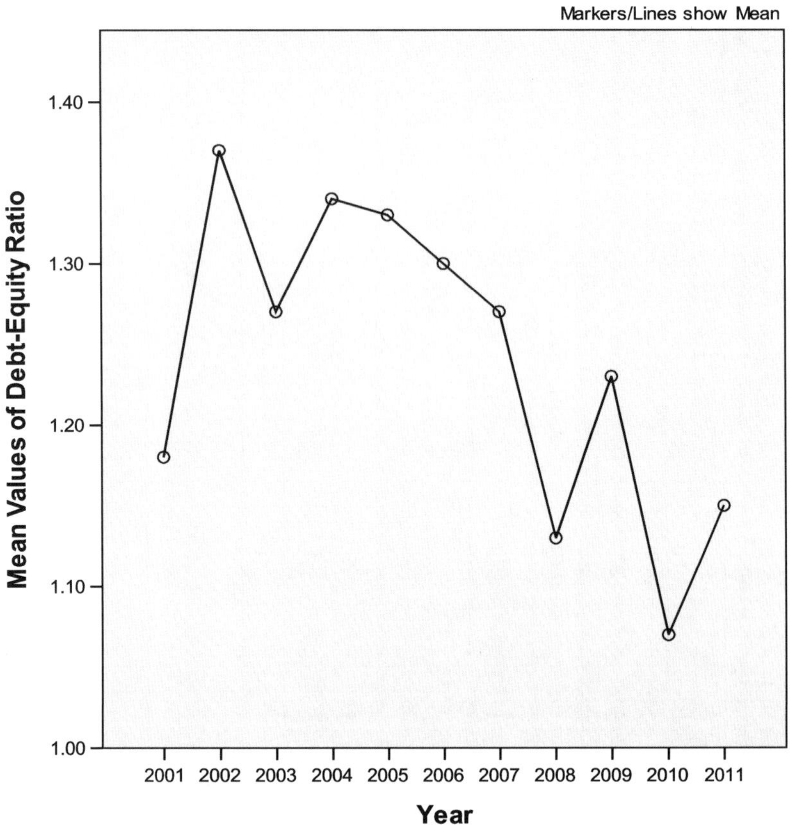

Fig. 3.1 Mean values of debt–equity ratio of the sample companies, 2001–2011

for the sample of nonfinancial BSE 200 companies. This finding, however, is in sharp contrast to the nearly 2:1 debt–equity ratio reported by Jain and Kumar (1997) on Indian private sector enterprises for the period 1985–1995; on the contrary, it is similar to the findings of later studies of Jain and Yadav (2000) on Indian private sector enterprises for a period of 1991–1998, which reported an average D/E ratio of 1.45 and of Jain and Yadav (2005) on Indian public sector enterprises over a period of 1991–2003, indicating a D/E ratio of 1.16. By and large (based on these studies), it appears safe to conclude that debt levels are reducing in Indian corporate enterprises over time. Figure 3.1 exhibits the trend of the D/E ratios.

Standard deviation and coefficient of variation figures indicate high degree of volatility within the sample. Skewness denotes that very few companies reported high values of D/E ratio (supported by kurtosis as well). However, there is no statistically significant change in the capital structure choices in phase 2 over phase 1 as well as phase 4 over phase 3 (evident through the paired samples *t*-test) indicating perhaps that the individual companies in the sample exhibited a varying range of D/E mix in their capital structures through the period of the study. This is also an

Table 3.2 Frequency distribution of debt–equity ratio of the sample companies, 2001–2011 (Figures are in percentages)

Debt–equity ratio	2001	2002	2003	2004	2005	2006	2007	2008	2009	2010	2011
0–1	45.14	40.94	38.06	41.94	40.63	45.34	43.29	49.40	50.30	54.60	56.97
1–2	29.86	26.17	31.61	28.39	35.00	31.68	35.98	32.74	27.54	27.61	26.67
2–5	14.58	24.83	18.06	20.00	18.13	18.63	17.68	12.50	18.56	13.50	15.76
5–10	3.47	2.68	6.45	5.81	3.75	1.86	1.83	2.98	1.20	2.45	0.61
Above 10	4.86	3.36	2.58	1.94	1.25	0.62	0.61	1.19	1.20	0.61	0.00

Frequency distribution data includes extreme values also. It applies to all tables related to frequency distribution data. A few companies having negative D/E ratios (ranging from 0 to 3.23% over the period of the study) have been excluded from the analysis (frequency distribution). Hence, the total does not tally to 100

indication of unique capital structures being followed by the sample companies and no uniform D/E mix emerging as the choice of majority of companies in framing their capital structure policies.

The frequency distribution (Table 3.2) of the D/E ratio is insightful. The companies having a D/E ratio of 0–1 showed a dip in the year 2003 but then has increased substantially towards around 50% of the sample companies in the subsequent years of phase 2. The companies having a debt–equity ratio of 2–5 have shown a decrease in proportion in phase 2 vis-à-vis phase 1. From the distribution, it is evident that companies have decreased debt in their capital structure from high proportions towards lower proportions.

Further, it was desired to understand the long-term vis-à-vis short-term components of the total debt of the sample companies. Therefore, long-term debt–equity and short-term obligations to equity ratios were calculated separately and analysed.

Long-Term Debt–Equity (LTD/E) Ratio

Relevant data in terms of mean, standard deviation, coefficient of variation, skewness, kurtosis, median and quartiles (1 and 3) for 2001–2011 are presented in Table 3.3. To present more representative and equitable picture, it has been desired to exclude extreme cases of LTD/E ratio less than zero and more than above 5 in computing long-term debt–equity ratio. The LTD/E ratio of the sample companies lies in the range of 0.52–0.71 during 2001–2011. The mean value of less than one (0.60) for the 11-year period covered by the study signifies that long-term debt has been relatively less important vis-à-vis equity as a source of financing for the sample of nonfinancial BSE 200 companies. Standard deviation and coefficient of variation figures indicate high degree of volatility within the sample. As with the D/E ratio, the skewness and kurtosis again indicate that only few companies reported a high value of LTD/E ratio. There is no statistically significant change in the capital

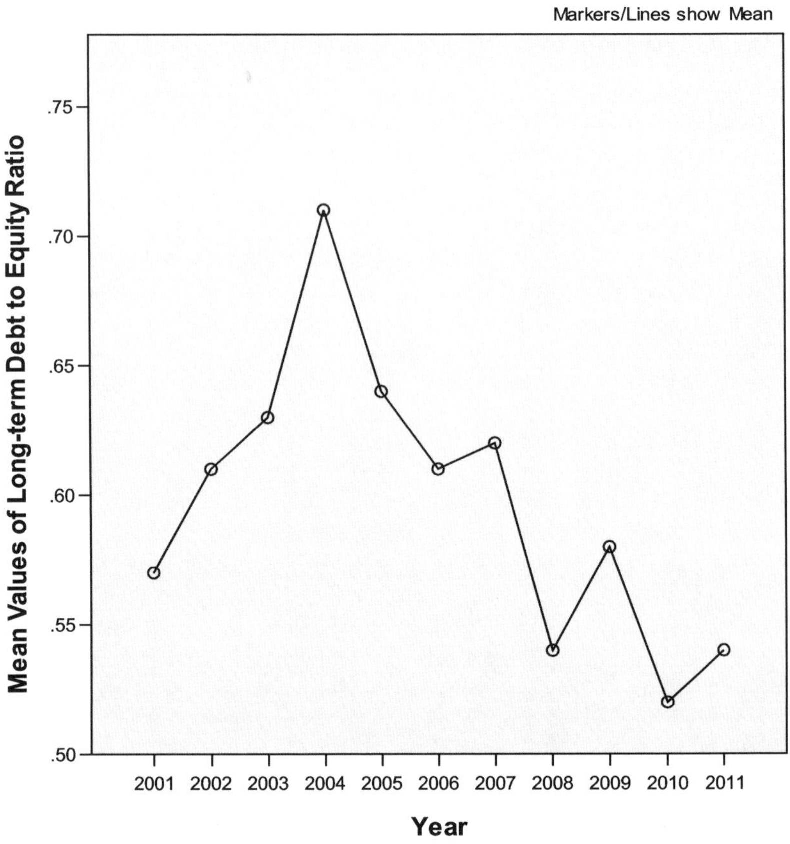

Fig. 3.2 Mean values of long-term debt–equity ratio of the sample companies, 2001–2011

structure choices in phase 2 over phase 1 as well as phase 4 over phase 3 (evident through the paired samples *t*-test).

The frequency distribution (Table 3.4) of the LTD/E ratio is revealing. The percentage of companies having a LTD/E ratio of 0–1 has hovered between 62.26 and 72.39 over the period of the study. The companies having a long-term debt–equity ratio of 5–10 have shown a decrease in proportion in phase 2 vis-à-vis phase 1 with a value of 0% in 2011.

Short-Term Obligations–Equity (STO/E) Ratio

Relevant data for 2001–2011 (and the four phases) are presented in Table 3.5. The STO/E ratio of the sample companies lies in the range of 0.64–0.99 during 2001–2011. The mean value 0.80 for the 11-year period covered by the study signifies that short-term obligations have been the larger component than long-term debt for the

Table 3.3 Mean, standard deviation, coefficient of variation, skewness, kurtosis, median and quartile values of long-term debt–equity ratio of the sample companies, 2001–2011

Year ending	Number	Mean	Standard deviation	Coefficient of variation (%)	Skewness	Kurtosis	Median	Quartile 1	Quartile 3
2001	133	0.57	0.71	124.48	2.46	8.12	0.35	0.07	0.75
2002	139	0.61	0.76	124.11	2.07	5.19	0.41	0.05	0.80
2003	142	0.63	0.84	134.65	2.22	5.66	0.35	0.02	0.78
2004	149	0.71	0.93	131.21	2.24	5.83	0.42	0.05	0.93
2005	155	0.64	0.75	117.01	1.92	5.26	0.45	0.04	0.92
2006	160	0.61	0.72	118.28	2.24	8.09	0.41	0.03	0.96
2007	160	0.62	0.72	115.36	1.94	5.57	0.43	0.06	0.91
2008	164	0.54	0.65	120.40	2.21	6.69	0.35	0.05	0.82
2009	161	0.58	0.66	113.34	1.75	3.93	0.40	0.05	0.90
2010	162	0.52	0.57	111.55	1.60	2.96	0.37	0.04	0.80
2011	163	0.54	0.63	116.35	1.86	3.95	0.33	0.07	0.77
2001–2011	153	0.60	0.72	120.61	2.05	5.57	0.39	0.05	0.85
Phase 1 (2000–2001 to 2005–2006)	146	0.63	0.78	124.96	2.19	6.36	0.40	0.04	0.86
Phase 2 (2006–2007 to 2010–2011)	162	0.56	0.65	115.40	1.87	4.62	0.37	0.05	0.84
Phase 3 (2006–2007 to 2007–2008)	162	0.58	0.68	117.88	2.07	6.13	0.39	0.06	0.86
Phase 4 (2008–2009 to 2010–2011)	162	0.55	0.62	113.75	1.74	3.61	0.37	0.05	0.82

	Paired differences							
	Mean	Standard deviation	Standard error mean	Lower	Upper	*t*	*df*	Significance (2-tailed)
Phase 1–Phase 2	0.07200	0.08672	0.03878	−0.03567	0.17967	1.857	160	0.137
Phase 3–Phase 4	−0.00973	0.37314	0.02905	−0.06709	0.04763	−0.335	164	0.738

Table 3.4 Frequency distribution of long-term debt–equity ratio of the sample companies, 2001–2011 (Figures are in percentages)

Long-term debt–equity ratio	2001	2002	2003	2004	2005	2006	2007	2008	2009	2010	2011
0–1	67.38	67.79	65.58	62.58	62.26	62.73	67.48	71.69	68.07	72.29	72.39
1–2	11.35	8.72	9.09	14.19	16.98	19.25	15.34	12.05	15.66	10.24	11.04
2–5	4.26	7.38	7.14	8.39	5.03	3.73	5.52	3.61	3.01	3.61	4.29
5–10	2.13	1.34	3.25	1.29	0.00	0.00	0.61	0.00	1.20	0.60	0.00
Above 10	1.42	4.03	1.30	0.00	0.63	0.00	0.00	0.00	0.00	0.60	0.00

A few companies having negative LTD/E ratios (ranging from 10.07 to 14.47% over the period of the study) have been excluded from the analysis (frequency distribution). Hence, the total does not tally to 100

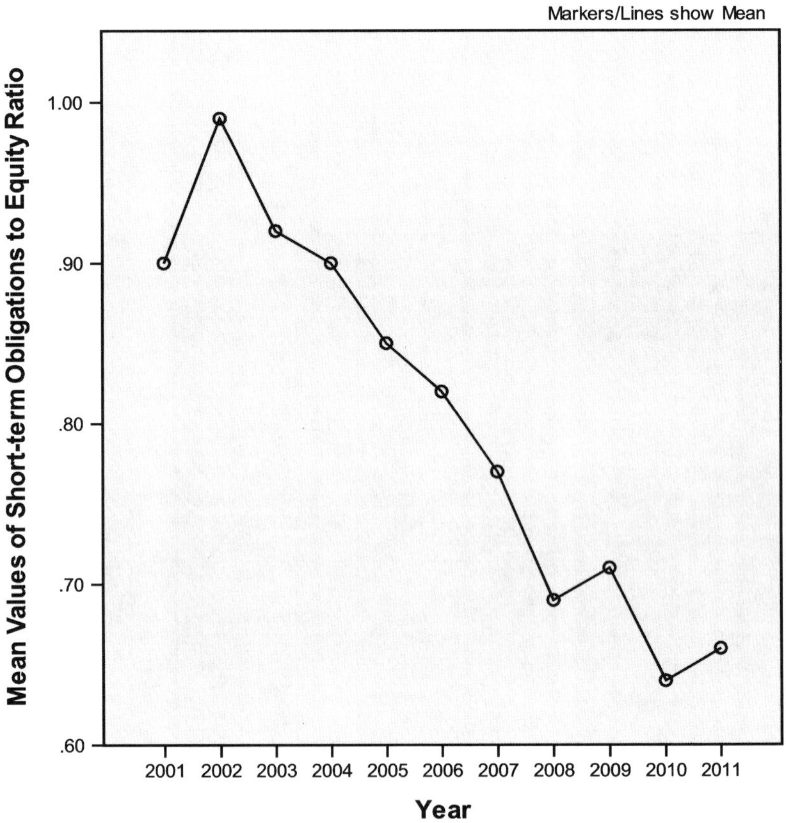

Fig. 3.3 Mean values of short-term obligations–equity ratio of the sample companies, 2001–2011

sample companies. Standard deviation and coefficient of variation figures indicate high degree of volatility within the sample. Keeping in with the D/E and LTD/E ratios, the skewness and kurtosis again indicate that few companies recorded large values of STD/E ratio. However, there is statistically significant change in the share

Table 3.5 Mean, standard deviation, coefficient of variation, skewness, kurtosis, median and quartile values of short-term obligations–equity ratio of the sample companies, 2001–2011

Year ending	Number	Mean	Standard deviation	Coefficient of variation (%)	Skewness	Kurtosis	Median	Quartile 1	Quartile 3
2001	137	0.90	0.95	106.51	2.01	3.97	0.59	0.28	1.13
2002	144	0.99	1.01	101.87	1.95	4.11	0.68	0.27	1.25
2003	146	0.92	0.88	95.72	2.08	5.88	0.69	0.28	1.35
2004	148	0.90	0.84	93.19	1.93	5.05	0.62	0.30	1.29
2005	153	0.85	0.78	91.36	1.58	2.30	0.56	0.30	1.08
2006	157	0.82	0.70	86.05	1.47	1.75	0.58	0.35	1.02
2007	159	0.77	0.68	87.92	1.99	6.19	0.57	0.30	1.00
2008	162	0.69	0.63	90.08	1.76	3.93	0.49	0.26	0.91
2009	162	0.71	0.68	96.71	2.17	6.91	0.51	0.25	0.98
2010	162	0.64	0.63	98.24	1.80	3.38	0.41	0.22	0.88
2011	164	0.66	0.64	96.99	1.57	2.01	0.43	0.23	0.81
2001–2011	154	0.80	0.77	94.97	1.85	4.13	0.56	0.28	1.06
Phase 1 (2000–2001 to 2005–2006)	148	0.90	0.86	95.78	1.84	3.84	0.62	0.30	1.19
Phase 2 (2006–2007 to 2010–2011)	162	0.69	0.65	93.99	1.86	4.48	0.48	0.25	0.92
Phase 3 (2006–2007 to 2007–2008)	161	0.73	0.65	89.00	1.87	5.06	0.53	0.28	0.96
Phase 4 (2008–2009 to 2010–2011)	163	0.67	0.65	97.31	1.85	4.10	0.45	0.23	0.89

	Paired differences							
	Mean	Standard deviation	Standard error mean	Lower	Upper	*t*	*df*	Significance (2-tailed)
Phase 1–Phase 2	0.20119	0.68661	0.05395	0.09466	0.30772	3.729	161	0.000
Phase 3–Phase 4	0.05873	0.52604	0.04108	−0.02238	0.13984	1.430	163	0.155

Table 3.6 Frequency distribution of short-term obligations–equity ratio of the sample companies, 2001–2011 (Figures are in percentages)

Short-term obligations–equity ratio	2001	2002	2003	2004	2005	2006	2007	2008	2009	2010	2011
0–1	70.92	58.39	57.79	59.35	64.78	71.43	72.39	74.10	73.49	76.51	78.18
1–2	14.18	26.17	25.97	25.16	21.38	16.77	19.02	18.67	18.07	16.27	16.36
2–5	10.64	10.74	8.44	9.03	7.55	8.07	5.52	4.22	5.42	4.22	4.24
5–10	0.00	1.34	1.30	1.29	1.89	0.62	1.23	1.81	1.81	1.81	0.61
Above 10	1.42	0.67	0.65	1.29	0.63	0.62	0.00	0.00	0.00	0.00	0.00

Frequency distribution data includes extreme values also. It applies to all tables related to frequency distribution data. A few companies having negative STO/E ratios (ranging from 0 to 5.19% over the period of the study) have been excluded from the analysis (frequency distribution). Hence, the total does not tally to 100

of short-term obligations as a component of debt in phase 2 over phase 1 as well as phase 4 over phase 3 (evident through the paired samples *t*-test) indicating that the sample companies exhibit a varying range of STO/E mix in their capital structures throughout the period of the study.

The frequency distribution (Table 3.6) of the STO/E ratio indicates that majority of the companies have a STO/E ratio of less than 2. Also, the percentage of companies having a STO/E ratio of 0–1 has hovered between 57.79% in 2003 and 78.18 in 2011. The companies having a debt–equity ratio of 5–10 have shown an increase in proportion in phase 2 vis-à-vis phase 1 with a value of 0% in 2001.

By and large, after considering the three ratios, and after comparing the findings with the three earlier studies, it appears that the Indian companies have offloaded debt (in their capital structure) in favour of equity (over time, i.e. the past two decades (1991–2011)). Also, within debt, there appears to be a shift from long-term debt to short-term debt instruments.

Total Debt to Total Assets (D/A) Ratio

That total debt (defined more comprehensively to include total borrowings + current liabilities and provisions, i.e. virtually all total external obligations) constitutes a significant source of financing assets (total assets – revaluation reserves – miscellaneous expenses not written off) of the sample companies is also corroborated by total debt to total assets ratio (Table 3.7). The mean value for the period of the study indicates that more than half of the total assets are funded by debt. Standard deviation figures are low indicating less volatility and are supported by the low coefficient of variation. Large number of companies reported low D/A ratios (denoted by the moderate negative skewness and kurtosis). Overall, the data is an indication of almost similar D/A ratios over the period of study (supported by the paired *t*-test results as well). This is in contrast to the findings of Jain and Yadav (2000) of a

Table 3.7 Mean, standard deviation, coefficient of variation, skewness, kurtosis, median and quartile values of percentage of total debt to total assets (D/A) of the sample companies, 2001–2011 (Figures are in percentages)

Year ending	Number	Mean	Standard deviation	Coefficient of variation (%)	Skewness	Kurtosis	Median	Quartile 1	Quartile 3
2001	109	54.83	25.54	46.59	−0.32	−0.80	58.08	36.61	74.05
2002	106	55.20	27.59	49.98	−0.31	−0.92	57.78	34.36	78.15
2003	102	54.22	27.09	49.97	−0.37	−0.91	58.98	34.53	75.31
2004	109	57.18	27.52	48.12	−0.31	−0.94	60.26	38.49	80.50
2005	118	57.40	25.85	45.03	−0.32	−0.72	58.66	39.62	79.51
2006	120	56.86	23.34	41.05	−0.40	−0.64	58.94	41.36	75.54
2007	128	58.18	24.61	42.30	−0.29	−0.80	59.81	39.58	78.01
2008	129	52.88	24.21	45.79	−0.43	−0.63	57.72	35.05	69.99
2009	134	55.13	26.46	47.99	−0.31	−0.75	56.72	38.63	75.63
2010	130	51.09	24.73	48.41	−0.12	−0.77	50.32	33.22	70.50
2011	134	50.63	24.48	48.34	−0.13	−0.86	50.90	30.87	71.21
2001–2011	120	54.87	25.58	46.69	−0.30	−0.80	57.11	36.57	75.31
Phase 1 (2000–2001 to 2005–2006)	111	55.95	26.16	46.79	−0.34	−0.82	58.78	37.49	77.18
Phase 2 (2006–2007 to 2010–2011)	131	53.58	24.90	46.57	−0.26	−0.76	55.09	35.47	73.07
Phase 3 (2006–2007 to 2007–2008)	129	55.53	24.41	44.04	−0.36	−0.72	58.76	37.32	74.00
Phase 4 (2008–2009 to 2010–2011)	133	52.28	25.22	48.25	−0.19	−0.80	52.65	34.24	72.45

Extreme cases of negative D/A ratio and the cases having ratio higher than one are excluded

	Paired differences							
	Mean	Standard deviation	Standard error mean	Lower	Upper	*t*	*df*	Significance (2-tailed)
Phase 1–Phase 2	0.21079	27.24321	2.27819	−4.29276	4.71435	0.093	142	0.926
Phase 3–Phase 4	−0.90424	21.59266	1.67592	−4.21324	2.40477	−0.540	165	0.590

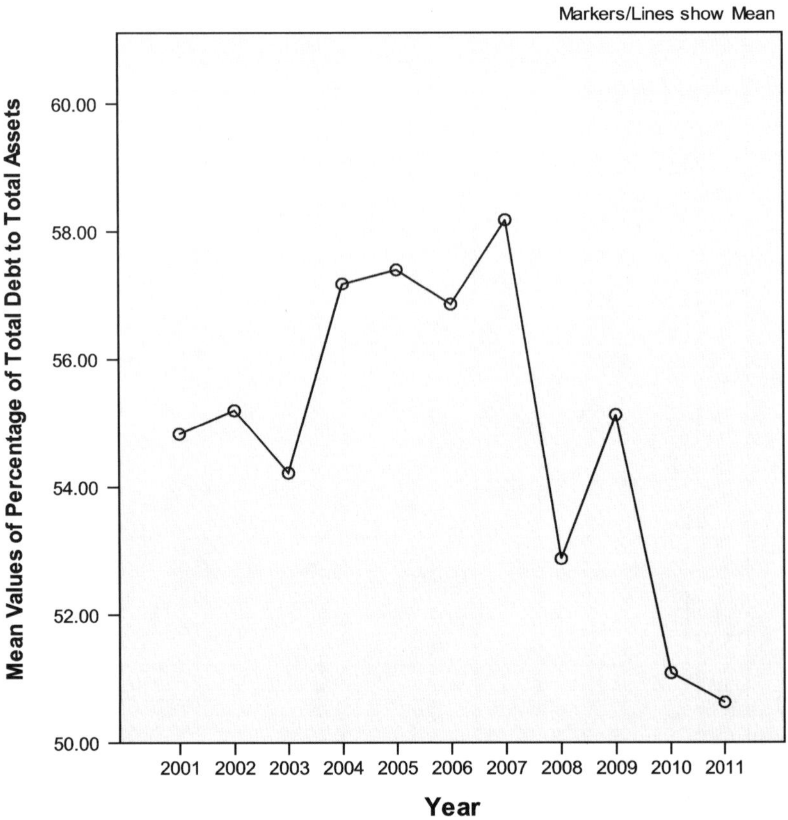

Fig. 3.4 Mean values of percentage of total debt to total assets of the sample companies, 2001–2011

mean D/A ratio of 0.38 for private sector enterprises over a period of 1991–1998, indicating that the usage of total debt to finance assets has perhaps increased over the past decade.

The frequency distribution (Table 3.8) also indicates similar distribution of values of D/A ratios through the period of study. It is similar to the findings of Jain and Kumar (1997) and to the findings of Jain and Yadav (2005).

There seems to be an almost even split in the opinion of the sample companies on whether debt is likely to be the mainstay of the sample companies in future also. It is eloquently borne out the relevant data contained in Table 3.9, which indicates that nearly half of the sample companies hold the view that the debt–equity ratio should be maintained around 2:1 or higher than 2:1. This is similar to the survey findings of Jain and Yadav (2000) on private sector enterprises and Jain and Yadav (2005) on public sector undertakings where nearly half of the sample companies preferred to have a D/E ratio of 2:1 or more.

The survey also sought from the sample companies the probable reasons for their preference for debt (if any). The survey identifies the two major reasons: (1) debt is

Table 3.8 Frequency distribution of total debt to total assets (D/A) ratio of the sample companies, 2001–2011 (Figures are in percentages)

Total debt to total assets ratio	2001	2002	2003	2004	2005	2006	2007	2008	2009	2010	2011
Less than 0.25	11.88	12.75	14.93	11.61	8.75	10.55	9.20	13.25	13.85	14.72	15.15
0.25–0.50	18.88	14.76	11.68	19.35	20.62	18.63	20.85	18.07	20.48	25.15	23.64
0.50–0.75	27.97	23.48	24.02	16.77	21.87	27.32	25.15	34.93	26.50	23.92	27.27
0.75–1.00	17.48	20.13	17.53	23.87	23.12	19.87	23.92	12.65	20.48	16.56	15.15
Above 1.00	23.77	28.85	31.81	28.38	25.62	23.60	20.85	21.08	18.67	19.63	18.79
Total (%)	100	100	100	100	100	100	100	100	100	100	100

Table 3.9 Opinion regarding desired level of debt–equity ratio to be maintained by the sample companies

Debt–equity ratio should be maintained around	Percentage
Less than 1	17.39
1:1	34.78
2:1	43.47
3:1	4.34
Greater than 3	0.00

Table 3.10 Reasons for preferring debt over equity as cited by the sample companies

Reasons for preferring debt over equity	Percentage
Debt is cheaper than equity	50.00 (30.76)
Debt is more flexible than equity in terms of callability clause, repayment schedules, etc.	46.15 (19.23)
It is easier to raise debt as investors are risk averse and equity is risk capital	23.07 (3.84)
The perceived advantage of flexibility in payment of dividend is more illusory than real	3.84 (–)
Any other[a]	15.38 (15.38)

Figures in brackets indicate that the reason mentioned has been cited exclusively by the respondents. (–) indicates not even one BSE 200 company uses the technique exclusively
These notes are applicable to all other tables prepared on the basis of survey
[a]Includes 'debt provides tax shelter'; it implies that debt is cheaper than equity

cheaper than equity and (2) debt is more flexible an instrument than equity in terms of callability clause, repayment schedule, etc. (Table 3.10). This is similar to the findings of Jain and Kumar (1997) and Jain and Yadav (2005).

It was of equal interest to ascertain the reasons of practicing managers of the sample companies for raising more equity (Table 3.11). 'Firm can go for projects involving higher risk' and 'firm is in a better position to face downturns' have been mentioned as the two major factors for the preference of equity. The factors 'flexibility in paying dividends' and 'the firm is not under obligations to pay dividends' are no longer the favoured factors for raising equity. It is a sign

Table 3.11 Reasons for using predominantly more equity as cited by the sample companies

Reasons for using predominantly more equity	Percentage
Equity is easy to raise	18.75
Firm is not under obligations to pay dividends	0.00
There is flexibility in paying dividends	0.00
Any other[a]	81.25

[a]Includes 'firm can go for projects involving higher risk' and 'firm is in a better position to face downturns'

Table 3.12 Opinion regarding utilisation of debt to maximum extent by the sample companies

Debt should be tapped to maximum extent	Percentage
Yes	37.50
No	62.50

of growing professionalism amongst the finance managers of the sample companies. In earlier studies carried out in India, the factor 'equity capital does not carry cost' has been cited as a major reason of using equity by a sizeable number of private corporate firms in India and Southeast Asia (Jain and Kumar 1997).

These factors are in conformity with sound principles of financial management to be followed in designing capital structure. These factors reinforce the earlier contention of greater professionalism in managing the sample companies.

It appears from the above that the sample companies are quite conscious of the advantages accruing from using equity; they also seem to be equally cautious being beset with debt-dominated capital structure. Perhaps, the sample companies are now more conscious about the bankruptcy costs associated with large debt (Titman 1984), lower agency costs due to greater equity and informational asymmetries and their impact on capital structures (Myers 1984). For these reasons, perhaps, the majority of the sample companies (62.50%) have stated that debt should not be tapped to the maximum extent (Table 3.12). The above findings are also similar to the findings of an earlier study of the public sector enterprises in India (Jain and Yadav 2005).

Section IV Composition of Debt

The preceding section has highlighted the share of debt in the capital structure of the sample companies. The present section examines the composition of debt from three perspectives: (1) the relative share of long-term debt in financing total assets, (2) the proportion of secured loans to total borrowings and (3) the percentage share of bank borrowings and borrowings from financial institutions to total borrowings.

Long-Term Debt to Total Assets Ratio

The long-term debt to total assets (LTD/TA) ratio would indicate the extent to which the total assets of the sample companies are financed by long-term debt. When this ratio is viewed along with D/A ratio (discussed in previous section) it would reflect *albeit* indirectly the level of short-term borrowings and other current liabilities.

Relevant data in terms of mean value and other statistics of LTD/TA ratio contained in Table 3.13 indicate that less than one-third (28.15%) of total assets have been financed from LTD. Standard deviation figures indicate fluctuations and are supported by the coefficient of variation. Skewness and kurtosis figures indicate approximate symmetry in distribution of values of LTD/TA. This is further supported by the statistically insignificant paired *t*-test results. This is similar to the findings of Jain and Yadav (2005) on public sector enterprises over a period of 1991–2003, which reported a mean LTD/A ratio of 0.32.

However, from operational point of view, the above data, *prima facie,* provide, though indirectly, the empirical evidence of a significant proportion of short-term external obligations in debt composition of the sample companies. This inference has been drawn when data related to LTD/DA ratio has been viewed along with TD/TA ratio. The frequency distribution also supports the above contention (Table 3.14). These findings are similar to the findings of Abor (2005) and not in tune with the findings of Chang et al. (2009).

Other things being equal, the sample companies, in general, should prefer long-term borrowings to short-term borrowings. The reason is that short-term debt poses a more serious threat to continued survival of corporate firms than the excessive long-term borrowings as per the empirical study of Gupta (1985).

Secured Loans (SL) to Total Borrowings (TB)

It was also of interest to ascertain the relative share of secured loans to total borrowings in the post-liberalisation period (Table 3.15). The mean value of secured loans has reduced by nearly 10 percentage points in phase 2 compared to phase 1, the respective figures being 54.17 and 64.46%. The quartile 1 value shows more pronounced decrease in this regard (more than two times decrease from 42.45% in phase 1 to 18.37% in phase 2). Standard deviation and coefficient of variation figures do not indicate large volatility in values within the sample. However, there has been a significant decrease in the relative share of secured loans to total borrowings as per the paired sample *t*-test in phase 2 over phase 1. Figure 3.6 portrays the decreasing trend of secured loans in total borrowings over the years of the study. The same is supported by Table 3.16 (frequency distribution). It may be noted here that the findings of Jain and Yadav (2005) on public sector enterprises over a period of 1991–2003 indicated a lower SL/TB percentage of 27.91.

Table 3.13 Mean, standard deviation, coefficient of variation, skewness, kurtosis, median and quartile values of percentage of long-term debt to total assets of the sample companies, 2001–2011

Year ending	Number	Mean	Standard deviation	Coefficient of variation (%)	Skewness	Kurtosis	Median	Quartile 1	Quartile 3
2001	138	27.83	22.92	82.37	0.69	0.15	26.95	6.54	41.84
2002	147	30.58	25.89	84.68	0.75	–0.10	27.73	5.77	42.60
2003	147	29.03	25.56	88.07	0.65	–0.49	27.42	4.82	43.32
2004	150	29.45	24.18	82.11	0.42	–0.83	28.91	5.07	47.78
2005	156	29.09	23.68	81.39	0.38	–0.67	30.42	4.26	45.43
2006	159	27.85	22.47	80.68	0.26	–1.04	28.02	3.58	46.03
2007	160	28.96	22.92	79.14	0.28	–1.00	29.43	6.52	46.86
2008	163	25.82	21.12	81.79	0.36	–0.99	24.56	5.36	42.88
2009	163	27.90	22.71	81.40	0.30	–1.07	28.49	4.52	46.94
2010	163	26.85	22.04	82.10	0.36	–0.89	26.88	4.15	44.16
2011	163	26.26	21.31	44.05	0.39	–0.90	24.04	6.20	41.67
2001–2011	155	28.15	23.16	78.89	0.44	–0.71	27.53	5.16	44.50
Phase 1 (2000–2001 to 2005–2006)	150	28.97	24.12	83.22	0.52	–0.49	28.24	5.01	44.50
Phase 2 (2006–2007 to 2010–2011)	162	27.16	22.02	73.70	0.34	–0.97	26.68	5.35	44.50
Phase 3 (2006–2007 to 2007–2008)	162	27.39	22.02	80.46	0.32	–0.99	27.00	5.94	44.87
Phase 4 (2008–2009 to 2010–2011)	163	27.00	22.02	69.18	0.35	–0.95	26.47	4.96	44.26

	Paired differences							
	Mean	Standard deviation	Standard error mean	Lower	Upper	*t*	*df*	Significance (2-tailed)
Phase 1–Phase 2	2.27312	16.98956	1.33483	–0.36291	4.90914	1.703	161	0.091
Phase 3–Phase 4	0.10687	12.65143	0.98194	–1.83192	2.04566	0.109	165	0.913

Table 3.14 Frequency distribution of percentage of long-term debt to total assets of the sample companies, 2001–2011 (Figures are in percentages)

Long-term debt to total assets ratio	2001	2002	2003	2004	2005	2006	2007	2008	2009	2010	2011
Less than 0.25	46.81	45.95	46.98	43.71	43.04	45.63	44.72	51.22	46.34	47.56	50.92
0.25–0.50	36.17	33.78	31.54	31.79	36.08	35.00	32.92	32.93	32.32	34.76	33.74
0.50–0.75	11.35	12.16	16.11	19.87	18.35	16.88	19.88	14.63	19.51	16.46	14.11
0.75–1.00	3.55	7.43	4.03	3.97	1.27	1.88	1.86	0.61	1.22	0.61	0.61
Above 1.00	2.13	0.68	1.34	0.66	1.27	0.63	0.62	0.61	0.61	0.61	0.61
Total (%)	100	100	100	100	100	100	100	100	100	100	100

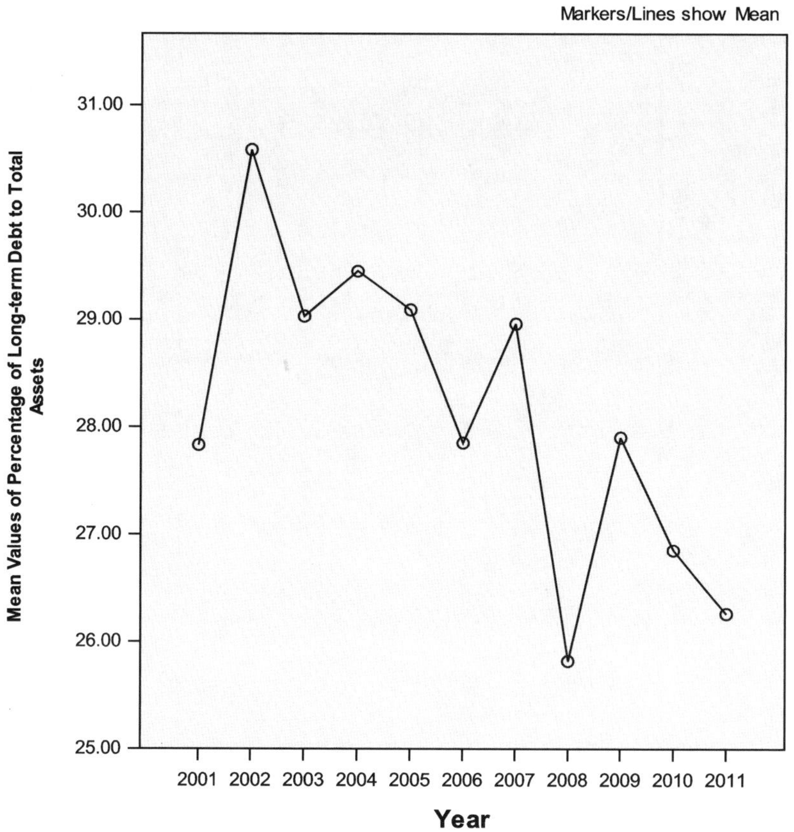

Fig. 3.5 Mean values of long-term debt to total assets of the sample companies, 2001–2011

Table 3.15 Mean, standard deviation, coefficient of variation, skewness, kurtosis, median and quartile values of percentage of secured loans (*SL*) to total borrowings (*TB*) of the sample companies, 2001–2011 (Figures are in percentages)

Year ending	Number	Mean	Standard deviation	Coefficient of variation (%)	Skewness	Kurtosis	Median	Quartile 1	Quartile 3
2001	126	64.44	30.47	47.29	−0.92	−0.18	70.52	50.06	89.15
2002	138	67.74	30.45	44.95	−0.85	−0.27	75.15	50.79	94.51
2003	140	66.55	32.01	48.09	−0.86	−0.45	75.61	45.53	92.80
2004	140	66.12	32.59	49.28	−0.81	−0.61	77.27	43.76	92.72
2005	143	63.29	33.34	52.67	−0.54	−1.08	75.17	34.13	94.39
2006	142	58.59	33.00	56.31	−0.29	−1.21	62.14	30.42	89.39
2007	149	54.05	35.21	65.14	−0.24	−1.38	60.31	22.65	85.57
2008	151	52.72	36.40	69.03	−0.13	−1.46	56.69	18.13	88.12
2009	151	54.35	36.81	67.72	−0.21	−1.48	61.42	17.05	91.99
2010	149	55.41	36.42	65.72	−0.31	−1.38	63.73	18.67	90.84
2011	151	54.34	36.23	66.68	−0.29	−1.36	60.48	15.35	87.37
2001–2011	144	59.78	33.90	57.53	−0.49	−0.99	67.14	31.50	90.62
Phase 1 (2000–2001 to 2005–2006)	138	64.46	31.98	49.77	−0.71	−0.63	72.64	42.45	92.16
Phase 2 (2006–2007 to 2010–2011)	150	54.17	36.21	66.86	−0.24	−1.41	60.53	18.37	88.78
Phase 3 (2006–2007 to 2007–2008)	150	53.39	35.81	67.08	−0.18	−1.42	58.50	20.39	86.85
Phase 4 (2008–2009 to 2010–2011)	150	54.70	36.49	66.70	−0.27	−1.41	61.88	17.02	90.07

	Paired differences							
	Mean	Standard deviation	Standard error mean	Lower	Upper	*t*	*df*	Significance (2-tailed)
Phase 1–Phase 2	9.82717	31.37162	2.55299	4.78271	14.87163	3.849	150	0.000
Phase 3–Phase 4	−7.02171	31.17186	2.41941	−11.79870	−2.24473	−2.902	165	0.004

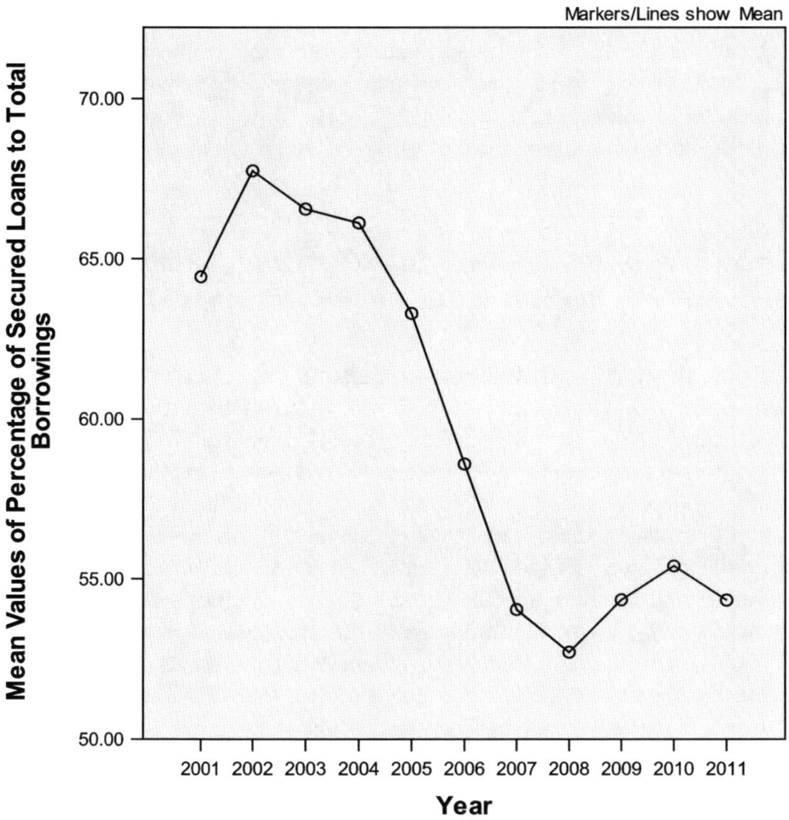

Fig. 3.6 Mean values of secured loans to total borrowings (in percentages) of the sample companies, 2001–2011

Table 3.16 Frequency distribution of secured loans to total borrowings ratio of the sample companies, 2001–2011 (Figures are in percentages)

Secured loans to total borrowings (%)	2001	2002	2003	2004	2005	2006	2007	2008	2009	2010	2011
Zero	9.52	5.79	8.57	8.57	6.29	6.33	8.72	9.27	8.60	9.39	11.26
0.01–10	2.38	2.17	2.85	1.428	2.79	3.52	10.73	11.25	11.92	11.40	9.93
10–30	3.96	5.79	5.00	7.85	12.58	14.78	10.73	11.92	11.92	7.38	8.61
30–50	9.52	9.42	10.71	11.42	13.98	14.78	12.08	12.58	11.25	14.76	11.92
Above 50	74.60	76.81	72.85	70.71	64.33	60.56	57.71	54.96	56.29	57.04	58.28
Total (%)	100	100	100	100	100	100	100	100	100	100	100

The finding is notable as these large sample companies with substantial asset bases should have preferred to raise finance from more secured loans as secured loans are likely to be cheaper source of finance compared to unsecured borrowings. The corporates should opt for more secured loans to reduce their cost of debt; this aspect merits consideration on the part of the practicing managers.

Relative Share of Bank Borrowings (BB) and Financial Institutions' (FI) Borrowings to Total Borrowings (TB)

Although the development/public financial institutions (DFIs/PFIs) constituted the backbone of the Indian financial system for a long time (say, 1950–2000), their relative significance in the emerging financial scenario has been declining, indicating a shift in corporate financing in India, in terms of greater reliance of industry on non-institutional sources of finance and greater recourse to the capital market. Secondly, in addition to the financing of industry by these institutions in the traditional form of rupee/foreign currency term loans for project finance, underwriting, lease financing and so on, they also started providing core working capital to industry (Khan 2011). This is amply evident from the findings of the present study as well. Borrowings from PFIs do not form major share in financing debt instruments of the sample companies. Borrowings from FIs have accounted for less than 10% in phase 1. In fact, as per the trend, a marked decrease (nearly halved) has been noted (4.35%) in the share of borrowings from FIs in phase 2 over phase 1. Standard deviation and coefficient of variation figures indicate extreme volatility. Skewness and kurtosis figures are high and positive indicating a predominance of smaller values of FI/TB ratio.

Bank borrowings, on the other hand, seem to occupy a significant position in meeting debt requirements of the sample companies (Table 3.17). In fact, the share of bank borrowings has increased substantially in phase 2 *vis-à-vis* phase 1. Standard deviation figures are high indicating volatility in the values and are supported by the coefficient of variation figures. Positive skewness and high kurtosis report that few companies recorded a high value to BB/TB. The increase in the share of bank borrowings to the total borrowings of the sample companies has been found to be statistically significant as per *t*-test for phase 2 over phase 1. Bank borrowings to total borrowings have increased significantly compared to the findings of Jain and Yadav (2005) on public sector enterprises over a period of 1991–2003, where the mean BB/TB was 23.08.

In sum, it can be said that bank borrowings form a major source of finance for the sample companies. The findings are not surprising as cash credit and advances from banks are the major sources of financing their working capital requirements. However, in the Indian banking scenario, for decades now, cash credit/overdraft continues to be the preponderant style of working capital funding. Cash credit constitutes about 70% of the total bank credit (Source: http://www.rbi.org.in/scripts/PublicationReportDetails.aspx?ID=190: *Report of the Working Group on Discounting of Bills by Banks*, Accessed on Sep 28, 2010). The reason is cash credit arrangement causes less financial costs, as explained hereunder.

Table 3.17 Mean, standard deviation, coefficient of variation, skewness, kurtosis, median and quartile values of relative share of bank borrowings (*BB*) and financial institution borrowings (*FIB*) to total borrowings (*TB*) of the sample companies, 2001–2011 (Figures are in percentages)

	Number		Mean		Standard deviation		Coefficient of variation (%)		Skewness		Kurtosis		Median		Quartile 1		Quartile 3	
Year ending	BB	FIB	BB	FIB	BB	FIB	BB	FIB	BB	FIB	BB	FIB	BB	FIB	BB	FIB	BB	FIB
2001	126	126	14.02	14.35	19.78	22.54	141.11	157.08	1.65	2.08	2.19	4.07	4.44	3.63	0.00	0.00	23.66	20.46
2002	138	138	17.35	10.69	23.82	21.52	137.33	201.32	1.59	2.62	2.10	6.52	4.22	0.22	0.00	0.00	27.90	11.62
2003	140	140	22.03	7.55	27.19	16.31	123.45	216.01	1.21	3.04	0.52	10.36	8.75	0.00	0.00	0.00	34.79	6.92
2004	140	140	27.08	7.61	28.50	16.81	105.24	220.81	0.84	2.95	−0.43	9.71	19.90	0.00	0.00	0.00	43.27	5.16
2005	143	143	28.69	6.38	29.36	15.80	102.34	247.78	0.83	3.92	−0.42	18.20	18.47	0.00	0.00	0.00	49.63	4.32
2006	142	142	34.98	5.26	31.10	14.35	88.91	272.85	0.55	4.01	−0.77	18.81	32.55	0.00	2.45	0.00	55.30	2.06
2007	149	149	38.51	5.19	32.77	13.94	85.09	268.83	0.32	4.24	−1.22	21.20	34.71	0.00	4.22	0.00	66.02	2.04
2008	151	151	42.96	4.96	34.27	13.95	79.76	281.25	0.10	4.14	−1.41	19.90	42.85	0.00	6.52	0.00	71.60	0.90
2009	151	151	44.24	4.10	34.17	12.58	77.23	306.60	0.02	4.81	−1.42	27.92	46.30	0.00	5.40	0.00	73.58	0.00
2010	149	149	37.57	3.79	32.80	12.20	87.30	322.23	0.39	4.79	−1.17	28.93	31.87	0.00	4.35	0.00	64.94	0.00
2011	150	151	38.54	3.42	32.98	11.81	85.58	345.42	0.32	5.16	−1.21	33.15	36.14	0.00	2.50	0.00	64.63	0.00
2001–2011	144	144	31.45	6.66	29.70	15.62	101.21	258.20	0.71	3.80	−0.29	18.07	25.47	0.35	2.31	0.00	52.30	4.86
Phase 1 (2000–2001 to 2005–2006)	138	138	24.02	8.64	26.63	17.89	116.40	219.31	1.11	3.10	0.53	11.28	14.72	0.64	0.41	0.00	39.09	8.42
Phase 2 (2006–2007 to 2010–2011)	150	150	40.37	4.29	33.40	12.90	82.99	304.87	0.23	4.63	−1.29	26.22	38.37	0.00	4.60	0.00	68.15	0.59
Phase 3 (2006–2007 to 2007–2008)	150	150	40.74	5.07	33.52	13.95	82.43	275.04	0.21	4.19	−1.32	20.55	38.78	0.00	5.37	0.00	68.81	1.47
Phase 4 (2008–2009 to 2010–2011)	150	150	40.12	3.77	33.32	12.20	83.37	324.75	0.24	4.92	−1.26	30.00	38.10	0.00	4.08	0.00	67.71	0.00

		Paired differences							
		Mean	Standard deviation	Standard error mean	Lower	Upper	*t*	*df*	Significance (2-tailed)
BB to TB	Phase 1–Phase 2	−16.04395	24.70048	2.05126	−20.09843	−11.98948	−7.821	144	0.000
	Phase 3–Phase 4	−5.43611	28.64834	2.22354	−9.82638	−1.04585	−2.445	165	0.016
FIB to TB	Phase 1–Phase 2	3.74016	12.12510	0.98673	1.79048	5.68984	3.790	150	0.000
	Phase 3–Phase 4	1.08158	7.62682	0.59196	−0.08721	2.25036	1.827	165	0.069

Table 3.18 Frequency distribution pertaining to relative share of bank borrowings to total borrowings of the sample of BSE 200 companies, 2001–2011 (Figures are in percentages)

Bank borrowings to total borrowings (%)	2001	2002	2003	2004	2005	2006	2007	2008	2009	2010	2011
Less than 5	50.78	49.27	42.14	35.00	32.86	26.05	26.00	23.84	25.16	26.71	26.00
5–10	8.59	5.07	8.57	5.00	2.79	4.92	4.00	5.29	1.98	4.10	4.00
10–20	12.50	11.59	7.14	10.71	14.68	11.26	8.00	4.63	5.29	8.21	8.67
20–30	11.71	9.42	10.71	10.00	8.39	4.22	7.33	7.28	6.62	10.27	7.33
30–40	5.46	10.14	8.57	10.00	9.79	9.85	8.00	7.28	5.96	5.47	6.67
40–50	3.90	3.62	5.71	7.85	5.59	11.97	8.00	5.96	8.60	7.53	9.33
Above 50	7.03	10.86	17.14	21.42	25.87	31.69	38.66	45.69	46.35	37.67	38.00
Total (%)	100	100	100	100	100	100	100	100	100	100	100

Table 3.19 Frequency distribution pertaining to relative share of financial institutions to total borrowings of the sample companies, 2001–2011 (Figures are in percentages)

Financial institution borrowings to total borrowings (%)	2001	2002	2003	2004	2005	2006	2007	2008	2009	2010	2011
Zero	39.84	49.27	58.57	61.42	64.33	65.49	67.33	70.86	76.00	82.19	82.12
0.01–10	21.87	23.18	18.57	18.57	15.38	21.12	18.00	15.89	12.66	6.84	7.28
10–30	23.43	17.39	15.00	10.00	14.68	6.33	9.33	7.947	7.33	6.84	5.96
30–50	4.68	1.44	2.85	6.42	3.49	4.92	3.33	1.98	2.00	2.73	3.31
Above 50	10.15	8.69	5.00	3.57	2.10	2.11	2.00	3.31	2.00	1.36	1.32
Total (%)	100	100	100	100	100	100	100	100	100	100	100

Under the cash credit arrangement, the bank sanctions a predetermined borrowings/ credit limit. The borrower (a company) can draw/borrow up to the stipulated credit limit. Within the specified limit, any number of drawls/drawings are possible to the extent of the requirement of the company periodically. Similarly, repayments can be made whenever desired during the period. The interest is determined on the basis of the running balance/amount actually utilised by the company and not on the sanctioned limit. Obviously, this form of bank financing of working capital is highly attractive to the borrowing company. The reasons are (1) it is flexible in that although borrowed funds are repayable on demand, banks usually do not recall cash advances/ roll them over; and (2) the company enjoys the freedom to draw the amount in advance as and when required as well as repay the amount whenever it so desires, while the interest is charged on the amount actually outstanding (Khan and Jain 2011).

Statistically too, the differences in mean values over the four phases of the study have been found significant (as per paired *t*-test). Similar conclusions follow on the basis of quartile 1 as well as frequency distribution data (Tables 3.18 and 3.19).

The preceding analysis related to composition of debt indicates that short-term debt from banks seems to form a significant component of total debt obligations of

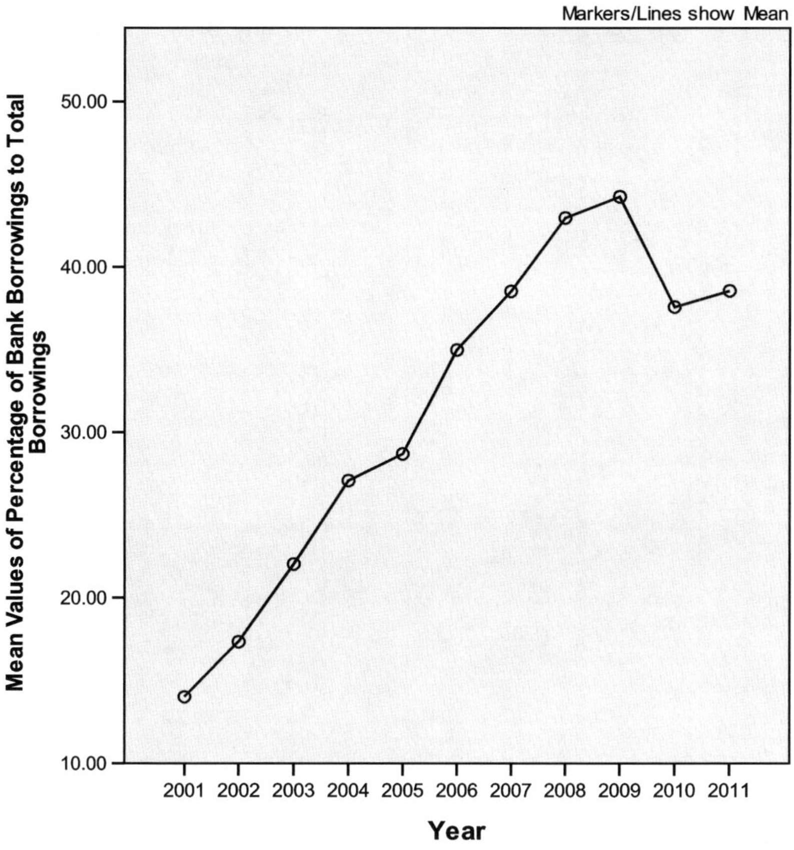

Fig. 3.7 Mean values of bank borrowings to total borrowings (in percentages) of the sample companies, 2001–2011

the sample companies. This finding is corroborated by the fact that banks have been the major providers of their debt requirements (perhaps in the form of cash credit to a marked extent which, *per se,* is short term in nature). In contrast, the contribution of financial institutions to the debt financing has been virtually negligible.

These findings are similar to the findings of Abor (2005) and dissimilar to the findings of Chang et al. (2009).

Section V Preferred Order of Long-Term Source of Funds

The objective of this section is to test the pecking order hypothesis on the sample companies. Donaldson (1961) was perhaps the first to have described firms' preferences for internal funds over external funds and firms' preferences for issuing debt over issuing equity (when acquiring external funds).

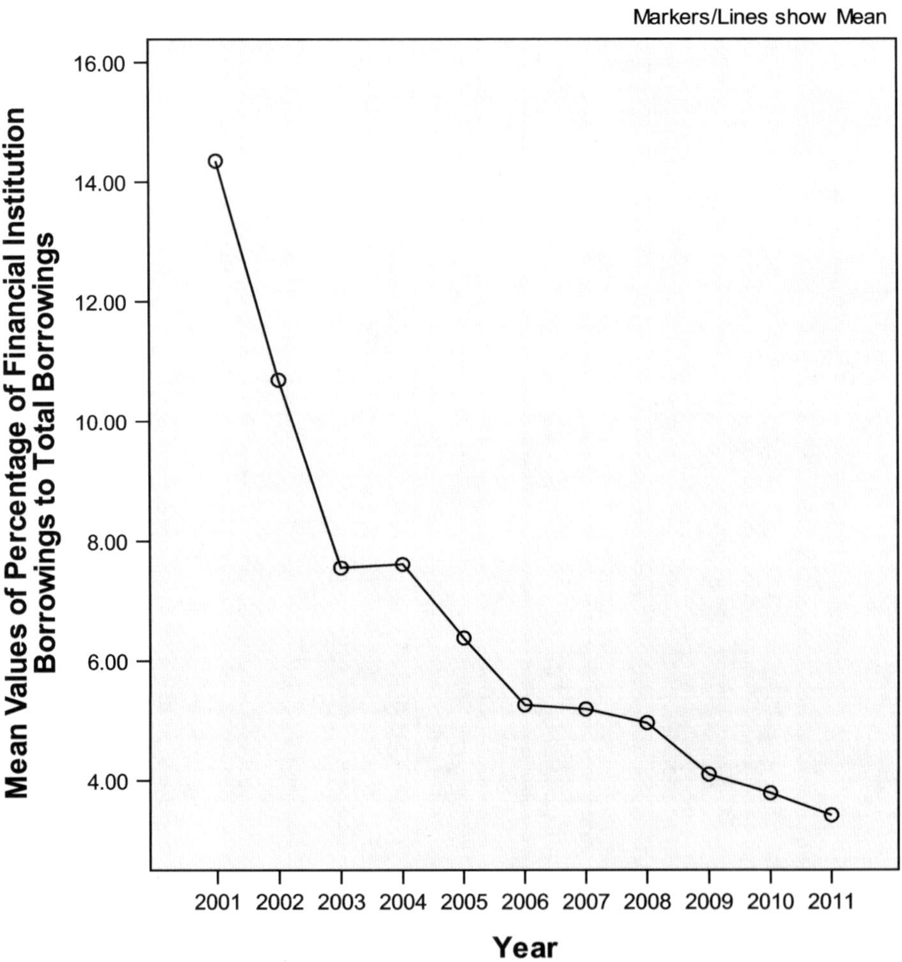

Fig. 3.8 Mean values of financial institution borrowings to total borrowings (in percentages) of the sample companies, 2001–2011

According to pecking order theory, firms adopt a hierarchical order of financing preferences; internal financing is preferred to external financing and when a company resorts to external financing (in case retentions are inadequate to support investments); debt is the first option and equity the last (Myers 1984). Shyam-Sunder and Myers (1999), through their empirical test, stated that following the pecking order, firms issued or retired an amount of debt equal to the funds flow deficit/surplus. Hence, the correlation between issue of debt and deficit and the redemption of debt and surplus would be high.

On the same lines, the funds flow deficit or surplus for the sample companies were calculated and a correlation matrix computed based on the funds flow deficit

Table 3.20 Correlation of deficit with debt issue, debt redemption and equity issue

Year ending	Correlation of deficit with debt issue	Correlation of deficit with debt redemption	Correlation of deficit with Equity issue	Correlation of deficit with equity redemption (buy-back)
2001	0.556 (0.000)	−0.249 (0.064)	–	–
2002	0.345 (0.034)	−0.244 (0.140)	0.462 (0.004)	–
2003	0.693 (0.000)	−0.699 (0.000)	0.457 (0.001)	0.010 (0.945)
2004	0.474 (0.002)	−0.574 (0.000)	0.217 (0.185)	–
2005	0.724 (0.000)	−0.734 (0.000)	0.263 (0.065)	–
2006	0.352 (0.014)	−0.139 (0.346)	0.127 (0.391)	–
2007	0.449 (0.000)	−0.209 (0.109)	0.095 (0.468)	–
2008	0.819 (0.000)	−0.864 (0.000)	0.348 (0.005)	0.037 (0.771)
2009	0.181 (0.182)	−0.189 (0.163)	0.098 (0.471)	0.011 (0.935)
2010	0.530 (0.000)	−0.620 (0.000)	0.555 (0.000)	–
2011	0.558 (0.000)	−0.565 (0.000)	0.576 (0.000)	0.023(0.868)

As per pecking order theory, deficits should have positive relationship with debt issued and equity issued and negative relationship with debt redeemed and equity redeemed (bought-back)
Cells with no values indicate that all the firms neither issued nor redeemed equity during that year
Values of equity redeemed and issued have been taken from 2002 onwards

and the issue of debt and/or equity; similarly, correlation was computed on the funds flow surplus and the retirement of debt and/or equity.

Deficit/Surplus was calculated as inflows/cash from operating activities minus investments. Companies with a positive value from the above calculations are surplus companies, and the companies with a negative value from of the above calculation are deficit companies. According to the pecking order hypothesis, companies with deficit would issue debt first and then issue equity as a last resort. Similarly, in terms of surplus companies, debt would be redeemed first.

Debt issued was calculated as proceeds from issue of debenture + bank borrowings + other long-term borrowings. Debt redemption was calculated as redemption of debentures + repayment of other long-term borrowings. Equity issued was taken as proceeds from issue of shares and equity redeemed was through share repurchases. Both deficit and surplus correlations on a yearly basis for the sample companies have been computed separately in Tables 3.20 and 3.21, respectively.

For the purpose of this analysis, only companies that have continuous data available (for the 11-year period for the variables defined above) have been considered. There were 115 such companies based on the criteria mentioned. For any given year, there were nearly half of the companies with a surplus or a deficit.

As is evident from the tables, the correlation values are very low between deficit and debt issue as well as surplus and debt redemption, for the sample companies. This indicates the non-adherence to the pecking order hypothesis (in its entirety) by the selected companies. In 2003 and 2004, however, there is an indication that the companies with deficit raised finance through debt. Similarly, in 2001 and 2005, companies with surplus redeemed debt.

Table 3.21 Correlation of surplus with debt issue, debt redemption and equity issue and equity redemption

Year ending	Correlation of surplus with debt issue	Correlation of surplus with debt redemption	Correlation of surplus with equity issue	Correlation of surplus with equity redemption (buy-back)
2001	−0.331 (0.822)	0.003 (0.981)	–	–
2002	−0.357 (0.002)	0.427 (0.000)	0.061 (0.606)	−0.044 (0.713)
2003	−0.522 (0.000)	0.641 (0.000)	−0.044 (0.729)	−0.099 (0.437)
2004	−0.321 (0.006)	0.527 (0.000)	0.053 (0.660)	−0.041 (0.731)
2005	−0.409 (0.001)	0.616 (0.000)	0.015 (0.912)	0.040 (0.762)
2006	−0.324 (0.010)	−0.238 (0.061)	0.093 (0.474)	0.053 (0.682)
2007	−0.309 (0.027)	0.161 (0.260)	−0.831 (0.000)	–
2008	−0.059 (0.698)	0.142 (0.346)	−0.198 (0.188)	0.089 (0.556)
2009	−0.561 (0.000)	0.185 (0.177)	−0.469 (0.000)	−0.034 (0.805)
2010	−0.366 (0.006)	0.302 (0.024)	−0.070 (0.611)	−0.095 (0.484)
2011	−0.693 (0.000)	0.346 (0.010)	0.001 (0.996)	0.153 (0.265)

As per pecking order theory, surplus should have negative relation with debt issued and equity issued and positive with debt redeemed and equity redeemed (bought-back)
Cells with no values indicate that firms neither issued nor redeemed the amount of equity
Values of equity redeemed and issued have been taken from 2002 onwards

Table 3.22 Use of a pecking order approach in financing projects (i.e. order of preference is using retained earnings first followed by debt and issue of additional equity capital as a last resort)

Option	Percentage
Yes	44.00
No	56.00

The findings from secondary data are corroborated by the primary data tabulated in Table 3.22 where more than half of the respondent companies indicate that they do not employ pecking order approach while making capital structure choices.

Section VI Risk Considerations

The risks which a business enterprise is exposed to are of several types. Two notable are business/operating risk and financial risk. Although we are primarily concerned with financial risk for capital structure decisions, the discussion of business risk is in order as it serves as a guideline for finance managers to decide about the type of capital structure. In operational terms, if business risk (caused by operating fixed costs) is high, the company is expected to opt for low financial risk (emanating from the use of debt and senior securities, necessitating payment of fixed financial charges) on the basis of sound tenets of financial management so that total risk is within 'safe/tolerable' limits.

Thus, from the perspective of designing capital structure, both business risk (measured by the degree of operating leverage, DOL) and financial risk (measured by the degree of financial leverage, DFL) are relevant. The objective of this section is to gain insight on the magnitude of business risk, financial risk and total risk (indicated by the degree of combined leverage, DCL) of the sample companies. Degree of operating leverage is calculated as percentage change in earnings before interest and taxes (EBIT) divided by percentage change in net sales. Degree of financial leverage is calculated as percentage change in earnings per share (EPS) divided by percentage change in EBIT. Degree of combined leverage is the product of DOL and DFL.

Further, it may be noted that the negative values have been excluded from analysis as they do not serve the intended purpose of measuring risk on the one hand and would have caused distortion in determination of average values on the other. To have better and more representative data on the subject, we have also excluded extreme values (exceeding 5) of DOL/DFL/DCL.

Relevant data pertaining to mean, standard deviation, coefficient of variation, skewness, kurtosis, median, and quartiles values of DOL, DFL and DCL of the sample companies are contained in Table 3.23. Frequency distribution pertaining to DOL, DFL and DCL of the sample companies is presented in Table 3.24.

Degree of operating leverage for the sample companies is 1.42 and has remained stable through phase 1 and 2; it increased in phase 3 but then decreased again in phase 4. The paired *t*-test does not indicate any statistically significant changes in mean values over the four phases indicating stable risk conditions.

Financial leverage in the sample companies has reduced marginally in phase 2 over phase 1 and remained stable during phases 3 and 4 indicating low risk.

Combined leverage has reduced marginally over the phases of the study. However, this change is not statistically significant as per the paired *t*-test. Thus, the sample companies have managed their combined risk within controllable limits, an indication of sound risk management practices.

The skewness and kurtosis figures also indicate that only few companies reported large values of the three measures of risk indicating low-risk statistics (for sizeable corporates). Similar conclusions follow on the basis of frequency distribution. Majority of the sample companies have low DOL of less than 1.5 (Table 3.23) throughout the period of the study (2001–2011). Likewise, DCL of less than 1.5 has also been noted in respect of sizeable number of the sample companies during the period under reference. This is in sharp contrast to the findings of Jain and Kumar (1997) where the sample of private sector companies reported high DOL and DFL of 2.58 and 2.10 for the 10-year period (1986–1995) and to the findings of Jain and Yadav (2000) for private sector enterprises over a period of 1991–1998, reporting a DOL and DFL of 1.83 and 1.99, respectively. The findings are similar, however, to the findings of Jain and Yadav (2005) on public sector enterprises over a period of 1991–2003, reporting a DOL of 1.18 and a DFL of 1.09, respectively. This aspect has to be seen in light of the fact that debt did occupy a significant portion of the capital structure of these companies over the period of the study unlike the current study's findings; the reduction in DFL is perhaps related to the same. These findings

Table 3.23 Mean, standard deviation, coefficient of variation, skewness, kurtosis, median and quartile values of degree of operating leverage (*DOL*), degree of financial leverage (*DFL*) and degree of combined leverage (*DCL*) of the sample companies, 2002–2011

Year ending	Leverage	Number	Mean	Standard deviation	Coefficient of variation (%)	Skewness	Kurtosis	Median	Quartile 1	Quartile 3
2002	DOL	88	1.27	0.95	74.39	1.16	0.87	0.96	0.58	1.67
	DFL	77	1.34	0.93	69.23	1.15	1.22	1.16	0.73	1.64
	DCL	60	1.70	1.13	73.11	0.77	–0.09	1.13	0.75	2.32
2003	DOL	103	1.62	1.16	71.44	0.83	0.09	1.3	0.67	2.41
	DFL	90	1.48	1.08	72.92	1.17	0.81	1.15	0.78	1.95
	DCL	63	2.40	1.14	78.34	1.13	0.80	1.20	0.56	1.87
2004	DOL	115	1.42	1.05	74.15	1.49	2.24	1.24	0.8	1.63
	DFL	102	1.55	1.07	69.06	1.04	0.79	1.38	0.82	1.84
	DCL	81	2.20	1.27	71.11	0.40	–0.79	1.72	0.61	2.65
2005	DOL	114	1.35	1.04	76.86	1.37	1.73	1.07	0.66	1.66
	DFL	101	1.36	0.80	58.54	1.60	3.60	1.2	0.89	1.57
	DCL	81	1.84	1.05	62.55	0.87	0.39	1.47	0.91	2.31
2006	DOL	112	1.41	1.01	71.87	1.45	2.08	1.17	0.81	1.76
	DFL	102	1.47	1.02	69.58	1.21	0.94	1.21	0.89	1.59
	DCL	77	2.07	1.09	75.84	1.08	0.67	1.29	0.65	1.76
2007	DOL	125	1.51	0.87	57.49	0.89	0.45	1.31	0.91	1.96
	DFL	105	1.31	0.87	66.75	1.84	4.01	1.11	0.82	1.45
	DCL	91	1.98	1.13	73.85	1.19	1.01	1.16	0.76	2.15
2008	DOL	135	1.56	0.92	59.45	1.40	2.04	1.23	0.95	1.95
	DFL	124	1.18	0.84	71.75	2.05	5.34	0.99	0.67	1.38
	DCL	103	1.84	1.14	76.79	1.19	0.68	1.19	0.67	1.94
2009	DOL	104	1.22	0.99	81.46	1.65	3.02	0.99	0.56	1.51
	DFL	117	1.41	0.83	58.67	1.54	3.48	1.18	0.91	1.69
	DCL	72	1.72	0.99	81.21	1.49	2.33	1.03	0.51	1.57

2010	DOL	102	1.70	1.23	72.06	0.84	−0.01	1.43	0.78	2.48
	DFL	107	1.50	0.81	54.35	0.97	1.86	1.35	0.98	1.97
	DCL	66	2.55	1.27	67.71	0.50	−0.58	1.81	0.82	2.71
2011	DOL	112	1.13	1.08	95.59	2.03	3.69	0.87	0.49	1.17
	DFL	95	1.11	0.76	68.61	0.58	0.12	1.02	0.55	1.7
	DCL	81	1.25	1.17	104.17	1.57	1.75	0.74	0.28	1.24
2002 – 2011	DOL	111	1.42	1.03	73.48	1.31	1.62	1.16	0.72	1.82
	DFL	102	1.37	0.90	65.95	1.32	2.22	1.18	0.80	1.68
	DCL	77	1.95	1.14	76.47	1.02	0.62	1.27	0.65	2.05
Phase 1 (2001–2002 to 2005–2006)	DOL	106	1.41	1.04	73.74	1.26	1.40	1.15	0.70	1.83
	DFL	94	1.44	0.98	67.87	1.23	1.47	1.22	0.82	1.72
	DCL	72	2.03	1.14	72.19	0.85	0.20	1.36	0.70	2.18
Phase 2 (2006–2007 to 2010–2011)	DOL	116	1.42	1.02	73.21	1.36	1.84	1.17	0.74	1.81
	DFL	110	1.30	0.82	64.03	1.40	2.96	1.13	0.79	1.64
	DCL	83	1.85	1.14	80.75	1.19	1.04	1.19	0.61	1.92
Phase 3 (2006–2007 to 2007–2008)	DOL	130	1.54	0.90	58.47	1.15	1.24	1.27	0.93	1.955
	DFL	115	1.25	0.86	69.25	1.95	4.67	1.05	0.75	1.42
	DCL	97	1.51	1.14	75.32	1.19	0.84	1.18	0.71	2.04
Phase 4 (2008–2009 to 2010–2011)	DOL	106	1.35	1.10	83.04	1.51	2.23	1.10	0.61	1.72
	DFL	106	1.34	0.80	60.54	1.03	1.82	1.18	0.81	1.79
	DCL	73	1.81	1.14	84.36	1.19	1.16	1.19	0.54	1.84

		Paired differences							
		Mean	Standard deviation	Standard error mean	Lower	Upper	*t*	*df*	Significance (2-tailed)
DOL	Phase 1–Phase 2	5.33819	38.63184	3.09302	−0.77173	11.44811	1.726	155	0.086
	Phase 3–Phase 4	.18581	1.58506	0.12302	−0.05710	0.42871	1.510	165	0.133
DFL	Phase 1–Phase 2	1.68243	14.11879	1.11272	−0.51508	3.87994	1.512	160	0.133
	Phase 3–Phase 4	−0.12079	1.03843	0.08060	−0.27993	0.03834	−1.499	165	0.136
DCL	Phase 1–Phase 2	4.16099	50.44162	4.17458	−4.08989	12.41188	0.997	145	0.321
	Phase 3–Phase 4	0.09682	1.52032	0.11800	−0.13617	0.32980	0.820	165	0.413

Table 3.24 Frequency distribution pertaining to operating leverage of the sample companies, 2002–2011

Leverage	Range	2002	2003	2004	2005	2006	2007	2008	2009	2010	2011
DOL	0.0–0.5	16.80	13.30	12.90	14.60	11.90	7.20	5.50	20.60	13.10	25.21
DFL		14.60	11.50	12.70	9.70	11.70	9.10	12.70	7.80	6.80	20.95
DCL		14.60	16.30	18.00	8.20	16.60	11.10	14.00	20.20	9.40	29.89
DOL	0.5–1.0	26.10	17.50	26.60	28.40	26.10	19.50	21.60	25.00	15.50	35.29
DFL		20.20	25.00	19.10	18.60	15.30	25.50	37.30	18.90	17.10	23.81
DCL		20.00	8.60	11.00	16.50	15.60	26.80	23.60	19.10	11.50	29.89
DOL	1.0–1.5	12.10	17.50	24.10	19.50	20.60	27.50	29.30	21.50	14.70	16.81
DFL		24.70	19.20	21.00	32.70	38.70	39.10	27.70	36.20	28.20	20.95
DCL		12.00	18.40	3.00	19.50	18.70	12.00	22.80	20.20	11.50	13.79
DOL	1.5–2.0	12.10	8.30	9.60	12.10	14.20	15.20	15.30	6.00	13.10	4.20
DFL		8.90	9.60	18.20	14.20	7.20	8.20	9.50	10.20	17.10	12.38
DCL		8.00	9.70	17.00	10.30	12.50	9.20	7.80	6.70	5.20	2.30
DOL	2.0–5.0	14.90	29.10	19.30	17.80	15.80	21.00	22.30	16.30	27.00	12.61
DFL		17.90	21.10	20.90	14.20	18.90	13.60	11.10	18.90	22.20	12.38
DCL		25.30	15.20	32.00	28.80	16.60	25.00	21.90	14.60	31.50	17.24
DOL	Above 5.0	17.70	14.10	7.20	7.30	11.10	9.40	5.50	10.30	16.30	5.88
DFL		13.40	13.40	7.20	10.60	8.10	4.50	1.60	7.80	8.50	9.52
DCL		20.00	31.50	19.00	16.40	19.70	15.70	9.60	19.10	30.50	6.90
	Total (%)	100	100	100	100	100	100	100	100	100	100

conform to the findings of Titman and Wessels (1988), Kremp et al. (1999) and Booth et al. (2001).

Section VII Debt Service Capacity

The soundness of a firm, from the point of view of long-term lenders, lies in its ability to service their claims. The objective of this section is to examine debt service capacity in terms of periodic payment of debt as well as interest of the sample companies. Debt service coverage ratio and interest coverage ratio (earnings before interest and taxes/interest) are well-accepted ratios for the purpose. Between the two, debt service coverage ratio (DSCR) has been considered a comprehensive measure to compute debt service capacity and provides the value in terms of the number of times the total debt service obligations consisting of interest and repayment of principal (in instalments) are covered by the total operating funds available after the payment of taxes. As the data regarding instalments was not available in the final accounts of the companies, the average period of long-term debt for the sample companies was determined. The period came out to be approximately 5 years. Hence, it is assumed that the loans were paid in 5 equal instalments and the instalment for each year, therefore, is computed as long-term loans divided by 5 (for the

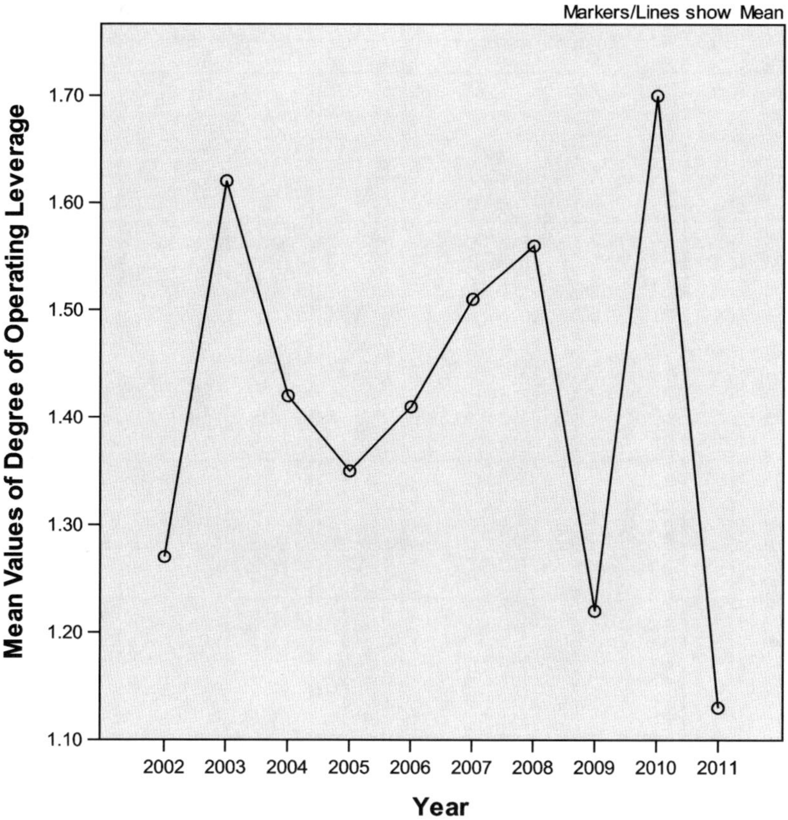

Fig. 3.9 Mean values of operating leverage of the sample companies, 2002–2011

purpose of our analysis). Interest coverage ratio, also known as 'time-interest-earned ratio' is determined, dividing the operating profits or earnings before interest and taxes (EBIT) by the fixed interest charges on loans. An attempt has been made to go a step further and compute the total external obligations coverage ratio (TEOCR) to understand the most comprehensive external obligations' service capacity of the sample companies. To compute TEOCR, long-term debt, short-term debt and current liabilities are added and the firm's ability to meet this complete external obligation is measured.

Relevant data of debt service coverage ratio (DSCR), interest coverage ratio (ICR) and total external obligations coverage ratio (TEOCR) in terms of mean, standard deviation, coefficient of variation, skewness, kurtosis, median and quartile values and frequency distribution of the sample companies have been shown in Tables 3.25, 3.26, 3.27, 3.28, 3.29 and 3.30. To have better and more representative data on the subject, both the negative values of DSCR, ICR and TEOCR and extreme values (exceeding the ratio of ten times) have been excluded.

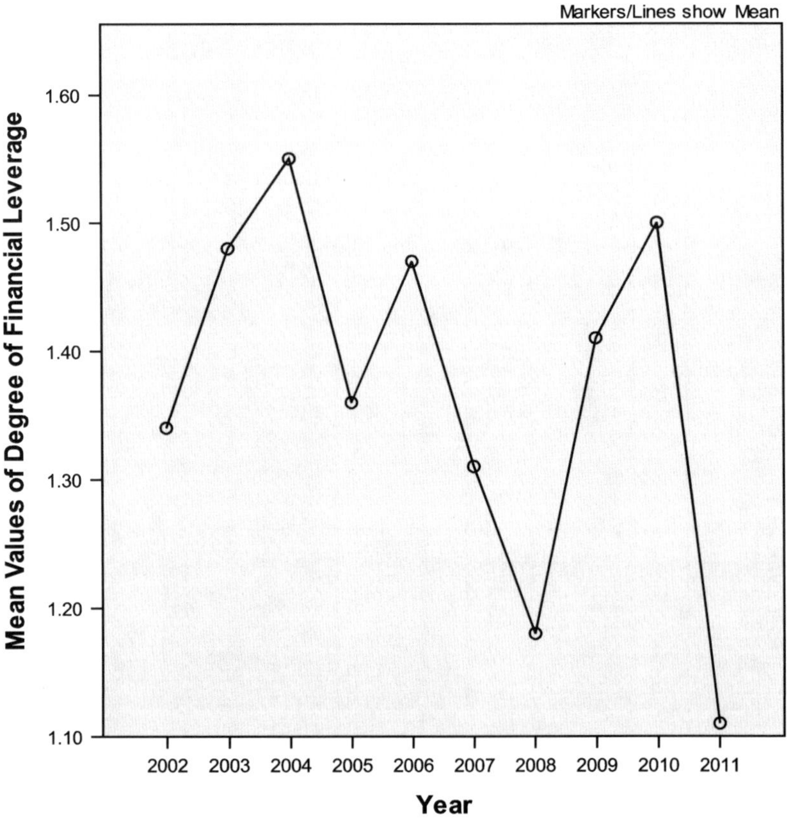

Fig. 3.10 Mean values of financial leverage of the sample companies, 2002–2011

In the form of equations, the three ratios could be stated as debt service coverage ratio = (EAT + interest + depreciation)/(total instalment + interest) where total instalment (is assumed to be) = total debt/5; interest coverage ratio (ICR) = EBIT/interest; and total external obligations coverage ratio (TEOCR) = (EAT + interest + depreciation)/(total instalment + interest + current liabilities & provisions).

Debt Service Coverage Ratio

The sample companies have had a debt service coverage ratio of an average of 2 through the period of the study (Table 3.25). The paired *t*-test indicates statistically significant changes in the mean values in phase 2 over phase 1. This is very satisfactory ratio; it implies that the sample companies have adequate funds (twice the amount required to be paid) to meet their obligations arising from

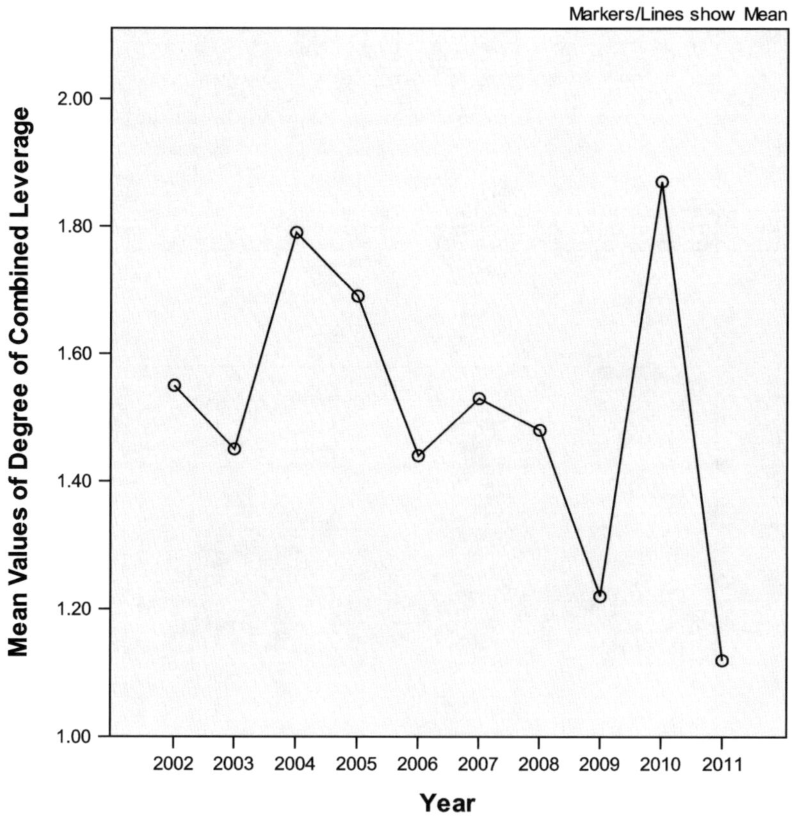

Fig. 3.11 Mean values of combined leverage of the sample companies, 2002–2011

long-term loans. They have sound financial position and, therefore, are not likely to encounter any problems in raising long-term loans to finance their investment projects.

Interest Coverage Ratio

The mean interest coverage ratio is very satisfactory, the average being 4.46 during the period of the study (2001–2011). The mean ICR of 4.44 signifies that the operating earnings of the sample companies are more than four times of their interest payment obligations (in operational terms, it implies that the firms have very high probability of meeting their interest schedules in time). In fact, over the years, there has been an improvement in the ICR during phase 2 over phase 1. Figure 3.13 portrays the rising trend of ICR. A significant difference in ICR of these two phases is

Table 3.25 Mean, standard deviation, coefficient of variation, skewness, kurtosis, median and quartile values related to debt service coverage ratio of the sample companies, 2001–2011 (Figures are in percentages)

Year ending	Number	Mean	Standard deviation	Coefficient of variation (%)	Skewness	Kurtosis	Median	Quartile 1	Quartile 3
2001	113	1.65	1.70	103.39	1.92	3.84	1.11	0.64	1.82
2002	116	2.03	2.10	103.26	2.02	3.62	1.26	0.89	2.51
2003	110	1.84	1.64	89.04	1.88	3.91	1.33	0.83	2.11
2004	113	2.31	2.11	91.60	1.61	2.28	1.61	0.90	2.99
2005	111	2.06	1.76	85.73	1.72	2.44	1.45	0.91	2.45
2006	111	2.05	1.78	87.08	1.98	3.87	1.43	0.92	2.53
2007	116	2.14	1.90	88.39	1.67	2.40	1.40	0.93	2.87
2008	118	2.29	1.99	87.22	2.00	3.86	1.53	1.03	2.80
2009	118	1.84	1.76	96.13	2.47	6.79	1.23	0.82	2.08
2010	115	2.07	2.31	111.57	2.48	6.89	1.15	0.78	2.31
2011	120	1.76	1.93	109.77	2.19	4.49	1.05	0.63	1.87
2001–2011	115	2.00	1.91	95.74	2.00	4.03	1.32	0.84	2.39
Phase 1 (2000–2001 to 2005–2006)	112	1.99	1.85	93.35	1.86	3.33	1.36	0.85	2.40
Phase 2 (2006–2007 to 2010–2011)	117	2.02	1.98	98.61	2.16	4.88	1.27	0.84	2.39
Phase 3 (2006–2007 to 2007–2008)	117	2.21	1.94	87.81	1.84	3.13	1.47	0.98	2.84
Phase 4 (2008–2009 to 2010–2011)	118	1.89	2.00	105.82	2.38	6.05	1.14	0.74	2.09

	Paired differences							
	Mean	Standard deviation	Standard error mean	Lower	Upper	t	df	Significance (2-tailed)
Phase 1–Phase 2	−0.40545	2.22138	0.19634	−0.79398	−0.01692	−2.065	127	0.041
Phase 3–Phase 4	0.15982	2.18644	0.16970	−0.17525	0.49488	0.942	165	0.348

Table 3.26 Frequency distribution pertaining to debt service coverage ratio of the sample companies, 2001–2011 (Figures are in percentages)

Debt service coverage ratio	2001	2002	2003	2004	2005	2006	2007	2008	2009	2010	2011
Less than 0	3.45	1.50	2.22	0.73	0.72	1.43	2.70	2.04	1.35	0.69	1.22
0–1	11.21	12.03	10.37	13.87	13.04	12.14	15.54	8.84	11.49	17.36	33.54
1–2	23.28	23.31	20.74	16.06	22.46	30.71	26.35	27.21	31.76	30.56	22.56
2–3	17.24	15.04	18.52	14.60	16.67	10.71	11.49	14.97	14.86	10.42	6.10
3–5	13.79	15.04	10.37	16.79	14.49	11.43	9.46	14.97	10.13	4.86	3.66
5–10	9.48	7.52	10.37	12.41	9.42	11.43	8.78	7.48	6.08	10.42	7.32
Above 10	21.55	25.56	27.41	25.55	23.19	22.14	25.68	24.49	24.32	25.69	25.61
Total (%)	100	100	100	100	100	100	100	100	100	100	100

supported by paired sample test also. Even during the recession phase, the ratio continued to be equally very high (4.39), making it possible for the sample companies to pay interest on time. The moderate skewness also supports the robustness in ICR for the entire sample, by and large. This is in sharp contrast to the findings of Jain and Kumar (1997) where the sample private sector companies reported an ICR of 2.4 and a DSCR of 2 (assuming debt repayments in 6 years), Jain and Yadav (2000) where the sample private sector enterprises for the period 1991–1998 had an ICR of 1.94 and a DSCR of 2.28 and Jain and Yadav (2005) study on public sector undertakings reporting an ICR of 2.52. The debt-bearing capacity of companies appears to have improved significantly in this regard. However, it has to be borne in mind that the component of debt in the capital structure has also reduced considerably over the given time; the betterment in debt servicing/paying capacity could be a result of this as well.

Total External Obligations Coverage Ratio

The mean total external obligations coverage ratio may be considered very satisfactory, the average being 0.73 during the period of the study (2001–2011). It signifies that the operating earnings (exclusively) of the sample companies are adequate to meet more than seven-tenths of their total external obligations. Given the fact that the current assets (in practice) are also available to pay current liabilities, the sample firms are not likely to encounter any difficulties in meeting their total obligations (emanating from long-term debt in terms of interest payments and short-term maturing obligations). The ratio did register a decline in phase 4 (due to recession) which was statistically significant. In spite of the same, however, the mean TEOCR remained close to 70% indicating the operational/financial soundness of the sample companies. The same is supported by the frequency distribution (Table 3.30). Figure 3.14 portrays the trend of TEOCR.

Table 3.27 Mean, standard deviation, coefficient of variation, skewness, kurtosis, median and quartile values related to interest coverage ratio of the sample companies, 2001–2011 (Figures are in percentages)

Year ending	Number	Mean	Standard deviation	Coefficient of variation (%)	Skewness	Kurtosis	Median	Quartile 1	Quartile 3
2001	93	3.17	1.94	61.22	1.35	1.79	2.61	1.94	3.85
2002	98	3.62	2.31	63.74	1.08	0.43	2.92	1.97	4.32
2003	88	3.86	2.17	56.23	0.68	0.01	3.69	2.28	4.97
2004	83	4.61	2.53	54.82	0.35	–0.98	4.12	2.55	6.73
2005	71	4.45	2.38	53.32	0.74	–0.41	3.73	2.73	5.79
2006	75	5.32	2.43	45.69	0.19	–0.64	5.08	3.39	6.87
2007	74	5.16	2.27	43.92	0.11	–0.98	5.22	3.23	6.74
2008	74	5.52	2.39	43.18	0.03	–1.01	5.54	3.59	7.39
2009	86	4.14	2.17	52.31	0.83	0.08	3.60	2.46	5.30
2010	78	4.52	2.24	49.47	0.45	–0.90	4.26	2.67	5.84
2011	87	4.51	2.51	55.57	0.57	–0.61	4.26	2.31	6.16
2001–2011	82	4.44	2.30	52.68	0.58	–0.29	4.09	2.65	5.81
Phase 1 (2000–2001 to 2005–2006)	85	4.17	2.29	55.84	0.73	0.03	3.69	2.48	5.42
Phase 2 (2006–2007 to 2010–2011)	80	4.77	2.31	48.89	0.40	–0.68	4.58	2.85	6.29
Phase 3 (2006–2007 to 2007–2008)	74	5.34	2.33	43.55	0.07	–1.00	5.38	3.41	7.07
Phase 4 (2008–2009 to 2010–2011)	84	4.39	2.30	52.45	0.61	-0.47	4.04	2.48	5.77

	Paired differences							
	Mean	Standard deviation	Standard error mean	Lower	Upper	*t*	*df*	Significance (2-tailed)
Phase 1–Phase 2	–0.72407	2.34881	0.24622	–1.21324	–0.23491	–2.941	90	0.004
Phase 3–Phase 4	–0.12444	2.88474	0.22390	–0.56651	0.31764	–0.556	165	0.579

Table 3.28 Frequency distribution pertaining to interest coverage ratio of the sample companies, 2001–2011 (Figures are in percentages)

Interest coverage ratio	2001	2002	2003	2004	2005	2006	2007	2008	2009	2010	2011
Less than 0	2.20	2.80	1.30	0.00	0.60	0.60	1.20	0.60	1.20	1.20	1.22
0–1	5.90	4.90	3.40	3.40	0.60	1.30	0.00	0.00	1.20	0.00	1.22
1–2	13.40	12.60	9.00	4.80	4.60	2.60	4.40	3.10	4.90	6.80	7.93
2–3	20.10	19.00	14.60	7.50	10.00	4.60	5.00	4.30	12.80	9.90	9.15
3–5	20.10	17.60	18.80	20.00	16.00	15.70	12.50	12.90	17.10	12.40	15.24
5–10	9.70	14.70	15.30	21.30	16.00	25.00	24.50	25.30	16.50	19.20	18.29
Above 10	28.30	28.10	37.00	42.70	52.00	50.00	52.20	53.70	46.00	50.30	46.95
Total (%)	100	100	100	100	100	100	100	100	100	100	100

Section VIII Sector-Wise Analysis

Debt–Equity Ratio

The debt–equity ratio of the constituent sectors (for details on sectors refer to Table 1.2, Chap. 1) of the sample companies remained stable throughout the period of the study. The housing sector had the highest average ratio at 1.92 (for details, refer to Appendix 3.1). The metals sector had a debt–equity ratio of 1. The sectors that reduced leverage to less than unity in phase 4 (2009–2011) of the study were healthcare and diversified (Appendix 3.2). The only sectors that reported a significant difference in their mean values were the healthcare and housing sector (between phases 1 and 2) through the paired *t*-test. Also, as per RBI's outlook (refer to Appendix 2.1, Chap. 2), the sectors which suffered due to recession (in terms of reduced investments) were housing, ICT, capital goods, healthcare, metal, miscellaneous, oil and gas and transport. However, from the capital structure point of view, the only sectors that altered capital structure practices significantly were healthcare and housing. The ANOVA test (Appendix 3.3) does not indicate any statistically significant difference amongst the variances for any constituent sectors, throughout the period of the study. Thus, the sample companies seem to have followed, by and large, a uniform capital structure policy for the period of the study in spite of the recession over phase 4. These findings are in tune with RBI's view of the resilience of the Indian economy (Appendix 2.1, Chap. 2).

Long-Term Debt–Equity Ratio

The housing sector remained highly leveraged in phase 1, but the LTD/E reduced substantially in phase 2 (Appendix 3.4). Similarly, the LTD/E ratio reduced considerably

Table 3.29 Mean, standard deviation, coefficient of variation, skewness, kurtosis, median and quartile values related to total external obligations coverage ratio of the sample companies, 2001–2011 (Figures are in percentages)

Year ending	Number	Mean	Standard deviation	Coefficient of variation (%)	Skewness	Kurtosis	Median	Quartile 1	Quartile 3
2001	129	0.78	1.50	191.37	3.04	9.42	0.25	0.04	0.63
2002	139	0.76	1.37	181.08	3.50	13.47	0.36	0.11	0.63
2003	144	0.74	1.27	172.34	3.47	13.42	0.36	0.14	0.67
2004	145	0.78	1.34	171.42	3.54	14.97	0.37	0.13	0.65
2005	149	0.75	1.26	168.48	3.71	15.48	0.37	0.16	0.68
2006	152	0.67	1.00	149.72	3.40	13.21	0.38	0.18	0.64
2007	156	0.78	1.22	156.82	3.84	17.39	0.41	0.20	0.77
2008	157	0.73	0.98	135.13	3.47	14.40	0.42	0.22	0.75
2009	161	0.82	1.33	162.86	3.99	18.21	0.45	0.21	0.73
2010	161	0.71	1.02	143.02	4.01	21.83	0.40	0.20	0.74
2011	162	0.55	0.58	105.29	3.21	12.67	0.38	0.23	0.66
2001–2011	150	0.73	1.17	157.96	3.56	14.95	0.38	0.16	0.69
Phase 1 (2000–2001 to 2005–2006)	143	0.75	1.29	172.40	3.44	13.33	0.35	0.13	0.65
Phase 2 (2006–2007 to 2010–2011)	159	0.72	1.03	140.63	3.70	16.90	0.41	0.21	0.73
Phase 3 (2006–2007 to 2007–2008)	157	0.75	1.10	145.97	3.66	15.90	0.42	0.21	0.76
Phase 4 (2008–2009 to 2010–2011)	161	0.69	0.98	137.06	3.74	17.57	0.41	0.21	0.71

	Paired differences							
				95% confidence interval of the difference				
	Mean	Standard deviation	Standard error mean	Lower	Upper	*t*	df	Significance (2-tailed)
Phase 1–Phase 2	0.11177	0.92305	0.07390	−0.03422	0.25775	1.512	155	0.132
Phase 3–Phase 4	0.09917	0.61286	0.04860	0.00317	0.19516	2.040	158	0.043

Table 3.30 Frequency distribution pertaining to total external obligations coverage ratio of the sample companies, 2001–2011 (Figures are in percentages)

Total external obligations coverage ratio	2001	2002	2003	2004	2005	2006	2007	2008	2009	2010	2011
Less than 0	2.84	2.03	1.31	1.31	1.27	1.88	2.45	1.81	1.20	1.20	1.22
0–1	76.60	78.38	77.12	78.43	79.62	82.50	77.30	77.11	78.92	79.52	89.02
1–2	4.26	6.08	8.50	7.19	8.28	5.00	9.20	11.45	10.84	10.84	6.71
2–3	2.84	4.05	2.61	2.61	2.55	3.13	6.13	2.41	2.41	3.01	1.22
3–5	4.26	2.03	2.61	4.58	1.91	3.13	0.00	2.41	2.41	3.01	1.83
5–10	3.55	3.38	3.27	1.96	2.55	1.25	3.07	1.20	2.41	0.60	0.00
Above 10	5.67	4.05	4.58	3.92	3.82	3.13	1.84	3.61	1.81	1.81	0.00
Total (%)	100	100	100	100	100	100	100	100	100	100	100

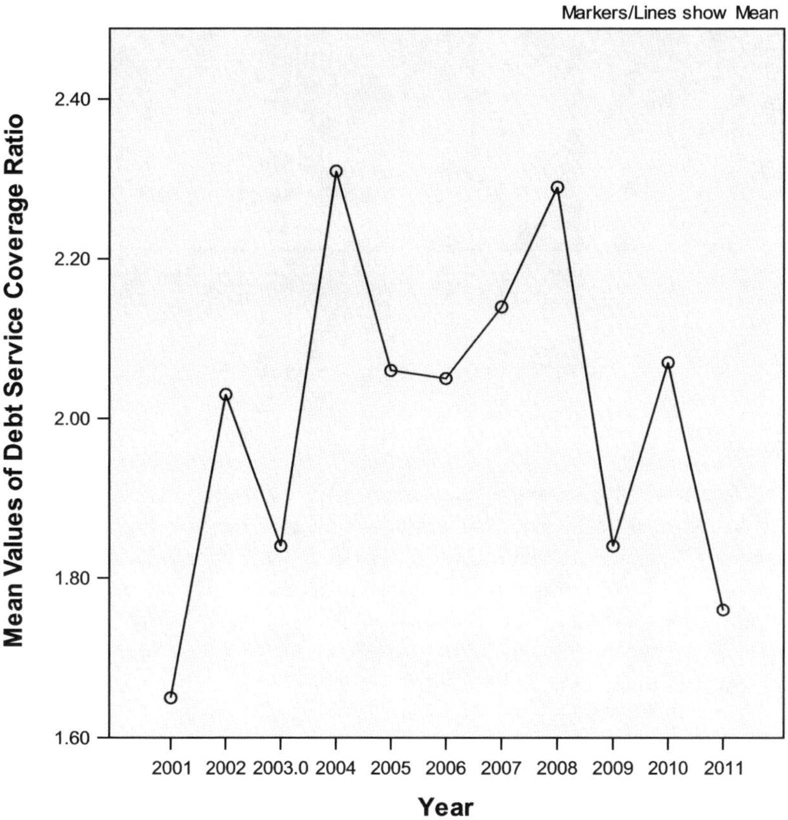

Fig. 3.12 Mean values of debt service coverage ratio of the sample companies, 2001–2011

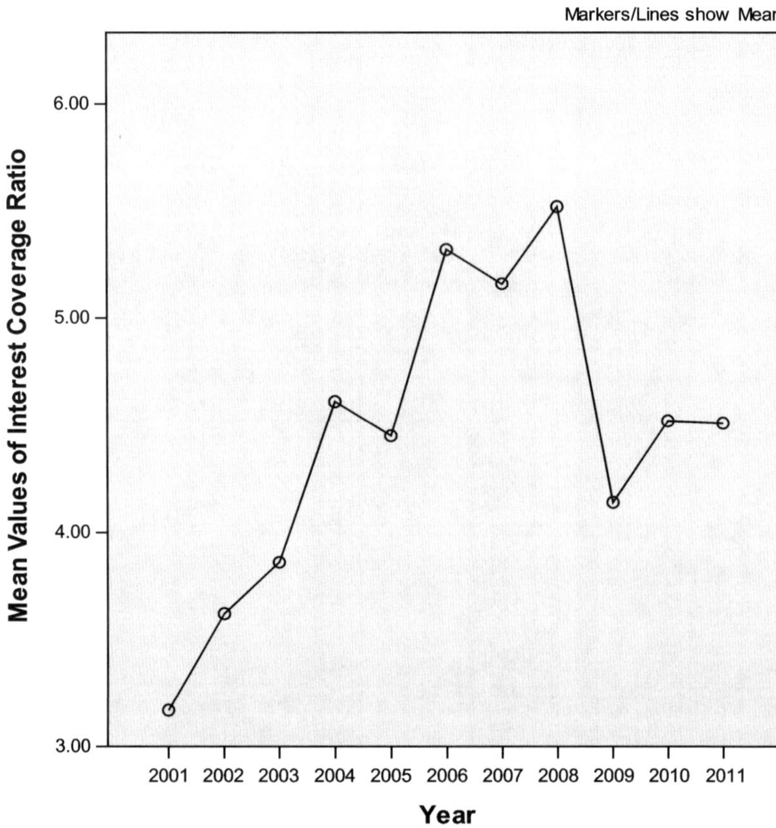

Fig. 3.13 Mean values of interest coverage ratio of the sample companies, 2001–2011

from 0.93 to 0.64 in phase 4 over phase 3 (Appendix 3.5). The only sector that reported a significant difference in its mean value was the housing sector (between phases 1 and 2) through the paired *t*-test. As per RBI's outlook, housing was one of the sectors which suffered due to recession (in terms of reduced investments) with ICT, capital goods, healthcare, metal, miscellaneous, oil and gas and transport being the others. However, the only sector that altered capital structure practices in terms of deployment of long-term debt significantly was housing. The ANOVA test (Appendix 3.6) does not indicate any statistically significant difference amongst the variances for any constituent sectors, throughout the period of the study except for the consolidated sample as a whole. Thus, the sample companies do not seem to have made major changes in capital structure policy for the period of the study including the recession period. These findings are in tune with RBI's view of the resilience of the Indian economy.

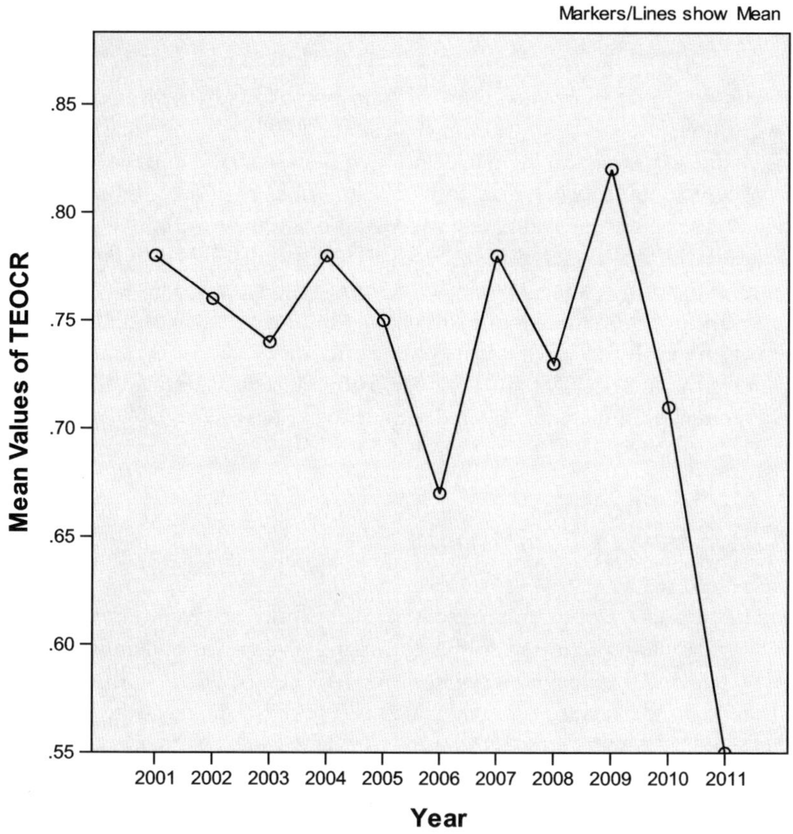

Fig. 3.14 Mean values of total external obligations coverage ratio of the sample companies, 2001–2011

Short-Term Obligations–Equity Ratio

Short-term obligations (including current liabilities) heavily funded the operations of the capital goods, FMCG, housing and miscellaneous sectors over the period of the study (Appendix 3.7). However, the STO/E ratio reduced in phases 3 and 4 of the study (compared to phases 1 and 2) for the housing and miscellaneous sectors (Appendix 3.8). The sectors that reported a significant difference in their mean values were the health (between phases 1 and 2 and phases 3 and 4) and housing sectors (between phases 1 and 2) as per the paired *t*-test. As per RBI's outlook, housing and healthcare were amongst the sectors which suffered due to recession. The ANOVA test (Appendix 3.9) indicates statistically significant differences amongst the variances for the consolidated sample as a whole throughout the period of the study and the housing sector for phases 1 and 2.

Total Debt to Total Assets Ratio

The sectors financing more than 60% of their total assets by debt in phase 1 of the study were housing, oil and gas and miscellaneous (Appendix 3.10). This could perhaps be due to the capital intensive nature of their business and the resultant large asset base which could be used as collateral to attract high debt. Of these, housing and oil and gas sectors (probably due to recession and the resultant loss in earnings) offloaded debt in phases 3 and 4, respectively (Appendix 3.11). In contrast, capital goods and transport sectors increased debt during the later phases of the study. The healthcare sector reported a significant change in mean values of total debt to total assets over phases 1 and 2. The ANOVA test did not report any statistically significant changes in variances for any of the constituent sectors. However, it reported a significant change for the consolidated sample over phases 3 and 4 (Appendix 3.12).

Long-Term Debt to Total Assets Ratio

All constituent sectors of the sample companies maintained long-term debt component in their capital structure over phases 1 and 2, except for housing; it recorded a decline by nearly 10 percentage points from 40.17 to 30.96% (statistically significant). Likewise, the healthcare sector also registered a decrease in the long-term debt component (Appendices 3.13 and 3.14). The ANOVA does not indicate any statistically significant changes in variances for the constituent sectors. However, there is a significant change in the variances of the consolidated sample, as a whole, over the four phases of the study (Appendix 3.15).

Secured Loans to Total Borrowings

The sample companies are some of the largest companies in India with a substantial asset base. A strong asset base attracts secured debt at cheaper rate than unsecured debt. It is rather disheartening to note, then, that the sample companies seem to have offloaded the secured debt component from their total borrowings over phases 1 and 2. In fact, healthcare reduced the secured loans component to total borrowings by nearly 16 percentage points (statistically significant). Healthcare, housing, oil and gas, power and miscellaneous sectors were the sectors that indicated an increase in secured loans to total borrowings in phase 4 (Appendices 3.16 and 3.17). The sectors to record a statistically significant change in mean values were healthcare over phases 1 and 2 and housing over phases 3 and 4. The ANOVA test did not report any statistically significant changes in variances for either the constituent sectors or the consolidated sample as a whole (for details, refer Appendix 3.18).

Bank Borrowings to Total Borrowings

The dependence of all the constituent sectors on bank borrowings (to total borrowings) has witnessed a significant increase over the period of the study. Such borrowings more than doubled in capital goods, FMCG and healthcare sectors and doubled in diversified and housing sectors (Appendix 3.19). The only sector to note a reduction in the component of bank borrowings to total borrowings was the oil and gas sector which offloaded bank borrowings by nearly 12 percentage points in phase 4 (Appendix 3.20). The changes in the above stated mean values were statistically significant as per the paired *t*-test for capital goods, diversified, FMCG, healthcare, housing, ICT, metals and miscellaneous over phases 1 and 2. Similarly, the ANOVA registered statistically significant changes in variances for the capital goods, diversified, FMCG and housing sectors over phases 1 and 2 (Appendix 3.21).

Financial Institution Borrowings to Total Borrowings

The already meagre share of financial institution borrowing to total borrowings in the constituent sectors of the sample companies was further reduced over the period of the study. The notable sectors were capital goods which reduced the percentage of financial institution borrowings from 2.37 to 0.53%, FMCG from 4.85 to 1.83%, transport from 14.52 to 0.72% and healthcare which brought it down from 6.89% to nil, over phases 1 and 2. The increase was noted only in respect of the diversified sector. Also, the miscellaneous sector maintained a nearly 8% share of financial institutional borrowings. This could perhaps be due to the presence of the agriculture sector under the miscellaneous category which attracts cheaper finance in the form of priority sector lending by certain financial institutions (Appendix 3.22). A similar scenario continued over phases 3 and 4 with the diversified sector being the only sector to increase the percentage share of financial institution borrowing to total borrowings (Appendix 3.23). The paired *t*-test reported statistically significant changes in mean values only for the healthcare sector over phases 1 and 2. The ANOVA test reported statistically significant changes in variances for the healthcare and transport sector for phases 1 and 2 and the consolidated sample for phases 3 and 4 (Appendix 3.24).

Degree of Operating Leverage

The degree of operating leverage (DOL) showed minor fluctuations for the constituent sectors of the sample companies. FMCG, amongst others showed an increase in DOL from 1.31 to 1.53 over phases 1 and 2. All sectors except metals and transport indicated a decline in DOL over phases 3 and 4 (Appendices 3.25 and 3.26). None of these fluctuations had any statistically significant changes in mean values or variances for the constituent sectors (Appendix 3.27).

Degree of Financial Leverage

The constituent sectors of the sample companies show fluctuating degrees of financial leverage (DFL) over the period of the study. Notable amongst them are FMCG which reduced DFL from 1.71 to 1.16 and transport (from 1.80 to 1.42) over phases 1 and 2. Over phases 3 and 4, diversified sector increased DFL from 1.16 to 1.48, health from 1.15 to 1.57, while ICT and power reduced DFL from 1.32 to 1.12 and from 1.22 to 0.85, respectively (Appendices 3.28 and 3.29). The paired *t*-test indicates significant changes in mean values for FMCG sector over phases 1 and 2. The ANOVA test reports statistically significant changes in variances for the consolidated sector (for both phases 1 and 2 and phases 3 and 4), the FMCG sector (phases 1 and 2), diversified and transport sectors for phases 3 and 4 (Appendix 3.30).

Degree of Combined Leverage

The constituent sectors of the sample companies exhibit the usual fluctuations in the degrees of combined leverage (DCL). Notables are ICT that showed a decline from 1.65 to 1.16 over phases 1 and 2 and from 1.34 to 0.98 over phases 3 and 4. Oil and gas registered a decline from 1.55 to 1.31 over phases 3 and 4 (Appendices 3.31 and 3.32). The paired *t*-test found the changes in mean values of DCL statistically significant for the ICT and transport sectors over phases 1 and 2. The ANOVA test did not indicate any statistically significant changes in variances over the period of the study for any of the constituent sectors except for transport over phases 1 and 2 and power over phases 3 and 4 (Appendix 3.33).

Debt Service Coverage Ratio

Amongst the constituent sectors, there has been a decline in the debt service capacity measured through the debt service coverage ratio (DSCR) over phases 1 and 2, except for the FMCG, healthcare and housing sectors which recorded an increase in their DSCR. Similarly, over phases 3 and 4, the FMCG and ICT sectors recorded an increase in their DSCR, indicative of sound earnings even during the recession (Appendices 3.34 and 3.35). Out of these, the changes in mean values of DSCR were statistically significant only for the capital goods sector over phases 3 and 4.

The ANOVA test also resulted in statistically significant changes in variances for the capital goods sector over phases 3 and 4 (Appendix 3.36).

Interest Coverage Ratio

Indicative of the sound earnings of the sample companies, all constituent sectors except healthcare and miscellaneous registered an increase in their interest coverage ratio (ICR) over phases 1 and 2. However, over phases 3 and 4, nine sectors except ICT and power registered a decline in their ICR (probably due to lower earnings attributable to recession in phase 4). Of these, the changes in mean values of ICR for metals was statistically significant for phases 1 and 2 and healthcare and miscellaneous were significant for phases 3 and 4. The ANOVA test concluded statistically significant changes in variances of ICR for the consolidated sample over phases 1 and 2 and for the healthcare sector over phases 3 and 4 (Appendices 3.37, 3.38 and 3.39).

Total External Obligations Coverage Ratio

ICT sector recorded the highest TEOCR of 1.29 with capital goods with the lowest at 0.20. All sectors, however, increased their TEOCR except for diversified, ICT, oil and gas, power and transport sectors. Even during the post-recession phase, the diversified, FMCG, healthcare, power and miscellaneous sectors noted increases in their TEOCR. These changes were significant for the capital goods sector in phases 1 and 2 and the housing and metals sectors for phases 3 and 4. ANOVA was significant for the consolidated sample through the study period (Appendices 3.40, 3.41 and 3.42).

Section IX Costs of Capital

There are two major findings of the survey (Table 3.30). The first is that half of the respondent companies rely on primary rate of return plus risk premium in estimating their cost of equity capital. The second is that another half of respondent companies use an absolute sum to denote cost of equity (ranging from 10 to more than 20%). Capital asset pricing model (CAPM) is used by 40% of the respondent companies, an indication of the sophistication in estimating costs of capital in the sample companies. However, none of the respondent companies uses the dividend valuation model (extensively cited in finance theory) to estimate cost of equity, perhaps signalling that returns in form of dividends do not constitute a major factor for Indian investors while making equity investment decisions.

Table 3.31 Equivalence of cost of equity capital in the firm

Option	Percentage
Primary rate of return plus risk premium	50.00 (36.36)
An absolute sum	50.00
(a) >20%	31.81
(b) 15–20%	9.09
(c) 10–14%	9.09
(d) Any other	–
Capital asset pricing model (CAPM)	40.90 (18.18)
No cost is considered	4.54
Dividend valuation model	0.00
Rate of return available to investors on securities of balanced mutual funds	0.00

As per the sound theory of financial management, nearly half of the respondent companies consider cost of equity capital as the proxy for estimating cost of retained earnings (Table 3.31). The external yield criterion is used by one-third of the companies. Although the vast majority uses sound measures of estimating cost of retained earnings, it is ironical to note that less than one-fifth of the respondent companies (16%) do not consider any cost of retained earnings which is indicative of unsound financial management practice.

Section X Emerging Factors Affecting Capital Structure Choice

The majority of the sample companies in the survey endorses that capital structure has been affected (towards relatively more equity) in the wake of India's liberalisation and globalisation (Tables 3.32 and 3.33).

A shift towards more equity in the capital structure of the companies is an indication of the increasingly important role that the capital markets of the country are to play in raising finance for the companies.

It is corroborated by the fact that nearly 60% of the respondent companies state that capital markets are increasingly being tapped to raise finance (Table 3.34).

The survey highlights financial risk, stability in sales and profits and corporate control as the three ors major factors governing the capital structure decision of Indian corporate (Table 3.35 and 3.36).

These findings are similar to the findings of Bancel and Mittoo (2004), Vasiliou and Daskalakis (2009), Chang et al. (2009) and Kayo and Kimura (2011).

Section XI Concluding Observations

The study succinctly brings to fore that debt (which was the most important constituent of corporate financing in pre-economic liberalisation) is steadily being replaced by equity for the majority of the sample companies in India. Equity financing

Table 3.32 Equivalence of cost of retained earnings in the company

Option	Percentage
Cost of equity capital	48.00 (44.00)
Opportunity cost of using these funds by company	28.00 (24.00)
No cost is considered	16.00
Opportunity cost of using these funds by equity holders	8.00 (8.00)
Any other	4.00 (4.00)

Table 3.33 Opinion regarding changes affected in the capital structure of the company, in the wake of liberalisation of the country's economy and globalisation

Option	Percentage
Yes	48.14
Expected in near future	7.40
No	44.44

Table 3.34 Nature of changes (if any) in the capital structure of the company, in the wake of liberalisation of the country's economy and globalisation

Option	Percentage
More equity	53.84
More debt	46.15

Table 3.35 Extent of dependence on the capital market in the wake of opening up of the economy

Option	Percentage
Increased	59.09
Remains unchanged	31.81
Decreased	9.09

Table 3.36 Opinion of the company regarding the importance of the following factors in the capital structure decision (1. very important, 2. important, 3. not so important, 4. not at all important)

Factors	1	2	3	4	Total
Financial risk	65.38	19.23	15.38	0.00	100.00
Stability in sales/profits	53.84	26.92	15.38	3.84	100.00
Corporate control	48.00	40.00	4.00	8.00	100.00
State of the capital market	40.00	36.00	12.00	12.00	100.00
Business/operational risk	40.00	56.00	4.00	0.00	100.00
Regulatory framework	40.00	44.00	8.00	8.00	100.00
Restrictions imposed by lenders	20.00	20.00	36.00	24.00	100.00
Corporate tax	20.00	60.00	16.00	4.00	100.00

Cost of servicing debt–equity was another option but was not accorded any rank

reduces agency costs (Jung et al. 1996) and helps in dealing with informational asymmetries (Myers 1984). These perhaps could also be important contributors to the increasing preference of equity vis-à-vis debt.

It is also pertinent to emphasise here that the development/public financial institutions (DFIs/PFIs) constituted the backbone of the Indian financial system until 2000. However, their relative significance in the emerging financial scenario has been declining, indicating a shift in corporate financing in India, in terms of greater reliance of industry on non-institutional sources of finance and greater recourse to the capital market. Secondly, in addition to the financing of industry by these institutions in the traditional form of rupee/foreign currency term loans for project finance, underwriting, lease financing and so on, they also started providing core working capital to industry (Khan 2011). This is amply evident from the findings of the present study as well.

After clause 49 of corporate governance becoming mandatory in India (from 1 April 2006), companies that disclose material information (as a part of being publicly traded) are assumed to have better financial discipline, diversified/pedigree ownership, better corporate governance and management and corporate social responsibility. It is our belief that these aspects (now and in the future) will increasingly affect the valuations of companies. This could be the possible future indication of our findings and the road ahead for corporate financing. This is also supported (in part) by the studies of Haque et al. (2011) stating that better corporate governance reduces agency costs and Jensen (1986) and Stulz (1990) which deal with financial discipline.

Also, the sample companies seem to be well conscious of the downside of a debt-dominated capital structure. This gets support from many aspects indicated by the survey: (1) retained earnings have been cited as the most preferred source by the sample companies; (2) the majority of the sample companies opine that debt should not be used to the maximum extent; and (3) while favouring equity they have stated, inter alia, the enterprise is in better position to face bad periods compared to firms having high D/E ratio, and the companies can go for projects involving higher risk. These findings of the survey lead us to believe that there is an emerging trend towards equity financing taking a dominant role (erstwhile occupied by debt) in corporate financing (in the times to come).

Another notable finding of the study is that there is a significant portion of short-term debt (primarily from banks) in the total debt. Reliance on short-term debt to such a marked extent in preference to long-term debt is not in conformity with sound tenets of finance theory as it causes grave risk, at least, in terms of risk of nonrenewal and interest rate fluctuations. Therefore, there is need for substitution of short-term debt with long-term sources, in particular, when the requirements are permanent in nature.

Further, the study suggests that banks have been the major providers of debt requirements of the sample companies. In contrast, there was modest/meagre contribution from financial institutions in their financing. The declining role of financial institutions (in corporate financing in India) is very evident.

Yet another notable finding of the study is that the sample companies seem to be comfortable with the servicing of debt in terms of both payment of interest and repayment of principal. Given the fact that the companies raise funds on their own externally to meet their financial needs, they are, *perforce,* to have sound fundamentals in terms of reasonable/low risk and so on. It is gratifying to note, then, that they have low operating and financial risk (as per operating and financial leverage).

It is revealing to note a low component of secured loans to total borrowings. These large sample companies with substantial asset bases should raise finance from secured loans as it will be relatively cheaper than unsecured loans. There is untapped opportunity of lowering cost of capital by having the relatively lower cost of debt; this can be achieved by having greater proportion of secured loans as companies have strong assets base.

Another important finding is that the sample companies show non-adherence to the pecking order hypothesis. This could perhaps be due to the robust capital markets in the country making it easier for the companies to raise equity. This further strengthens our contention that equity for aspects like signalling theory, reduction in agency costs, etc., is finding favour with the sample companies over the traditional model of debt being utilised first and equity finance only being raised as the last resort.

The sample companies (having profitable operations) in view of large internal cash accruals at their disposal to meet their investment requirements are using less amount of debt as external financing requirement not because they have low target debt ratios, but because of preference for internally generated funds. This again flouts sound tenets of finance theory. Such firms, due to favourable financial leverage, could have magnified their RoR (rate of return) for their equity owners by employing higher debt. In this regard, hence, the tax shield on interest is now being regarded as a secondary consideration in designing capital structure.

Normative Framework

Guidelines for Practitioners

Given the interactions with managers, and based on the literature survey, the following guidelines are suggested for business executives to make better and sound capital structure choices.

- *Long-term debt* – whenever possible long-term investments should be financed through equity and long-term debt as short-term debt is a riskier proposition.
- *Secured loans* – in large companies (with substantial asset base) secured loans should be preferred over unsecured borrowings as the secured loans are likely to be cheaper an. would enable to bring down the overall cost of capital.
- *Cost of capital* – sophisticated techniques like CAPM may be encouraged to be used in estimation of the cost of equity capital.

Appendices

Appendix 3.1: Mean, median and quartile values of debt–equity ratio of constituent sectors of the sample companies over phase 1 (2001–2006) and phase 2 (2007–2011)

	Phase 1 (2001–2006)				Phase 2 (2007–2011)			
Sector	Mean	Median	Quartile 1	Quartile 3	Mean	Median	Quartile 1	Quartile 3
Housing	1.92	1.80	1.07	2.70	1.19	1.03	0.52	1.49
Capital goods	1.54	1.37	1.05	2.00	1.35	1.27	0.84	1.78
Power	1.46	1.14	0.54	2.36	1.10	0.99	0.46	1.64
Oil and gas	1.37	1.25	0.77	1.81	1.25	1.04	0.34	1.75
Miscellaneous	1.34	1.27	0.75	1.77	1.35	1.14	0.77	1.84
Transport	1.23	1.03	0.62	1.47	1.08	0.98	0.53	1.44
Healthcare	1.17	0.97	0.60	1.52	0.85	0.67	0.37	1.32
Diversified	1.16	0.87	0.55	1.85	1.10	0.70	0.32	1.70
Fast-moving consumer goods (FMCG)	1.16	0.92	0.43	1.53	1.43	1.08	0.64	2.04
Internet and communications technology (ICT)	1.03	0.66	0.23	1.52	1.18	1.02	0.62	1.65
Metals	1.00	0.79	0.39	1.43	1.03	0.79	0.49	1.39

Paired samples *t*-test of constituent sectors of the sample companies based on debt–equity ratio over phase 1 (2001–2006) and phase 2 (2007–2011)

	Phase 1 and Phase 2		
Sector	*t*	*df*	Significance (2-tailed)
Housing	2.819	16	0.012
Healthcare	2.412	13	0.031
Transport	1.319	16	0.206
ICT	−1.070	17	0.299
Metals	1.045	16	0.312
Power	0.744	12	0.471
Capital goods	0.677	12	0.511
Diversified	0.674	8	0.519
Miscellaneous	0.269	15	0.791
FMCG	0.259	10	0.801
Oil and gas	0.096	14	0.925

Appendix 3.2: Mean, median and quartile values of debt–equity ratio of constituent sectors of the sample companies over phase 3 (2007–2008) and phase 4 (2009–2011)

	Phase 3 (2007–2008)				Phase 4 (2009–2011)			
Sector	Mean	Median	Quartile 1	Quartile 3	Mean	Median	Quartile 1	Quartile 3
FMCG	1.43	1.06	0.50	2.08	1.43	1.10	0.73	2.01
Miscellaneous	1.40	1.08	0.75	1.91	1.33	1.18	0.79	1.80
ICT	1.38	1.36	0.74	2.03	1.05	0.79	0.54	1.39
Capital goods	1.32	1.22	0.84	1.75	1.37	1.30	0.84	1.80

(continued)

Appendix 3.2: (continued)

	Phase 3 (2007–2008)				Phase 4 (2009–2011)			
Sector	Mean	Median	Quartile 1	Quartile 3	Mean	Median	Quartile 1	Quartile 3
Diversified	1.31	0.93	0.44	1.81	0.97	0.56	0.24	1.64
Oil and gas	1.19	1.17	0.27	1.73	1.29	0.96	0.38	1.76
Housing	1.17	1.08	0.59	1.39	1.21	1.00	0.47	1.56
Metals	1.08	0.86	0.66	1.25	1.00	0.74	0.37	1.49
Power	1.07	1.04	0.49	1.62	1.12	0.96	0.44	1.66
Transport	1.02	0.97	0.56	1.44	1.13	0.98	0.50	1.44
Healthcare	0.98	0.72	0.40	1.57	0.77	0.64	0.35	1.15

Paired samples *t*-test of constituent sectors of the sample companies based on debt–equity ratio over phase 3 (2007–2008) and phase 4 (2009–2011)

	Phase 3 and Phase 4		
Sector	*t*	d*f*	Significance (2-tailed)
ICT	2.094	17	0.052
Healthcare	1.713	13	0.110
Diversified	1.262	8	0.242
Miscellaneous	−0.870	14	0.399
Metals	0.770	16	0.452
Power	−0.756	13	0.463
Transport	−0.714	16	0.486
Oil and gas	−0.626	15	0.541
Housing	−0.451	17	0.658
FMCG	0.368	10	0.721
Capital goods	−0.326	12	0.750

Appendix 3.3: ANOVA of the consolidated sample and the constituent sectors of the sample companies based on debt–equity ratio over phase 1 (2001–2006) and phase 2 (2007–2011) and phase 3 (2007–2008) and phase 4 (2009–2011)

	Phase 1 and Phase 2		Phase 3 and Phase 4	
Sector	*F*	Significance	*F*	Significance
Housing	4.268	0.047	0.032	0.860
Healthcare	1.510	0.230	0.747	0.395
Metals	1.222	0.277	0.068	0.796
Consolidated	1.174	0.308	1.254	0.256
Transport	0.790	0.380	0.112	0.740
ICT	0.531	0.471	1.872	0.180
Power	0.519	0.478	0.118	0.734
Capital goods	0.490	0.491	0.039	0.845
Oil and gas	0.071	0.792	0.022	0.882
Miscellaneous	0.047	0.829	0.058	0.811
FMCG	0.039	0.846	0.005	0.947
Diversified	0.035	0.853	0.510	0.485

Appendix 3.4: Mean, median and quartile values of long-term debt–equity ratio of constituent sectors of the sample companies over phase 1 (2001–2006) and phase 2 (2007–2011)

	Phase 1 (2001–2006)				Phase 2 (2007–2011)			
Sector	Mean	Median	Quartile 1	Quartile 3	Mean	Median	Quartile 1	Quartile 3
Housing	1.05	0.86	0.43	1.49	0.64	0.46	0.19	0.88
Miscellaneous	0.74	0.55	0.15	1.00	0.68	0.56	0.15	1.02
Power	0.72	0.35	0.09	1.23	0.55	0.50	0.04	0.84
Transport	0.71	0.55	0.09	0.86	0.55	0.44	0.05	0.88
Metals	0.69	0.43	0.15	0.99	0.76	0.48	0.22	0.92
Oil and gas	0.66	0.36	0.09	0.80	0.69	0.44	0.05	0.99
ICT	0.55	0.17	0.01	0.67	0.56	0.40	0.11	0.73
Diversified	0.47	0.40	0.22	0.67	0.55	0.36	0.08	0.72
Healthcare	0.42	0.29	0.03	0.55	0.31	0.15	0.04	0.41
FMCG	0.38	0.17	0.02	0.51	0.44	0.17	0.02	0.73
Capital goods	0.36	0.18	0.04	0.59	0.30	0.17	0.02	0.46

Paired samples *t*-test of constituent sectors of the sample companies based on long-term debt–equity ratio over phase 1 (2001–2006) and phase 2 (2007–2011)

	Phase 1 and Phase 2		
Sector	*t*	*df*	Significance (2-tailed)
Housing	2.506	16	0.023
Healthcare	1.457	13	0.169
Transport	1.389	16	0.184
Capital goods	0.666	12	0.518
Power	0.659	12	0.523
Diversified	−0.598	8	0.567
FMCG	0.457	11	0.656
Oil and gas	−0.454	14	0.657
Metals	0.447	17	0.660
ICT	−0.323	17	0.750
Miscellaneous	0.301	15	0.768

Appendix 3.5: Mean, median and quartile values of long-term debt–equity ratio of constituent sectors of the sample companies over phase 3 (2007–2008) and phase 4 (2009–2011)

	Phase 3 (2007–2008)				Phase 4 (2009–2011)			
Sector	Mean	Median	Quartile 1	Quartile 3	Mean	Median	Quartile 1	Quartile 3
Metals	0.93	0.52	0.27	1.05	0.64	0.45	0.19	0.84
Miscellaneous	0.66	0.54	0.13	0.91	0.70	0.57	0.17	1.10
Diversified	0.65	0.37	0.09	0.81	0.49	0.35	0.07	0.67
Housing	0.65	0.45	0.16	0.94	0.63	0.46	0.20	0.84
Oil and gas	0.64	0.38	0.00	0.93	0.72	0.49	0.08	1.03
ICT	0.59	0.42	0.03	0.85	0.55	0.38	0.15	0.65
FMCG	0.56	0.21	0.02	0.91	0.36	0.15	0.01	0.61
Power	0.50	0.43	0.01	0.86	0.58	0.55	0.06	0.83
Transport	0.49	0.47	0.05	0.83	0.59	0.42	0.05	0.91
Healthcare	0.34	0.16	0.06	0.41	0.29	0.15	0.02	0.41
Capital goods	0.29	0.19	0.01	0.39	0.30	0.15	0.02	0.51

(continued)

Appendix 3.5: (continued)

Paired samples *t*-test of constituent sectors of the sample companies based on long-term debt–equity ratio over phase 3 (2007–2008) and phase 4 (2009–2011)

	Phase 3 and Phase 4		
Sector	*t*	*df*	Significance (2-tailed)
Miscellaneous	−2.100	15	0.053
FMCG	1.483	11	0.166
Oil and gas	−1.332	15	0.203
Healthcare	1.180	13	0.259
Diversified	1.115	8	0.297
Power	−0.972	13	0.349
Transport	−0.859	16	0.403
Metals	0.554	15	0.588
ICT	0.326	17	0.748
Housing	0.146	17	0.885
Capital goods	0.073	12	0.943

Appendix 3.6: ANOVA of the consolidated sample and the constituent sectors of the sample companies based on long-term debt–equity ratio over phase 1 (2001–2006) and phase 2 (2007–2011), phase 3 (2007–2008) and phase 4 (2009–2011)

	Phase 1 and Phase 2		Phase 3 and Phase 4	
Sector	*F*	Significance	*F*	Significance
Consolidated	2.328	0.012	1.879	0.047
Housing	3.482	0.071	0.002	0.964
Transport	1.190	0.283	0.112	0.740
Healthcare	0.526	0.475	0.211	0.650
Power	0.425	0.520	0.373	0.547
Capital goods	0.397	0.535	0.003	0.957
Diversified	0.169	0.687	0.293	0.596
ICT	0.066	0.799	0.049	0.827
Miscellaneous	0.056	0.815	0.287	0.596
Metals	0.046	0.831	0.876	0.356
FMCG	0.021	0.885	0.744	0.398
Oil and gas	0.001	0.971	0.093	0.763

Appendix 3.7: Mean, median and quartile values of short-term obligations–equity ratio of constituent sectors of the sample companies over phase 1 (2001–2006) and phase 2 (2007–2011)

	Phase 1 (2001–2006)				Phase 2 (2007–2011)			
Sector	Mean	Median	Quartile 1	Quartile 3	Mean	Median	Quartile 1	Quartile 3
Housing	1.32	1.04	0.47	1.69	0.60	0.44	0.23	0.77
Capital goods	1.23	1.26	0.47	1.94	1.07	1.10	0.50	1.55
Miscellaneous	1.08	0.77	0.36	1.43	0.72	0.54	0.34	0.95
FMCG	1.07	0.72	0.37	1.35	1.08	0.57	0.37	1.72
Power	0.90	0.75	0.26	1.12	0.58	0.41	0.24	0.66
Healthcare	0.84	0.61	0.46	1.18	0.61	0.46	0.26	0.75
Oil and gas	0.78	0.75	0.32	1.03	0.74	0.54	0.20	1.15
Metals	0.71	0.47	0.29	0.87	0.55	0.47	0.25	0.72

(continued)

Appendix 3.7: (continued)

	Phase 1 (2001–2006)				Phase 2 (2007–2011)			
Sector	Mean	Median	Quartile 1	Quartile 3	Mean	Median	Quartile 1	Quartile 3
Transport	0.71	0.65	0.31	0.93	0.58	0.51	0.29	0.82
Diversified	0.70	0.39	0.23	1.01	0.56	0.32	0.19	0.79
ICT	0.59	0.36	0.22	0.81	0.66	0.43	0.26	0.79

Paired samples *t*-test of constituent sectors of the sample companies based on short-term obligations–equity ratio over phase 1 (2001–2006) and phase 2 (2007–2011)

	Phase 1 and Phase 2		
Sector	*t*	*df*	Significance (2-tailed)
Housing	2.821	16	0.012
Healthcare	2.781	13	0.016
ICT	−1.891	17	0.076
Transport	1.599	16	0.129
Miscellaneous	1.496	15	0.155
Power	1.483	12	0.164
Metals	1.173	17	0.257
Diversified	1.162	8	0.279
Capital goods	0.791	12	0.444
FMCG	0.588	11	0.568
Oil and gas	−0.389	14	0.703

Appendix 3.8: Mean, median and quartile values of short-term obligations–equity ratio of constituent sectors of the sample companies over phase 3 (2007–2008) and phase 4 (2009–2011)

	Phase 3 (2007–2008)				Phase 4 (2009–2011)			
Sector	Mean	Median	Quartile 1	Quartile 3	Mean	Median	Quartile 1	Quartile 3
FMCG	1.19	0.59	0.38	1.66	1.01	0.55	0.36	1.75
Capital goods	1.07	1.04	0.48	1.61	1.07	0.99	0.49	1.47
ICT	0.82	0.53	0.32	1.02	0.55	0.37	0.21	0.64
Healthcare	0.75	0.51	0.31	0.85	0.52	0.42	0.22	0.68
Miscellaneous	0.73	0.59	0.37	0.88	0.71	0.51	0.32	0.99
Oil and gas	0.71	0.52	0.19	1.08	0.76	0.55	0.21	1.21
Diversified	0.63	0.39	0.26	0.88	0.51	0.27	0.14	0.73
Power	0.60	0.46	0.28	0.63	0.57	0.38	0.21	0.67
Metals	0.58	0.52	0.26	0.79	0.53	0.44	0.25	0.68
Transport	0.58	0.55	0.34	0.81	0.59	0.47	0.26	0.82
Housing	0.55	0.47	0.22	0.79	0.64	0.42	0.23	0.75

Paired samples *t*-test of constituent sectors of the sample companies based on short-term obligations–equity ratio over phase 3 (2007–2008) and phase 4 (2009–2011)

	Phase 3 and Phase 4		
Sector	*t*	*df*	Significance (2-tailed)
ICT	2.036	17	0.058
Healthcare	1.918	13	0.077
FMCG	1.330	11	0.211

(continued)

Appendix 3.8: (continued)

Sector	Phase 3 and Phase 4		
	t	*df*	Significance (2-tailed)
Housing	–0.972	17	0.345
Diversified	0.837	8	0.427
Metals	–0.624	17	0.541
Oil and gas	–0.581	15	0.570
Power	0.175	13	0.864
Miscellaneous	–0.103	14	0.920
Transport	0.041	16	0.968
Capital goods	–0.036	12	0.972

Appendix 3.9: ANOVA of the consolidated sample and the constituent sectors of the sample companies based on short-term obligations–equity ratio over phase 1 (2001–2006) and phase 2 (2007–2011), phase 3 (2007–2008) and phase 4 (2009–2011)

Sector	Phase 1 and Phase 2		Phase 3 and Phase 4	
	F	Significance	*F*	Significance
Consolidated	2.407	0.009	2.726	0.003
Housing	6.389	0.016	0.334	0.567
Miscellaneous	1.996	0.168	0.000	0.987
Healthcare	1.745	0.198	1.450	0.239
Power	1.358	0.255	0.003	0.954
Metals	0.667	0.420	0.171	0.682
Transport	0.658	0.423	0.014	0.906
ICT	0.391	0.536	2.274	0.141
Capital goods	0.347	0.561	0.000	0.987
Diversified	0.264	0.614	0.234	0.635
FMCG	0.096	0.760	0.462	0.504
Oil and gas	0.000	0.990	0.061	0.807

Appendix 3.10: Mean, median and quartile values of total debt to total assets (d/a) ratio of constituent sectors of the sample companies over phase 1 (2001–2006) and phase 2 (2007–2011)

Sector	Phase 1 (2001–2006)				Phase 2 (2007–2011)			
	Mean	Median	Quartile 1	Quartile 3	Mean	Median	Quartile 1	Quartile 3
Housing	64.33	74.83	50.33	86.00	52.49	57.47	35.88	66.85
Oil and gas	63.09	71.01	51.85	81.39	48.21	52.35	22.95	71.23
Miscellaneous	62.67	70.00	54.50	79.50	64.80	69.04	52.75	81.48
Transport	59.17	64.00	45.33	75.33	55.70	55.23	43.54	72.30
Capital goods	57.33	58.83	45.83	72.17	62.12	60.95	51.60	73.16
Healthcare	55.67	57.33	47.17	67.50	45.78	45.84	30.88	58.81
Power	55.14	49.74	38.09	80.97	53.48	49.07	36.20	75.30
Metals	53.33	51.67	36.83	70.83	55.96	60.24	40.89	75.60

(continued)

Appendix 3.10: (continued)

	Phase 1 (2001–2006)				Phase 2 (2007–2011)			
Sector	Mean	Median	Quartile 1	Quartile 3	Mean	Median	Quartile 1	Quartile 3
Diversified	47.18	46.87	36.06	57.38	42.21	38.39	26.57	54.05
FMCG	47.17	42.17	30.17	64.33	51.64	53.36	39.05	66.94
ICT	46.83	50.50	21.50	68.33	53.82	55.57	37.03	70.43

Paired samples *t*-test of constituent sectors of the sample companies based on total debt to total assets (D/A) ratio over phase 1 (2001–2006) and phase 2 (2007–2011)

	Phase 1 and Phase 2		
Sector	*t*	*df*	Significance (2-tailed)
Healthcare	2.686	12	0.020
Housing	1.892	13	0.081
ICT	−1.686	14	0.114
Diversified	1.283	7	0.240
Transport	1.208	15	0.246
Oil and gas	1.124	9	0.290
Power	−0.530	11	0.607
Metals	0.390	15	0.702
Capital goods	0.274	6	0.793
FMCG	0.219	6	0.834
Miscellaneous	−0.058	14	0.955

Appendix 3.11: Mean, median and quartile values of total debt to total assets (d/a) ratio of constituent sectors of the sample companies over phase 3 (2007–2008) and phase 4 (2009–2011)

	Phase 3 (2007–2008)				Phase 4 (2009–2011)			
Sector	Mean	Median	Quartile 1	Quartile 3	Mean	Median	Quartile 1	Quartile 3
Miscellaneous	65.50	69.50	52.50	83.00	64.33	68.73	52.92	80.46
Capital goods	62.50	64.50	52.00	73.00	61.87	58.59	51.34	73.27
Transport	60.00	62.50	49.00	73.00	52.83	50.38	39.90	71.84
Metals	59.50	61.50	50.50	75.00	53.59	59.40	34.49	75.99
ICT	59.00	62.50	36.50	78.00	50.37	50.95	37.38	65.39
Housing	53.00	58.50	38.50	68.00	52.16	56.78	34.14	66.08
Power	52.83	44.82	35.72	74.68	53.92	51.91	36.52	75.71
Healthcare	49.00	49.50	32.00	65.00	43.63	43.39	30.13	54.69
Oil and gas	47.29	48.81	17.46	71.30	48.83	54.71	26.62	71.19
Diversified	45.68	45.82	36.03	51.20	39.90	33.44	20.27	55.96
FMCG	45.50	45.50	26.50	65.00	55.73	58.60	47.41	68.23

Paired samples *t*-test of constituent sectors of the sample companies based on total debt to total assets (D/A) ratio over phase 3 (2007–2008) and phase 4 (2009–2011)

	Phase 3 and Phase 4		
Sector	*t*	*df*	Significance (2-tailed)
ICT	2.324	12	0.038
Transport	1.646	13	0.124
Metals	1.524	16	0.147

(continued)

Appendix 3.11: (continued)

	Phase 3 and Phase 4		
Sector	*t*	*df*	Significance (2-tailed)
Capital goods	1.295	6	0.243
Diversified	1.235	6	0.263
Healthcare	0.892	10	0.393
Oil and gas	−0.826	11	0.426
FMCG	−0.527	5	0.621
Housing	0.196	16	0.847
Power	−0.168	12	0.870
Miscellaneous	−0.149	13	0.884

Appendix 3.12: ANOVA of the consolidated sample and the constituent sectors of the sample companies based on total debt to total assets (d/a) ratio over phase 1 (2001–2006) and phase 2 (2007–2011) and phase 3 (2007–2008) and phase 4 (2009–2011)

	Phase 1 and Phase 2		Phase 3 and Phase 4	
Sector	*F*	Significance	*F*	Significance
Healthcare	3.753	0.065	0.351	0.560
Consolidated	1.543	0.124	1.917	0.043
Housing	1.450	0.238	0.005	0.942
Oil and gas	1.426	0.244	0.067	0.798
Diversified	0.527	0.479	0.262	0.617
ICT	0.469	0.499	0.935	0.342
Transport	0.367	0.549	0.925	0.344
Metals	0.149	0.702	0.458	0.504
FMCG	0.124	0.729	1.037	0.326
Capital goods	0.043	0.839	0.166	0.690
Power	0.021	0.887	0.066	0.799
Miscellaneous	0.009	0.924	0.001	0.970

Appendix 3.13: Mean, median and quartile values of long-term debt to total assets (d/a) ratio of constituent sectors of the sample companies over phase 1 (2001–2006) and phase 2 (2007–2011)

	Phase 1 (2001–2006)				Phase 2 (2007–2011)			
Sector	Mean	Median	Quartile 1	Quartile 3	Mean	Median	Quartile 1	Quartile 3
Housing	40.17	42.33	27.00	56.33	30.96	28.66	14.03	46.95
Metals	34.50	32.17	16.67	48.83	34.97	32.66	19.00	49.66
Transport	32.41	33.32	9.36	47.36	28.03	29.64	5.01	46.40
Power	32.36	26.68	8.08	53.37	26.16	29.43	3.18	41.15
Miscellaneous	31.53	31.25	12.53	46.95	30.70	31.73	12.81	48.80
Oil and gas	30.40	31.42	7.72	43.39	28.42	28.03	3.52	47.81
Diversified	25.69	25.23	17.11	36.60	25.79	24.83	7.13	34.44
ICT	23.92	16.67	0.64	39.91	27.84	26.70	7.74	41.99
Healthcare	22.50	22.67	4.83	33.67	17.91	12.42	4.12	27.71

(continued)

Appendix 3.13: (continued)

	Phase 1 (2001–2006)				Phase 2 (2007–2011)			
Sector	Mean	Median	Quartile 1	Quartile 3	Mean	Median	Quartile 1	Quartile 3
Capital goods	19.01	15.40	3.79	31.88	18.22	14.02	1.51	31.81
FMCG	19.00	13.17	1.67	30.50	21.24	15.27	2.03	39.46

Paired samples *t*-test of constituent sectors of the sample companies based on long-term debt to total assets (D/A) ratio over phase 1 (2001–2006) and phase 2 (2007–2011)

	Phase 1 and Phase 2		
Sector	*t*	*df*	Significance (2-tailed)
Housing	2.723	16	0.015
Transport	1.737	16	0.102
Healthcare	1.697	13	0.114
ICT	−1.019	17	0.322
Power	0.710	12	0.491
FMCG	0.502	11	0.625
Metals	0.495	17	0.627
Capital goods	0.392	12	0.702
Miscellaneous	0.304	15	0.766
Oil and gas	0.275	14	0.788
Diversified	−0.008	8	0.994

Appendix 3.14: Mean, median and quartile values of long-term debt to total assets (d/a) ratio of constituent sectors of the sample companies over phase 3 (2007–2008) and phase 4 (2009–2011)

	Phase 3 (2007–2008)				Phase 4 (2009–2011)			
Sector	Mean	Median	Quartile 1	Quartile 3	Mean	Median	Quartile 1	Quartile 3
Metals	38.00	34.50	23.00	54.00	32.95	31.44	16.33	46.77
Housing	32.00	29.50	14.00	48.00	30.27	28.10	14.05	46.24
ICT	28.27	28.12	2.27	47.06	27.55	25.75	11.38	38.61
Miscellaneous	28.04	30.81	11.49	41.32	32.48	32.35	13.68	53.79
Diversified	27.52	23.91	8.59	35.60	24.64	25.44	6.15	33.67
Oil and gas	27.38	27.69	0.49	48.03	29.11	28.26	5.55	47.66
Transport	27.10	30.96	4.63	44.16	28.65	28.75	5.27	47.90
Power	25.66	28.09	1.40	41.72	26.50	30.33	4.37	40.76
FMCG	24.00	17.00	3.00	44.00	19.39	14.11	1.39	36.43
Healthcare	19.50	13.00	7.00	27.50	16.84	12.03	2.21	27.86
Capital goods	17.41	16.54	0.88	26.44	18.77	12.34	1.92	35.38

Paired samples *t*-test of constituent sectors of the sample companies based on long-term debt to total assets (D/A) ratio over phase 3 (2007–2008) and phase 4 (2009–2011)

	Phase 3 and Phase 4		
Sector	*t*	*df*	Significance (2-tailed)
Healthcare	1.459	12	0.170
Miscellaneous	−1.211	15	0.244
FMCG	1.020	11	0.330

(continued)

Appendix 3.14: (continued)

	Phase 3 and Phase 4		
Sector	*t*	*df*	Significance (2-tailed)
Metals	0.906	16	0.378
Housing	0.897	17	0.382
Oil and gas	−0.469	15	0.646
ICT	0.438	17	0.667
Power	−0.361	13	0.724
Diversified	0.337	8	0.745
Capital goods	0.079	12	0.939
Transport	−0.004	16	0.997

Appendix 3.15: ANOVA of the consolidated sample and the constituent sectors of the sample companies based on long-term debt to total assets (d/a) ratio over phase 1 (2001–2006) and phase 2 (2007–2011) and phase 3 (2007–2008) and phase 4 (2009–2011)

	Phase 1 and Phase 2		Phase 3 and Phase 4	
Sector	*F*	Significance	*F*	Significance
Consolidated	2.702	0.003	2.193	0.018
Housing	3.153	0.085	0.097	0.757
Transport	0.632	0.432	0.013	0.911
ICT	0.530	0.472	0.043	0.837
Power	0.483	0.494	0.026	0.872
Healthcare	0.445	0.510	0.299	0.589
Oil and gas	0.118	0.733	0.018	0.896
Capital goods	0.103	0.751	0.003	0.957
Metals	0.085	0.772	0.475	0.496
FMCG	0.035	0.854	0.281	0.601
Miscellaneous	0.029	0.866	0.244	0.625
Diversified	0.000	0.996	0.015	0.903

Appendix 3.16: Mean, median and quartile values of relative share of secured loans to total borrowings of constituent sectors of the sample companies over phase 1 (2001–2006) and phase 2 (2007–2011)

	Phase 1 (2001–2006)				Phase 2 (2007–2011)			
Sector	Mean	Median	Quartile 1	Quartile 3	Mean	Median	Quartile 1	Quartile 3
Diversified	72.89	76.46	59.41	88.73	52.10	57.82	30.56	74.60
Miscellaneous	72.27	78.41	54.00	91.35	70.72	77.55	59.06	91.26
Housing	68.78	77.76	55.79	90.15	65.35	67.30	51.50	88.39
ICT	68.49	69.92	46.36	97.55	53.58	65.42	15.81	86.81
Metals	65.55	77.01	48.64	90.70	55.76	63.94	33.13	83.90
Power	64.71	78.14	36.11	93.92	58.06	65.98	27.89	87.28
Capital goods	62.05	72.24	39.62	87.26	51.98	59.54	15.02	84.85
Oil and gas	62.02	68.10	35.09	94.21	51.74	52.43	14.52	91.25
Transport	59.22	65.82	36.57	88.79	46.27	44.54	14.09	79.23

(continued)

Appendix 3.16: (continued)

	Phase 1 (2001–2006)				Phase 2 (2007–2011)			
Sector	Mean	Median	Quartile 1	Quartile 3	Mean	Median	Quartile 1	Quartile 3
FMCG	57.32	60.44	33.38	83.62	44.70	34.82	13.22	75.75
Healthcare	56.51	61.59	33.32	79.89	40.21	34.70	4.44	74.42

Paired samples *t*-test of constituent sectors of the sample companies based on relative share of secured loans to total borrowings over phase 1 (2001–2006) and phase 2 (2007–2011)

	Phase 1 and Phase 2		
Sector	*t*	*df*	Significance (2-tailed)
Transport	3.722	14	0.002
Healthcare	3.051	12	0.010
Diversified	1.988	8	0.082
Metals	1.759	16	0.098
ICT	1.559	15	0.140
FMCG	1.494	10	0.166
Oil and gas	1.338	12	0.206
Capital goods	1.034	12	0.321
Miscellaneous	0.472	14	0.644
Power	−0.423	11	0.681
Housing	−0.218	16	0.830

Appendix 3.17: Mean, median and quartile values of relative share of secured loans to total borrowings of constituent sectors of the sample companies over phase 3 (2007–2008) and phase 4 (2009–2011)

	Phase 3 (2007–2008)				Phase 4 (2009–2011)			
Sector	Mean	Median	Quartile 1	Quartile 3	Mean	Median	Quartile 1	Quartile 3
Miscellaneous	68.08	72.36	62.85	86.29	72.48	81.02	56.53	94.58
Housing	59.29	61.80	45.16	82.77	69.40	70.97	55.73	92.14
ICT	58.67	72.67	18.28	96.48	50.19	60.59	14.17	80.37
Metals	56.43	61.26	34.46	91.07	55.32	65.73	32.25	79.11
Power	53.32	56.45	22.49	84.90	61.22	72.34	31.49	88.87
Diversified	52.22	62.28	28.60	75.94	52.03	54.84	31.87	73.70
Capital goods	50.93	53.81	12.31	84.93	52.68	63.36	16.82	84.80
Oil and gas	49.02	42.71	12.01	87.83	53.55	58.92	16.20	93.52
Transport	48.26	45.20	17.81	82.50	44.95	44.10	11.61	77.06
FMCG	47.96	36.29	24.91	73.66	42.54	33.84	5.43	77.15
Healthcare	37.76	28.82	4.24	72.14	41.84	38.62	4.58	75.94

Paired samples *t*-test of constituent sectors of the sample companies based on relative share of secured loans to total borrowings over phase 3 (2007–2008) and phase 4 (2009–2011)

	Phase 3 and Phase 4		
Sector	*t*	*df*	Significance (2-tailed)
Housing	−2.384	16	0.030
ICT	1.069	15	0.302
Power	−0.956	12	0.358

(continued)

Appendix 3.17: (continued)

	Phase 3 and Phase 4		
Sector	*t*	*df*	Significance (2-tailed)
FMCG	0.685	10	0.509
Oil and gas	–0.628	11	0.543
Miscellaneous	–0.576	13	0.575
Transport	0.431	15	0.673
Healthcare	–0.346	12	0.736
Diversified	–0.344	8	0.740
Metals	0.167	17	0.870
Capital goods	0.026	12	0.979

Appendix 3.18: ANOVA of the consolidated sample and the constituent sectors of the sample companies based on relative share of secured loans to total borrowings over phase 1 (2001–2006) and phase 2 (2007–2011) and phase 3 (2007–2008) and phase 4 (2009–2011)

	Phase 1 and Phase 2		Phase 3 and Phase 4	
Sector	*F*	Significance	*F*	Significance
Diversified	3.571	0.077	0.075	0.788
Consolidated	1.699	0.080	2.207	0.017
ICT	3.135	0.086	0.316	0.578
Healthcare	1.851	0.186	0.005	0.944
Transport	1.502	0.230	0.055	0.816
Metals	1.488	0.231	0.010	0.922
Oil and gas	1.264	0.271	0.021	0.886
FMCG	1.170	0.292	0.179	0.676
Capital goods	0.951	0.339	0.000	0.995
Miscellaneous	0.067	0.797	0.344	0.562
Housing	0.022	0.884	1.383	0.248
Power	0.010	0.922	0.351	0.559

Appendix 3.19: Mean, median and quartile values of relative share of bank borrowings to total borrowings of constituent sectors of the sample companies over phase 1 (2001–2006) and phase 2 (2007–2011)

	Phase 1 (2001–2006)				Phase 2 (2007–2011)			
Sector	Mean	Median	Quartile 1	Quartile 3	Mean	Median	Quartile 1	Quartile 3
Oil and gas	36.94	36.76	6.18	63.38	49.76	57.05	23.82	77.10
Metals	27.21	20.14	5.27	38.27	43.71	43.82	12.02	72.65
Diversified	26.68	22.39	6.61	41.05	50.64	55.42	26.88	77.19
Miscellaneous	26.45	21.00	3.64	42.12	39.48	41.64	9.95	63.93
Power	25.34	15.26	1.88	37.10	34.32	35.41	4.37	56.26
Housing	24.48	20.32	10.96	34.00	40.90	42.40	21.02	59.23
ICT	24.15	10.69	1.88	33.91	33.07	25.65	1.79	52.43
Transport	20.29	10.93	0.00	32.94	33.73	20.99	0.46	66.58
Healthcare	19.15	14.26	0.39	28.03	40.35	37.07	9.28	66.69

(continued)

Appendix 3.19: (continued)

	Phase 1 (2001–2006)				Phase 2 (2007–2011)			
Sector	Mean	Median	Quartile 1	Quartile 3	Mean	Median	Quartile 1	Quartile 3
FMCG	18.91	10.65	0.86	29.02	43.85	44.02	22.31	66.04
Capital goods	14.03	8.22	0.00	22.87	38.00	31.00	0.00	69.24

Paired samples *t*-test of constituent sectors of the sample companies based on relative share of bank borrowings to total borrowings over phase 1 (2001–2006) and phase 2 (2007–2011)

	Phase 1 and Phase 2		
Sector	*t*	*df*	Significance (2-tailed)
Capital goods	–3.455	12	0.005
Housing	–3.230	16	0.005
FMCG	–3.513	10	0.006
Healthcare	–3.333	12	0.006
Miscellaneous	–2.517	13	0.026
ICT	–2.365	15	0.032
Diversified	–2.556	8	0.034
Metals	–2.137	16	0.048
Transport	–1.910	15	0.075
Oil and gas	–1.692	13	0.114
Power	–0.881	11	0.397

Appendix 3.20: Mean, median and quartile values of relative share of bank borrowings to total borrowings of constituent sectors of the sample companies over phase 3 (2007–2008) and phase 4 (2009–2011)

	Phase 3 (2007–2008)				Phase 4 (2009–2011)			
Sector	Mean	Median	Quartile 1	Quartile 3	Mean	Median	Quartile 1	Quartile 3
Oil and gas	60.62	69.74	49.80	81.81	42.52	48.59	6.50	73.97
FMCG	50.02	55.25	32.75	70.20	39.74	36.54	15.35	63.26
Diversified	48.27	60.49	16.41	70.36	50.85	47.24	32.52	78.38
Housing	44.80	47.06	26.03	66.12	38.31	39.29	17.68	54.64
Metals	41.93	34.89	13.16	75.48	44.90	49.78	11.26	70.77
Healthcare	41.51	42.58	5.01	65.59	39.34	33.27	11.47	68.72
Miscellaneous	40.83	45.38	7.44	65.01	38.58	39.15	11.62	63.21
Capital goods	38.35	33.04	0.00	69.55	37.76	29.65	0.00	69.03
Transport	34.12	27.68	1.16	61.52	33.47	16.53	0.00	69.95
ICT	28.15	13.66	0.35	44.87	36.34	33.64	2.76	57.47
Power	27.55	24.14	0.00	47.17	38.84	42.92	7.28	62.31

Paired samples *t*-test of constituent sectors of the sample companies based on relative share of bank borrowings to total borrowings over phase 3 (2007–2008) and phase 4 (2009–2011)

	Phase 3 and Phase 4		
Sector	*t*	*df*	Significance (2-tailed)
Oil and gas	2.329	11	0.040
Power	–2.037	12	0.064
ICT	–1.579	15	0.135

(continued)

Appendix 3.20: (continued)

	Phase 3 and Phase 4		
Sector	*t*	*df*	Significance (2-tailed)
FMCG	1.234	10	0.245
Housing	1.038	16	0.315
Metals	−0.617	17	0.545
Healthcare	0.554	12	0.589
Diversified	−0.458	8	0.659
Miscellaneous	0.309	13	0.762
Transport	−0.085	15	0.933
Capital goods	−0.047	12	0.963

Appendix 3.21: ANOVA of the consolidated sample and the constituent sectors of the sample companies based on relative share of bank borrowings to total borrowings over phase 1 (2001–2006) and phase 2 (2007–2011) and phase 3 (2007–2008) and phase 4 (2009–2011)

	Phase 1 and Phase 2		Phase 3 and Phase 4	
Sector	*F*	Significance	*F*	Significance
Capital goods	6.831	0.015	0.000	0.984
FMCG	5.591	0.028	0.453	0.509
Housing	5.044	0.032	0.993	0.326
Healthcare	4.781	0.038	0.069	0.795
Diversified	4.781	0.044	0.132	0.721
Metals	3.868	0.058	0.097	0.758
Oil and gas	2.711	0.111	2.148	0.155
Miscellaneous	1.821	0.188	0.038	0.846
Power	1.701	0.205	2.038	0.166
ICT	1.639	0.210	0.699	0.409
Transport	1.255	0.271	0.003	0.953
Consolidated	0.980	0.460	1.114	0.351

Appendix 3.22: Mean, median and quartile values of relative share of financial institution borrowings to total borrowings of constituent sectors of the sample companies over phase 1 (2001–2006) and phase 2 (2007–2011)

	Phase 1 (2001–2006)				Phase 2 (2007–2011)			
Sector	Mean	Median	Quartile 1	Quartile 3	Mean	Median	Quartile 1	Quartile 3
Transport	14.52	1.37	0.00	16.79	0.72	0.00	0.00	0.00
Metals	12.81	0.93	0.00	13.98	11.64	0.01	0.00	2.18
Power	11.25	4.82	0.00	14.88	4.61	0.87	0.00	2.86
ICT	9.25	0.70	0.00	7.68	3.63	0.00	0.00	0.18
Oil and gas	8.13	0.00	0.00	6.58	5.31	0.00	0.00	7.41
Housing	7.85	2.36	0.05	9.12	3.37	0.15	0.00	3.69
Miscellaneous	7.61	1.22	0.35	7.65	7.51	2.79	0.00	6.37
Healthcare	6.89	3.58	0.37	7.92	0.00	0.00	0.00	0.00

(continued)

Appendix 3.22: (continued)

	Phase 1 (2001–2006)				Phase 2 (2007–2011)			
Sector	Mean	Median	Quartile 1	Quartile 3	Mean	Median	Quartile 1	Quartile 3
FMCG	4.85	0.05	0.00	3.86	1.83	0.00	0.00	1.64
Diversified	4.32	0.10	0.00	3.11	5.36	0.00	0.00	0.00
Capital goods	2.37	0.66	0.00	1.91	0.36	0.00	0.00	0.00

Paired samples *t*-test of constituent sectors of the sample companies based on relative share of financial institution borrowings to total borrowings over phase 1 (2001–2006) and phase 2 (2007–2011)

	Phase 1 and Phase 2		
Sector	*t*	*df*	Significance (2-tailed)
Healthcare	2.654	12	0.021
Capital goods	2.559	12	0.025
Transport	2.087	15	0.054
ICT	1.776	15	0.096
FMCG	1.751	10	0.111
Oil and gas	1.567	13	0.141
Power	1.570	11	0.145
Housing	1.512	16	0.150
Diversified	−0.327	8	0.752
Metals	0.216	16	0.832
Miscellaneous	0.090	14	0.929

Appendix 3.23: Mean, median and quartile values of relative share of financial institution borrowings to total borrowings of constituent sectors of the sample companies over phase 3 (2007–2008) and phase 4 (2009–2011)

	Phase 3 (2007–2008)				Phase 4 (2009–2011)			
Sector	Mean	Median	Quartile 1	Quartile 3	Mean	Median	Quartile 1	Quartile 3
Metals	14.03	0.04	0.00	4.71	10.04	0.00	0.00	0.50
Miscellaneous	9.51	6.98	0.00	11.71	6.18	0.00	0.00	2.81
Oil and gas	6.15	0.00	0.00	7.07	4.75	0.00	0.00	7.64
ICT	4.62	0.00	0.00	0.13	2.97	0.00	0.00	0.21
Housing	4.44	0.38	0.00	5.56	2.67	0.00	0.00	2.44
Diversified	3.59	0.00	0.00	0.00	6.55	0.00	0.00	0.00
FMCG	3.30	0.00	0.00	4.10	0.86	0.00	0.00	0.00
Power	3.20	0.00	0.00	0.00	5.56	1.45	0.00	4.76
Capital goods	0.89	0.00	0.00	0.00	0.29	0.00	0.00	0.00
Transport	0.50	0.00	0.00	0.00	0.86	0.00	0.00	0.00
Healthcare	0.00	0.00	0.00	0.00	0.00	0.00	0.00	0.00

Paired samples *t*-test of constituent sectors of the sample companies based on relative share of financial institution borrowings to total borrowings over phase 3 (2007–2008) and phase 4 (2009–2011)

	Phase 3 and Phase 4		
Sector	*t*	*df*	Significance (2-tailed)
FMCG	1.751	10	0.111
Metals	1.524	17	0.146

(continued)

Appendix 3.23: (continued)

	Phase 3 and Phase 4		
Sector	*t*	*df*	Significance (2-tailed)
Housing	1.249	16	0.230
ICT	1.069	15	0.302
Miscellaneous	1.062	13	0.308
Capital goods	1.000	12	0.337
Healthcare	1.000	12	0.337
Diversified	−1.000	8	0.347
Power	−0.931	12	0.370
Transport	−0.521	15	0.610
Oil and gas	0.446	11	0.664

Appendix 3.24: ANOVA of the consolidated sample and the constituent sectors of the sample companies based on relative share of financial institution borrowings to total borrowings over phase 1 (2001–2006) and phase 2 (2007–2011) and phase 3 (2007–2008) and phase (4 2009–2011)

	Phase 1 and Phase 2		Phase 3 and Phase 4	
Sector	*F*	Significance	*F*	Significance
Healthcare	7.608	0.011	1.080	0.309
Transport	4.240	0.048	0.254	0.618
Capital goods	3.187	0.087	1.000	0.327
Consolidated	1.617	0.101	2.802	0.002
Housing	2.183	0.149	1.005	0.323
ICT	2.049	0.162	0.215	0.646
FMCG	1.582	0.223	1.974	0.175
Oil and gas	0.830	0.370	0.435	0.515
Power	0.296	0.592	1.239	0.276
Metals	0.046	0.831	0.168	0.685
Diversified	0.046	0.833	0.190	0.669
Miscellaneous	0.007	0.933	0.712	0.406

Appendix 3.25: Mean, median and quartile values of operating leverage of constituent sectors of the sample companies over phase 1 (2001–2006) and phase 2 (2007–2011)

	Phase 1 (2001–2006)				Phase 2 (2007–2011)			
Sector	Mean	Median	Quartile 1	Quartile 3	Mean	Median	Quartile 1	Quartile 3
ICT	1.54	1.40	0.83	2.04	1.39	1.05	0.71	1.58
Diversified	1.52	1.20	0.78	2.03	1.52	1.49	1.05	1.83
Metals	1.50	1.15	0.70	1.80	1.59	1.18	0.79	1.95
Capital goods	1.45	1.14	0.81	2.02	1.42	1.13	0.69	1.98
Power	1.45	1.34	0.90	1.90	1.32	1.08	0.82	1.54
Healthcare	1.43	1.28	0.90	1.81	1.38	1.20	0.79	1.77
Miscellaneous	1.38	1.13	0.55	1.78	1.41	1.42	0.75	1.96
Transport	1.35	1.12	0.76	1.68	1.44	1.23	0.89	1.67
FMCG	1.31	1.23	0.73	1.69	1.53	1.21	0.87	1.94

(continued)

Appendix 3.25: (continued)

	Phase 1 (2001–2006)				Phase 2 (2007–2011)			
Sector	Mean	Median	Quartile 1	Quartile 3	Mean	Median	Quartile 1	Quartile 3
Oil and gas	1.31	1.16	0.80	1.76	1.37	1.12	0.78	1.91
Housing	1.26	1.02	0.61	1.62	1.43	1.14	0.78	1.79

Paired samples *t*-test of constituent sectors of the sample companies based on operating leverage over phase 1 (2001–2006) and phase 2 (2007–2011)

	Phase 1 and Phase 2		
Sector	*t*	*df*	Significance (2-tailed)
Oil and gas	−1.405	13	0.184
ICT	1.034	15	0.317
Healthcare	1.027	13	0.323
Metals	−0.812	16	0.429
FMCG	−0.797	11	0.443
Miscellaneous	−0.657	13	0.522
Power	0.608	10	0.557
Diversified	0.562	8	0.589
Transport	−0.355	15	0.727
Capital goods	0.223	11	0.828
Housing	−0.071	12	0.945

Appendix 3.26: Mean, median and quartile values of operating leverage of constituent sectors of the sample companies over phase 3 (2007–2008) and phase 4 (2009–2011)

	Phase 3 (2007–2008)				Phase 4 (2009–2011)			
Sector	Mean	Median	Quartile 1	Quartile 3	Mean	Median	Quartile 1	Quartile 3
Oil and gas	1.76	1.28	0.92	2.48	1.11	1.01	0.68	1.52
FMCG	1.66	1.36	0.94	2.38	1.45	1.11	0.83	1.65
Housing	1.59	1.34	1.11	1.97	1.32	1.00	0.57	1.68
Miscellaneous	1.58	1.62	0.98	2.03	1.31	1.29	0.60	1.91
Metals	1.56	1.26	0.99	1.84	1.62	1.13	0.66	2.02
ICT	1.51	1.25	1.06	1.57	1.31	0.91	0.47	1.59
Healthcare	1.50	1.27	1.00	1.94	1.30	1.16	0.64	1.65
Capital goods	1.49	1.19	0.87	2.04	1.37	1.09	0.58	1.94
Diversified	1.41	1.29	1.08	1.82	1.59	1.63	1.03	1.84
Power	1.39	1.04	0.78	1.92	1.28	1.10	0.85	1.29
Transport	1.39	1.21	0.88	1.57	1.47	1.25	0.90	1.74

Paired samples *t*-test of constituent sectors of the sample companies based on operating leverage phase 3 (2007–2008) and phase 4 (2009–2011)

	Phase 3 and Phase 4		
Sector	*t*	*df*	Significance (2-tailed)
Miscellaneous	1.509	12	0.157
Oil and gas	1.241	11	0.240
Healthcare	1.028	13	0.323

(continued)

Appendix 3.26: (continued)

Sector	Phase 3 and Phase 4		
	t	d*f*	Significance (2-tailed)
ICT	1.011	14	0.329
FMCG	0.751	9	0.472
Capital goods	0.514	9	0.620
Transport	0.330	15	0.746
Housing	0.289	14	0.777
Diversified	−0.164	7	0.874
Metals	−0.068	15	0.946
Power	0.051	10	0.960

Appendix 3.27: ANOVA of the consolidated sample and the constituent sectors of the sample companies based on operating leverage over phase 1 (2001–2006) and phase 2 (2007–2011) and phase 3 (2007–2008) and phase 4 (2009–2011)

Sector	Phase 1 and Phase 2		Phase 3 and Phase 4	
	F	Significance	*F*	Significance
Oil and gas	1.171	0.288	3.239	0.084
Healthcare	1.132	0.297	1.392	0.249
FMCG	0.909	0.351	0.707	0.410
ICT	0.760	0.390	1.660	0.207
Metals	0.482	0.492	0.069	0.794
Transport	0.342	0.563	0.005	0.941
Capital goods	0.342	0.564	0.040	0.844
Power	0.257	0.617	0.460	0.504
Diversified	0.241	0.630	0.115	0.740
Miscellaneous	0.101	0.753	1.917	0.178
Housing	0.090	0.767	0.486	0.491
Consolidated	0.467	0.910	0.631	0.787

Appendix 3.28: Mean, median and quartile values of financial leverage of constituent sectors of the sample companies over phase 1 (2001–2006) and phase 2 (2007–2011)

Sector	Phase 1 (2001–2006)				Phase 2 (2007–2011)			
	Mean	Median	Quartile 1	Quartile 3	Mean	Median	Quartile 1	Quartile 3
Transport	1.80	1.66	0.96	2.41	1.42	1.33	1.02	1.73
FMCG	1.71	1.45	1.17	1.96	1.16	1.04	0.64	1.41
Miscellaneous	1.69	1.50	1.01	2.02	1.40	1.19	0.78	1.80
Housing	1.67	1.19	0.86	2.34	1.37	1.03	0.68	1.63
Diversified	1.40	1.42	1.00	1.89	1.48	1.35	1.13	1.68
Capital goods	1.39	1.15	0.84	1.79	1.29	1.12	0.91	1.62
Metals	1.32	1.20	0.82	1.59	1.33	1.25	0.92	1.42
ICT	1.28	1.07	0.80	1.61	1.16	1.02	0.77	1.40

(continued)

Appendix 3.28: (continued)

	Phase 1 (2001–2006)				Phase 2 (2007–2011)			
Sector	Mean	Median	Quartile 1	Quartile 3	Mean	Median	Quartile 1	Quartile 3
Healthcare	1.24	1.12	0.76	1.42	1.35	1.19	0.88	1.57
Oil and gas	1.18	1.09	0.67	1.54	1.30	1.26	0.87	1.70
Power	0.88	0.90	0.53	1.12	1.05	0.80	0.56	1.27

Paired samples *t*-test of constituent sectors of the sample companies based on financial leverage over phase 1 (2001–2006) and phase 2 (2007–2011)

	Phase 1 and Phase 2		
Sector	*t*	*df*	Significance (2-tailed)
FMCG	2.254	9	0.051
Transport	2.067	15	0.056
Housing	1.997	15	0.064
ICT	1.382	14	0.189
Capital goods	1.314	12	0.213
Oil and gas	−1.086	11	0.301
Diversified	0.209	7	0.840
Power	−0.095	7	0.927
Metals	−0.072	16	0.943
Healthcare	0.036	13	0.972
Miscellaneous	−0.011	14	0.991

Appendix 3.29: Mean, median and quartile values of financial leverage of constituent sectors of the sample companies over phase 3 (2007–2008) and phase 4 (2009–2011)

	Phase 3 (2007–2008)				Phase 4 (2009–2011)			
Sector	Mean	Median	Quartile 1	Quartile 3	Mean	Median	Quartile 1	Quartile 3
Diversified	1.48	1.18	1.03	1.58	1.48	1.46	1.19	1.75
Oil and gas	1.46	1.45	0.88	1.82	1.19	1.14	0.86	1.62
Miscellaneous	1.44	1.13	0.87	1.50	1.38	1.24	0.73	2.00
Power	1.34	0.83	0.59	1.46	0.85	0.79	0.54	1.14
Housing	1.33	0.82	0.56	1.48	1.40	1.17	0.77	1.73
ICT	1.23	1.12	0.87	1.44	1.12	0.96	0.71	1.38
Transport	1.20	1.07	0.79	1.38	1.57	1.50	1.17	1.97
Metals	1.15	1.09	0.95	1.20	1.45	1.36	0.90	1.57
Capital goods	1.13	1.13	0.98	1.30	1.33	1.12	0.91	1.71
FMCG	1.08	0.87	0.57	1.14	1.22	1.16	0.68	1.59
Healthcare	1.04	1.00	0.77	1.25	1.57	1.33	0.95	1.79

Paired samples *t*-test of constituent sectors of the sample companies based on financial leverage over phase 3 (2007–2008) and phase 4 (2009–2011)

	Phase 3 and Phase 4		
Sector	*t*	*df*	Significance (2-tailed)
Transport	−2.287	16	0.036
Healthcare	−2.079	12	0.060
Metals	−1.165	14	0.264

(continued)

Appendix 3.29: (continued)

	Phase 3 and Phase 4		
Sector	*t*	d*f*	Significance (2-tailed)
Capital goods	–0.985	10	0.348
FMCG	–0.656	10	0.527
Housing	0.525	14	0.608
Power	0.486	10	0.637
Miscellaneous	–0.066	11	0.948
Diversified	–0.057	8	0.956
ICT	–0.027	16	0.979
Oil and gas	–0.020	10	0.985

Appendix 3.30: ANOVA of the consolidated sample and the constituent sectors of the sample companies based on financial leverage over phase 1 (2001–2006) and phase 2 (2007–2011) and phase 3 (2007–2008) and phase 4 (2009–2011)

	Phase 1 and Phase 2		Phase 3 and Phase 4	
Sector	*F*	Significance	*F*	Significance
Consolidated	2.694	0.004	1.670	0.087
FMCG	4.530	0.046	0.728	0.404
Transport	3.707	0.063	5.131	0.030
Housing	2.011	0.166	0.599	0.445
Oil and gas	1.745	0.198	0.445	0.511
Capital goods	1.508	0.231	1.714	0.204
ICT	0.271	0.607	0.001	0.981
Power	0.014	0.906	0.282	0.600
Miscellaneous	0.009	0.926	0.017	0.898
Diversified	0.005	0.945	0.004	0.949
Metals	0.005	0.945	0.879	0.356
Healthcare	0.001	0.976	5.379	0.029

Appendix 3.31: Mean, median and quartile values of combined leverage of constituent sectors of the sample companies over phase 1 (2001–2006) and phase 2 (2007–2011)

	Phase 1 (2001–2006)				Phase 2 (2007–2011)			
Sector	Mean	Median	Quartile 1	Quartile 3	Mean	Median	Quartile 1	Quartile 3
Transport	1.86	1.74	1.09	2.22	1.48	1.29	0.95	1.76
Oil and gas	1.77	1.78	0.85	2.77	1.36	1.03	0.52	1.72
FMCG	1.71	1.76	1.25	2.09	1.44	1.06	0.68	2.13
Diversified	1.69	1.63	1.07	2.26	1.52	1.37	1.13	1.76
Power	1.69	1.73	1.02	2.29	1.41	1.28	0.70	1.87
ICT	1.65	1.43	0.94	2.41	1.16	0.84	0.60	1.47
Miscellaneous	1.65	1.48	0.94	2.14	1.44	1.08	0.69	1.94
Capital goods	1.59	1.33	0.69	2.15	1.69	1.48	0.78	2.65

(continued)

Appendix 3.31: (continued)

	Phase 1 (2001–2006)				Phase 2 (2007–2011)			
Sector	Mean	Median	Quartile 1	Quartile 3	Mean	Median	Quartile 1	Quartile 3
Healthcare	1.59	1.48	0.83	2.24	1.50	1.28	0.86	1.88
Metals	1.30	1.08	0.61	1.40	1.73	1.45	0.76	2.22
Housing	1.16	0.95	0.51	1.55	1.38	1.21	0.63	1.73

Paired samples *t*-test of constituent sectors of the sample companies based on combined leverage over phase 1 (2001–2006) and phase 2 (2007–2011)

	Phase 1 and Phase 2		
Sector	*t*	*df*	Significance (2-tailed)
ICT	2.567	13	0.023
Transport	2.184	14	0.046
Metals	−1.255	14	0.230
Diversified	1.098	7	0.308
Oil and gas	1.054	12	0.313
FMCG	0.833	11	0.422
Healthcare	0.716	12	0.488
Capital goods	−0.574	10	0.579
Housing	0.382	11	0.710
Miscellaneous	0.213	10	0.836
Power	−0.004	9	0.997

Appendix 3.32: Mean, median and quartile values of combined leverage of constituent sectors of the sample companies over phase 3 (2007–2008) and phase 4 (2009–2011)

	Phase 3 (2007–2008)				Phase 4 (2009–2011)			
Sector	Mean	Median	Quartile 1	Quartile 3	Mean	Median	Quartile 1	Quartile 3
Metals	1.95	1.71	0.82	2.50	1.59	1.28	0.73	2.03
Power	1.91	1.40	1.00	2.48	1.09	1.21	0.50	1.47
FMCG	1.80	1.30	0.99	2.45	1.20	0.90	0.48	1.92
Healthcare	1.62	1.47	1.06	2.06	1.41	1.16	0.73	1.76
Capital goods	1.47	1.14	0.85	2.27	1.84	1.70	0.73	2.90
Miscellaneous	1.47	1.14	0.85	2.27	1.84	1.70	0.73	2.90
ICT	1.43	1.07	0.77	1.79	0.98	0.68	0.49	1.25
Oil and gas	1.42	0.94	0.48	1.80	1.31	1.09	0.54	1.67
Transport	1.30	1.04	0.71	1.38	1.59	1.47	1.11	2.02
Diversified	1.26	1.15	0.62	1.77	1.70	1.53	1.47	1.75
Housing	1.13	0.93	0.65	1.11	1.56	1.40	0.61	2.15

Paired samples *t*-test of constituent sectors of the sample companies based on combined leverage over phase 3 (2007–2008) and phase 4 (2009–2011)

	Phase 3 and Phase 4		
Sector	*t*	*df*	Significance (2-tailed)
Power	1.631	10	0.134
Oil and gas	1.344	10	0.209
Healthcare	1.073	10	0.309

(continued)

Appendix 3.32: (continued)

Sector	Phase 3 and Phase 4		
	t	*df*	Significance (2-tailed)
Housing	–0.912	11	0.381
Miscellaneous	–0.867	8	0.411
Capital goods	–0.787	8	0.454
Diversified	–0.801	5	0.459
Metals	0.778	8	0.459
FMCG	0.762	8	0.468
ICT	0.567	9	0.585
Transport	–0.022	13	0.983

Appendix 3.33: ANOVA of the consolidated sample and the constituent sectors of the sample companies based on combined leverage over phase 1 (2001–2006) and phase 2 (2007–2011) and phase 3 (2007–2008) and phase 4 (2009–2011)

Sector	Phase 1 and Phase 2		Phase 3 and Phase 4	
	F	Significance	*F*	Significance
Transport	4.667	0.039	0.011	0.916
ICT	3.395	0.076	1.584	0.221
Diversified	1.305	0.271	1.721	0.214
Metals	1.019	0.321	1.009	0.326
FMCG	0.700	0.412	1.652	0.214
Healthcare	0.640	0.431	0.866	0.362
Consolidated	0.926	0.509	0.797	0.632
Oil and gas	0.352	0.558	1.376	0.252
Capital goods	0.152	0.701	0.537	0.473
Power	0.130	0.722	4.958	0.036
Housing	0.124	0.728	0.860	0.362
Miscellaneous	0.068	0.796	0.336	0.569

Appendix 3.34: Mean, median and quartile values of debt service coverage ratio of constituent sectors of the sample companies over phase 1 (2001–2006) and phase 2 (2007–2011)

Sector	Phase 1 (2001–2006)				Phase 2 (2007–2011)			
	Mean	Median	Quartile 1	Quartile 3	Mean	Median	Quartile 1	Quartile 3
Capital goods	4.42	4.23	2.98	5.63	2.88	2.78	2.08	3.45
Healthcare	3.40	2.86	1.64	4.92	3.75	3.76	2.14	5.07
Oil and gas	3.10	2.23	1.01	4.91	2.14	1.57	1.07	2.23
ICT	2.99	2.35	1.57	4.10	2.50	2.05	1.29	3.10
Transport	2.69	2.63	1.79	3.46	2.45	1.86	1.27	2.97
Metals	2.60	1.89	1.15	2.80	2.19	1.79	1.31	2.36
Diversified	2.50	2.51	1.78	3.14	1.78	1.39	0.95	2.30
FMCG	2.26	1.57	1.11	2.80	3.21	2.15	1.53	4.32
Miscellaneous	2.20	1.78	1.34	2.65	1.66	1.18	0.95	1.85
Power	2.03	1.46	0.94	2.73	1.35	1.34	0.84	1.77
Housing	1.88	1.63	1.16	2.18	1.90	1.61	1.00	2.23

(continued)

Appendix 3.34: (continued)

Paired samples *t*-test of constituent sectors of the sample companies based on debt service coverage ratio over phase 1 (2001–2006) and phase 2 (2007–2011)

	Phase 1 and Phase 2		
Sector	*t*	*df*	Significance (2-tailed)
FMCG	−1.754	7	0.123
Power	1.629	11	0.132
Transport	1.057	12	0.311
Oil and gas	0.890	11	0.393
Capital goods	0.902	6	0.402
Healthcare	−0.845	10	0.418
Housing	−0.445	15	0.662
Metals	−0.383	13	0.708
Diversified	0.346	7	0.739
ICT	−0.142	5	0.893
Miscellaneous	0.017	12	0.986

Appendix 3.35: Mean, median and quartile values of debt service coverage ratio of constituent sectors of the sample companies over phase 3 (2007–2008) and phase 4 (2009–2011)

	Phase 3 (2007–2008)				Phase 4 (2009–2011)			
Sector	Mean	Median	Quartile 1	Quartile 3	Mean	Median	Quartile 1	Quartile 3
Capital goods	4.03	4.03	3.11	4.95	2.11	1.94	1.39	2.45
Healthcare	3.79	4.10	2.18	4.99	3.72	3.53	2.12	5.13
FMCG	3.11	2.04	1.56	4.23	2.83	1.97	1.38	3.81
Transport	3.06	2.67	1.76	4.30	2.05	1.32	0.95	2.09
ICT	2.43	1.80	1.22	2.86	2.55	2.21	1.34	3.26
Housing	2.39	2.29	1.21	2.98	1.57	1.16	0.87	1.73
Metals	2.36	2.03	1.40	2.57	2.09	1.62	1.24	2.23
Oil and gas	2.25	1.77	1.27	2.44	2.08	1.44	0.93	2.08
Miscellaneous	2.00	1.38	1.11	2.29	1.44	1.05	0.84	1.56
Diversified	1.84	1.41	1.04	2.35	1.74	1.38	0.90	2.28
Power	1.48	1.45	0.84	1.81	1.27	1.27	0.83	1.75

Paired samples *t*-test of constituent sectors of the sample companies based on debt service coverage ratio over phase 3 (2007–2008) and phase 4 (2009–2011)

	Phase 3 and Phase 4		
Sector	*t*	*df*	Significance (2-tailed)
Housing	3.218	16	0.005
Diversified	−0.426	7	0.0683
Capital goods	2.858	2	0.104
Transport	1.256	12	0.233
Healthcare	0.875	8	0.407
Miscellaneous	0.820	10	0.431
ICT	0.652	9	0.531
FMCG	−0.624	6	0.556
Power	0.514	9	0.619
Oil and gas	0.486	10	0.637
Metals	0.382	12	0.709

Appendix 3.36: ANOVA of the consolidated sample and the constituent sectors of the sample companies based on debt service coverage ratio over phase 1 (2001–2006) and phase 2 (2007–2011) and phase 3 (2007–2008) and phase 4 (2009–2011)

	Phase 1 and Phase 2		Phase 3 and Phase 4	
Sector	*F*	Significance	*F*	Significance
Consolidated	3.819	0.000	3.229	0.001
Capital goods	3.887	0.067	2.896	0.123
FMCG	2.123	0.164	0.309	0.588
Power	1.320	0.262	1.606	0.219
Oil and gas	0.641	0.431	0.209	0.652
Diversified	0.503	0.489	0.054	0.820
Miscellaneous	0.469	0.499	0.039	0.846
Transport	0.441	0.512	0.383	0.541
Healthcare	0.220	0.643	0.283	0.601
ICT	0.114	0.739	0.023	0.881
Housing	0.092	0.764	0.867	0.359
Metals	0.030	0.865	0.000	0.991

Appendix 3.37: Mean, median and quartile values of interest coverage ratio of constituent sectors of the sample companies over phase 1 (2001–2006) and phase 2 (2007–2011)

	Phase 1 (2001–2006)				Phase 2 (2007–2011)			
Sector	Mean	Median	Quartile 1	Quartile 3	Mean	Median	Quartile 1	Quartile 3
Healthcare	5.79	5.87	4.60	7.03	5.66	5.56	5.01	6.27
Transport	5.41	5.29	4.36	6.26	5.46	5.35	4.14	6.62
Oil and gas	4.87	4.66	3.24	6.46	4.87	4.93	3.48	6.19
Capital goods	4.50	4.19	2.77	6.27	5.59	5.86	4.28	6.77
Power	4.18	3.85	2.74	5.41	5.16	4.91	3.74	6.61
Miscellaneous	4.01	3.66	2.68	5.14	3.84	3.27	2.53	5.11
ICT	3.67	2.87	1.89	5.14	3.75	3.52	2.35	4.97
Diversified	3.64	3.04	2.23	5.01	3.88	3.27	2.17	5.38
Metals	3.50	3.33	2.49	4.40	5.62	5.61	4.82	6.77
Housing	3.45	3.26	2.80	4.05	4.44	3.71	2.98	6.00
FMCG	3.16	2.74	1.94	4.00	3.85	3.72	2.74	4.43

Paired samples *t*-test of constituent sectors of the sample companies based on interest coverage ratio over phase 1 (2001–2006) and phase 2 (2007–2011)

	Phase 1 and Phase 2		
Sector	*t*	d*f*	Significance (2-tailed)
Metals	–4.984	10	0.001
FMCG	–2.225	5	0.077
Housing	–1.895	11	0.085
Diversified	–0.819	6	0.444
Miscellaneous	0.432	12	0.674
Power	–0.388	7	0.710
Healthcare	–0.380	5	0.719

(continued)

Appendix 3.37: (continued)

Sector	Phase 1 and Phase 2		
	t	*df*	Significance (2-tailed)
ICT	−0.357	3	0.745
Oil and gas	−0.312	8	0.763
Capital goods	−0.279	6	0.790
Transport	−0.142	8	0.890

Appendix 3.38: Mean, median and quartile values of interest coverage ratio of constituent sectors of the sample companies over phase 3 (2007–2008) and phase 4 (2009–2011)

	Phase 3 (2007–2008)				Phase 4 (2009–2011)			
Sector	Mean	Median	Quartile 1	Quartile 3	Mean	Median	Quartile 1	Quartile 3
Healthcare	7.16	7.03	6.41	7.84	4.66	4.58	4.08	5.22
Transport	6.49	6.46	5.18	7.77	4.78	4.61	3.45	5.86
Metals	6.42	6.64	5.61	7.80	5.09	4.93	4.29	6.09
Oil and gas	6.13	6.31	5.38	7.56	4.04	4.02	2.22	5.28
Capital goods	5.51	5.51	4.45	6.58	5.64	6.10	4.17	6.90
Housing	5.18	4.73	3.84	6.71	3.95	3.04	2.41	5.53
Power	5.18	5.12	3.77	6.60	5.14	4.76	3.72	6.62
FMCG	5.03	5.44	3.17	6.15	3.06	2.57	2.45	3.29
Miscellaneous	4.26	3.59	2.85	5.74	3.57	3.05	2.33	4.70
Diversified	4.12	3.07	2.43	5.90	3.73	3.41	1.99	5.04
ICT	3.46	3.18	2.35	4.43	3.94	3.74	2.35	5.33

Paired samples *t*-test of constituent sectors of the sample companies based on interest coverage ratio over phase 3 (2007–2008) and phase 4 (2009–2011)

Sector	Phase 3 and Phase 4		
	t	*df*	Significance (2-tailed)
Healthcare	9.605	3	0.002
Metals	2.228	9	0.053
FMCG	2.706	4	0.054
Miscellaneous	1.584	10	0.144
Oil and gas	1.588	8	0.151
Transport	1.563	4	0.193
Housing	1.366	11	0.199
Power	1.072	8	0.315
ICT	0.499	3	0.652
Diversified	0.242	5	0.818
Capital goods	−0.042	1	0.973

Appendix 3.39: ANOVA of the consolidated sample and the constituent sectors of the sample companies based on interest coverage ratio over phase 1 (2001–2006) and phase 2 (2007–2011) and phase 3 (2007–2008) and phase 4 (2009–2011)

	Phase 1 and Phase 2		Phase 3 and Phase 4	
Sector	*F*	Significance	*F*	Significance
Consolidated	2.928	0.002	1.933	0.044
Metals	4.616	0.042	2.149	0.159
Housing	3.840	0.060	1.469	0.237
FMCG	1.356	0.269	3.051	0.115
Power	0.453	0.510	0.070	0.794
Healthcare	0.208	0.655	9.833	0.014
Oil and gas	0.204	0.656	4.419	0.048
ICT	0.178	0.682	0.317	0.587
Miscellaneous	0.125	0.727	0.457	0.506
Capital goods	0.058	0.813	0.002	0.967
Diversified	0.022	0.884	0.003	0.955
Transport	0.000	0.999	3.503	0.086

Appendix 3.40: Mean, median and quartile values of total external obligations coverage ratio of constituent sectors of the sample companies over phase 1 (2001–2006) and phase 2 (2007–2011)

	Phase 1 (2001–2006)				Phase 2 (2007–2011)			
Sector	Mean	Median	Quartile 1	Quartile 3	Mean	Median	Quartile 1	Quartile 3
Power	1.52	0.49	0.06	2.21	0.81	0.31	0.12	0.72
ICT	1.29	0.74	0.19	1.44	1.05	0.59	0.32	1.00
Metals	1.02	0.56	0.30	1.01	1.22	0.54	0.31	1.20
Transport	0.96	0.59	0.38	1.19	0.74	0.57	0.42	0.98
Oil and gas	0.81	0.38	0.20	0.59	0.69	0.42	0.22	0.63
Diversified	0.61	0.29	0.14	0.58	0.56	0.33	0.19	0.52
Healthcare	0.55	0.39	0.19	0.59	0.63	0.52	0.24	0.81
Housing	0.54	0.25	0.14	0.42	0.59	0.45	0.22	0.78
FMCG	0.30	0.31	0.10	0.47	0.48	0.46	0.25	0.63
Miscellaneous	0.28	0.23	0.11	0.40	0.39	0.25	0.14	0.46
Capital goods	0.20	0.15	0.09	0.19	0.34	0.19	0.15	0.30

Paired samples *t*-test of constituent sectors of the sample companies based on total external obligations coverage ratio over phase 1 (2001–2006) and phase 2 (2007–2011)

	Phase 1 and Phase 2		
Sector	*t*	d*f*	Significance (2-tailed)
Capital goods	−2.745	11	0.019
FMCG	−2.084	11	0.061
Power	1.668	10	0.126
Miscellaneous	−1.273	15	0.223

(continued)

Appendix 3.40: (continued)

	Phase 1 and Phase 2		
Sector	*t*	d*f*	Significance (2-tailed)
Transport	1.175	16	0.257
ICT	0.917	16	0.373
Healthcare	–0.739	13	0.473
Oil and gas	0.578	12	0.574
Housing	–0.494	16	0.628
Diversified	0.286	8	0.782
Metals	0.276	16	0.786

Appendix 3.41: Mean, median and quartile values of total external obligations coverage ratio of constituent sectors of the sample companies over phase 3 (2007–2008) and phase 4 (2009–2011)

	Phase 3 (2007–2008)				Phase 4 (2009–2011)			
Sector	Mean	Median	Quartile 1	Quartile 3	Mean	Median	Quartile 1	Quartile 3
Metals	1.51	0.64	0.35	1.38	1.03	0.48	0.28	1.08
ICT	1.09	0.53	0.27	0.96	1.02	0.63	0.36	1.03
Transport	0.85	0.59	0.46	1.24	0.67	0.56	0.40	0.81
Power	0.80	0.35	0.07	0.60	0.82	0.29	0.16	0.79
Oil and gas	0.76	0.47	0.27	0.61	0.64	0.39	0.20	0.65
Housing	0.70	0.52	0.21	0.97	0.51	0.39	0.22	0.66
Healthcare	0.58	0.43	0.19	0.77	0.66	0.57	0.27	0.83
FMCG	0.45	0.46	0.29	0.65	0.51	0.46	0.22	0.62
Capital goods	0.43	0.21	0.17	0.29	0.27	0.17	0.14	0.30
Miscellaneous	0.33	0.23	0.12	0.47	0.42	0.27	0.15	0.45
Diversified	0.32	0.31	0.20	0.37	0.71	0.35	0.18	0.62

Paired samples *t*-tes t of constituent sectors of the sample companies based on total external obligations coverage ratio over phase 3 (2007–2008) and phase 4 (2009–2011)

	Phase 3 and Phase 4		
Sector	*t*	d*f*	Significance (2-tailed)
Metals	2.436	17	0.026
Housing	2.413	17	0.027
Transport	1.914	17	0.073
Capital goods	1.280	12	0.225
Diversified	–1.244	8	0.249
Miscellaneous	–1.093	15	0.292
Healthcare	–0.924	13	0.373
Oil and gas	0.916	11	0.379
ICT	0.878	17	0.392
Power	0.815	10	0.434
FMCG	–0.664	11	0.520

Appendix 3.42: ANOVA of the consolidated sample and the constituent sectors of the sample companies based on total external obligations coverage ratio over phase 1 (2001–2006) and phase 2 (2007–2011) and phase 3 (2007–2008) and phase 4 (2009–2011)

	Phase 1 and Phase 2		Phase 3 and Phase 4	
Sector	*F*	Significance	*F*	Significance
Consolidated	3.231	0.001	3.234	0.001
FMCG	2.905	0.102	0.163	0.690
Capital goods	1.427	0.244	0.712	0.407
Transport	0.961	0.334	1.156	0.290
Power	0.689	0.415	0.004	0.953
Miscellaneous	0.644	0.429	0.562	0.459
Healthcare	0.183	0.672	0.162	0.691
Metals	0.120	0.731	0.774	0.385
Oil and gas	0.110	0.743	0.123	0.728
Housing	0.032	0.859	1.427	0.241
Diversified	0.006	0.941	1.329	0.266
ICT	0.003	0.957	0.138	0.712

References

Abor J (2005) The effect of capital structure on profitability: an empirical analysis of listed firms in Ghana. J Risk Finance 6(5):438–445

Afza T, Hussain A (2011) Determinants of capital structure: a case study of automobile sector of Pakistan. Interdiscip J Contemp Res Bus 2(10):219–230

Agca S, Mozumdar A (2007) Corporate finance choices constrained by the amount of debt firms can support. George Washington University and Virginia Tech Working Paper

Bancel F, Mittoo UR (2004) Cross-country determinants of capital structure choice: a survey of European Firms. Finance Manage 33:103–132

Bombay Stock Exchange (BSE) website. http://www.bseindia.com/about/abindices/bse200.asp. Accessed 1 Apr 2010

Booth L, Aivazian V, Demirgue-Kunt A, Maksimovic V (2001) Capital structure in developing countries. J Finance 56:87–130

Brounen D, de Jong A, Koedjik K (2004) Corporate finance in Europe: confronting theory with practice. Finance Manage 33:71–101

Chakraborty SK (1977) Corporate capital structure and cost of capital. Institute of Cost and Works Accountants of India (ICWA), Calcutta, pp 62–65

Chang C, Lee AC, Lee CF (2009) Determinants of capital structure choice: a structural equation modeling approach. Q Rev Econ Finance 49:197–213

Donaldson G (1961) Corporate debt capacity: a study of corporate debt policy and the determination of corporate debt capacity. Graduate School of Business Administration, Harvard University, Boston

Ebaid SI (2009) The impact of capital structure choice on firm performance: empirical evidence from Egypt. J Risk Finance 10(5):477–487

Fama EF, French KR (2002) Testing trade-off and pecking order predictions about dividends and debt. Rev Finance Stud 15:1–33

Faulkender M, Petersen AM (2006) Does the source of capital affect capital structure? Rev Finance Stud 19(1):45–79

Fox RJ, Crask MR, Jonghoon K (1988) Mail survey response rate – a meta-analysis of selected techniques for inducing response. Public Opin Q 52(4):467–491

Frank MZ, Goyal VK (2003) Testing the pecking order theory of capital structure. J Finance Econ 67:217–248

Gaud P, Jani E, Hoesli M, Bender A (2005) The capital structure of Swiss companies: an empirical analysis using dynamic panel data. Eur Finance Manage 11(1):51–69

Graham JR, Harvey CR (2001) The theory and practice of corporate finance: evidence from the field. J Finance Econ 60:187–243

Gupta LC (1985) Financial ratios for monitoring corporate sickness. Oxford University Press, New Delhi

Haque F, Arun GT, Kirkpatrick C (2011) Corporate governance and capital structure in developing countries: a case study of Bangladesh. Appl Econ 43(6):673

Jain PK, Kumar M (1997) Comparative financial management: practices of India and South East Asia. Hindustan Publishing Corporation, New Delhi, pp 43–44

Jain PK, Yadav SS (2000) Financial management practices in select private corporate enterprises – a comparative study of India, Thailand and Singapore. Hindustan Publishing Corporation, New Delhi

Jain PK, Yadav SS (2005) Financial management practices – a study of public sector enterprises in India. Hindustan Publishing Corporation, New Delhi

Jensen M (1986) Agency costs of free cash flow, corporate finance and takeovers. Am Econ Rev 76:323–329

Jung K, Kim Y, Stulz R (1996) Timing, investment opportunities, managerial discretion and the security issue decision. J Finance Econ 42(2):159–185

Kayo KE, Kimura H (2011) Hierarchical determinants of capital structure. J Bank Finance 35:358–371

Khan MY (2011) Indian financial system, 7th edn. Tata McGraw Hill, New Delhi

Khan MY, Jain PK (2011) Financial management: text, problems and cases. Tata McGraw Hill, New Delhi

Korteweg A (2010) The net benefits to leverage. J Finance 65(6):2137–2170

Kremp E, Stoss E, Gerdesmeier D (1999) Estimation of a debt function: evidence from French and German firm panel data. In: Sauve A, Scheuer M (eds) Corporate finance in Germany and France, A joint research project of Deutsche Bundesbank and the Banque de France. SSRN working paper

Lemmon ML, Zender JF (2010) Debt capacity and tests of capital structure theories. J Finance Quant Anal 45(5):1161–1187

Margaritis D, Psillaki M (2010) Capital structure, equity ownership and firm performance. J Bank Finance 34:621–632

Miller M (1977) Debt and taxes. J Finance 32:261–275

Modigliani F, Miller MH (1958) The cost of capital, corporate finance, and the theory of investment. Am Econ Rev 48:261–297

Myers SC (1984) The capital structure puzzle. J Finance 39:575–592

Paolo AM, Bonaminio GA, Gibson C, Patridge T, Kallai K (2009) Response rate comparisons of e-mail and mail distributed student evaluations. Teach Learn Med Int J 12(2):81–84

Rajan RG, Zingales L (1995) What do we know about capital structure? Some evidence from international data. J Finance 50:1421–1460

Sen A (1979) Problems of raising long-term finance. Chart Acc 28(1):38–46

Shyam-Sunder L, Myers SC (1999) Testing static tradeoff against pecking order models of capital structure. J Finance Econ 51:219–244

Stulz R (1990) Managerial discretion and optimal financing policies. J Finance Econ 26:3–27

Templeton L, Deehan A, Taylor C, Drummond C, Strang J (1997) Surveying general practitioners: does a low response rate matter? J Gen Pract 47(415):91–94

Titman S (1984) The effect of capital structure on the Firms's liquidation decision. J Finance Econ 13:137–152

Titman S, Wessels R (1988) The determinants of capital structure choice. J Finance 43:1–19

Vasiliou D, Daskalakis N (2009) Institutional characteristics and capital structure: a cross-national comparison. Glob Finance J 19:286–306

Weston JF, Brigham EF (1992) Essentials of managerial finance. The Dryden Press, Hinsdale

Chapter 4
Dividend Policy

Introduction

Dividend policy/decision constitutes yet another major financial decision for corporate firms. Decision relates to the share of dividends to be paid out of profits earned. The company should prefer the decision which has a salutary effect on the wealth of the shareholders. The two major objectives of this chapter are first, to ascertain/identify the practices followed by the sample companies in this regard and second, to assess whether the sample companies follow a stable dividend policy or not.

For better exposition, this chapter has been divided into six sections. Section I enumerates a brief literature review on the dividend decision. Dividend payout ratios of the sample companies form the subject matter of section II. In section III, data has been analyzed to determine the type of dividend policy followed. In particular, this section aims at ascertaining whether Indian companies are pursuing stable dividend policy or not. Section IV examines considerations affecting dividend policy. The sectoral variations (both pertaining to dividend payout ratio and dividend policy) are enumerated in Section V. Section VI recapitulates the major findings.

Section I Literature Review

Literature is rife with debates on the relevance of the dividend policy followed by a company and its impact on the future growth and valuation of the company. More theories and research do, however, indicate a relationship between dividend decisions and valuation. Walter (1956) contended that if the return of a firm's investment was greater than the cost of capital, the company would do well to retain the earnings (as this way, the firm would be maximising the wealth of its shareholders) and

P.K. Jain et al., *Financial Management Practices: An Empirical Study of Indian Corporates*, India Studies in Business and Economics,
DOI 10.1007/978-81-322-0990-4_4, © Springer India 2013

distribute its earnings in case the shareholders could earn more than the company. However, according to Miller and Modigliani (1961), dividend policy had no relevance and significance in determining the value of a company.

Jensen et al. (1997) explained that the size of the firm and the price-to-book (P/B) value ratios were important determinants of stock returns' performance for companies. Examining historical returns, it was observed that the average return on the shares of small capitalisation firms with low P/B ratios exceeded the average return of large capitalisation firms with high P/B ratios. Fama and French (1995) confirmed that high book-to-market equity ratio (BE/ME) signalled persistent poor earnings and a low BE/ME ratio signalled persistent good earnings. Consistent with the life cycle theory of dividends, the percentage of companies paying dividends was high when retained earnings were a large portion of total equity and became almost negligible when the equity was contributed rather than earned (DeAngelo et al. 2006). On similar lines, Denis and Osobov (2008) stated that in the USA, Canada, UK, Germany, France and Japan, the propensity to pay dividends was higher amongst larger, more profitable firms and those for which retained earnings comprised a large fraction of total equity.

Aivazian et al. (2003) noted that firms in emerging markets had more unstable dividend payments than their US counterparts due to the institutional structures of these developing markets. Farinha (2003) analysed the agency explanation for the cross-sectional variation of corporate dividend policy in the UK by looking at the managerial entrenchment hypothesis drawn from the agency literature. The results strongly suggested the possibility of managerial entrenchment when insider ownership reached a threshold of around 30%. Allen and Michaely (2003) suggested that the rise in the popularity of repurchases increased overall payout and increased firms' financial flexibility.

Dutta and Reichelstein (2004) developed a multi-period, principal-agent model which suggested that the stock market drew information about future cash flows from current investments. The stock price is said to reflect all value-relevant information. On the other hand, Collins et al. (1999) raised questions about the basic equity capitalisation model which works on the assumptions of a positive and homogeneous relationship between price and earnings. They also confirmed a negative price–earnings relationship for loss firms. Penman (1996) observed that the price/earnings (P/E) ratio indicated future growth in earnings and the price/book (P/B) values indicated only the expected future return on equity. The two could be reconciled on comparing the current and expected future return on equity.

Black and Scholes (1974) model emphasised the fact that investors paid a lot of importance to the dividends paid out by the companies and valued such investments higher than the companies that retain their earnings. Ezra Solomon (1969) also reflected the same views. Beaver (1968) stated that market prices reflected the investor sentiments as investors relied upon ratio analysis as the basis of their assessment. Lintner (1956) propounded the importance and significance of a stable dividend policy and so did Joy (1977). Pruitt and Gitman (1991) contended that the earnings risk faced by the company is an important determinant of the kind of dividend policy it adopted.

Brigham (1971) had focused on a trade-off between the concept of current income for investors and future investment potentials/growth of the company with the eventual aim of maximising the wealth of the shareholders/owners of the company.

Menzly and Ozbas (2010) provided evidence to support that value-relevant information diffused gradually in financial markets due to investor specialisation and market segmentation. Fang and Peress (2008) observed that stocks with no media coverage earn higher returns than stocks with high media coverage even after controlling for well-known risk factors. Short et al. (2002) stated that a positive association exists between dividend payout policy and institutional ownership.

The literature review reveals gaps for further inquiry into dividend decisions of companies. The available literature consists of examples of corporate practices from Western countries. To the best of our knowledge, there is no in-depth study regarding the dividend decisions and practices of Indian companies (covering the post-recession period). The present chapter is a modest attempt to fill this gap.

Section II Dividend Payout Ratio

A major aspect of the dividend policy of a company is the dividend payout (D/P) ratio, that is, the percentage share of its net earnings after taxes distributed to the shareholders as dividends. In other words, dividend policy involves the decision to pay out earnings or to retain them for reinvestment in the firm itself.

The retained earnings constitute an easily accessible source of financing investment opportunities. In case the firm is unable to raise external funds, its growth is likely to be impeded as the payment of dividends entail cash outflow. At the same time, skipping dividends may also have an adverse impact on the market price per share (MPS). Witness in this context an apt observation: 'The most common argument is that the corporation can increase the value of its share by increasing the payout ratio. The feeling is that the investors prefer a dollar of dividend to a dollar of capital gains because "a bird in the hand is worth more than two in the bush" (Black and Scholes 1974)'. Also, as per Brigham (1971), the optimum dividend policy should strike a balance between current dividends and future growth (which maximises the price of the firm's share).

Thus, the D/P ratio of a corporate should be determined with reference to two basic objectives – maximising the wealth of the firm's owners and providing sufficient funds to finance growth. The practices of the sample companies (in this regard) have been enumerated in this section.

The relevant data (in terms of mean, standard deviation, coefficient of variation, skewness, kurtosis, median and quartile values of D/P ratio) contained in Table 4.1 indicates that the sample companies seem to have a policy of paying less than one-fourth (22.58%) of net earnings to the equity shareholders during the entire 11-year period of the study under reference. This is lower than the mean D/P ratio of 25.19% reported by the Indian public sector enterprises for the period 1991–2003 (Jain and Yadav 2005). It is notable that in the post-recession year of 2010–2011, the D/P ratio of the sample corporate enterprises was at the highest level of 25.54%.

This is in sharp contrast to the D/P ratio of 45% reported by the private sector enterprises over a period of 1984–1995 (Jain and Kumar 1997) and the subsequent D/P ratio of 32% reported by the private sector companies studied over 1991–1998

Table 4.1 Mean, standard deviation, coefficient of variation, skewness, kurtosis, median and quartile values of dividend payout (D/P) ratio of the sample companies, 2001–2011

Year ending[a]	Number	Mean	Standard deviation	Coefficient of variation (%)	Skewness	Kurtosis	Median	Quartile 1	Quartile 3
2001	133	20.63	18.23	88.34	0.85	0.38	19.30	4.90	30.11
2002	136	23.39	21.55	92.13	0.82	−0.09	20.01	3.32	36.25
2003	141	22.65	19.34	85.40	0.70	−0.11	19.18	5.35	36.10
2004	148	22.46	19.52	86.94	0.92	0.45	18.96	7.07	33.08
2005	149	22.95	18.37	80.03	0.87	0.45	19.92	10.14	33.85
2006	154	24.17	18.30	75.70	0.80	0.36	21.04	11.47	34.64
2007	159	22.37	17.81	79.61	0.87	0.61	20.31	8.19	31.74
2008	159	21.75	17.92	82.38	0.98	0.83	19.87	7.68	31.32
2009	163	21.00	17.78	84.67	1.04	0.90	18.73	6.87	29.83
2010	157	21.52	18.17	84.44	1.03	0.80	18.85	7.46	30.04
2011	157	25.54	20.99	82.20	1.08	1.00	22.80	10.02	33.67
2001–2011	151	22.58	18.91	83.80	0.91	0.51	19.91	7.50	32.78
Phase 1 (2000–2001 to 2005–2006)	144	22.71	19.22	84.76	0.83	0.24	19.74	7.04	34.01
Phase 2 (2006–2007 to 2010–2011)	159	22.44	18.53	82.66	1.00	0.83	20.11	8.04	31.32
Phase 3 (2006–2007 to 2007–2008)	159	22.06	17.86	81.00	0.93	0.72	20.09	7.94	31.53
Phase 4 (2008–2009 to 2010–2011)	159	22.69	18.98	83.77	1.05	0.90	20.13	8.12	31.18

	Paired differences							
				95% confidence interval of the difference				
	Mean	Standard deviation	Standard error mean	Lower	Upper	t	df	Significance (2-tailed)
Phase 1–Phase 2	4.26796	27.09980	2.13576	0.05004	8.48588	1.998	160	0.047
Phase 3–Phase 4	3.85798	31.89973	2.47590	−1.03055	8.74650	1.558	165	0.121

[a]In the paired t-test, in case the value of significance (2-tailed) is 0.05 or less, the alternate hypothesis that there is significant difference in two phases is accepted; when its value exceeds 0.05, the alternate hypothesis is rejected implying that there is no significant difference in the two phases. The same holds true for all paired t-test tables

[b]The Indian financial year begins on April 1 and ends on March 31 of the following year. The same holds true for all subsequent tables and notations

Table 4.2 Frequency distribution related to dividend payout (D/P) ratio of the sample companies, 2001–2011 (Figures are in percentages)

Dividend payout (D/P)	2001	2002	2003	2004	2005	2006	2007	2008	2009	2010	2011
Less than 10	33.81	30.77	29.05	26.80	23.72	20.63	30.67	34.15	33.54	30.25	24.22
10–20	15.11	16.78	19.59	25.49	25.00	21.88	15.95	14.63	18.90	20.37	18.63
20–30	21.58	15.38	15.54	13.73	17.95	21.88	20.86	20.73	21.95	21.60	23.60
30–40	11.51	11.19	9.46	15.03	12.82	13.75	16.56	11.59	10.98	10.49	11.80
40–50	6.47	7.69	14.86	5.88	7.05	8.13	5.52	8.54	6.71	4.32	6.21
50–80	7.19	13.29	6.76	9.80	8.97	10.00	7.98	7.32	7.32	9.88	11.80
Above 80	4.32	4.90	4.73	3.27	4.49	3.75	2.45	3.05	0.61	3.09	3.72
Total	100	100	100	100	100	100	100	100	100	100	100

(Jain and Yadav 2000) probably indicating the decrease in dividend payouts over the past two decades.

Based on the median, the dividend payment is lower at less than one-fifth (19.91%). Quartile values (7.50–32.78%) further reinforce the assertion in that one-fourth of the sample companies (affiliated to the lower quartile) have paid 7.50% only as dividends and even the top quartile affiliated corporate have paid less than one-third (32.78%) of their net earnings as dividends. Similar conclusions follow from frequency distribution table of D/P ratio for the period (Table 4.2). The sample companies (about 15–20%) have dividend payout ratio of more than 40%.

Skewness and kurtosis are moderate denoting that a large number of the sample companies have not declared large dividends (as percentage of net earnings). The coefficient of variation figures is high probably due to the varying nature of the dividend policies being pursued by the constituent sectors of the sample.

The segregation of statistics related to D/P ratio of the sample companies on the basis of the four phases has also not been distinctly different. It is corroborated by the fact that the mean D/P ratio in terms of paired *t*-test (the difference at 95% level of confidence) has been observed to be statistically insignificant.

In sum, the available data on the subject (in unmistakable terms) brings out the fact that the sample firms (on aggregative basis) have paid less than one-fourth of their earnings as dividends. This finding may partially be attributed to the fact that the sample companies are high growth firms and hence would do well to retain their earnings to finance their expansion needs; it is expected that this would, in turn, help the corporates to maximise wealth of their shareholders in the long run (Fig. 4.1).

Section III Stable Dividend Policy

The term stability of dividends refers to the consistency or lack of variability in the stream of dividend payment. In operational terms, this policy means that a certain amount of dividend is paid out regularly. The corporate firms (while taking decisions

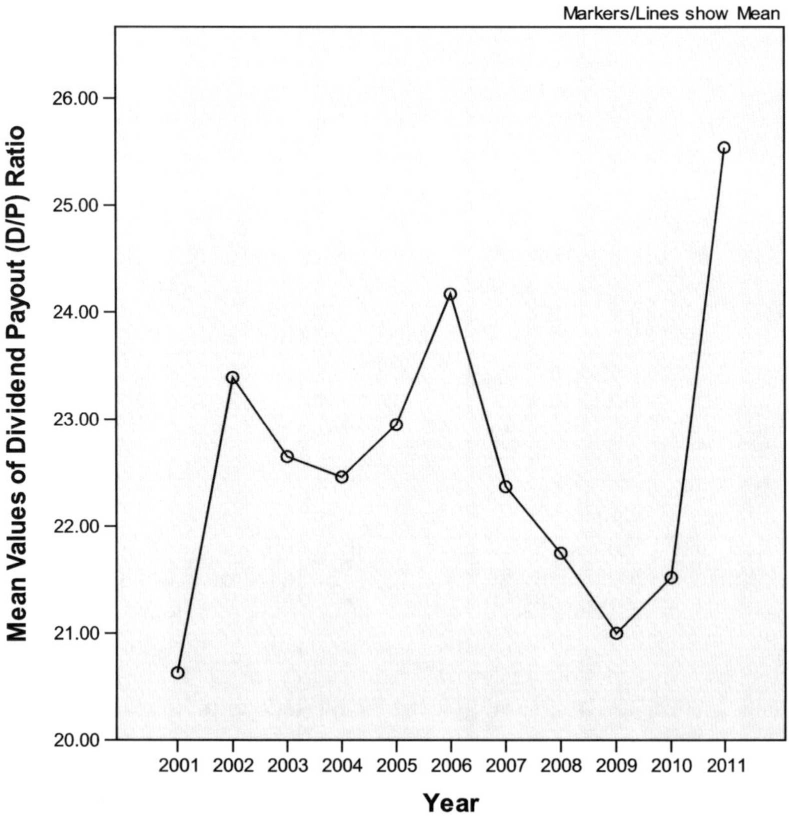

Fig. 4.1 Mean values of dividend payout (D/P) ratio of the sample companies, 2001–2011

on the payment of dividends) bear in mind the dividend sum paid in the previous years. There is resistance on their part to reduce dividends below the amount paid in previous years. Actually, firms practising this policy, favour a policy of establishing/paying a non-decreasing dividends-per-share stream over time. Firms are extremely careful not to raise dividends per share above a level than what can safely be sustained in the future. The cautious 'creep-up' of dividends per share results in a stable dividend-per-share pattern during fluctuating earnings per share periods and a rising 'step-function' pattern of dividends per share during increasing earnings per share periods (Joy 1977).

Stable dividend policy is generally accepted as the best policy and is adopted by most firms, inter alia, in view of the following: investors view constant dividends as a source of funds to meet their current living expenses; stability of dividends (where such dividends are based upon long-run earning power of the company) is a means of reducing share riskiness and consequently increasing share value to investors; and also, financial institutions are constrained by rules to invest in only those equity shares which have good and stable dividend record and investments by these institutions (which represent a significant force in the market) can have an enhancing effect on the market price of the share of the firm.

Apart from theoretical postulates for the desirability of stable dividends, there are also many empirical studies, classic amongst them being that of Lintner (1956) to support the viewpoint that companies pursue a stable dividend policy. According to him, corporate firms make changes in dividend per share (DPS) slowly and these changes lag behind changes in earnings per share (EPS) by one or more periods. The firms generally have long-run dividend payout ratio regardless of its policy towards dividend stability which they attempt to achieve. The firms avoid reducing the dividends in a lean year and, to ensure that they progress towards target D/P ratio, raise DPS gradually as the EPS rises. According to his model, DPS is a function of EPS of that year, existing dividend rate, target payout ratio and speed of adjustment.

Lintner's model has been tested over the years by a number of other empirical research studies. For example, it has been applied to financial market data in the United States by Fama and Babiak (1968), in Canada by Chateau (1979), in the United Kingdom by Ryan (1974) and in Australia by Shelvin (1982). In general, the results of all these studies are consistent with the model (Kester et al. 1994).

In view of the above, it is believed, ex hypothesi, that the corporate firms in India are also likely to adopt stable dividend policy. This section examines the extent to which the sample companies are practising stable dividend policy.

Each year's data was considered as one observation and was compared with the previous year's data. The firms were considered to be implementing stable dividend policy if they paid either constant dividend per year in the following year with fluctuating EPS or increased the dividend with increase in EPS. The relevant data so determined has been presented in Table 4.3.

The results support the hypothesis that nearly two-third (65.69%) of the sample companies in India followed a stable dividend policy (akin to Lintner's model) during the period of the study. Indian public sector undertakings studied during 1991–2003 also reported 68.18% companies carrying a preference for stable dividends (Jain and Yadav 2005) as did 60% of private sector companies studied over 1984–1995 (Jain and Kumar 1997). As per trend (Fig. 4.2), there appears a growth in the percentage of companies pursuing a stable dividend policy in phase 3. The change is not statistically significant though (as per the paired *t*-test). However, a decline has been noted in phase 4; this decrease could be attributed to the recession during which the companies perhaps decided to retain earnings due to the uncertain economic and financial climate.

The survey findings on the subject of the desirability of following stable dividend policy are most revealing in that more than nine-tenth (92.59%) of the respondent firms hold the view that a firm should strive to maintain uninterrupted dividend payments and should avoid making changes in dividends that might later have to be reversed (Table 4.4). This is similar to the findings on private sector companies studied by Jain and Kumar (1997) where 93.33% pursued/desired stable dividend policy. However, the finding is in contrast with the much lower value of 75.59% companies desiring to pursue stable dividend policy amongst the private sector enterprises studied over 1991–1998 (Jain and Yadav 2000).

Table 4.3 Percentage of the sample companies adhering to a stable dividend policy, 2002–2011

Year ending	Total observations	Observations conforming to stable dividend policy	Percentage of companies conforming to stable dividend policy
2002	109	64	58.72
2003	114	82	71.93
2004	122	97	79.51
2005	130	98	75.38
2006	135	85	62.96
2007	141	95	67.38
2008	143	106	74.13
2009	141	71	50.35
2010	142	93	65.49
2011	141	72	51.06
2001–2011	132	86	65.69
Phase 1 (2000–2001 to 2005–2006)	122	85	69.70
Phase 2 (2006–2007 to 2010–2011)	142	87	61.68
Phase 3 (2006–2007 to 2007–2008)	142	101	70.76
Phase 4 (2008–2009 to 2010–2011)	141	79	55.63

	Paired differences							
				95% confidence interval of the difference				
	Mean	Standard deviation	Standard	Lower	Upper	t	df	Significance (2-tailed)
Phase 1–Phase 2	8.01800	14.56126	6.51200	−10.06220	26.09820	1.231	4	0.286
Phase 3–Phase 4	12.83500	5.93263	4.19500	−40.46753	66.13753	3.060	1	0.201

Further, the survey indicates that 86.20% companies adopt a constant payout ratio (Table 4.5). Nearly two-third (64%) of the sample companies (following a constant dividend payout ratio) pay out one-fourth to half of their earnings as dividends to their shareholders (Table 4.6). These findings corroborate that the Indian companies, by and large, follow/desire to follow stable dividend policy; in operational terms, they have preference for such a policy.

Section IV Consideration Affecting Dividend Policy

It was desirable to enquire about the considerations which affected dividend policy for the sample companies over the past decade (Table 4.7). 'Returns to shareholders' emerged as the preferred choice for more than two-fifth (42.30%) of companies (for 38.46% as an exclusive consideration). Thus, the survey findings indicate that

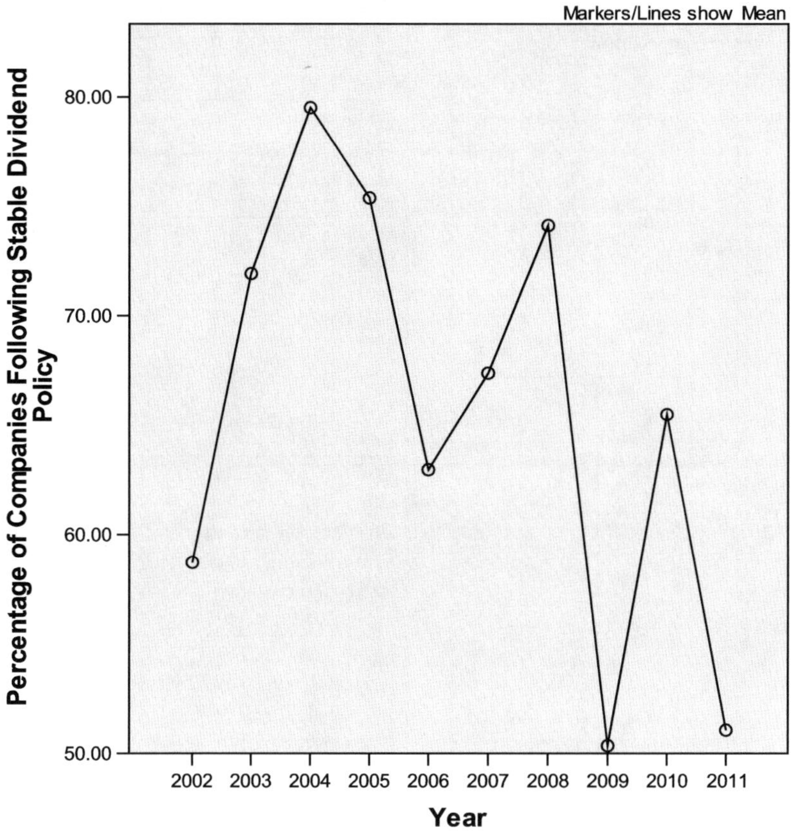

Fig. 4.2 Percentage of companies following stable dividend policy, 2002–2011

Table 4.4 Stable dividend policy followed by the sample companies

Options	Percentage
Yes	92.59
No	7.40

dividend policy in the case of two-fifth of the respondent companies (only) are guided by the consideration of returns to shareholders; this guiding factor is in tune with the sound tenets of financial management and the primary objective of maximising the wealth of its shareholders. It is desired that a greater number of companies is influenced by such a consideration.

'Cash flow constraints' was the consideration affecting dividend policy for more than one-fourth companies. 'Government of India directives (in the case of public sector enterprises)', 'constant payout policy' and 'internal cash generations' remained the other factors considered by the sample companies in designing their dividend policy.

Table 4.5 Constant payout ratio followed by the sample companies

Options	Percentage
Yes	86.20
No	13.79

Table 4.6 Percentage of earnings (if constant payout ratio followed) paid out as dividends by the sample companies

Percentage of earning	Percentage
Less than 10%	4.00
10–25%	16.00
25–50%	64.00
Above 50%	16.00

Table 4.7 Considerations affecting the dividend policy in the past decade for the sample companies

Considerations	Percentage
Consideration of returns	42.30 (38.46)
Cash flow constraints	26.92 (23.07)
Consideration of taxes	7.69 (3.84)
Legal constraints	3.84 (–)
Contractual constraints	0.00 (–)
Any other[a]	26.92 (26.92)

Figures in brackets indicate that the consideration is adopted exclusively by the sample companies. The same applies to other tables

[a]Includes 'Government of India directives', 'constant payout policy' and 'internal cash generation for future growth'

Table 4.8 Issue of bonus shares in the past decade by the sample companies

Options	Percentage
Yes	40.00
No	60.00

Sometimes, instead of paying cash dividends, companies issue bonus shares (stock dividends) by capitalising reserves thereby conserving (the required) cash. The rationale/genesis of issuing bonus shares (instead of cash dividend), by and large, is that the company has growth plans; it desires to use that cash for investment (which would ultimately result in higher returns for the owners). As per Table 4.8, 40% of the sample companies issued bonus shares in the past decade. As per a large majority (75%) of respondents, the issue of bonus shares sent a positive signal about the firm's future prospects to the public and made the stock more attractive to the investors (58.33%) as per Table 4.9.

The objective of stock splits (breaking down the face value of the shares into smaller denominations) is different; they are issued by companies in order to bring the prevailing market price of the shares to popular trade-able levels. The majority

Table 4.9 Benefits of issuing bonus shares (if issued) for the sample companies

Benefits	Percentage
Sent a positive signal about the firm's future prospects	75.00 (25.00)
Made the stock more attractive to the investors	58.33 (8.33)
Eased the sale of new common stock	8.33 (8.33)
Helped conserve cash	8.33 (–)
Any other[a]	16.66 (8.33)

[a]Includes 'capitalisation of reserves' and 'increased liquidity'

Table 4.10 Announcement of stock split in the past decade by the sample companies

Options	Percentage
Yes	44.82
No	55.17

of the respondent companies (55.17%) did not announce a stock split in the past decade (Table 4.10) indicating that there were perhaps no trading issues related to the prevalent price of their shares.

Section V Sectoral Analysis

The objective of this section is to examine whether there exists industry-wise variations in dividend payment pattern amongst the sample companies.

The sector with the highest dividend payout was FMCG at 43.90% (perhaps because of the presence of large cash-rich multinationals in this sector), and the lowest dividend payout was for the metals sector at 14.64% in phase 1. All constituent sectors of the sample reported a decrease in their dividend payout in phase 2 over phase 1 except for the housing, ICT, metals, power and miscellaneous sectors (for details, refer to Appendix 4.1). Expectedly (due to recession), all sectors registered a decline in their dividend payout in phase 4 over phase 3 except for the diversified, FMCG, transport and miscellaneous sectors (Appendix 4.2). The decrease in the dividend payout for the ICT sector was statistically significant for phases 3 and 4. The sample showed significant variances for the entire period of the study and the housing sector for phases 1 and 2 (Appendix 4.3).

Appendix 4.4 lists the percentage of companies adhering to a stable dividend policy amongst the constituent sectors of the sample. All sectors save the oil and gas, power and miscellaneous sectors reported a decline in the percentage of companies following a stable dividend policy in phase 2 over phase 1. Expectedly, all sectors (except the power and miscellaneous) reported a decline in companies pursuing stable dividend policy in the post-recession phase 4 over phase 3 (pre-recession). These fluctuations suggest similarities with the findings of Aivazian et al. (2003) on emerging markets.

Section VI Concluding Observations

The important conclusions emerging out of the study may now be underlined.

It is gratifying to note from 11-year (2001–2011) period of the study that the majority of the sample companies follow stable dividend policy. They seem to follow an approach similar to Lintner's model. The survey findings on the preference to adopt stable dividend policy (by sectors like oil and gas and ICT amongst others) were in fact more revealing. This practice is in tune with the sound principles of financial management.

The empirical evidence, further, suggests that the sample firms have dividend payout ratio of much less than 25% for the entire period of the study perhaps suggesting that the sample consists of companies with good growth opportunities. It is worthwhile to mention here that the dividend payout ratios have been gradually decreasing over the past two decades (as is evident after comparing results with previous studies, viz. Jain and Kumar (1997), Jain and Yadav (2000) and Jain and Yadav (2005)), perhaps indicating better growth opportunities for companies now, necessitating the ploughing back of cash into the business.

The study has also brought out industry-wise variations, to some extent, as far as dividend policy and practices are concerned. For instance, FMCG and healthcare sectors had high D/P ratios whereas sectors like metals and diversified reported low D/P ratios.

Normative Framework

Stable dividend policy is perhaps the best policy to follow for dividend paying firms in view of the following: investors view constant dividends as a source of cash/income to meet their current living expenses and stability of dividends is a means of reducing share riskiness (consequently increasing share value to investors). Further, financial institutions are constrained by rules to invest in only those equity shares which have good and stable dividend record, and investments by these institutions (which represent a significant force in the market) can have an enhancing effect on the market price of the share of the firm. It merits consideration on the part of the management of the sample firms not following hitherto a stable dividend policy to adopt it.

Appendices

Appendix 4.1: Mean, median and quartile values of dividend payout ratio of constituent sectors of the sample companies over phase 1 (2001–2006) and phase 2 (2007–2011)

	Phase 1 (2001–2006)				Phase 2 (2007–2011)			
Sector	Mean	Median	Quartile 1	Quartile 3	Mean	Median	Quartile 1	Quartile 3
Fast-moving consumer goods (FMCG)	43.90	49.89	16.57	68.70	43.55	45.79	18.66	65.90
Transport	28.66	27.56	13.58	38.70	26.62	23.37	15.45	38.26
Healthcare	27.83	25.83	15.16	40.05	26.25	22.51	15.30	32.55
Oil and gas	27.48	31.58	15.27	36.28	23.54	24.78	9.02	32.36
Miscellaneous[a]	26.53	23.98	5.44	41.54	29.70	28.28	16.30	41.21
Capital goods	23.87	19.29	12.27	30.60	19.74	21.03	13.96	24.12
Diversified	20.34	21.44	5.13	28.20	16.54	17.16	3.99	23.04
Power	19.33	20.50	9.50	27.17	20.99	24.93	2.50	33.53
Internet and communications technology (ICT)	18.39	12.34	4.58	26.39	20.67	15.73	5.38	32.40
Housing	16.88	14.87	2.67	26.17	20.27	11.69	5.64	24.21
Metals	14.64	13.45	3.48	20.21	14.72	12.30	6.25	20.99

[a]Miscellaneous sectors comprises of the media and publishing sector; agriculture, chemicals and petrochemicals; and tourism, textiles and miscellaneous sectors

Paired samples *t*-test of constituent sectors of the sample companies based on dividend payout ratio over phase 1 (2001–2006) and phase 2 (2007–2011)

	Phase 1 and Phase 2		
	t	*df*	Significance (2-tailed)
Diversified	1.763	8	0.116
Capital goods	1.644	12	0.126
ICT	1.591	17	0.130
Power	−1.095	11	0.297
Housing	1.043	16	0.312
Healthcare	0.881	13	0.395
Oil and gas	0.574	14	0.575
Metals	−0.445	17	0.662
Transport	0.407	16	0.690
Miscellaneous	0.398	15	0.697
FMCG	0.327	11	0.750

Appendix 4.2: Mean, median and quartile values of dividend payout ratio of constituent sectors of the sample companies over phase 3 (2007–2008) and phase 4 (2009–2011)

	Phase 3 (2007–2008)				Phase 4 (2009–2011)			
Sector	Mean	Median	Quartile 1	Quartile 3	Mean	Median	Quartile 1	Quartile 3
FMCG	41.12	44.33	14.78	63.43	44.85	45.79	23.01	66.57
Healthcare	28.00	22.82	12.26	36.34	24.93	22.64	17.62	29.49
Miscellaneous	27.65	25.23	14.49	38.32	31.78	31.37	18.24	43.94
Oil and gas	23.94	22.11	8.82	34.05	22.27	24.43	7.35	30.85
Housing	23.62	9.24	6.02	21.97	20.43	13.39	7.11	27.12
Transport	23.44	25.36	15.02	31.87	28.26	22.08	14.26	43.11
ICT	22.57	19.01	5.19	33.52	16.27	10.68	2.02	26.66
Power	22.00	26.50	2.00	33.50	19.31	22.20	1.00	32.72
Capital goods	19.97	20.93	11.87	24.58	18.54	21.27	14.17	23.41
Metals	15.78	13.46	5.24	21.34	13.40	10.80	6.52	20.83
Diversified	15.44	14.54	4.03	24.29	17.18	17.31	5.29	22.39

Paired samples *t*-test of constituent sectors of the sample companies based on dividend payout ratio over phase 3 (2007–2008) and phase 4 (2009–2011)

	Phase 3 and Phase 4		
	t	*df*	Significance (2-tailed)
ICT	2.214	17	0.041
Power	2.154	13	0.051
Miscellaneous	−2.040	14	0.061
Capital goods	1.619	12	0.131
Transport	−1.417	17	0.174
Oil and gas	1.136	15	0.274
Metals	0.833	17	0.416
Housing	0.675	17	0.509
Healthcare	0.586	13	0.568
Diversified	−0.525	8	0.614
FMCG	−0.171	11	0.867

Appendix 4.3: ANOVA of the consolidated sample and the constituent sectors of the sample companies based on dividend payout ratio over phase 1 (2001–2006) and phase 2 (2007–2011) and phase 3 (2007–2008) and phase 4 (2009–2011)

	Phase 1 and Phase 2		Phase 3 and Phase 4	
Sector	*F*	Significance	*F*	Significance
Consolidated	6.154	0.000	3.392	0.000
Housing	5.544	0.027	0.027	0.871
Capital goods	1.535	0.227	0.485	0.493
ICT	0.547	0.466	0.229	0.636
Diversified	0.335	0.571	0.071	0.794
Miscellaneous	0.272	0.606	0.002	0.961
Metals	0.215	0.647	0.953	0.338
Healthcare	0.071	0.792	0.186	0.670
Oil and gas	0.048	0.828	0.036	0.851
FMCG	0.007	0.935	0.005	0.942
Power	0.000	0.985	0.175	0.679
Transport	0.000	0.989	0.603	0.444

Appendix 4.4: Adherence to stable dividend policy by the constituents sectors of the sample companies (Figures are in percentages)

Sector	2002	2003	2004	2005	2006	2007	2008	2009	2010	2011	Phase1	Phase2	Phase3	Phase4
Capital goods	70.00	90.00	91.67	84.62	53.85	69.23	53.85	41.67	50.00	66.67	78.03	56.28	61.54	52.78
Healthcare	75.00	75.00	83.33	61.54	85.71	78.57	71.43	66.67	69.23	57.14	76.12	68.61	75.00	64.35
Diversified	57.14	85.71	85.71	83.33	66.67	66.67	100.00	66.67	66.67	50.00	75.71	70.00	83.34	61.11
FMCG	37.50	90.00	90.00	80.00	80.00	75.00	58.33	50.00	83.33	33.33	75.50	60.00	66.67	55.55
Metals	58.33	75.00	83.33	92.85	66.67	80.00	62.50	25.00	50.00	56.25	75.24	54.75	71.25	43.75
Housing	70.00	81.82	81.82	83.33	50.00	50.00	92.86	42.86	66.67	43.75	73.39	59.23	71.43	51.09
Miscellaneous	45.45	72.73	76.92	85.71	62.50	43.75	62.50	43.75	87.50	33.33	68.66	54.17	53.13	54.86
Oil and gas	80.00	70.00	70.00	75.00	41.67	76.92	76.92	66.67	75.00	53.85	67.33	69.87	76.92	65.17
Transport	41.67	69.23	85.71	64.29	60.00	81.25	93.75	35.29	76.47	62.50	64.18	69.85	87.50	58.09
Power	50.00	28.57	85.71	75.00	75.00	55.56	77.78	100.00	66.67	77.78	62.86	75.56	66.67	81.48
ICT	54.55	45.45	50.00	50.00	57.14	61.54	78.57	50.00	28.57	33.33	51.43	50.40	70.06	37.30

References

Aivazian V, Booth L, Cleary S (2003) Dividend policy and the organization of capital markets. J Multinatl Financ Manage 13:101–121

Allen F, Michaely R (2003) Chapter 7: Payout policy. In: Handbook Econ Finance, vol 1, part 1. Elsevier, Dordrecht, pp 337–429

Beaver WH (1968) Market prices, financial ratios, and the prediction of failure. J Account Res 6(2):179–192

Black FM, Scholes M (1974) The effect of dividend yield and dividend policy on common stock prices and returns. J Financ Econ 1(1):1–22

Brigham EF (1971) Readings in managerial finance. Rinehart and Winston, New York, p 675

Chateau JPD (1979) Dividend policy revisited: within and out-of sample tests. J Bus Finance Account 6(3):355–372

Collins DW, Pincus M, Xie H (1999) Equity valuation and negative earnings: the role of book value of equity. Account Rev 74(1):29–67

DeAngelo H, DeAngelo L, Stulz RM (2006) Dividend policy and the earned/contributed capital mix: a test of the lifecycle theory. J Financ Econ 81(2):227–254

Denis DJ, Osobov I (2008) Why do firms pay dividends? International evidence on the determinants of dividend policy. J Financ Econ 89:62–82

Dutta S, Reichelstein S (2004) Stock price, earnings and book value in managerial performance measures. Research paper no. 1873, Research paper series, Stanford Graduate School of Business

Fama EF, Babiak H (1968) Dividend policy: an empirical analysis. J Am Stat Assoc 63(4):1132–1161

Fama EF, French KR (1995) Size and book-to-market factors in earnings and returns. J Finance 50(1):131–155

Fang Lily H, Peress J (2008) Media coverage and the cross-section of stock returns. San Francisco Meetings Paper. J Finance (forthcoming). Available at SSRN: http://ssrn.com/abstract=971202. Accessed April 15, 2011

Farinha J (2003) Dividend policy, corporate governance and the managerial entrenchment hypothesis: an empirical analysis. J Bus Finance Account, JEL Classification: G32, G35

Jain PK, Kumar M (1997) Comparative financial management: practices of India and South East Asia. Hindustan Publishing Corporation, New Delhi, pp 43–44

Jain PK, Yadav SS (2000) Financial management practices in select private corporate enterprises – a comparative study of India, Thailand and Singapore. Hindustan Publishing Corporation, New Delhi

Jain PK, Yadav SS (2005) Financial management practices – a study of public sector enterprises in India. Hindustan Publishing Corporation, New Delhi

Jensen GR, Johnson RR, Mercer JF (1997) New evidence on size and price-to-book effects in stock returns. Financ Analysts J 53(6):34–42

Joy OM (1977) Introduction to financial management. Richard D. Irwin, Skokie, p 274

Kester GW et al (1994) Corporate financial policy in the pacific basin; Hong Kong and Singapore. Financ Practice Edu 4(1):118–127

Lintner J (1956) Distribution of income of corporations among dividends, retained earnings and taxes. Am Econ Rev 46(2):97–113

Menzly L, Ozbas O (2010) Market segmentation and cross-predictability of returns. J Finance 65:1555–1580

Miller MH, Modigliani F (1961) Dividend policy, growth and the valuation of shares. J Business 34:411–33

Penman SH (1996) The articulation of price-earnings ratios and market-to-book ratios and the evaluation of growth. J Account Res 34(2):235–259

Pruitt SW, Gitman LW (1991) The interactions between the investment, financing and dividend decisions of major US firms. Financ Rev 26(33):409–430

Ryan TM (1974) Dividend policy and market valuation in British industry. J Bus Finance Account 1(3):57–76
Shelvin T (1982) Austrian corporate dividend policy: empirical evidence. Account Finance 22(2):1–22
Short H, Zhang H, Keasey K (2002) The link between dividend policy and institutional ownership. J Corporate Finance 8:105–122
Solomon E (1969) Theory of financial management. Columbia University Press, New York, p 142
Walter JE (1956) Dividend policies and common stock prices. J Finance 11(1):29–41

Chapter 5
Working Capital Management

Introduction

Working capital management is concerned with the problems that arise in managing current assets (CA), current liabilities (CL) and the interrelationships that exist between them. The term current assets refer to those assets which, in the normal course of business, can be/will be converted into cash within 1 year or length of operating cycle (whichever is longer). The major current assets are cash and bank balances, debtors and inventory. Current liabilities are those liabilities which are intended, at their inception, to be paid in the normal course of business, within a year. The major current liabilities are creditors, short-term loan and outstanding expenses. Business success heavily depends on the ability of financial executives to effectively manage receivables, inventory and payables (Filbeck and Krueger 2005).

While inadequate working capital has the potential to disrupt production/sales operations of otherwise well-run business enterprises, excessive working capital adversely impacts profitability. Therefore, the firms should strive to maintain adequate amount of working capital to ensure smooth production and sales operations. Firms are able to reduce financing costs and/or increase the funds available for expansion by minimising the amount of funds tied up in current assets (Lamberson 1995). The importance of efficient working capital management (WCM) is therefore indisputable. This chapter is a modest attempt to gain insight on the working capital management practices of the sample companies.

For better exposition, this chapter has been divided into ten sections. Section I lays down the objective, rationale, scope and methodology of the chapter. Section II contains a brief literature review on aspects related to working capital management. Section III presents aggregative analysis of CA and CL in terms of major liquidity ratios. Disaggregative analysis in terms of management of individual current assets as well as gross working capital cycle has been delineated in section IV. Section V is devoted to the examination of aspects such as creditors' payment period and net working capital cycle. Other allied aspects relating to working

P.K. Jain et al., *Financial Management Practices: An Empirical Study of Indian Corporates*, India Studies in Business and Economics,
DOI 10.1007/978-81-322-0990-4_5,

capital management, say, planning, determination, financing, policy for dealing with situations like its excess/shortage, and so on, constitute the subject matter of section VI. Components of total current assets constitute the subject matter of section VII. The emerging concept of zero working capital and its practice amongst the sample companies is taken up in section VIII. Sector-wise analysis on all aspects of working capital management is presented in section IX. Concluding observations are listed in section X.

Section I Scope and Methodology

The Bombay Stock Exchange BSE 200 index comprises of the top 200 companies listed with the Bombay Stock Exchange, based on their market capitalisation. The scope of this study is limited to the 166 nonfinancial BSE 200 companies engaged in manufacturing and service rendering businesses (for details, kindly refer to Chap. 1).

The relevant data (secondary) on the first aspect were collected from the Capitaline database, for 11 years (2001–2011). The period of the study is of particular importance because of the recession (originating due to the US financial crisis) that impacted the world economy towards the second half of 2008. Consequently, phase 2 of the study (2007–2011) has been divided into two subphases to ascertain the impact of recession. The 2 years from 2005–2006 to 2007–2008 denote the pre-recession phase (phase 3) and the subsequent 3 years (2008–2009 to 2010–2011) denote the post-recession phase (phase 4) for the purpose of this study.

The *t*-test as well as ANOVA (analysis of variance) has been administered to assess whether financing pattern changed during the second phase compared to the first phase, as well as during the fourth phase as compared to the third phase, for the sample companies. To study trends and its implications, the descriptive statistical values/positional values, that is, mean, standard deviation, coefficient of variation, skew, kurtosis, median, quartile 1 and quartile 3, have been computed for each year.

The research instrument for primary data consisted of a questionnaire (Appendix 1.3, Chap. 1). This part of the analysis is based on 31 responses received out of 166 after 2 reminders (a response rate of 18.67%). The entire set of data has been analysed using Microsoft Excel spreadsheets and the statistics software SPSS, namely, Statistical Package for the Social Sciences.

Section II Literature Review

The objective of working capital management is to maintain the optimum balance of each of the working capital components. An optimal level would be one in which a balance is achieved between risk and efficiency.

Smith (1973) noted that working capital management had received adequate attention as an area of inquiry within the broader field of finance. Sokoloff (1983) found that most of the firms invested bulk of their investment in working capital and most manufacturing industries had made modest investments in fixed assets. Working capital practices change significantly within industries over time (Long et al. 1993). Most of the financial managers' time and effort was allocated in bringing nonoptimal levels of current assets and liabilities back towards optimal levels (Lamberson 1995).

Components/Factors Affecting Working Capital Management

Gitman et al. (1979) found that large firms appeared to utilise more sophisticated techniques in cash management and as a result turned over their cash more quickly than did the smaller firms. Richards and Laughlin (1980) found that cash conversion cycle analysis provided more explicit insights for managing a firm's working capital position (in a manner that will assure the proper amount and timing of funds available) to meet a firm's liquidity needs. Sastry (1970) developed models for analysing the transactions demand for cash at the firm level. Barth et al. (2001) developed models which showed how each accrual component reflected different information relating to future cash flows.

Gentry et al. (1990) took into account both the timing of the flows and the amount of funds used in each segment of the cycle by introducing the concept of weighted cash conversion cycle (WCCC) which provided management, Boards of Directors, credit analysts and students of finance insightful information for evaluating short-run financial management performance.

Dechow (1994) developed a simple model of earnings, cash flows and accruals by assuming a random walk sales process, variable and fixed costs, accounts receivables and payables and inventory. The model implied that earnings better predict future operating cash flows than does current operating cash flows.

Fazzari and Petersen (1993) found that working capital investment was excessively sensitive to cash flow fluctuations. Opler et al. (1999) found that firms with strong growth opportunities and riskier cash flows held relatively high ratios of cash to total noncash assets.

Long et al. (1993) showed that credit could stimulate sales because it allowed customers to assess product quality before paying. According to Cheng and Pike (2003), trade credit was a vehicle to attract new customers. Many firms were prepared to change their standard credit terms in order to win new customers and to gain large orders.

Mramor and Valentincic (2003) suggested the use of financial ratios to forecast the cash shortage of the company in the near future. According to them, the liquidity of a company was an important aspect of its financial soundness for creditors, suppliers, equity holders, employees and other stakeholders.

Ward (2004) provided an easily understood view to measure the operating output – the cash-to-cash (C2C) cycle time. Banomyong (2005) observed that the cash conversion cycle was a powerful performance metric for assessing how well a company was managing capital. Chiou and Cheng (2006) assessed working capital management. Results indicated that though debt ratios and operating cash flows affected the company's working capital management yet there was lack of consistent evidence for the influence of the business cycle, industry effect, growth of the company, performance of the company and firm size on the working capital management.

Bates et al. (2009) discovered that there was an increase from 1980 through 2006 in the average cash held by American firms. Raheman et al. (2010) estimated and compared sector-wise impact of working capital management on performance of manufacturing firms in terms of collection policy, inventory policy, payment policy, cash conversion cycle and net trading cycle using financial data for 204 firms listed on Karachi Stock Exchange (classified in 9 sectors) during period 1998–2007. The results indicated that there were variations in sectoral performance in terms of different measures of working capital management.

Hill et al. (2010) analysed the factors affecting net operating working capital on a large sample of companies; they observed that operating conditions and financing ability influence the working capital requirements. Kusnad and Wei (2011) examined the determinants of international firms' corporate cash management policies. It was reported that firms in countries with strong legal protection of minority investors exhibit lower cash flow sensitivity of cash than do firms in countries with weak legal protection.

Relationship Between Risk and Profitability

In literature, there has been a long debate on the risk–return trade-off between different working capital policies (Gitman et al. 1979). Working capital management is important in view of its effects on the firm's profitability and risk and consequently its value (Smith 1973). Ali (1994) observed non-linear relations between returns and each of three performance variables (earnings, working capital from operations and cash flows).

Deloof (2003) analysed a sample of large Belgian firms during the period 1992–1996, and the results confirmed that Belgian firms could improve their profitability by reducing the number of days accounts receivable were outstanding and by reducing inventories. Van Horne and Wachowicz (2004) pointed out that excessive level of current assets may have a negative effect on a firm's profitability whereas a low level of current assets may lead to lower liquidity and stock-outs resulting in difficulties in maintaining smooth operations. Lazaridis and Tryfonidis (2006) investigated relationship between working capital management and corporate profitability of listed company at the Athens Stock Exchange. There was a statistically significant relationship between profitability (measured in terms of gross operating profit) and cash conversion cycle.

Teruel and Solano (2007) studied effects of working capital management on the profitability of a sample of small- and medium-sized Spanish firms and found that managers could create value by reducing their inventories and the number of days for which their accounts were outstanding. Afza and Nazir (2009) investigated the traditional relationship between working capital management policies and firm's profitability for a sample of 204 nonfinancial firms listed on Karachi Stock Exchange (KSE) for the period 1998–2005. This study noted significant difference between the working capital requirements and financing policies across different industries.

Raheman et al. (2010) analysed the impact of working capital management on firm's performance in Pakistan for a decade from 1998 to 2007. They concluded that cash conversion cycle, net trade cycle and inventory turnover were significantly affecting the performance of the firms.

Saad and Mohamad (2010) studied the working capital management in Malaysia. Their results showed significant negative association between working capital variables and firm's performance. Dong and Su (2010) investigated the relationship existing between profitability and the cash conversion cycle for listed firms in Vietnam stock market for the period 2006–2008. Their findings showed a strong negative relationship between profitability (measured through gross operating profit) and the cash conversion cycle.

Kaur (2010) performed a two-dimensional study which examined the policy and practices of cash management and evaluated the principles, procedures and techniques of investment management, receivables and payables management. The findings indicated a stand-off between liquidity and profitability (the selected corporates had been achieving a trade-off between risk and return). Gill et al. (2010) noted a significant relationship between the cash conversion cycle and profitability (measured through gross operating profit).

Sur and Chakraborty (2011) studied the relationship between working capital management and profitability of the Indian pharmaceutical industry during the period 1996–1997 to 2007–2008 and observed that the joint influence of the liquidity management, inventory management and credit management on corporate profitability was not statistically significant.

Some of the variations in the findings of working capital research can be partially explained by the fact that there are industry benchmarks to which the firms adhere to when setting their policies. Thus, studies of different sectors would yield different results because of the inherent differences in their business situations. Undoubtedly then, it remains a challenge to determine the exact nature of influence that working capital exerts on a corporate.

Section III Liquidity Management

The importance of adequate liquidity to meet current/short-term maturing obligations as and when they become due for payment needs no emphasis. In fact, maintenance of adequate liquidity without impairing profitability is the foremost requirement of sound and efficient working capital management.

From this perspective, while excessive liquidity may be desired by the short-term creditors (as they are interested in the ability of the sample companies to pay them in time), it may be undesirable/unwarranted to carry excessive funds on the part of business firms as such funds are either nonearning or earn very little. This apart, excessive liquidity may be indicative of slack management practices as it might signal excessive inventories for the current requirements and poor credit management in terms of overextended accounts receivables. For a typical manufacturing firm, the current assets may account for over half of its total assets. For a distribution company, they may account for even more.

The companies should, therefore, maintain adequate liquidity in terms of satisfactory current ratio (CR) and acid-test ratio (ATR). What constitutes satisfactory level of these ratios depends on their access to sources of funds and ease with which these funds can be tapped in times of need. In general, it appears that the sizeable number of the sample companies in India have arrangements of short-term needs say, in the form of bank borrowings/overdraft and cash credit limit from banks (for more details on cash credit limit, kindly refer to Chap. 3 on capital structure). These facilities, then, should enable finance managers of the sample companies to operate on lower margins of working capital reflected in relatively lower current ratio (CR) as well as acid-test ratio (ATR). It may be worth mentioning here that conventionally current ratio 2:1 and acid-test ratio of 1:1 are considered satisfactory.

While Table 5.1 exhibits mean, standard deviation, coefficient of variation, skewness, kurtosis, median and quartile values of CR (based on year-end relevant data) of the sample companies, the ATR measured on these parameters has been shown in Table 5.3. Data contained in these two tables is exclusive of extreme values (of greater than 5 for CR and of greater than 3 for ATR). The mean values of CR and ATR, year-wise, in respect of the sample companies are portrayed in Figs. 5.1 and 5.2, respectively. Frequency distribution data pertaining to CR and ATR of these the sample companies are contained in Tables 5.2 and 5.4, respectively.

A high current ratio indicates a larger investment in current assets which, in general, means a low rate of return on investment for the firm. On the contrary, a low ratio indicates a smaller investment in current assets which, prima facie, yields a high rate of return on investment for the firm (in view of lower investments in current assets). However, a low current ratio could also entail interrupted production and sales, because of frequent stock-outs and inability to pay to creditors in time. Thus, the inverse relationship between profitability and liquidity may not always hold good; it may apply up to a certain level of liquidity only. Beyond that level, a decline in liquidity (in fact) is likely to cause a decline in profitability. A very poor liquidity position in a firm will create problems in smooth running of business, thereby obstructing the growth of business and causing a decline in profitability.

Data contained in Table 5.1 indicate that mean as well as median current ratio of the sample companies has been around the theoretically desired 2:1 for the entire 11-year period (2001–2011) of the study. Also, the acid-test ratio has been higher than the desired 1:1 (mean and median) for the entire period covered by the study (Table 5.3). Conclusions are similar on the basis of quartile values for both sets of ratios. However, the distribution has a high positive skewness indicating that only few companies had very high liquidity (higher values of CR) amongst the sample companies.

Table 5.1 Mean, standard deviation, coefficient of variation, skewness, kurtosis, median and quartile values of current ratio of the sample companies, 2001–2011

Year ending[a]	Number	Mean	Standard deviation	Coefficient of variation (%)	Skewness	Kurtosis	Median	Quartile 1	Quartile 3
2001	130	2.16	0.94	43.47	0.66	0.03	2.02	1.55	2.61
2002	139	2.16	1.05	48.45	0.85	0.95	2.01	1.36	2.75
2003	141	1.97	0.95	48.72	0.56	0.38	1.84	1.33	2.56
2004	143	1.82	0.90	49.36	0.80	0.81	1.65	1.23	2.27
2005	147	1.90	0.89	46.93	0.79	0.56	1.76	1.26	2.35
2006	151	1.93	0.98	50.48	0.85	0.58	1.71	1.31	2.34
2007	148	1.99	0.98	49.48	0.96	0.49	1.73	1.35	2.36
2008	151	2.05	1.01	49.71	0.72	−0.20	1.78	1.32	2.69
2009	145	2.00	0.96	48.26	0.78	−0.06	1.80	1.33	2.55
2010	145	2.00	0.96	48.26	0.78	−0.06	1.80	1.33	2.55
2011	143	2.00	0.98	49.10	0.72	0.04	1.86	1.27	2.56
2001–2011	144	2.00	0.96	48.38	0.77	0.32	1.82	1.33	2.51
Phase 1 (2000–2001 to 2005–2006)	142	1.99	0.95	47.90	0.75	0.55	1.83	1.34	2.48
Phase 2 (2006–2007 to 2010–2011)	146	2.01	0.98	48.96	0.79	0.04	1.79	1.32	2.54
Phase 3 (2006–2007 to 2007–2008)	150	2.02	1.00	49.60	0.84	0.14	1.76	1.34	2.52
Phase 4 (2008–2009 to 2010–2011)	144	2.00	0.97	48.54	0.76	−0.03	1.82	1.31	2.55

[a](1) The Indian financial year begins on April 1 and ends on March 31 of the following year. The same holds true for all subsequent tables and notations
(2) Extreme values of CR above 5 have been excluded

		Paired differences							
					95% confidence interval of the difference				
		Mean	Standard deviation	Standard error mean	Lower	Upper	*t*	*df*	Significance (2-tailed)
Pair 1	Phase 1–Phase 2	−.11195	.78435	.06280	−.23600	.01210	−1.783	155	0.077
Pair 2	Phase 3–Phase 4	−.02992	.73037	.06024	−.14898	.08913	−.497	146	0.620

In the paired t-test, in case the value of sig. (2-tailed) is 0.05 or less, the alternate hypothesis that there is significant difference in two phases is accepted; when its value exceeds 0.05, the alternate hypothesis is rejected implying that there is no significant difference in the two phases. The same holds true for all paired t-test tables

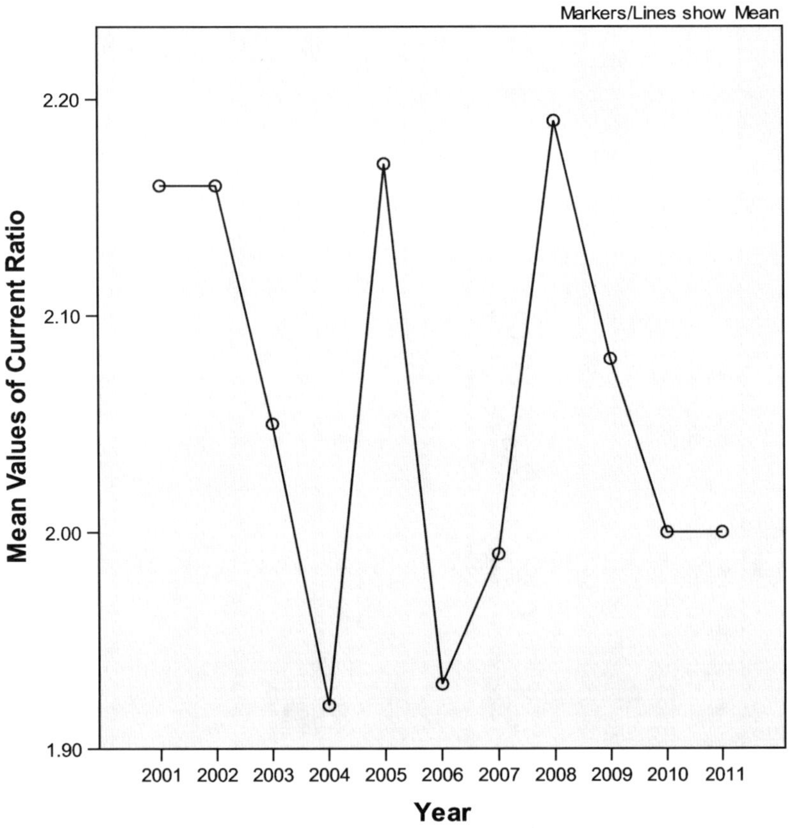

Fig. 5.1 Mean values of current ratio of the sample companies, 2001–2011

The findings are significant as they are indicative of better short-term liquidity position when compared to the findings of Jain and Kumar (1997) on private sector enterprises for the period 1985–1995, when the mean current ratio reported was 1.47; a marginally higher mean current ratio of 1.53 was reported in the findings of Jain and Yadav (2000) on private sector enterprises for the period 1991–1998. However, a much lower liquidity (current ratio) of 1.19 was indicated by public sector undertakings for the period 1991–2003 in the study of Jain and Yadav (2005).

From the frequency distributions (Tables 5.2 and 5.4), it is evident that more than half of the sample companies have a CR and ATR of between 1 and 3 indicating adequate liquidity. The paired samples *t*-test signifies that there is no significant difference in mean CR of phase 2 (2007–2011) compared to mean values of the ratios in phase 1 (2001–2006) unlike the mean ATR changes (statistically significant).

Between ATR and CR, ATR is a more rigorous measure as it excludes, apart from prepaid expenses, all types of inventories (considered to be the least liquid in

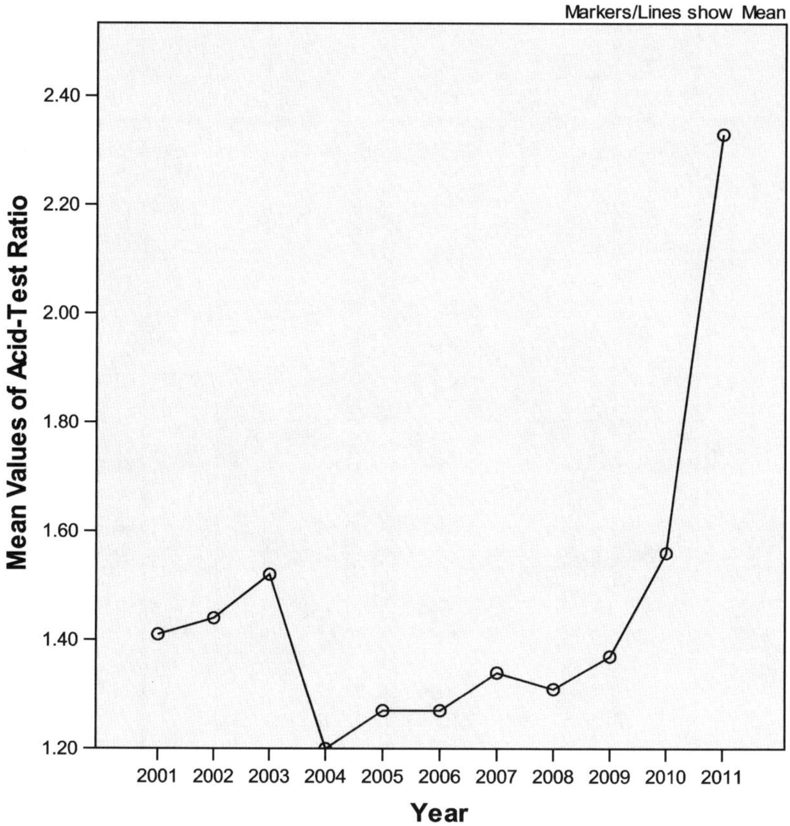

Fig. 5.2 Mean values of acid-test ratio of the sample companies, 2001–2011

Table 5.2 Frequency distribution of current ratio of the sample companies, 2001–2011 (Figures are in percentages)

Current ratio	2001	2002	2003	2004	2005	2006	2007	2008	2009	2010	2011
0.0–1.0	5.63	8.73	13.82	14.93	10.26	12.42	9.81	12.65	9.03	10.42	10.91
1.0–1.5	14.79	20.13	20.40	22.73	26.93	26.70	21.47	19.88	19.88	26.38	22.43
1.5–2.0	23.24	18.12	17.76	19.48	21.15	15.53	25.15	18.67	22.29	11.04	13.33
2.0–3.0	28.17	29.53	27.63	25.32	24.36	24.22	20.25	20.48	21.69	28.22	24.85
3.0–5.0	18.31	16.78	13.15	10.39	11.53	14.91	14.11	18.68	14.46	12.88	15.15
Above 5.0	9.86	6.71	7.24	7.14	5.77	6.21	9.20	9.04	12.65	11.04	13.33
Total (%)	100	100	100	100	100	100	100	100	100	100	100.00

Total (100) may not tally due to rounding off. The same holds true for other frequency distribution tables

Table 5.3 Mean, standard deviation, coefficient of variation, skewness, kurtosis, median and quartile values of acid-test ratio of the sample companies, 2001–2011

Year ending	Number	Mean	Standard deviation	Coefficient of variation (%)	Skewness	Kurtosis	Median	Quartile 1	Quartile 3
2001	111	1.41	0.79	61.17	0.97	2.68	1.29	0.83	1.94
2002	116	1.39	0.75	57.67	0.29	–0.78	1.29	0.84	1.92
2003	122	1.38	0.74	57.46	0.34	–0.62	1.29	0.83	1.90
2004	123	1.20	0.65	56.81	0.53	–0.18	1.15	0.68	1.60
2005	127	1.27	0.70	59.64	0.58	–0.27	1.18	0.72	1.66
2006	125	1.24	0.64	53.78	0.34	–0.49	1.19	0.72	1.71
2007	124	1.34	0.72	57.46	0.62	–0.20	1.25	0.81	1.75
2008	121	1.31	0.70	58.97	0.48	–0.57	1.18	0.70	1.78
2009	121	1.37	0.65	49.74	0.39	–0.73	1.31	0.88	1.84
2010	122	1.43	0.78	61.71	0.76	0.62	1.27	0.84	1.97
2011	133	1.36	0.68	55.74	0.32	–0.84	1.23	0.83	1.92
2001–2011	122	1.34	0.71	57.29	0.51	–0.13	1.24	0.79	1.82
Phase 1 (2000–2001 to 2005–2006)	121	1.32	0.71	57.76	0.51	0.06	1.23	0.77	1.79
Phase 2 (2006–2007 to 2010–2011)	124	1.36	0.71	56.72	0.52	–0.34	1.25	0.81	1.85
Phase 3 (2006–2007 to 2007–2008)	123	1.33	0.71	58.22	0.55	–0.38	1.21	0.75	1.77
Phase 4 (2008–2009 to 2010–2011)	125	1.39	0.70	55.73	0.49	–0.32	1.27	0.85	1.91

Extreme values of ATR above 3 have been excluded

		Paired differences							
					95% confidence interval of the difference				
		Mean	Standard deviation	Standard error mean	Lower	Upper	*t*	*df*	Significance (2-tailed)
Pair 1	Phase 1–Phase 2	–.12889	.80075	.06411	–.25553	–.00224	–2.010	155	0.046
Pair 2	Phase 3–Phase 4	.00701	.82133	.06706	–.12550	.13953	.105	149	0.917

Table 5.4 Frequency distribution related to acid-test ratio of the sample companies, 2001–2011 (Figures are in percentages)

Acid-test ratio	2001	2002	2003	2004	2005	2006	2007	2008	2009	2010	2011
0.0–1.0	28.03	28.67	29.93	36.18	34.96	33.11	28.00	28.76	25.97	25.32	27.27
1.0–2.0	37.88	36.03	38.69	39.72	39.86	38.51	41.33	36.60	38.31	37.33	36.36
2.0–3.0	18.18	20.59	20.44	11.35	13.99	12.84	13.33	13.73	14.29	18.67	16.97
Above 3.0	15.91	14.71	10.95	12.77	11.19	15.54	17.33	20.92	21.43	18.67	19.39
Total	100	100	100	100	100	100	100	100	100	100	100

the category of CAs). The ATR median value of 1.24 for the 11-year period (in conjunction with median CR of 1.82), prima facie, leads us to infer that the sample companies would not be encountering problems in meeting/paying their short-term maturing obligations in time. This is in tune with the findings on the importance of liquidity for a firm's survival and is supported by a number of empirical studies on the subject; the select list includes Lamberson (1995) and Mramor et al. (2003). There are many factors in today's economic conditions which may trigger the need to have more cash – growth without raising additional funds, funding acquisitions, rising costs, market developments, etc. (explaining the rationale of higher set of liquidity ratios of the sample companies).

In terms of the acid-test ratio as well, the findings are indicative of better short-term liquidity position when compared to the findings of Jain and Kumar (1997) on private sector enterprises for the period 1985–1995, when the mean acid-test ratio reported was 0.89. An even lower average ratio of 0.57 was reported in the findings of Jain and Yadav (2000) on private sector enterprises for the period 1991–1998 and Jain and Yadav (2005) on public sector undertakings (0.59) for the period 1991–2003.

Thus, the empirical evidence on the subject does not seem to support the ex hypothesi expectation stated above, that is, the sample companies are likely to opt for lower CR as well as lower ATR than the norm stated in literature.

However, the sample companies could do well to be less conservative with their working capital management as they are large and stable companies and may attempt a better trade-off between risk and profitability as has been propounded by researches on the subject by Gitman et al. (1979), Fazzari and Peterson (1993), Opler et al. (1999), Deloof (2003), Teruel and Solano (2007) and Van Horne and Wachowicz (2004).

Section IV Current Assets Management

Current assets management is considered to be the primary goal of working capital management. Each current asset must be managed efficiently in order to maintain liquidity of a business enterprise while not maintaining too high a level of any one of them. The major current assets are cash and bank balances, inventories and debtors.

What have been the major policies for their management? Are there significant changes in holding period of various types of inventories and collection period of debtors? These and other important aspects related to the management of current assets constitute the subject matter of this section.

For better exposition, this section has been divided in four subsections. While subsection one deals with cash/bank balances, subsections two and three dwell on inventory management and debtors' management. Subsection four pertains to gross working capital cycle.

Cash Management

Cash management is one of the key areas of current assets management. In fact, the two major current assets, that is, receivables and inventory, get converted into cash eventually. Further, cash and bank balances are the most commonly used mode of making all payments in ordinary course of business. Therefore, the sample companies should carry adequate cash (commensurate with their requirements) so that all dues are paid in time. However, at the same time, these enterprises should not carry cash more than warranted since cash, per se, is a nonearning asset. What have been the practices of the sample companies primarily in terms of the modus operandi of utilising excess cash and arrangement to cater to emergent cash needs/shortages (shown by survey) form the subject matter of this part.

While some of the sample companies might be encountering cash shortage situation, some others might be looking out for avenues/investment outlets for utilising surplus cash with them. Our survey sought responses of the sample companies on both these counts.

Bank overdraft/cash credit (in tune with ex hypothesi expectation) has been cited as the major source of dealing with cash deficit situations by the vast majority (64.28%) of the sample companies (Table 5.5). This is similar to the findings of Jain and Kumar (1997), Jain and Yadav (2000) and Jain and Yadav (2005).

More than one-third (35.71%) companies maintain a minimum cash balance over and above the required amount to meet exigencies (if any). The other two methods, namely, discounting bill receivables and having special arrangement with some lending agency, are less frequently used techniques by them. The methods, such as selling marketable securities and raising loans against warehouse receipt are not in vogue.

The notable finding of the survey is that the sample companies are/seem to be highly conscious of the fact that it is not desirable to carry more cash than required. The survey also brings to fore the multiple ways of dealing with surplus cash situations amongst the sample companies (Table 5.6). Temporary investment in marketable securities has been singled out as the major source of deploying cash by majority of the sample companies (90%); the findings of Jain and Kumar (1997) on private sector enterprises for the period 1985–1995, apart from the temporary investment in marketable securities, also cited the payment of short-term debt. Jain and Yadav (2000),

Table 5.5 Management of emergency requirements of cash by the sample companies

Management of emergency requirements of cash	Percentage
Utilisation of cash credit limit from bank	50.00 (25.00)
Always maintain minimum cash balance over and above the required amount	35.71 (17.85)
Bank overdraft	14.28 (3.57)
Have special arrangements with some lending agency for such purposes	14.28 (7.14)
Any other[a]	14.28 (–)
Discount bill receivables	10.71 (–)
Sell marketable securities	10.71 (7.14)
Raise loan against warehouse receipt	0.00 (–)

Figures in brackets indicate the exclusive method of cash management adopted by the sample companies
[a]There were no details provided against this option

Table 5.6 Use of excess cash by the sample companies

Use of excess cash	Percentage
Temporarily invested (say, in marketable securities)	90.00 (70.00)
Invested in long-term securities	0.00 (–)
Invested in fixed assets	10.00 (5.00)
Utilised for repayment of debt	20.00 (–)
Any other	5.00 (5.00)

Figures in brackets indicate the exclusive use of excess cash by the sample companies

in their study of private sector enterprises for the period 1991–1998 reported temporary investments in marketable securities as the first mode of utilisation of excess cash; the present survey also supports the same.

The above findings related to cash management (in broad terms) are in conformity with sound tenets of financial management and are indicative of professionalism amongst practising managers of the sample companies. These findings are similar to the findings of Deloof (2003), Teruel and Solano (2005) and Van Horne and Wachowicz (2004).

Inventory Management

Inventory management constitutes yet another major aspect of current assets management. The objective of inventory management consists of two counter-balancing parts, namely, to minimise investments in inventory (with a view to reduce its carrying costs) and to meet demand for products by efficient production and sales operations (to minimise stock-out costs). In operational terms, its goal is to have a trade-off between costs and benefits associated with holding of inventory.

This part discusses the inventory management (primarily in terms of holding period of raw materials and spare parts, work-in-process and finished goods) of the sample companies. The ex hypothesi expectation is that there is likely to be decrease in holding period of all types of inventories on account of significant improvement in facilities and means of communication, liberalisation (making the firms/products more competitive and therefore greater possibility/need of the forms following improved manufacturing practices), improved logistics and distribution and, above all, globalisation of the Indian economy (perhaps bringing out better availability of raw materials and other supplies, in general).

Raw Materials and Spare Parts (RMSP) Inventory

While mean, standard deviation, coefficient of variation, skewness, kurtosis, median and quartile value of raw materials and spare parts holding period of the sample companies have been exhibited in Table 5.7, frequency distribution in this respect is contained in Table 5.8. There are two inferences from the data. First, average raw materials inventory holding period of less than a month (20.64 days) for the entire period of the study, prima facie, indicates efficient RMSP inventory management by the sample companies. This is in sharp contrast to the findings of the study conducted on public sector undertakings which brought out the average RMSP inventory holdings of 170 days (Jain and Yadav 2005). The lower and upper quartile values reconfirm the indication as per the mean; one-fourth of the sample companies have RMSP holding period of less than 4 days (quartile 1 of 3.49 days) with a quartile 3 value of less than a month (28.9 days). Frequency distribution data is equally revealing. An overwhelming majority of companies (nearly 90%) have RMSP inventory holdings of less than 40 days. The skewness and kurtosis figures support the above (in the sense) that only few companies report very high values of RMSP holdings.

The RMSP inventory holding has risen sharply in 2011 (Fig. 5.3) over 2010 perhaps due to the recessionary pressure on the operations of the sample companies in phase 4 of the study. However, despite this increase, the holding period has been a month. There is a high degree of variation in the mean amongst the sample companies indicated by the coefficient of variation (which is expected due to the different nature of business of the sample firms).

Frequency distribution data is more revealing on the subject (Tables 5.10 and 5.12). More than half of the sample companies maintained WIP and FG inventory for less than 5 days during the period of the study except for the year 2011, when both WIP and FG inventory holdings have risen sharply indicating perhaps the lag in the operational efficiency of the sample companies due to the recession affecting the Indian economy during phase 4 of the study (Table 5.11).

Table 5.7 Mean, standard deviation, coefficient of variation, skewness, kurtosis, median and quartile values of holding period (in days) of raw materials and spare parts inventory for the sample companies, 2001–2011

Year ending	Number	Mean	Standard deviation	Coefficient of variation (%)	Skewness	Kurtosis	Median	Quartile 1	Quartile 3
2001	126	21.53	19.46	90.39	1.46	3.25	19.27	6.35	31.36
2002	142	19.68	18.05	91.75	1.63	4.34	17.23	5.86	28.59
2003	145	19.15	18.03	94.16	1.29	2.04	16.16	3.53	28.97
2004	148	18.06	18.07	100.05	1.60	3.48	15.42	3.64	25.95
2005	155	19.57	18.50	94.55	1.36	2.51	17.66	3.34	26.91
2006	157	19.79	19.14	96.73	1.12	1.00	16.10	2.12	30.26
2007	160	18.83	18.44	97.92	1.18	1.25	15.84	1.25	28.80
2008	162	19.47	18.62	95.63	1.06	0.84	16.32	1.70	29.78
2009	163	21.58	28.88	133.82	4.29	30.14	15.16	1.62	28.96
2010	162	19.27	21.02	109.05	1.55	2.57	14.28	0.56	26.95
2011	133	30.10	55.32	183.82	6.31	44.74	19.38	8.42	32.17
2001–2011	145	20.64	23.05	100.41	2.08	8.74	16.62	3.49	28.97
Phase 1 (2000–2001 to 2005–2006)	142	19.63	18.54	94.61	1.41	2.77	16.97	4.14	28.67
Phase 2 (2006–2007 to 2010–2011)	148	21.85	28.46	124.05	2.88	15.91	16.20	2.71	29.33
Phase 3 (2006–2007 to 2007–2008)	161	19.15	18.53	96.77	1.12	1.04	16.08	1.48	29.29
Phase 4 (2008–2009 to 2010–2011)	148	23.65	35.07	142.23	4.05	25.82	16.27	3.53	29.36

Extreme values above 770 days have been excluded

		Paired differences							
					95% confidence interval of the difference				
		Mean	Standard deviation	Standard error mean	Lower	Upper	*t*	*df*	Significance (2-tailed)
Pair 1	Phase 1–Phase 2	−1.84995	13.27007	1.04583	−3.91536	.21546	−1.769	160	0.079
Pair 2	Phase 3–Phase 4	−2.92329	19.42537	1.51226	−5.90930	.06273	−1.933	164	0.055

Table 5.8 Frequency distribution related to holding period (in days) of raw materials and spare parts inventory for the sample companies, 2001–2011 (Figures are in percentages)

Days	2001	2002	2003	2004	2005	2006	2007	2008	2009	2010	2011
0–10	30.16	30.99	31.72	36.49	33.55	36.94	38.27	38.65	40.49	43.21	28.57
10–20	22.22	28.17	28.28	24.32	20.65	19.75	20.37	17.79	20.25	16.05	24.06
20–40	37.30	32.39	30.34	30.41	34.84	29.30	28.40	31.29	25.15	28.40	29.32
Above 40	10.32	8.45	9.66	8.79	10.98	14.01	11.79	12.26	14.11	12.34	18.04
Total	100	100	100	100	100	100	100	100	100	100	100

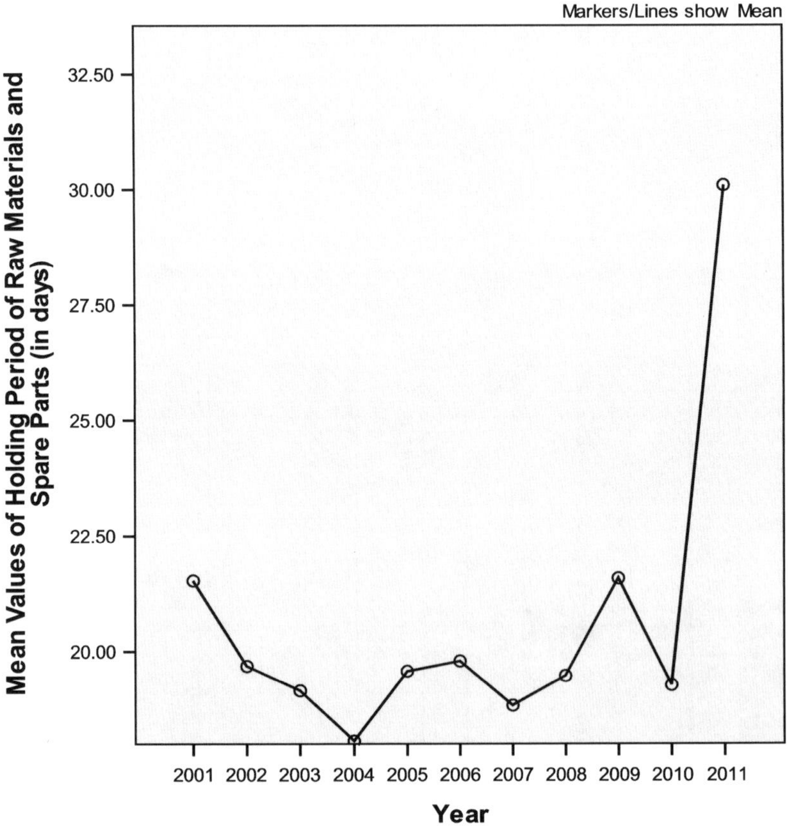

Fig. 5.3 Mean values of holding period (in days) of raw materials and spare parts inventory for the sample companies, 2001–2011

It is worth noting here that in comparison, Indian public sector undertakings reported average WIP inventory holding period of 29.29 days and FG inventory holding of 34.49 days for the period 1991–2003 (Jain and Yadav 2005).

There is expectedly a high degree of variation within the sample companies for all types of inventory (Long et al. (1993), Raheman et al. (2010) and Hill et al. (2010)). However, the high skewness and kurtosis figures indicate that only few

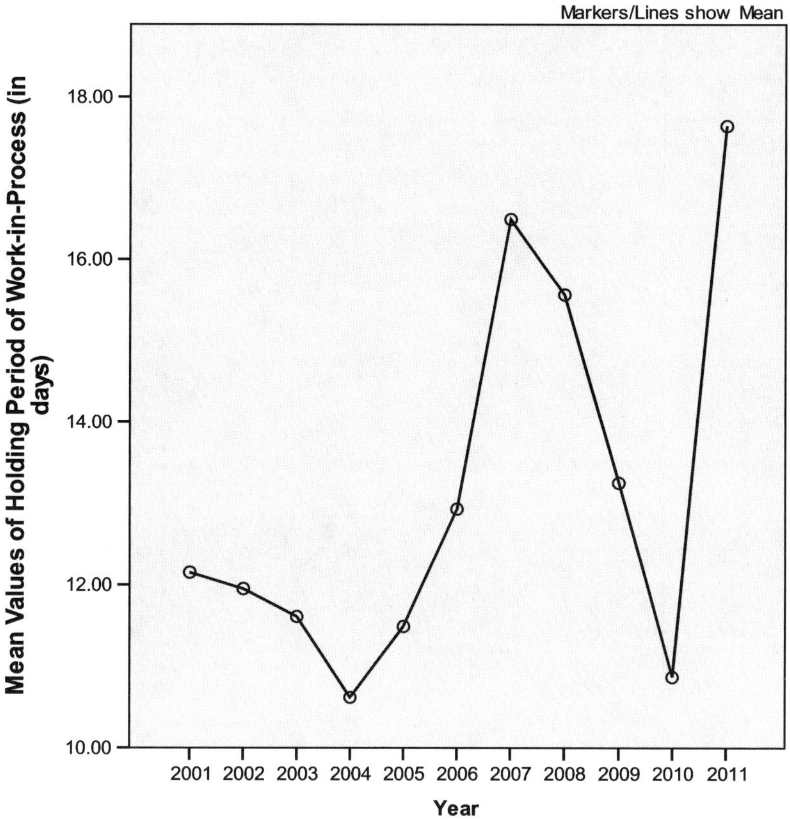

Fig. 5.4 Mean values of holding period (in days) of work-in-process inventory for the sample companies, 2001–2011

companies report very high values of WIP and FG holdings, an indication perhaps of professional/aggressive inventory management, by and large.

'Materials management is one of the key factors for improving performance of any unit. Higher inventories saddle an organisation with avoidable costs besides blocking scarce funds which might be required by the enterprise for its own operations. Proper management of materials, therefore, assumes considerable importance in corporate functioning. The sample companies, on the whole, appear to be conscious about this aspect and exhibit efficient inventory management.

Debtors Management

Debtors/receivables represent an important component of current assets amongst all business corporate enterprises as credit sales form an essential part of the modern

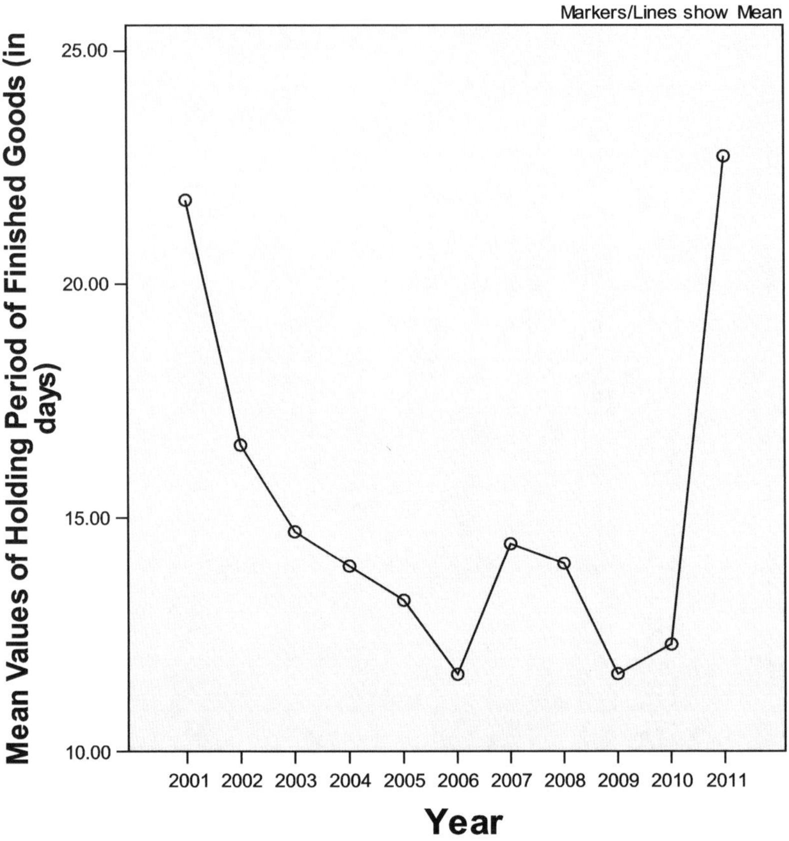

Fig. 5.5 Mean values of holding period (in days) of finished goods inventory for the sample companies, 2001–2011

competitive economic system. In fact, credit sales and, therefore, receivables are treated as a marketing tool to promote sales and thereby profits (Long et al. (1993) and Cheng and Pike (2003)).

For obvious reasons, extension of credit involves both risk and cost. Management, therefore, should weigh both costs and benefits of granting/extending credit as per risk–return trade-off approach. Discussion that follows in this part examines various facets of receivables management, such as debtors' collection period, credit policy and objectives, credit terms and risk analysis of debtors as practised by the sample companies in India.

The data contained in Table 5.13 indicate that one-fourth of the sample companies have debtors collection period of 1 month or less (as per lower quartile) and another one-fourth of the sample companies have the average debtors' collection period of more than 3 months (evidenced by upper quartile).

The findings are similar to the findings of Jain and Kumar (1997) on private sector enterprises for the period 1985–1995 and to the findings of Jain and Yadav

Table 5.9 Mean, standard deviation, coefficient of variation, skewness, kurtosis, median and quartile values of holding period (in days) of work-in-process inventory for the sample companies, 2001–2011

Year ending	Number	Mean	Standard deviation	Coefficient of variation (%)	Skewness	Kurtosis	Median	Quartile 1	Quartile 3
2001	125	12.15	27.48	226.08	6.09	48.68	3.17	0.00	14.10
2002	141	11.95	28.84	241.32	6.93	61.49	3.11	0.00	12.64
2003	143	11.61	25.15	216.60	5.23	35.83	3.19	0.00	11.81
2004	145	10.62	20.40	192.13	4.21	24.72	3.06	0.00	11.96
2005	152	11.49	22.38	194.72	3.33	11.90	3.11	0.00	12.19
2006	155	12.93	30.12	232.95	4.23	19.78	2.24	0.00	12.34
2007	159	16.49	47.73	289.50	5.02	26.74	1.81	0.00	12.42
2008	160	15.56	44.31	284.80	5.28	30.56	1.90	0.00	11.61
2009	159	13.25	36.54	275.79	6.01	44.00	1.49	0.00	10.44
2010	157	10.87	25.62	235.67	4.84	28.92	1.43	0.00	8.87
2011	98	17.64	32.00	181.45	4.98	33.00	8.15	2.35	17.94
2001–2011	129	13.14	30.96	233.73	5.10	33.24	2.97	0.21	12.39
Phase 1 (2000–2001 to 2005–2006)	139	11.79	25.73	217.30	5.00	33.73	2.98	0.00	12.51
Phase 2 (2006–2007 to 2010–2011)	129	14.76	37.24	253.44	5.23	32.64	2.96	0.47	12.26
Phase 3 (2006–2007 to 2007–2008)	160	16.02	46.02	287.15	5.15	28.65	1.85	0.00	12.02
Phase 4 (2008–2009 to 2010–2011)	129	13.92	31.39	230.97	5.27	35.31	3.69	0.78	12.42

Extreme values above 365 days have been excluded

		Paired differences							
					95% confidence interval of the difference				
		Mean	Standard deviation	Standard error mean	Lower	Upper	t	*df*	Significance (2-tailed)
Pair 1	Phase 1–Phase 2	−5.33944	33.60700	2.68213	−10.63742	−.04146	−1.991	156	0.048
Pair 2	Phase 3–Phase 4	.55857	27.14663	2.15287	−3.69354	4.81069	.259	158	0.796

Table 5.10 Frequency distribution related to holding period (in days) of work-in-process inventory for the sample companies, 2001–2011 (Figures are in percentages)

Days	2001	2002	2003	2004	2005	2006	2007	2008	2009	2010	2011
Below 5	55.56	52.82	57.24	56.76	58.71	57.32	59.26	58.28	58.28	58.64	37.31
5–10	11.11	16.20	12.41	15.54	14.19	13.38	12.35	13.50	12.88	15.43	16.42
10–20	16.67	14.79	13.10	9.46	14.84	13.38	10.49	9.20	10.43	8.02	23.88
20–40	8.73	10.56	8.28	9.46	5.81	7.01	8.02	9.82	7.36	8.02	13.43
Above 40	7.13	5.62	8.97	8.80	7.11	8.91	9.88	9.20	11.05	9.88	8.96
Total	100	100	100	100	100	100	100	100	100	100	100

(2000) on private sector enterprises for the period 1991–1998. However, the public sector undertakings (Jain and Yadav 2005) reported a higher debtors' collection period of 86.48 days (for a period of 1991–2003).

Frequency distribution data (which include extreme values of average debtors' collection period of more than a year) further reinforce the above findings (Table 5.14).

As far as objectives of credit policy are concerned, the survey indicates that 'growth in sales' is the most favoured objective of credit policy for nearly two-thirds of the sample companies (Table 5.15). 'Matching credit terms with those of competitors' is the second desired objective amongst the sample companies.

The most notable finding of the survey is that the vast majority of the sample companies do not reckon 'offering credit terms better than those of competitors' as the primary objective of their credit policy. The reason for low reckoning of better credit terms may be expected from some of the sample companies which are in monopoly/quasi-monopoly situation (say oil firms).

'Full coverage through LC (letter of credit)', 'market conditions and brand strength', 'rebate provided to customers as per norms' and 'matching with credit risk' are the other cited objectives of credit policy from the sample companies.

From the foregoing, it is apparent that the vast majority of the sample companies recognise credit sales as an essential element of promoting sales. Further, they are conscious of risk inherent in such sales. To minimise the risk, all the respondent companies assess the financial health of customers before granting credit (Table 5.16). Similarly, there is a practice of preparing 'ageing schedule of debtors' amongst all the sample companies (Table 5.17). These findings are in tune with the findings of Gentry et al. (1990) and Opler et al. (1999) (Table 5.18).

Gross Working Capital Cycle

Gross working capital cycle (GWCC) refers to the length of time necessary to complete the following three events: (i) conversion of cash into inventory, (ii) conversion of inventory into debtors and (iii) conversion of debtors into cash. The longer is the

Table 5.11 Mean, standard deviation, coefficient of variation, skewness, kurtosis, median and quartile values of holding period (in days) of finished goods inventory for the sample companies, 2001–2011

Year ending	Number	Mean	Standard deviation	Coefficient of variation (%)	Skewness	Kurtosis	Median	Quartile 1	Quartile 2
2001	126	21.80	42.07	192.95	5.28	32.38	12.49	0.00	26.99
2002	142	16.55	23.61	142.61	3.76	22.28	9.49	0.00	24.61
2003	145	14.70	21.45	145.95	3.68	20.55	9.63	0.00	21.64
2004	148	13.96	22.33	159.96	4.58	32.34	6.45	0.00	20.60
2005	155	13.23	21.12	159.70	4.15	26.62	6.42	0.00	18.80
2006	157	11.65	14.54	124.78	1.90	5.61	5.47	0.00	18.96
2007	162	14.44	32.00	221.55	6.37	52.08	4.37	0.00	18.61
2008	163	14.02	29.27	208.85	6.43	54.86	4.76	0.00	19.61
2009	163	11.66	18.50	158.61	3.52	16.86	4.03	0.00	17.20
2010	162	12.29	21.23	172.71	4.03	20.88	4.61	0.00	16.46
2011	107	22.74	41.98	184.56	5.85	41.96	13.85	4.61	24.72
2001–2011	148	15.19	26.19	170.20	4.50	29.67	7.42	0.42	20.75
Phase 1 (2000–2001 to 2005–2006)	146	15.32	24.19	154.32	3.89	23.30	8.33	0.00	21.93
Phase 2 (2006–2007 to 2010–2011)	151	15.03	28.59	189.26	5.24	37.33	6.32	0.92	19.32
Phase 3 (2006–2007 to 2007–2008)	163	14.23	30.63	215.20	6.40	53.47	4.56	0.00	19.11
Phase 4 (2008–2009 to 2010–2011)	144	15.57	27.23	171.96	4.47	26.57	7.50	1.54	19.46

Extreme values above 365 days are excluded

		Paired differences							
					95% confidence interval of the difference				
		Mean	Standard deviation	Standard error mean	Lower	Upper	*t*	*df*	Significance (2-tailed)
Pair 1	Phase 1–Phase 2	.55238	16.02051	1.27452	−1.96504	3.06981	.433	157	0.665
Pair 2	Phase 3–Phase 4	.94467	27.27041	2.13598	−3.27329	5.16263	.442	162	0.659

Table 5.12 Frequency distribution related to holding period of finished goods inventory for the sample companies, 2001–2011 (Figures are in percentages)

Days	2001	2002	2003	2004	2005	2006	2007	2008	2009	2010	2011
Less than 5	37.30	40.14	41.38	45.27	47.74	48.41	51.85	50.31	52.15	51.23	26.85
5–15	16.67	19.71	21.38	16.90	18.06	17.19	16.66	17.79	20.25	20.99	24.07
15–25	18.25	15.49	17.24	20.95	18.71	18.47	14.20	14.11	14.11	12.96	24.07
25–50	22.22	18.31	15.86	12.84	11.61	14.01	12.96	14.11	11.04	11.11	17.59
Above 50	5.55	6.33	4.14	4.06	3.88	1.91	4.32	3.68	2.45	3.70	7.42
Total	100	100	100	100	100	100	100	100	100	100	100

duration of the GWCC, the larger is the need of working capital for a business enterprise. Therefore, it was considered useful to know the GWCC of the sample companies.

Relevant data in terms of mean, standard deviation, coefficient of variation, skewness, kurtosis, median and quartile values pertaining to GWCC have been presented in Table 5.19 for the aggregate period of the study (supported by t-test).

The length of the GWCC, prima facie, appears to be adequate (123 days) leading us to infer that the sample companies, in general, do not seem to carry a larger amount of working capital. This is supported by the moderate coefficient of variation amongst the sample values. These findings are, however, in sharp contrast to the GWCC of 291.03 days reported by the public sector undertakings in India over the period 1991–2003 (Jain and Yadav 2005) indicating perhaps lower level of professionalism in the sense of carrying a larger amount of working capital (than required). The net working capital cycle (GWCC – creditors' payment period) has been computed in the subsequent section (Table 5.20).

As per trend, it is encouraging to note that there has been a decrease in GWCC of the sample companies in the two subphases of the study. Statistically, however, the difference is not significant.

Section V Current Liabilities Management

Current liabilities form another significant component of working capital management. The major current liabilities arising in the normal course of business accrue from sundry creditors/trade credit. What is the creditors' payment period of the sample companies constitutes the subject matter of this section. Besides, this section also aims at ascertaining the impact of trade credit on working capital cycle. As a result of credit purchases of inventories, the gross working capital cycle gets reduced, referred to as net working capital cycle (NWCC).

Trade Credit/Trade Creditors

Trade credit represents credit extended by suppliers of goods and services in the normal course of business to the buyers/companies. Relevant data of the average

Table 5.13 Mean, standard deviation, coefficient of variation, skewness, kurtosis, median and quartile values of debtors' collection period (in days) of the sample companies, 2001–2011 (Figures are in days)

Year ending	Number	Mean	Standard deviation	Coefficient of variation (%)	Skewness	Kurtosis	Median	Quartile 1	Quartile 2
2001	125	73.11	54.18	74.11	1.11	1.33	64.98	33.26	97.65
2002	141	80.17	65.46	81.65	1.56	2.82	66.15	35.93	109.23
2003	143	73.28	66.25	90.40	1.91	4.57	52.33	29.36	102.30
2004	148	64.40	53.38	82.90	1.40	2.42	51.75	25.64	85.56
2005	155	61.21	52.88	86.40	1.63	3.56	48.91	22.33	85.77
2006	157	61.02	52.07	85.34	1.49	2.45	49.94	20.85	82.34
2007	161	67.88	63.09	92.95	1.77	4.08	51.81	21.95	93.07
2008	162	66.11	62.00	93.78	1.77	4.18	50.06	19.36	89.53
2009	163	62.18	54.51	87.67	1.25	1.22	49.57	17.82	86.38
2010	162	65.64	60.74	92.53	1.79	4.20	50.09	20.32	90.47
2011	159	63.03	57.38	91.03	1.51	3.00	47.88	19.69	89.05
2001–2011	152	67.09	58.36	87.16	1.56	3.08	53.04	24.23	91.94
Phase 1 (2000–2001 to 2005–2006)	149	68.87	57.37	83.46	1.52	2.86	55.68	27.89	93.81
Phase 2 (2006–2007 to 2010–2011)	161	64.97	59.54	91.59	1.62	3.34	49.88	19.83	89.70
Phase 3 (2006–2007 to 2007–2008)	162	66.99	62.54	93.36	1.77	4.13	50.94	20.66	91.30
Phase 4 (2008–2009 to 2010–2011)	161	63.61	57.54	90.41	1.52	2.81	49.18	19.28	88.63

		Paired differences							
					95% confidence interval of the difference				
		Mean	Standard deviation	Standard error mean	Lower	Upper	t	df	Significance (2-tailed)
Pair 1	Phase 1–Phase 2	4.01709	34.21153	2.72172	−1.35883	9.39301	1.476	157	0.142
Pair 2	Phase 3–Phase 4	2.67292	37.51578	2.93846	−3.12971	8.47555	.910	162	0.364

Table 5.14 Frequency distribution related to debtors collection period (in days) for the sample companies, 2001–2011 (Figures are in percentages)

Days	2001	2002	2003	2004	2005	2006	2007	2008	2009	2010	2011
Less than 30	23.81	20.98	25.52	29.56	32.26	35.03	35.80	37.42	37.42	34.57	38.65
30–60	20.63	27.28	29.66	22.64	29.03	26.75	17.90	17.18	18.41	24.07	19.63
60–90	23.02	16.08	13.79	25.79	16.13	16.56	18.52	20.86	22.70	16.05	15.34
90–120	11.90	15.38	11.03	6.92	10.97	10.83	12.96	9.20	8.59	10.49	9.82
120–180	14.29	12.59	13.10	10.69	7.74	7.64	7.41	8.59	7.98	9.88	10.43
Above 180	6.35	7.69	6.90	4.40	3.87	3.82	7.40	6.75	4.91	4.94	6.13
Total	100	100	100	100	100	100	100	100	100	100	100

Table 5.15 Ranking of the objectives of credit policy of the sample companies

Objectives of credit policy	1	2	3	4
Growth in sales	65.21 (43.47)	4.34	0.00	0.00
Match credit terms with that of competitors	26.08 (–)	0.00	4.34	0.00
Better credit terms than those of competitors	13.04 (–)	4.34	4.34	0.00
Any other[a]	17.39 (17.39)	0.00	0.00	0.00

Figures in brackets represent the opinion chosen exclusively. The same holds true for all tables
[a]Includes ‘fully covered by LC’, ‘driven by market conditions and brand strength’, ‘rebate given to customers as per norms’ and ‘match with credit risk’

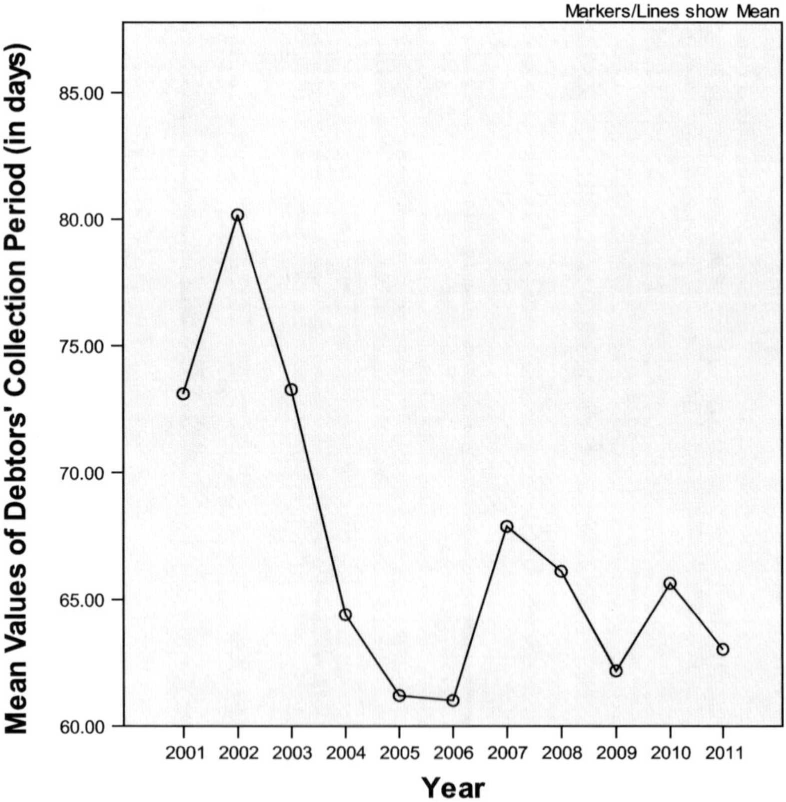

Fig. 5.6 Mean values of debtors collection period (in days) for the sample companies, 2001–2011

Table 5.16 Risk analysis of customers carried out before granting credit by the sample companies

Risk analysis of customers before granting credit	Percentage
Yes	100.00
No	0.00

Table 5.17 Preparation of ageing schedule of debtors by the sample companies

Preparation of ageing schedule of debtors	Percentage
Yes	100.00
No	0.00

Table 5.18 Schedule of receipt of payment from debtors by the sample companies

	Never	Infrequently	Frequently	Always
Before due date	0.00	44.82	31.03	10.34
On due date	0.00	3.44	68.96	17.24
After due date	0.00	51.72	17.24	3.44

period of credit (shown in Table 5.21) indicates that the sample companies have been extended credit for nearly 4 months. It may be recapitulated that debtors have been extended credit period of marginally higher than 2 months. In operational terms, the sample companies are favourably placed as they extend only half the period of credit to debtors compared to the period they receive from their creditors. This may perhaps be attributed to the fact that the sample companies are large, well-established companies enabling them to negotiate favourable credit terms from their suppliers.

As per the trend, though decrease has been noted in respect of creditors' payment period, the period still remained close to 4 months. Similar conclusions follow on the basis of frequency distribution (Table 5.22). For instance, more than three-fifths of the sample companies had creditors' payment period of more than 3 months.

It is worth noting here that the public sector undertakings in India over the period 1991–2003 (Jain and Yadav 2005) reported a creditors' payment period of less than 2 months (57.35 days) indicating unfavourable placement as far as their debtors' collection period (86.48 days) was concerned, an indication of a lower level of professionalism in the management of their credit policy (vis-à-vis the sample companies).

Given the fact that the net working capital cycle (GWCC credit availed from creditors) is a major determinant of the working capital needs of a business enterprise, it has been determined for the sample companies.

Table 5.19 Mean, standard deviation, coefficient of variation, skewness, kurtosis, median and quartile values of gross working capital cycle (in days) of the sample companies, 2001–2011

Year ending	Number	Mean	Standard deviation	Coefficient of variation (%)	Skewness	Kurtosis	Median	Quartile 1	Quartile 3
2001	114	141.99	82.52	58.11	1.30	1.85	123.74	86.88	178.95
2002	129	134.87	80.97	60.03	1.27	1.66	120.62	79.03	164.84
2003	129	135.65	90.14	66.45	1.57	2.71	113.74	77.82	171.95
2004	133	121.29	89.01	73.38	2.89	14.32	99.65	66.78	153.29
2005	139	118.72	77.54	65.31	2.06	8.60	103.56	64.96	148.85
2006	143	117.12	72.95	62.29	1.33	2.47	102.31	68.38	151.10
2007	144	121.98	91.02	74.62	2.27	8.75	100.71	59.19	150.51
2008	147	118.76	80.30	67.62	1.50	2.98	95.92	59.09	160.99
2009	148	119.47	90.37	75.65	1.74	4.05	91.61	56.92	153.13
2010	148	120.40	92.19	76.57	1.85	4.91	94.35	55.86	160.55
2011	145	123.00	93.64	76.13	1.57	2.68	101.18	60.00	169.81
2001–2011	131	124.84	85.51	68.74	1.76	5.00	104.31	66.81	160.36
Phase 1 (2000–2001 to 2005–2006)	129	128.27	82.19	64.26	1.74	5.27	110.60	73.97	161.50
Phase 2 (2006–2007 to 2010–2011)	146	120.72	89.51	74.12	1.78	4.67	96.75	58.21	159.00
Phase 3 (2006–2007 to 2007–2008)	146	120.37	85.66	71.12	1.88	5.87	98.32	59.14	155.75
Phase 4 (2008–2009 to 2010–2011)	147	120.95	92.07	76.12	1.72	3.88	95.71	57.59	161.16

Extreme values above 770 days are excluded

		Paired differences							
					95% confidence interval of the difference				
		Mean	Standard deviation	Standard error mean	Lower	Upper	*t*	*df*	Significance (2-tailed)
Pair 1	Phase 1–Phase 2	2.40678	50.94382	4.05287	–5.59841	10.41197	.594	157	0.553
Pair 2	Phase 3–Phase 4	4.39385	69.57664	5.44966	–6.36768	15.15539	.806	162	0.421

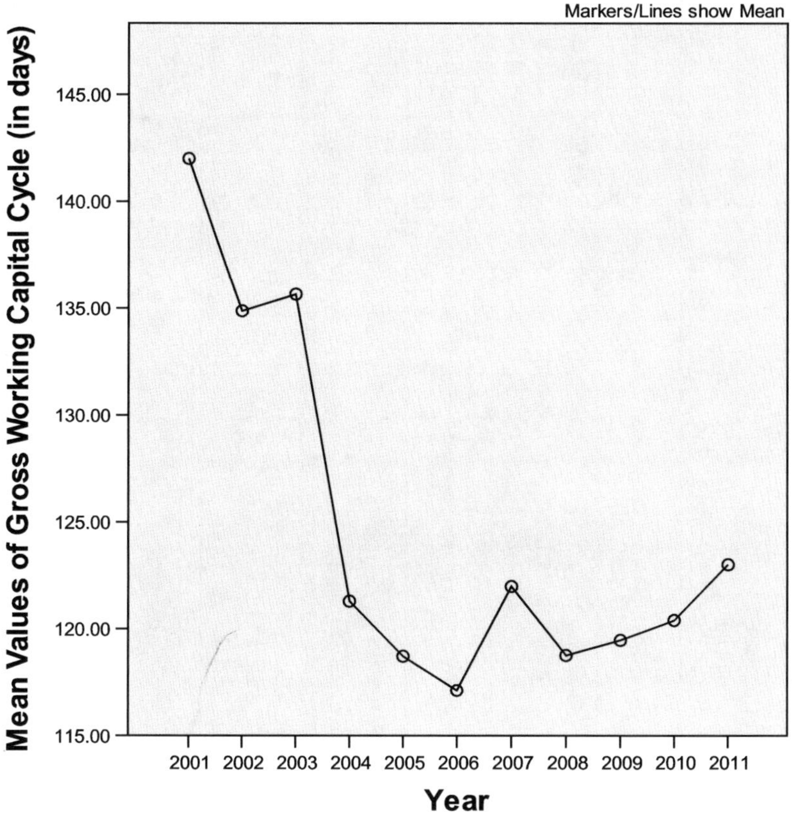

Fig. 5.7 Mean values of gross working capital cycle (in days) for the sample companies, 2001–2011

Table 5.20 Frequency distribution related to gross working capital cycle (in days) of the sample companies, 2001–2011 (Figures are in percentages)

Days	2001	2002	2003	2004	2005	2006	2007	2008	2009	2010	2011
Less than 60	13.04	15.04	15.04	20.74	21.28	19.44	25.00	25.17	26.32	28.29	24.50
60–120	33.04	33.08	38.35	42.96	36.17	44.44	35.14	33.11	33.55	34.21	35.76
120–180	27.83	30.83	24.06	15.56	22.70	18.75	18.92	23.18	16.45	15.13	14.57
180–240	13.91	8.28	9.03	14.82	12.76	7.64	9.46	9.27	13.81	10.53	9.93
Above 240	12.18	12.79	13.55	5.92	7.10	9.72	11.49	9.27	9.87	11.84	15.22
Total	100	100	100	100	100	100	100	100	100	100	100

Net Working Capital Cycle (NWCC)

Relevant data contained in Table 5.23 indicates that the sample companies have NWCC of less than 3 months. The high skewness and kurtosis also indicates that only very few companies report very high duration of the NWCC.

Table 5.21 Mean, standard deviation, coefficient of variation, skewness, kurtosis, median and quartile values of creditors payment period (in days) of the sample companies, 2001–2011

Year ending	Number	Mean	Standard deviation	Coefficient of variation (%)	Skewness	Kurtosis	Median	Quartile 1	Quartile 3
2001	80	96.38	83.95	87.11	0.92	0.36	106.70	62.88	171.86
2002	88	107.59	79.59	73.98	1.07	0.81	104.10	64.86	146.57
2003	88	114.23	79.12	69.26	1.09	0.89	98.99	66.20	155.33
2004	90	110.18	69.78	63.34	1.02	1.16	97.25	64.79	143.96
2005	99	108.89	66.86	61.40	1.10	1.25	95.63	62.08	132.30
2006	98	111.21	75.53	67.91	1.31	1.56	93.85	60.35	138.68
2007	98	114.91	76.21	66.32	1.00	0.33	91.41	54.08	146.91
2008	97	111.95	63.67	56.87	1.04	1.46	94.12	57.18	147.74
2009	97	105.72	69.70	65.93	1.28	1.40	87.77	52.99	132.99
2010	95	119.96	81.59	68.01	1.27	1.06	94.51	60.78	148.18
2011	94	107.24	71.03	66.24	0.99	1.02	93.81	50.38	139.42
2001–2011	90	109.84	74.28	67.85	1.10	1.03	96.19	59.69	145.81
Phase 1 (2000–2001 to 2005–2006)	90	108.08	75.81	70.50	1.09	1.01	99.42	63.53	148.12
Phase 2 (2006–2007 to 2010–2011)	96	111.96	72.44	64.67	1.12	1.05	92.32	55.08	143.05
Phase 3 (2006–2007 to 2007–2008)	98	113.43	69.94	61.60	1.02	0.89	92.77	55.63	147.32
Phase 4 (2008–2009 to 2010–2011)	96	110.97	74.11	66.73	1.18	1.16	92.03	54.72	140.19

Extreme values of above 365 days are excluded

		Paired differences							
					95% confidence interval of the difference				
		Mean	Standard deviation	Standard error mean	Lower	Upper	t	df	Significance (2-tailed)
Pair 1	Phase 1–Phase 2	5.21717	68.91654	5.48271	−5.61221	16.04655	.952	157	0.343
Pair 2	Phase 3–Phase 4	11.71587	82.57027	6.46740	−1.05542	24.48715	1.812	162	0.072

Table 5.22 Frequency distribution related to creditors payment period (in days) of the sample companies, 2001–2011 (Figures are in percentages)

Days	2001	2002	2003	2004	2005	2006	2007	2008	2009	2010	2011
Less than 30	10.11	24.17	6.06	8.91	7.41	7.55	11.11	8.04	11.71	9.43	12.39
30–60	7.87	10.00	12.12	9.90	13.89	14.15	12.04	15.18	15.32	11.32	12.39
60–90	22.47	11.67	19.19	15.84	22.22	22.64	20.37	17.86	20.72	19.81	14.16
90–120	11.24	17.50	15.15	21.78	20.37	16.98	13.89	14.29	14.41	17.92	18.58
120–180	20.22	15.00	20.20	16.83	14.81	16.98	18.52	24.11	13.51	17.92	15.04
180–365	17.98	12.50	16.16	15.84	12.96	14.15	14.81	7.14	11.71	13.21	10.62
Above 365	10.11	9.17	11.11	10.89	8.33	7.55	9.26	13.39	12.61	10.38	16.81
Total	100	100	100	100	100	100	100	100	100	100	100

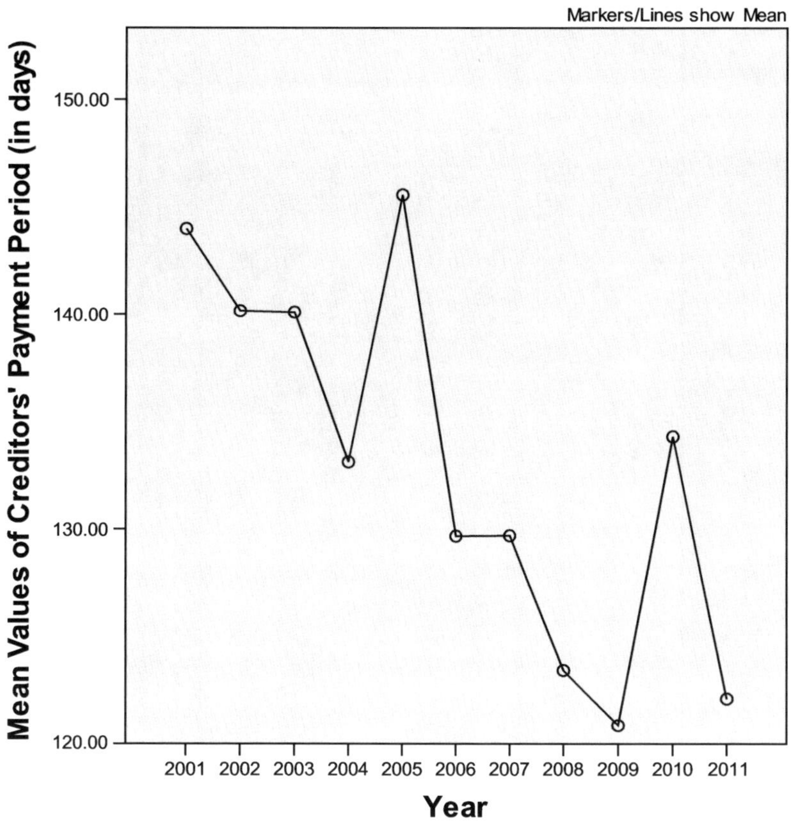

Fig. 5.8 Mean values of creditors payment period (in days) for the sample companies, 2001–2011

As per trend (Fig. 5.9), it is gratifying to note that the span of NWCC has declined in the sample companies. In fact, nearly half of the sample companies have a negative NWCC indicating that trade creditors finance their working capital needs (Table 5.24); these companies are not to arrange finances to meet their working capital requirements. Evidently, such firms are likely to register better/higher profitability.

Table 5.23 Mean, standard deviation, coefficient of variation, skewness, kurtosis, median and quartile values of net working capital cycle (in days) of the sample companies, 2001–2011

Year ending	Number	Mean	Standard deviation	Coefficient of variation (%)	Skewness	Kurtosis	Median	Quartile 1	Quartile 3
2001	49	77.65	62.01	79.85	1.33	1.51	61.24	31.86	96.79
2002	54	66.05	61.34	92.86	1.82	3.89	47.44	24.94	96.94
2003	55	68.29	57.83	84.69	1.31	1.46	50.97	24.45	95.78
2004	49	68.07	61.31	90.07	1.13	0.40	39.30	24.06	91.51
2005	56	69.81	55.23	79.11	0.55	−1.01	55.58	22.30	117.01
2006	55	69.74	60.66	86.98	1.14	0.91	56.10	24.66	107.87
2007	62	63.50	63.92	100.66	1.91	4.22	37.92	19.22	80.77
2008	56	73.55	68.51	93.15	1.85	4.13	54.66	22.86	92.36
2009	56	86.57	87.41	100.97	1.79	3.65	56.48	27.72	117.64
2010	56	73.20	86.38	118.01	2.62	8.83	50.50	23.14	91.48
2011	55	90.25	108.46	120.18	2.99	12.73	55.96	22.97	124.84
2001–2011	56	73.34	70.28	95.14	1.68	3.70	51.47	24.38	101.18
Phase 1 (2000–2001 to 2005–2006)	53	69.94	59.73	85.59	1.21	1.19	51.77	25.38	100.99
Phase 2 (2006–2007 to 2010–2011)	59	77.41	82.94	106.59	2.23	6.71	51.10	23.18	101.42
Phase 3 (2006–2007 to 2007–2008)	59	68.53	66.21	96.90	1.88	4.18	46.29	21.04	86.57
Phase 4 (2008–2009 to 2010–2011)	56	83.34	94.08	113.05	2.47	8.41	54.31	24.61	111.32

Extreme values above 770 days are excluded

		Paired differences							
					95% confidence interval of the difference				
		Mean	Standard deviation	Standard error mean	Lower	Upper	*t*	*df*	Significance (2-tailed)
Pair 1	Phase 1–Phase 2	−1.74218	85.92275	6.83565	−15.24387	11.75952	−.255	157	0.799
Pair 2	Phase 3–Phase 4	10.29940	89.63617	7.02085	−3.56477	24.16358	1.467	162	0.144

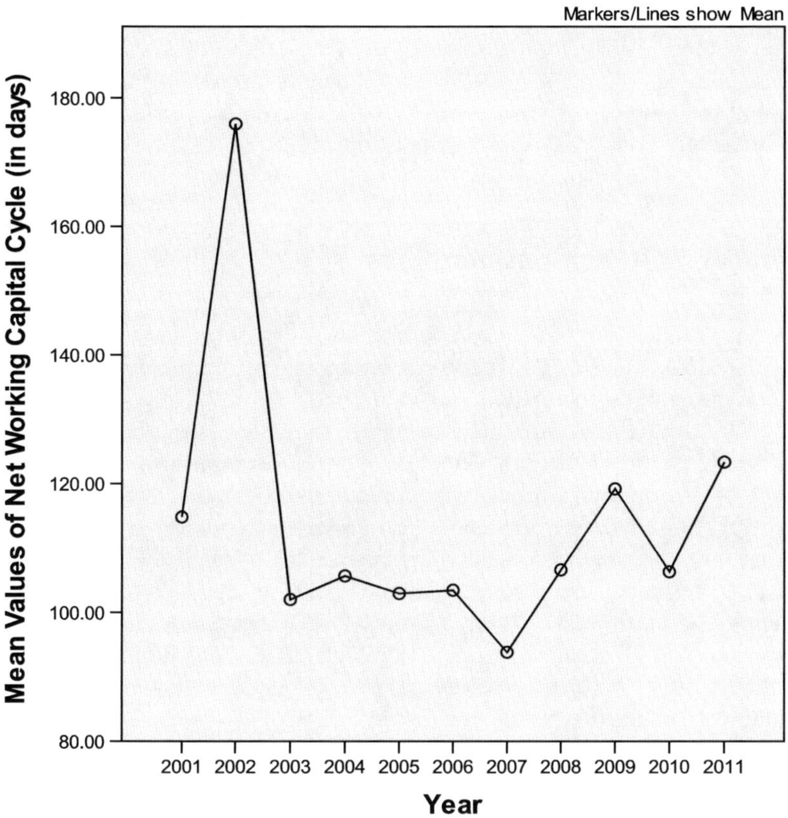

Fig. 5.9 Mean values of net working capital cycle (in days) for the sample companies, 2001–2011

Table 5.24 Frequency distribution related to net working capital cycle of the sample companies, 2001–2011 (Figures are in percentages)

Days	2001	2002	2003	2004	2005	2006	2007	2008	2009	2010	2011
Less than 0	44.32	45.45	44.44	52.48	48.15	48.11	41.12	48.65	49.09	47.17	48.62
0–60	26.14	29.29	30.30	27.72	26.85	27.36	37.38	28.83	27.27	31.13	26.61
60–120	21.59	18.18	17.17	7.92	13.89	12.26	10.28	11.71	10.91	13.21	11.01
120–180	3.41	3.03	4.04	8.91	10.19	9.43	7.48	7.21	5.45	3.77	7.34
Above 180	4.55	4.04	4.04	2.97	0.93	2.82	3.72	3.60	7.28	4.71	6.44
Total	100	100	100	100	100	100	100	100	100	100	100

In sum, it is reasonable to contend that the vast majority of the sample corporates do not seem to have 'excessive' investment in working capital. The reason for inference is that only less than one-tenth of the companies have NWCC span of more than 4 months. In brief, working capital investment (component of working capital management) is commendable.

It seems worthwhile to draw a comparison here with the NWCC of 242.72 days reported by the public sector undertakings in India (Jain and Yadav 2005) indicating that these companies have been saddled with long duration of NWCC, necessitating substantial working capital to be carried by them, eventually affecting their profitability adversely (vis-à-vis our the sample companies).

Section VI Other Considerations

The present section examines various other major policies pertaining to working capital decisions, such as its determination and financing, dealing with working capital surplus/shortage situations and so on.

As far as the basis of working capital determination is concerned, the survey indicates that a vast majority (85.71%) of the sample companies adopt a scientific approach of determining working capital requirements in that their computation is based on the individual components of current assets and current liabilities (with more than half of the companies adopting this method exclusively) indicating a high degree of professionalism in the estimation of working capital. This finds support in the findings of Barth et al. (2001), Ward (2004), Banomyong (2005) and Filbeck and Krueger (2005). 'Length of operating cycle' is the second most widely used method with little over one-fifth of the sample companies following it, followed by percentage of budgeted sales method (Table 5.25).

As far as company's policy towards financing working capital is concerned, 'hedging/matching approach' (permanent needs from long-term sources and temporary needs from short-term sources) is followed by the majority of the sample companies (Table 5.26). The findings find support in the findings of Jain and Kumar (1997), Jain and Yadav (2000) and Jain and Yadav (2005). Moreover, these findings are in conformity with sound theory of financial management. Net working capital requirements are, by and large, permanent in nature and hence need to be financed from long-term sources.

Another important aspect pertaining to working capital management is the ways of dealing with extraordinary/special situations, say, shortage and surplus of working

Table 5.25 Basis for working capital determination adopted by the sample companies

Basis for working capital determination	Percentage
Determination of individual components of current assets and current liabilities (based on raw material holding period, debtors' collection period, creditors' payment period and so on)	85.71(64.28)
Length of operating cycle	21.42 (–)
Percentage of budgeted sales	14.28(7.14)
Percentage of budgeted production	7.14 (3.57)
Any other	0.00 (–)

Table 5.26 Policy regarding financing of working capital adopted by the sample companies

Policy regarding financing of working capital	Percentage
Permanent needs from long-term sources and temporary/seasonal needs from short-term sources	51.85(51.85)
Mainly from short-term sources	25.92(18.51)
Temporary/seasonal needs from short-term sources and only for period needed	25.92(18.51)
Mainly from long-term sources	3.70 (3.70)
Any other	3.70 (3.70)

Table 5.27 Experiences pertaining to working capital shortage by the sample companies

Experience of working capital shortage	Percentage
Yes	17.24
No	82.75

Table 5.28 Reasons for working capital shortage of the sample companies

Reasons for working capital shortage	Percentage
Less than expected sales	75.00 (25.00)
Excess in inventories	50.00 (–)
Any other	25.00 (–)
Default from debtors	0.00 (–)

capital situations. This aspect assumes significance in view of the fact that howsoever sound may be the working capital planning, there is a likelihood of such situations to occur as the sample companies operate in highly uncertain, turbulent and dynamic environment.

The survey reveals that the majority of the sample companies have not experienced working capital shortage (Table 5.27). The findings are in contrast to the findings of Jain and Kumar (1997) and Jain and Yadav (2000) on private sector enterprises for the period 1985–1995 and 1991–1998, respectively, where a substantial six-tenths of the companies reported a working capital shortage occasionally.

These findings are in tune with sound financing policies followed by the majority of the sample companies as indicated by data contained in Table 5.26 as well as by adequate CR and ATR (Tables 5.1 and 5.3).

'Less than expected sales' is the major cause cited for working capital shortage (if any). It is worth mentioning here that 'excess in inventories' (the second probable cause for the sample companies as per Table 5.28) was the first cause reported by the private sector enterprises in the study of Jain and Kumar (1997) for the period 1985–1995 and that of Jain and Yadav (2000) for the period 1991–1998.

As far as the nature of working capital (WC) shortage is concerned, at the outset, it is useful to mention that a vast majority of the sample companies (82.75%) have responded to this question by stating that it is not applicable to them. In operational

Table 5.29 Terms of lending in emergency situations for the sample companies

Terms of lending in emergency situations	Percentage
At normal rate of interest	73.68
At more than normal rate of interest	15.78
Any other	10.52

Table 5.30 Experiences pertaining to surplus working capital situation in the sample companies

Excess working capital situation	Percentage
Yes	74.07
No	25.92

Table 5.31 Mode of utilisation of surplus working capital by the sample companies

Use of the excess working capital	Percentage
Temporarily invested (in marketable securities)	90.00 (70.00)
Utilised for repayment of debt	20.00 (–)
Invested in fixed assets	10.00 (5.00)
Any other	5.00 (5.00)
Invested in long-term securities	0.00 (–)

terms, this response signifies that the sample corporate, by and large, seems to carry required working capital (helping to avoid situations entailing working capital shortage) (Table 5.29).

Equally significant observation from the survey is that majority of the sample companies have experienced excess working capital situations (Table 5.30). The vast majority (90%) of the sample companies mention that such funds are temporarily invested (Table 5.31). This finding is in tune with sound finance theory as surplus working capital is, by and large, seasonal or temporary in nature and, therefore, not normally available (and hence should not be deployed) in financing long-term assets or investments in long-term securities.

The findings are similar to the findings of Jain and Kumar (1997) and Jain and Yadav (2000) on private sector enterprises for the period 1985–1995 where more than two-thirds companies reported a similar situation. However, the primary utilisation of the surplus working capital was in the repayment of debt unlike the sample companies where only one-fifth of the sample companies utilise their working capital in paying off debt. This shift may also be due to the fact that debt as a source of finance is gradually decreasing over time in Indian corporate (for more insight, kindly refer to Chap. 3 on capital structure).

These findings, however, are in contrast with the findings of Jain and Yadav (2005) on public sector undertakings where nearly six-tenths of the sample companies (58.33%) did not report an excess working capital situation.

Section VII Components of Current Assets

As a part of the disaggregative analysis, this section attempts to ascertain the relative share of each major current asset, namely, cash and bank, inventory and receivables to the total current assets in order to determine the composition of current assets.

Mean, standard deviation, coefficient of variation, skewness, kurtosis, median and quartile values of percentage of cash and bank to total current assets, percentage of inventory to total current assets and percentage of debtors and bills receivables to total current assets have been presented in Tables 5.32, 5.34 and 5.36, respectively. Similarly, their corresponding frequency distributions have been presented in Tables 5.33, 5.35 and 5.37, respectively.

It is useful to note here that the ‘cash and bank’ component denotes the ‘cash and cash equivalents’. Cash equivalents include short-term deposits (of less than 3 months) and investment in marketable securities. This point should be borne in mind while interpreting the results based on carrying cash and bank balances.

Cash and bank balances constitute nearly one-fifth of the total current assets (Table 5.32) with more than half of the sample companies reporting this (Table 5.33). There has also been a statistically significant decrease in the holding of current assets in the form of cash in phase 2 over phase 1 of the study (as per the t-test) indicating growing professionalism in cash management over the period of the study (as cash is a ‘nonearning’ asset).

Inventory constitutes nearly one-fourth of the total current assets (Table 5.34). The findings are significant as they are indicative of lesser holding of inventory when compared to the findings of Jain and Kumar (1997) on private sector enterprises for the period 1985–1995, where the average was nearly four-tenths of total current assets (39.39%), and to the findings of Jain and Yadav (2000) on private sector enterprises for the period 1991–1998 that also reported nearly the same figures (40.78%).

There has been a marked decrease in the percentage of debtors and bills receivables as components of current assets over the period of the study for all the four phases (as evidenced by the paired t-tests). More than half of the sample companies have reported to hold less than 20% of their current assets in the form of debtors since 2008, perhaps an indication of tightening collection norms and credit policy as an aftermath of the recession (Table 5.37).

There has been a notable decrease in the percentage share of debtors to total current assets when viewed against the findings of Jain and Kumar (1997) on private sector enterprises for the period 1985–1995, when one-third of the total current assets (33.28%) were held in the form of debtors and bills receivables. A similar case is made when the findings are compared with the findings of Jain and Yadav (2000) on private sector enterprises and Jain and Yadav (2005) on public sector undertakings.

However, when viewed in the entirety of the study period, the reduction in the relative share of debtors in the current assets appears to be a uniform trend for the sample companies.

Table 5.32 Mean, standard deviation, coefficient of variation, skewness, kurtosis, median and quartile values of percentage of cash and bank to total current assets of the sample companies, 2001–2011

Year ending	Number	Mean	Standard deviation	Coefficient of variation (%)	Skewness	Kurtosis	Median	Quartile 1	Quartile 3
2001	143	13.47	17.91	132.92	2.61	7.76	7.16	2.81	17.63
2002	149	14.32	16.39	114.42	1.92	3.52	8.14	3.17	19.79
2003	154	14.02	17.06	121.65	2.20	5.52	6.72	3.54	18.94
2004	155	17.54	20.06	114.36	1.82	3.51	8.74	3.40	23.17
2005	159	21.99	23.66	107.58	1.41	1.53	12.68	3.73	34.30
2006	161	20.54	20.07	97.72	1.18	0.49	12.56	5.43	31.56
2007	163	23.08	23.30	100.97	1.35	1.04	13.40	5.52	33.97
2008	166	21.13	21.93	103.79	1.22	0.52	10.83	4.90	34.47
2009	166	23.28	22.42	96.30	1.00	0.11	15.34	4.19	35.56
2010	163	22.15	21.77	98.30	1.10	0.46	14.99	3.52	33.72
2011	165	21.06	22.22	105.47	1.30	0.94	13.43	3.36	30.68
2001–2011	154	19.33	20.62	108.50	1.55	2.31	11.27	3.96	28.53
Phase 1 (2000–2001 to 2005–2006)	152	16.98	19.19	114.78	1.86	3.72	9.33	3.68	24.23
Phase 2 (2006–2007 to 2010–2011)	164	22.14	22.33	100.97	1.19	0.61	13.60	4.30	33.68
Phase 3 (2006–2007 to 2007–2008)	165	22.10	22.62	102.38	1.29	0.78	12.12	5.21	34.22
Phase 4 (2008–2009 to 2010–2011)	165	22.16	22.13	100.02	1.13	0.50	14.58	3.69	33.32

		Paired differences							
					95% confidence interval of the difference				
		Mean	Standard deviation	Standard error mean	Lower	Upper	*t*	*df*	Significance (2-tailed)
Pair 1	Phase 1–Phase 2	−3.88204	15.66900	1.23107	−6.31317	−1.45091	−3.153	161	.002
Pair 2	Phase 3–Phase 4	−.02621	14.94995	1.16034	−2.31724	2.26482	−.023	165	.982

Table 5.33 Frequency distribution related to percentage of cash and bank to total current assets of the sample companies, 2001–2011 (Figures are in percentages)

Cash and bank (%)	2001	2002	2003	2004	2005	2006	2007	2008	2009	2010	2011
Less than 10	61.54	56.38	61.04	54.25	47.80	43.48	38.65	47.59	43.37	41.10	41.21
10–20	16.08	18.79	15.58	15.69	10.69	19.88	23.93	15.66	11.45	14.72	22.42
20–40	14.69	16.11	14.94	15.69	20.13	19.88	17.18	16.27	24.10	24.54	18.18
40–60	3.50	4.70	4.55	11.11	13.21	9.94	10.43	11.45	11.45	11.66	9.70
Above 60	4.20	4.03	3.90	3.27	8.18	6.83	9.82	9.04	9.64	7.97	8.48
Total	100	100	100	100	100	100	100	100	100	100	100

Table 5.34 Mean, standard deviation, coefficient of variation, skewness, kurtosis, median and quartile values of percentage of inventory to total current assets of the sample companies, 2001–2011

Year ending	Number	Mean	Standard deviation	Coefficient of variation (%)	Skewness	Kurtosis	Median	Quartile 1	Quartile 3
2001	143	26.26	20.78	79.12	0.72	0.20	24.66	8.97	38.92
2002	149	24.67	20.57	83.38	0.86	0.47	22.37	7.67	36.99
2003	154	24.34	20.28	83.31	0.67	−0.18	22.62	6.37	37.44
2004	155	25.37	20.66	81.45	0.69	0.21	24.04	6.20	37.82
2005	159	25.62	21.08	82.30	0.54	−0.50	23.80	5.55	41.85
2006	161	23.75	19.89	83.75	0.50	−0.86	20.28	4.73	40.35
2007	163	23.54	20.29	86.21	0.68	−0.38	19.29	5.18	37.84
2008	166	23.12	20.56	88.96	0.82	−0.11	19.08	5.72	34.11
2009	166	22.10	19.19	86.83	0.81	0.21	19.39	4.94	34.34
2010	163	22.68	20.52	90.47	0.80	−0.21	18.69	4.48	35.02
2011	165	22.76	20.59	90.46	0.78	−0.40	17.87	5.01	35.54
2001–2011	154	24.02	20.40	85.11	0.71	−0.14	21.10	5.89	37.29
Phase 1 (2000–2001 to 2005–2006)	152	25.00	20.55	82.22	0.66	−0.11	22.96	6.58	38.90
Phase 2 (2006–2007 to 2010–2011)	164	22.84	20.23	88.59	0.78	−0.18	18.86	5.07	35.37
Phase 3 (2006–2007 to 2007–2008)	165	23.33	20.43	87.59	0.75	−0.25	19.18	5.45	35.97
Phase 4 (2008–2009 to 2010–2011)	165	22.51	20.10	89.25	0.80	-0.13	18.65	4.81	34.96

		Paired differences							
					95% confidence interval of the difference				
		Mean	Standard deviation	Standard error mean	Lower	Upper	*t*	*df*	Significance (2-tailed)
Pair 1	Phase 1–Phase 2	1.02244	11.03442	.86695	−.68961	2.73449	1.179	161	0.240
Pair 2	Phase 3–Phase 4	.71486	7.64618	.59346	−.45689	1.88661	1.205	165	0.230

Table 5.35 Frequency distribution related to percentage of inventory to total current assets of the sample companies, 2001–2011 (Figures are in percentages)

Inventories to total current assets (%)	2001	2002	2003	2004	2005	2006	2007	2008	2009	2010	2011
Less than 10	26.57	28.86	31.82	29.03	30.19	32.92	33.74	34.34	34.34	36.81	35.15
10–20	16.08	15.44	14.94	15.48	15.72	16.77	17.18	16.27	17.47	18.40	17.58
20–30	16.78	18.12	16.88	14.19	15.09	13.66	11.04	18.67	16.27	11.66	15.76
30–40	16.08	16.78	13.64	17.42	11.95	11.18	15.34	10.84	12.05	12.88	9.70
40–60	17.48	14.77	17.53	18.06	21.38	20.50	16.56	12.65	17.47	14.72	14.55
Above 60	6.99	6.04	5.20	5.81	5.66	4.97	6.13	7.22	2.40	5.52	7.27
Total	100	100	100	100	100	100	100	100	100	100	100

Table 5.36 Mean, standard deviation, coefficient of variation, skewness, kurtosis, median and quartile values of percentage of debtors and bills receivables to total current assets of the sample companies, 2001–2011

Year ending	Number	Mean	Standard deviation	Coefficient of variation (%)	Skewness	Kurtosis	Median	Quartile 1	Quartile 3
2001	142	27.67	17.73	64.06	0.37	−0.48	27.05	13.69	40.05
2002	148	28.56	17.35	60.76	0.36	−0.48	27.51	16.88	37.96
2003	153	27.70	18.56	67.00	0.48	−0.28	26.79	12.33	39.78
2004	154	26.53	18.75	70.68	0.89	1.10	24.01	11.66	37.32
2005	158	24.77	17.54	70.80	0.74	−0.04	20.87	12.02	35.70
2006	160	23.48	16.97	72.28	0.81	0.33	21.42	10.00	33.65
2007	162	23.61	17.06	72.26	0.62	−0.20	20.57	10.05	36.06
2008	165	22.51	16.85	74.86	0.73	−0.22	19.66	9.10	32.98
2009	165	20.82	15.46	74.25	0.66	−0.40	16.89	8.70	33.25
2010	162	20.56	14.88	72.38	0.80	0.10	17.99	9.10	29.72
2011	164	20.18	15.31	75.88	0.88	0.42	17.36	8.23	30.00
2001–2011	154	24.22	16.95	70.47	0.67	−0.01	21.83	11.07	35.13
Phase 1 (2000–2001 to 2005–2006)	151	26.45	17.82	67.60	0.61	0.02	24.61	12.76	37.41
Phase 2 (2006–2007 to 2010–2011)	164	21.54	15.91	73.93	0.74	−0.06	18.49	9.04	32.40
Phase 3 (2006–2007 to 2007–2008)	164	23.06	16.95	73.56	0.68	−0.21	20.12	9.57	34.52
Phase 4 (2008–2009 to 2010–2011)	164	20.52	15.22	74.17	0.78	0.04	17.41	8.68	30.99

		Paired differences							
					95% confidence interval of the difference				
		Mean	Standard deviation	Standard error mean	Lower	Upper	*t*	*df*	Significance (2-tailed)
Pair 1	Phase 1–Phase 2	4.23393	10.80751	.84912	2.55709	5.91078	4.986	161	0.000
Pair 2	Phase 3–Phase 4	2.55887	9.04774	.70224	1.17233	3.94541	3.644	165	0.000

Table 5.37 Frequency distribution related to percentage of debtors and bills receivables to total current assets of the sample companies, 2001–2011 (Figures are in percentages)

Debtors and bills receivables to total current assets (%)	2001	2002	2003	2004	2005	2006	2007	2008	2009	2010	2011
Less than 20	35.66	34.23	35.06	43.23	47.80	47.20	48.47	50.60	56.02	55.21	56.97
20–40	39.16	42.95	40.26	34.84	33.33	37.89	34.97	33.13	28.31	31.29	32.73
40–60	21.68	18.12	20.13	17.42	13.84	11.80	14.11	14.46	14.46	12.27	8.48
Above 60	3.50	4.70	4.55	4.52	5.03	3.11	2.45	1.81	1.20	1.23	1.82
Total	100	100	100	100	100	100	100	100	100	100	100

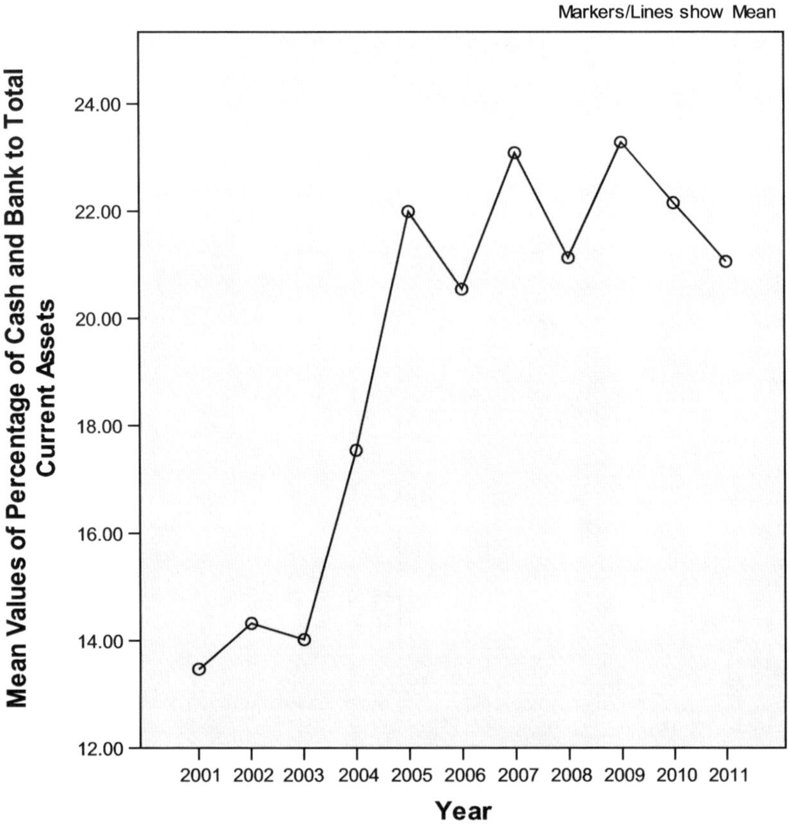

Fig. 5.10 Mean values of percentage of cash and bank to total current assets of the sample companies, 2001–2011

In sum, it appears that the components of cash and bank, inventory and debtors and bills receivables account for more than 60% of the total current assets for the sample companies indicating a high degree of advances payments and/or prepaid expenses in the balance sheets of the companies.

Section VIII Zero Working Capital

The proponents of the concept of zero working capital define it as inventories + receivables − payables = 0. The rationale is inventories and receivables contribute to sales and inventories can be financed from the payables. Though zero working capital is not an easy target to be achieved for most of the business firms, there could

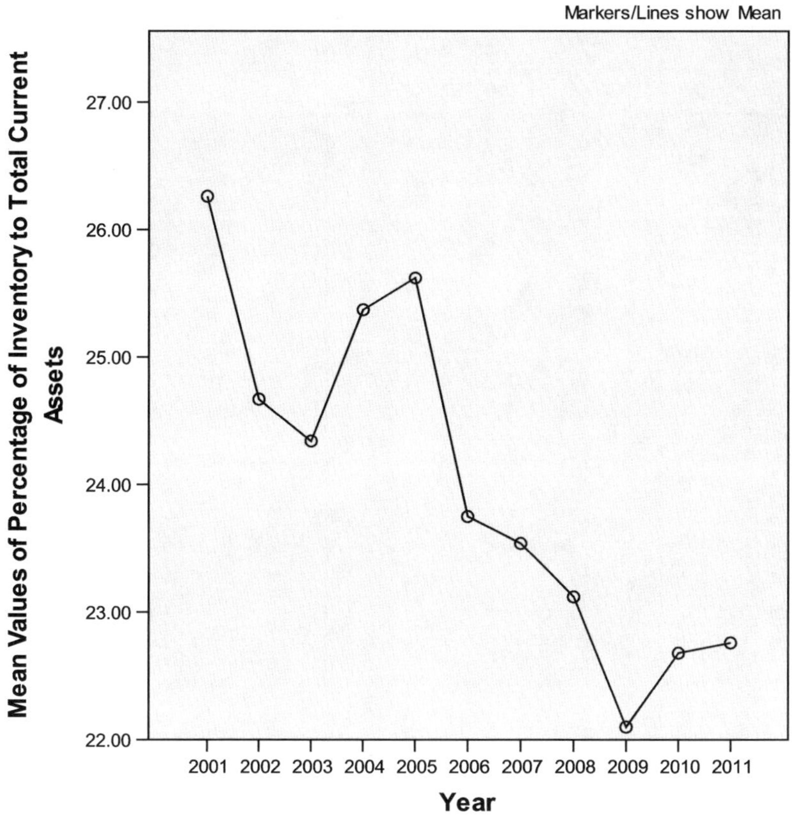

Fig. 5.11 Mean values of percentage of inventory to total current assets of the sample companies, 2001–2011

still be a focus on minimising the investment in working capital to achieve financial and production economies (Fig. 5.13).

The frequency distribution (Table 5.39) is the most revealing in this regard. The sample companies have increasingly become more aggressive in managing their working capital with more than one-fourth companies operating at a zero working capital ratio of less than 1 in 2011, up from 14.18% in 2001. These changes are statistically significant as per the paired t-test (Table 5.38) throughout the period of the study. Even though the statistics supporting zero working capital seem modest, the trend does support growing aggressiveness/professionalism in the management of working capital by the sample companies. Future studies would perhaps be a better indicator of whether the concept of zero working capital would become more popular in the years to come. The finding of this section is an attempt to contribute to the sparse literature available on the concept of zero working capital and its practice amongst companies.

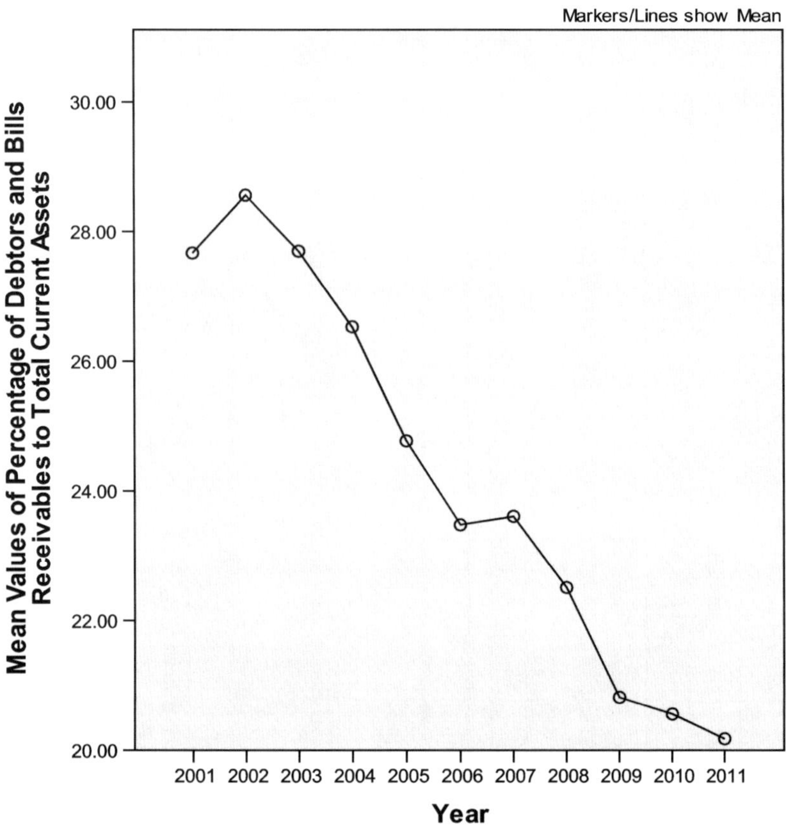

Fig. 5.12 Mean values of percentage of debtors and bills receivables to total current assets of the sample companies, 2001–2011

Section IX Sector-Wise Analysis

A summary of how the constituent sectors fare at the varied aspects of working capital management has been presented in this section.

Current Ratio

The current ratio of the constituent sectors (for details on sectors, refer to Table 1.2, Chap. 1) of the sample companies remained stable throughout the period of the study. The healthcare sector had the highest average ratio at 2.61 in

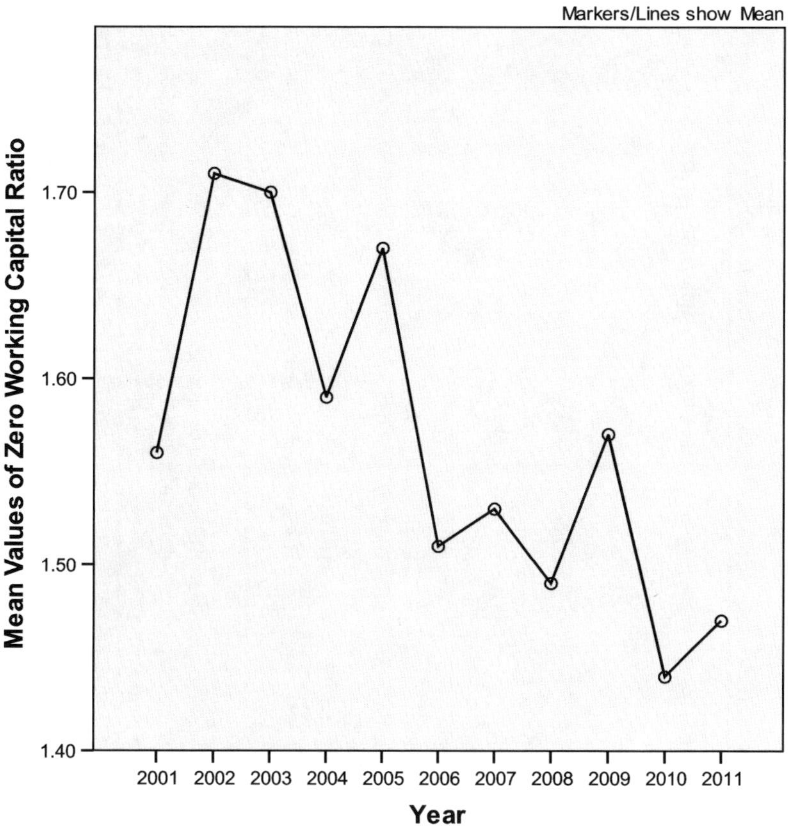

Fig. 5.13 Mean values of zero working capital ratio of the sample companies, 2001–2011

phase 1 (for details, refer to Appendix 5.1). The sectors that increased liquidity in phase 2 over phase 1 were healthcare, housing, metals, oil and gas, power and miscellaneous. The sectors that reduced liquidity in phase 4 over phase 3 were diversified, FMCG, housing, metals, transport and miscellaneous (Appendix 5.2). However, there were no statistically significant changes in mean values of current ratios for any of the sectors over the period of the study. The ANOVA test (Appendix 5.3) also does not indicate any statistically significant difference amongst the variances for any constituent sectors but does so for the sample as a whole. Thus, the sample companies seem to have maintained stable liquidity positions for the period of the study in spite of the recession over phase 4. These findings are in tune with RBI's view of the resilience of the Indian economy (Appendix 2.1, Chap. 2).

Table 5.38 Mean, standard deviation, coefficient of variation, skewness, kurtosis, median and quartile values of zero working capital ratio of the sample companies, 2001–2011

Year ending	Number	Mean	Standard deviation	Coefficient of variation (%)	Skewness	Kurtosis	Median	Quartile 1	Quartile 3
2001	78	1.56	0.73	46.82	–0.31	–0.43	1.64	1.02	2.09
2002	87	1.54	0.83	53.43	–0.21	–0.79	1.60	0.96	2.20
2003	96	1.58	0.81	51.27	–0.21	–0.69	1.60	1.11	2.18
2004	109	1.59	0.80	50.49	–0.25	–0.87	1.56	1.05	2.27
2005	107	1.67	0.78	46.74	0.10	0.31	1.70	1.13	2.21
2006	109	1.51	0.76	50.23	–0.08	–0.56	1.57	1.02	2.00
2007	115	1.53	0.76	49.90	–0.01	–0.71	1.52	0.99	2.17
2008	114	1.49	0.79	52.96	–0.03	–0.82	1.46	0.92	2.10
2009	114	1.45	0.80	55.41	0.04	–0.88	1.37	0.81	2.03
2010	111	1.44	0.76	52.98	0.08	–0.56	1.45	0.87	1.97
2011	118	1.47	0.78	53.28	0.05	–0.96	1.47	0.82	2.04
2001–2011	98	1.53	0.78	51.23	–0.08	–0.63	1.54	0.97	2.11
Phase 1 (2000–2001 to 2005–2006)	94	1.58	0.79	49.83	–0.16	–0.50	1.61	1.05	2.16
Phase 2 (2006–2007 to 2010–2011)	115	1.48	0.78	52.91	0.03	–0.74	1.46	0.88	2.06
Phase 3 (2006–2007 to 2007–2008)	115	1.51	0.78	51.43	–0.02	–0.77	1.49	0.96	2.13
Phase 4 (2008–2009 to 2010–2011)	115	1.45	0.78	53.89	0.06	–0.80	1.43	0.83	2.01

		Paired differences							
					95% confidence interval of the difference				
		Mean	Standard deviation	Standard error mean	Lower	Upper	*t*	*df*	Significance (2-tailed)
Pair 1	Phase 1–Phase 2	2.81465	9.62039	.58013	1.67257	3.95673	4.852	274	0.000
Pair 2	Phase 3–Phase 4	2.04812	8.67276	.52879	1.00702	3.08923	3.873	268	0.000

Table 5.39 Frequency distribution related to zero working capital ratio of the sample companies, 2001–2011 (Figures are in percentages)

Zero working capital ratio	2001	2002	2003	2004	2005	2006	2007	2008	2009	2010	2011
Less than 1.0	14.18	17.73	15.18	17.68	14.38	16.66	18.75	20.74	20.74	23.42	26.09
1.0–1.5	11.19	9.22	15.17	17.01	14.38	15.38	16.88	15.85	16.46	12.66	11.18
1.5–2.0	17.91	12.77	13.10	12.93	13.73	20.51	15.00	14.63	14.02	18.35	16.15
2.0–3.0	15.67	21.28	22.07	26.53	26.80	17.31	21.25	18.90	17.68	14.56	19.88
Above 3.0	41.04	39.01	34.48	25.85	30.72	30.13	28.13	29.88	31.10	31.01	26.71
Total	100	100	100	100	100	100	100	100	100	100	100

Acid-Test Ratio

The acid-test ratio of the constituent sectors of the sample companies remained well above 1 throughout the period of the study. The only sector to report an ATR of less than 1 in phase 2 over phase 1 was the FMCG sector (Appendix 5.4). It continued to be the only sector with an ATR of less than 1 in phases 3 and 4 as well (Appendix 5.5). However, there were no statistically significant changes in mean values of acid-test ratios for any of the sectors over the period of the study except for housing in phases 1 and 2. The ANOVA test (Appendix 5.6) does indicate a statistically significant difference amongst the variances for the sample as a whole but not for any of the constituent sectors, throughout the period of the study. Thus, the sample companies seem to have maintained stable liquidity position for the period of the study in spite of the recession during phase 4.

Holding Period (in Days) for Raw Material and Spare Parts (RMSP) Inventory

The RMSP inventory holding period of the constituent sectors of the sample companies presents a wide variation (as is expected due to the vastly different nature of each sector from each other). The metals sector had the highest holding period for RMSP in phase 1 at 34.14 days which further increased to 36.85 days in phase 4. The internet and communications technology (ICT) sector had the lowest RMSP holding at 1.02 days in phase 1 (Appendix 5.7). Power sector decreased its RMSP holding from 16.50 days in phase 3 to 12.48 days in phase 4 which was statistically significant (Appendix 5.8). The sectors that reported a RMSP holding of more than 30 days over phases 3 and 4 were capital goods, healthcare, metals and oil and gas. The ANOVA test (Appendix 5.9) does report a statistically significant difference amongst the variances for the sample as a whole but not for any of the constituent sectors.

Holding Period (in Days) for Work-in-Process (WIP) Inventory

As with the RMSP inventory holding, the WIP inventory holding period for the constituent sectors exhibits a large variation. Housing sector had the highest WIP holding at 30.41 days in phase 1 which went up to 49.40 days in phase 2. ICT sector went down to 1.06 days in phase 2 from 2.25 days in phase 1. Oil and gas sector went up to 1.63 days in phase 2 from 1.16 days in phase 1. Power sector remained the lowest with WIP holding of 0.95 day in phase 1 which went down to 0.36 day in phase 2 (Appendix 5.10). The housing sector reported a rather high WIP inventory holding of 62.43 days in phase 3 which reduced to 40.71 in phase 4 (Appendix 5.11).

There were statistically significant changes in mean values of WIP holding period for the transport sector over phases 1 and 2. The ANOVA test (Appendix 5.12), however, indicated a statistically significant difference amongst the variances for the sample as a whole, though not for any of the constituent sectors.

Holding Period (in Days) for Finished Goods (FG) Inventory

Continuing with the RMSP and WIP inventory holding, the FG inventory holding period for the constituent sectors presents a large variation. The miscellaneous sector had the largest FG holding of 33.47 days in phase 1 (Appendix 5.13). The FMCG sector reported the highest FG holding of 31.42 days in phase 3 (Appendix 5.14). There were, however, no statistically significant changes in mean values of FG holding period for the constituent sectors over the period of the study. The ANOVA test (Appendix 5.15) indicated a statistically significant difference amongst the variances for the sample as a whole.

Debtors' Collection Period (in Days)

Like the inventory holding period, the debtors' collection period (DCP) continued to vary with the constituent sectors. The longest DCP was 118.11 days for the capital goods sector in phase 1 while the shortest was 27.28 days for the FMCG sector during the same phase (Appendix 5.16). Notable changes in mean values came in phase 1 for the diversified sector which brought down its DCP to 46.82 days in phase 2 from 62.63 days in phase 1, the housing sector which on the other hand, increased its DCP from 52.67 days in phase 1 to 71.43 days in phase 2, the ICT sector which brought down its DCP from 106.03 days in phase 1 to 87.18 days in phase 2 and the metals sector brought down its DCP from 51.75 days in phase 1 to 34.73 days in phase 2. All these changes were statistically significant. The ANOVA test (Appendix 5.18) indicated a statistically significant difference amongst the variances for the sample as a whole for DCP, though not for any of the constituent sectors. Overall, there appears to be a conscious effort made by the sample companies in decreasing their DCP.

Gross Working Capital Cycle (in Days)

The gross working capital cycle (GWCC) for the capital goods sector increased from 192.36 days in phase 1 to 214.17 days in phase 2 and from a mean of 195.77 days in phase 3 to 226.43 days in phase 4. Sectors that reported a decrease in mean values of GWCC in phase 2 over phase 1 were FMCG, healthcare, ICT, metals, power, transport and miscellaneous (Appendix 5.19). Similarly, the sectors that reported reductions in their GWCC in phase 4 over phase 3 were diversified, healthcare, housing, ICT, transport and miscellaneous (Appendix 5.20). Out of these, the changes in metals sector's GWCC were statistically significant for phases 1 and 2 and for the capital goods sector for phases 3 and 4. The ANOVA test (Appendix 5.21) indicated a statistically significant difference amongst the variances for the sample as a whole only.

Creditors' Payment Period (in Days)

Similar to the debtors' collection period, the creditors' payment period (CPP) continued to vary between approximately 2–6 months amongst the constituent sectors. The longest CPP was 165.36 days for the housing sector in phase 1 (Appendix 5.22). The capital goods, diversified, FMCG, housing, metals, oil and gas and transport sectors brought down their CPP in phase 2 over phase 1. The healthcare, housing and metals sector increased their CPP in phase 4 over phase 3 while capital goods, diversified, FMCG, ICT, oil and gas, transport and miscellaneous sectors reduced their CPP (Appendix 5.23). None of these changes were statistically significant. The ANOVA test (Appendix 5.24) indicated a statistically significant difference amongst the variances for the sample as a whole for CPP and not for any of the constituent sectors.

Net Working Capital Cycle (in Days)

The net working capital cycle (NWCC) reduced in phase 2 over phase 1 for the diversified, FMCG, ICT, oil and gas, transport and miscellaneous sectors (Appendix 5.25). On the other hand, the sectors that reported an increase in their NWCC in phase 4 over phase 3 were capital goods, housing, transport and miscellaneous (Appendix 5.26). This perhaps indicates the effect of recession in reducing the operational efficiency of the said sectors. Out of these, however, none of the changes were statistically significant. The ANOVA test (Appendix 5.27) indicated a statistically significant difference amongst the variances in the NWCC for the sample as a whole, only.

Percentage of Cash and Bank to Total Current Assets

The percentage of cash and bank to total current assets was expectedly 26.18 for the ICT (with low required investments in operations) sector and surprisingly low at 9.03% for the healthcare sector in phase 1 (Appendix 5.28). In perhaps an indication of cash lying idle in phase 2 (with recession impacting in subphase 4), FMCG increased cash holdings from 8.84 to 15.11%, metals reported increase from 13.59 to 23.49% and miscellaneous sector reported an increase in cash holdings from 14.71 to 20.93%. Similarly, in phase 4 over phase 3, the diversified sector increased cash component from 12.02 to 14.73%, FMCG from 10.43 to 18.23% and power from 32.84 to 34.80%. Housing sector, on the other hand, reduced the component of cash from 21.98 to 14.14% during the same period (Appendix 5.29). Out of these, the changes in FMCG, metals and miscellaneous sectors were statistically significant for phase 2 over phase 1 and for the FMCG and housing sectors in phase 4 over phase 3. The ANOVA test (Appendix 5.30) indicated a statistically significant difference amongst the variances, only for the sample.

Percentage of Inventories to Total Current Assets

Expectedly, FMCG continued to be the sector with the highest percentage of inventories to total current assets throughout the period of the study. Its share of inventories increased from 36.40% of total current assets in phase 1 to 41.52% in phase 2, reducing from 42.77% in phase 3 to 40.70% in phase 4 (Appendix 5.31). In perhaps an indication of the growing retail segment in the country, ICT (the sector with the lowest percentage of inventories to total current assets due to the nature of its business) decreased its inventories to total current assets share from 2.39% in phase 1 to 1.38% in phase 2. The other sectors that reported reduced inventories in phase 2 over phase 1 were housing, healthcare, metals, power, transport and miscellaneous. The sectors that increased inventories in phase 4 over phase 3 (perhaps due to the onset of recession in phase 4) were housing, ICT and miscellaneous (Appendix 5.32). Out of these, the changes in the housing sector were statistically significant for phase 4 over phase 3. The ANOVA test (Appendix 5.33) indicated a statistically significant difference amongst the variances for the sample as a whole.

Percentage of Debtors and Bills Receivables to Total Current Assets

Debtors continued to be an important constituent of current assets with the percentage of debtors and bills receivables to total current assets being the highest for the capital goods sector at 41.43% in phase 1 with the oil and gas sector reporting the lowest percentage of debtors and bills receivables to total current assets at 14.67% for the same period (Appendix 5.34). Interestingly, all sectors reduced the composition of debtors to total current assets in phase 2 over phase 1 and in phase 4 over phase 3 except for the housing and oil and gas sectors which reported an increase in phase 4 over phase 3 (Appendix 5.35). Out of these, the reductions in the metals sector from 23.12 to 14.12% (in phase 2 over phase 1) and from 18.11 to 11.46% (in phase 4 over phase 3) were statistically significant. The decrease in the power sector from 32.23 to 18.63% and that of the transport sector from 26.25 to 21.57% were statistically significant for phase 2 over phase 1. The ANOVA test (Appendix 5.36) indicated a statistically significant difference amongst the variances for the sample as a whole and the metals sector for the entire period of the study.

Zero Working Capital Ratio

The ICT sector exhibited ratios closest to the concept of zero working capital at 1.21 in phase 1 which further came down to 1.08 in phase 2 (Appendix 5.37). Diversified sector remained the farthest from the concept with a ratio of 2.22 in phase 1. ICT reported close to zero working capital figures at 1.11 in phase 3 which reduced further to 1.06 in phase 4 (Appendix 5.38). The ANOVA test (Appendix 5.39) indicated a statistically significant difference amongst the variances for the sample as a whole. This supports the frequency distribution statistics discussed above for the sample as a whole.

Expectedly, the sectors exhibit variations in all aspects of working capital management. Some sectors (FMCG, housing, metals and power) appear to have been impacted from the recession but overall most of the sectors seem to have withered the post-recession period with little/no alterations in their working capital management. These variations are also reported by the studies of Long et al. (1993), Raheman and Abdul (2010) and Hill et al. (2010).

Section X Concluding Observations

The major findings related to working capital management practices of the sample companies are summarised in this section.

The sample companies do not appear to face any problems in meeting their short-term maturing obligations. The importance of liquidity is not lost on the sample companies. This is in tune with the findings on the importance of liquidity for a firm's survival (Lamberson 1995). However, the sample companies could do well to be less conservative with their working capital management as they are large and stable companies and may attempt a better trade-off between risk and profitability.

As far as cash management is concerned, it is gratifying to note that the sample companies are following sound cash management practices. While cash credit limit (from the banks) constitutes the major source of dealing with cash deficit situations, deposit with banks for short-term has been identified as the important method of deploying cash by majority of the sample companies.

Debtors and creditors form other significant constituents of working capital cycle. The survey reveals that 'growth in sales' is the most favoured objective of credit policy amongst the sample companies. Credit sales/receivables are treated as a marketing tool to promote sales and thereby profits (Long et al. (1993) and Cheng and Pike (2003)). It is common practice amongst the sample companies to assess the financial health of customers before granting credit and to prepare ageing schedule of debtors for monitoring purposes.

Another notable finding is that the sample companies adopt the scientific method of 'determination of individual components of current assets and current liabilities (based on raw material holding period, debtors' collection period, creditors' payment period and so on)' as the basis of working capital determination. As far as the policy towards financing working capital is concerned, 'permanent needs from long-term sources and temporary/seasonal needs from short-term sources' seems to be favoured by the majority. These findings are in conformity with sound theory of financial management.

It is encouraging to note that majority of the sample companies have not experienced working capital shortage. Further, the survey indicates that the sample companies experiencing working capital shortage face it occasionally only.

It appears that the components of cash and bank, inventory, and debtors and bills receivables accounts for more than 60% of the total current assets for the sample companies indicating a high degree of advances payments and/or prepaid expenses in the balance sheets of the companies.

Perhaps for the first time, the concept of zero working capital and its practice amongst the sample companies was studied. It is encouraging to note one-fourth of the sample companies are operating on zero working capital. Even though the statistics supporting zero working capital seem to be modest, the trend does support growing professionalism in the management of working capital by the sample companies.

The constituent sectors exhibit variations in all aspects of working capital management. Some sectors appear to have been impacted from the recession, but overall, the sample companies seem to have withered the post-recession period with little/no alterations in their working capital management.

Normative Framework

- *Determine individual components of the company's operating cycle with their duration and cash flows* – to be able to match receivables with payables better and plan the working capital financing accordingly.
- *Manage trade-off between risk and profitability* – cash is important but not at the cost of returns and profitability.
- *Usage of facilities like cash credit* – to be able to avail financing at low/no cost in times of shortage of working capital.
- *Collection and payment policies of the firms in manufacturing sectors (in general) need to be thoroughly reviewed* – this can be possible with some professional advice and supervision (Raheman et al. 2010).
- *Managers/executives can enhance performance of firms by reducing the number of days in cash conversion cycle* – this is only possible if its components are dealt individually and an optimal/effective policy is formulated for these components (Raheman et al. 2010).
- *Explore the feasibility of operating with zero working capital* – for companies in a position to negotiate better credit terms (with both creditors and debtors), this could be an option towards holding less cash (in favour of increased profitability).

Appendices

Appendix 5.1: Mean, median and quartile values of current ratio of constituent sectors of the sample companies over phase 1 (2001–2006) and phase 2 (2007–2011)

	Phase 1 (2001–2006)				Phase 2 (2007–2011)			
Sector	Mean	Median	Quartile 1	Quartile 3	Mean	Median	Quartile 1	Quartile 3
Healthcare	2.61	2.27	1.98	3.38	2.76	2.73	2.17	3.22
Miscellaneous[a]	2.32	2.25	1.71	2.77	2.33	2.25	1.70	2.88
Diversified	2.20	2.22	1.83	2.51	1.94	1.64	1.45	2.40
Internet and communications technology (ICT)	2.13	2.22	1.44	2.80	2.02	1.89	1.43	2.28
Metals	2.00	1.90	1.19	2.59	2.07	1.89	1.50	2.40
Housing	1.93	1.80	1.36	2.31	2.29	2.16	1.60	2.71
Transport	1.84	1.75	1.36	2.33	1.78	1.59	1.19	2.13
Power	1.79	1.73	1.23	2.36	1.91	1.78	1.18	2.53
Capital goods	1.71	1.55	1.41	1.71	1.60	1.38	1.28	1.63
Oil and gas	1.64	1.43	1.20	1.85	1.78	1.47	1.31	1.79
Fast-moving consumer goods (FMCG)	1.58	1.23	0.92	1.93	1.43	1.08	0.95	1.57

[a]Miscellaneous sectors comprises of the media and publishing sector; agriculture, chemicals and petrochemicals; and tourism, textiles and miscellaneous sectors

	Phase 1 and Phase 2		
Sector	*t*	*df*	Significance (2-tailed)
Healthcare	−1.594	13	0.135
Housing	−1.413	16	0.177
Metals	−1.050	15	0.311
Power	−0.845	11	0.416
Capital goods	0.759	12	0.462
FMCG	−0.685	11	0.508
Transport	−0.673	16	0.511
ICT	−0.587	16	0.566
Miscellaneous	0.499	15	0.625
Oil and gas	−0.216	13	0.832
Diversified	0.039	7	0.970

Appendix 5.2: Mean, median and quartile values of current ratio of constituent sectors of the sample companies over phase 3 (2007–2008) and phase 4 (2009–2011)

	Phase 3 (2007–2008)				Phase 4 (2009–2011)			
Sector	Mean	Median	Quartile 1	Quartile 3	Mean	Median	Quartile 1	Quartile 3
Healthcare	2.68	2.58	1.99	3.30	2.81	2.83	2.30	3.16
Miscellaneous	2.39	2.28	1.91	2.74	2.29	2.24	1.56	2.97
Housing	2.31	2.09	1.55	2.98	0.72	1.20	1.64	3.86

(continued)

Appendix 5.2: (continued)

	Phase 3 (2007–2008)				Phase 4 (2009–2011)			
Sector	Mean	Median	Quartile 1	Quartile 3	Mean	Median	Quartile 1	Quartile 3
Metals	2.12	1.94	1.62	2.44	2.03	1.86	1.41	2.37
Diversified	2.06	1.79	1.52	2.76	1.87	1.54	1.41	2.16
ICT	1.93	1.61	1.36	2.20	2.08	2.09	1.47	2.33
Transport	1.87	1.57	1.25	2.21	1.72	1.60	1.15	2.07
Oil and gas	1.75	1.58	1.37	1.78	1.80	1.40	1.28	1.80
Power	1.75	1.44	0.95	2.50	2.02	2.01	1.34	2.54
FMCG	1.72	1.03	0.86	1.87	1.23	1.12	1.01	1.38
Capital goods	1.51	1.37	1.23	1.60	1.66	1.39	1.31	1.65

	Phase 3 and Phase 4		
Sector	*t*	*df*	Significance (2-tailed)
Capital goods	−1.316	12	0.213
Miscellaneous	1.009	14	0.330
ICT	−0.982	15	0.341
FMCG	0.601	9	0.563
Power	−0.575	11	0.577
Transport	−0.545	16	0.594
Metals	0.478	14	0.640
Housing	−0.459	13	0.654
Healthcare	−0.290	11	0.777
Oil and gas	0.146	14	0.886
Diversified	0.142	6	0.892

Appendix 5.3: ANOVA of the consolidated sample and the constituent sectors of the sample companies based on current ratio over phase 1 (2001–2006) and phase 2 (2007–2011) and phase 3 (2007–2008) and phase 4 (2009–2011)

	Phase 1 and Phase 2		Phase 3 and Phase 4	
Sector	*F*	Significance	*F*	Significance
Consolidated	4.562	0.000	4.061	0.000
Housing	2.470	0.126	0.030	0.864
Power	1.383	0.251	0.542	0.469
Healthcare	0.659	0.424	0.043	0.838
Oil and gas	0.298	0.589	0.004	0.953
FMCG	0.242	0.628	1.560	0.226
Capital goods	0.230	0.636	0.388	0.539
Diversified	0.189	0.670	0.142	0.713
Miscellaneous	0.164	0.689	0.421	0.522
Transport	0.061	0.806	0.018	0.894
Metals	0.035	0.852	0.251	0.620
ICT	0.034	0.855	0.122	0.729

Appendix 5.4: Mean, median and quartile values of acid-test ratio of constituent sectors of the sample companies over phase 1 (2001–2006) and phase 2 (2007–2011)

	Phase 1 (2001–2006)				Phase 2 (2007–2011)			
Sector	Mean	Median	Quartile 1	Quartile 3	Mean	Median	Quartile 1	Quartile 3
Power	1.61	1.67	1.27	2.01	1.47	1.32	0.89	2.07
Healthcare	1.59	1.32	1.04	1.97	1.80	1.77	1.45	2.14
Oil and gas	1.50	1.58	1.09	1.95	1.22	1.21	0.64	1.46
Miscellaneous	1.39	1.29	0.93	1.82	1.59	1.61	1.11	2.04
ICT	1.36	1.25	0.87	1.93	1.40	1.49	1.00	1.81
Diversified	1.31	1.21	1.07	1.43	1.34	1.16	0.94	1.71
Transport	1.26	1.24	0.70	1.75	1.22	1.13	0.68	1.54
Metals	1.23	1.18	0.75	1.57	1.44	1.30	1.12	1.89
Capital goods	1.22	1.11	0.80	1.49	1.17	1.15	0.95	1.26
FMCG	1.18	1.12	0.74	1.45	0.77	0.71	0.52	0.81
Housing	1.07	0.80	0.44	1.68	1.40	1.33	0.78	1.92

	Phase 1 and Phase 2		
Sector	*t*	*df*	Significance (2-tailed)
Housing	−2.231	15	0.041
Metals	−2.058	14	0.059
Transport	−0.914	16	0.374
FMCG	0.757	10	0.466
Diversified	−0.715	6	0.501
Miscellaneous	−0.671	13	0.514
Oil and gas	0.392	14	0.701
ICT	−0.351	13	0.731
Capital goods	0.346	11	0.736
Power	−0.296	10	0.773
Healthcare	0.001	12	0.999

Appendix 5.5: Mean, median and quartile values of acid-test ratio of constituent sectors of the sample companies over phase 3 (2007–2008) and phase 4 (2009–2011)

	Phase 3 (2007–2008)				Phase 4 (2009–2011)			
Sector	Mean	Median	Quartile 1	Quartile 3	Mean	Median	Quartile 1	Quartile 3
Healthcare	1.66	1.66	1.37	1.83	1.90	1.84	1.50	2.35
Diversified	1.55	1.29	1.00	2.12	1.21	1.07	0.90	1.43
Metals	1.50	1.47	0.98	1.92	1.40	1.19	1.21	1.88
Miscellaneous	1.50	1.52	1.08	1.93	1.64	1.68	1.14	2.11
Housing	1.36	1.19	0.78	1.80	1.43	1.42	0.78	2.00
ICT	1.32	1.34	1.00	1.65	1.46	1.60	1.00	1.91
Oil and gas	1.26	1.34	0.65	1.62	1.19	1.12	0.64	1.35
Transport	1.25	1.24	0.66	1.39	1.20	1.06	0.70	1.64
Power	1.23	1.02	0.57	1.91	1.63	1.52	1.11	2.17
Capital goods	1.15	1.13	0.85	1.23	1.19	1.17	1.02	1.27
FMCG	0.65	0.63	0.45	0.71	0.84	0.76	0.56	0.88

(continued)

Appendix 5.5: (continued)

	Phase 3 and Phase 4		
Sector	*t*	*df*	Significance (2-tailed)
Metals	2.157	15	0.048
Power	−1.657	11	0.126
Diversified	1.836	4	0.140
Healthcare	−1.300	7	0.235
Transport	0.668	13	0.516
Housing	−0.620	13	0.546
ICT	−0.599	13	0.559
Oil and gas	0.543	13	0.596
Capital goods	−0.410	10	0.691
Miscellaneous	−0.174	10	0.865
FMCG	−0.160	7	0.878

Appendix 5.6: ANOVA of the consolidated sample and the constituent sectors of the sample companies based on acid-test ratio over phase 1 (2001–2006) and phase 2 (2007–2011) and phase 3 (2007–2008) and phase 4 (2009–2011)

	Phase 1 and Phase 2		Phase 3 and Phase 4	
Sector	*F*	Significance	*F*	Significance
Consolidated	2.633	0.004	3.124	0.001
Housing	2.830	0.102	0.144	0.707
Metals	2.759	0.107	0.603	0.443
FMCG	1.087	0.309	0.655	0.429
Diversified	0.581	0.459	1.662	0.226
Transport	0.243	0.625	0.063	0.804
Miscellaneous	0.195	0.662	0.518	0.479
Oil and gas	0.140	0.711	0.015	0.905
Capital goods	0.097	0.758	0.058	0.812
Power	0.092	0.765	2.379	0.137
ICT	0.054	0.817	0.156	0.697
Healthcare	0.022	0.884	1.894	0.188

Appendix 5.7: Mean, median and quartile values of holding period (in days) of raw materials and spare parts inventory of constituent sectors of the sample companies over phase 1 (2001–2006) and phase 2 (2007–2011)

	Phase 1 (2001–2006)				Phase 2 (2007–2011)			
Sector	Mean	Median	Quartile 1	Quartile 3	Mean	Median	Quartile 1	Quartile 3
Metals	34.14	29.49	23.01	44.95	34.11	29.58	21.74	42.29
Healthcare	30.37	25.96	18.55	35.82	31.22	28.56	20.01	38.19
Capital goods	29.29	20.72	14.06	32.43	31.73	18.67	10.17	37.87
Diversified	20.57	25.00	0.44	34.96	19.44	23.03	3.95	31.49
FMCG	20.10	15.43	11.44	22.31	23.29	17.30	10.63	27.26
Power	19.63	19.63	10.55	23.69	14.09	10.28	5.44	16.16
Oil and gas	17.76	16.16	9.00	24.28	28.35	19.97	11.67	27.44

(continued)

Appendix 5.7: (continued)

Sector	Phase 1 (2001–2006) Mean	Median	Quartile 1	Quartile 3	Phase 2 (2007–2011) Mean	Median	Quartile 1	Quartile 3
Miscellaneous	15.91	12.83	1.77	25.46	15.77	12.68	0.64	24.56
Transport	14.51	14.75	1.73	22.61	13.95	11.11	2.44	21.31
Housing	14.38	15.06	–	24.02	16.24	13.34	3.36	27.72
ICT	1.02	–	–	–	2.10	0.12	0.07	1.36

'–' denotes indeterminate/missing values. The same holds for other tables

Sector	Phase 1 and Phase 2 *t*	*df*	Significance (2-tailed)
Diversified	1.854	8	0.101
Power	1.290	10	0.226
FMCG	−1.203	11	0.254
Oil and gas	−1.187	13	0.256
Capital goods	−0.763	12	0.460
ICT	−0.472	16	0.644
Housing	−0.376	16	0.712
Healthcare	−0.369	13	0.718
Miscellaneous	−0.109	15	0.915
Metals	0.095	17	0.925
Transport	−0.047	16	0.963

Appendix 5.8: Mean, median and quartile values of holding period (in days) of raw materials and spare parts inventory of constituent sectors of the sample companies over phase 3 (2007–2008) and phase 4 (2009–2011)

Sector	Phase 3 (2007–2008) Mean	Median	Quartile 1	Quartile 3	Phase 4 (2009–2011) Mean	Median	Quartile 1	Quartile 3
Healthcare	32.09	27.19	21.57	38.69	30.64	29.47	18.96	37.86
Metals	29.99	29.70	23.37	37.69	36.85	29.50	20.65	45.35
Capital goods	29.64	18.20	10.01	37.25	33.13	18.99	10.28	38.28
Oil and gas	24.35	20.26	13.02	28.55	31.01	19.77	10.77	26.70
FMCG	22.03	17.15	9.05	29.03	24.13	17.41	11.68	26.07
Diversified	18.41	24.57	1.39	31.45	20.13	22.00	5.66	31.52
Miscellaneous	17.95	15.77	0.42	26.43	14.31	10.62	0.79	23.31
Power	16.50	12.76	6.23	18.77	12.48	8.63	4.91	14.41
Housing	13.86	9.88	–	25.79	17.83	15.65	5.60	29.01
Transport	12.12	10.66	1.05	20.56	15.16	11.42	3.38	21.81
ICT	1.44	–	–	0.21	2.54	0.20	0.12	2.13

Sector	Phase 3 and Phase 4 t	*df*	Significance (2-tailed)
Power	2.560	10	0.028
Metals	−1.930	17	0.070
Miscellaneous	1.819	15	0.089
ICT	−0.996	16	0.334

(continued)

Appendix 5.8: (continued)

Sector	Phase 3 and Phase 4 t	*df*	Significance (2-tailed)
Transport	−0.785	17	0.443
Oil and gas	−0.746	13	0.469
Capital goods	−0.667	12	0.517
Housing	−0.516	17	0.613
Healthcare	0.447	13	0.662
FMCG	−0.257	11	0.802
Diversified	0.181	8	0.861

Appendix 5.9: ANOVA of the consolidated sample and the constituent sectors of the sample companies based on holding period (in days) of raw materials and spare parts inventory over phase 1 (2001–2006) and phase 2 (2007–2011) and phase 3 (2007–2008) and phase 4 (2009–2011)

	Phase 1 and Phase 2		Phase 3 and Phase 4	
Sector	*F*	Significance	*F*	Significance
Consolidated	10.805	0.000	8.901	0.000
Oil and gas	1.889	0.181	0.349	0.559
Power	0.823	0.374	0.779	0.387
ICT	0.391	0.536	0.014	0.906
FMCG	0.228	0.638	0.005	0.946
Diversified	0.086	0.774	0.001	0.981
Capital goods	0.047	0.830	0.048	0.828
Healthcare	0.023	0.879	0.042	0.839
Transport	0.009	0.926	0.202	0.656
Metals	0.003	0.956	1.185	0.284
Housing	0.002	0.961	0.028	0.869
Miscellaneous	0.000	0.986	0.622	0.437

Appendix 5.10: Mean, median and quartile values of holding period (in days) of work-in-process inventory of constituent sectors of the sample companies over phase 1 (2001–2006) and phase 2 (2007–2011)

	Phase 1 (2001–2006)				Phase 2 (2007–2011)			
Sector	Mean	Median	Quartile 1	Quartile 3	Mean	Median	Quartile 1	Quartile 3
Housing	30.41	10.84	3.61	22.52	49.40	9.30	3.80	34.91
Capital goods	28.36	20.87	8.06	41.50	33.02	23.36	9.88	42.28
Healthcare	17.31	15.97	8.32	19.68	20.85	16.81	9.88	26.25
Metals	13.79	4.13	1.27	14.06	13.25	5.33	1.43	13.42
Diversified	10.96	3.59	–	6.78	17.9	3.14	0.39	7.12
Transport	10.16	6.01	0.72	12.97	7.50	2.61	0.23	8.83
FMCG	5.88	2.64	1.14	7.45	5.09	2.94	0.94	6.24
Miscellaneous	5.39	1.50	0.10	5.43	4.82	1.20	0.15	7.37
ICT	2.25	–	–	–	1.06	0.09	0.05	0.59
Oil and gas	1.16	–	–	1.45	1.95	0.90	0.60	2.70
Power	0.95	0.04	–	0.91	0.36	–	–	0.01

(continued)

Appendix 5.10: (continued)

Sector	Phase 1 and Phase 2 *t*	*df*	Significance (2-tailed)
Transport	2.400	16	0.029
Housing	−1.774	15	0.096
Healthcare	−1.677	13	0.117
Capital goods	−1.397	12	0.188
Diversified	−1.038	8	0.330
Oil and gas	−0.874	13	0.398
Miscellaneous	0.812	15	0.430
Power	−0.789	10	0.448
ICT	0.564	16	0.580
Metals	0.447	17	0.661
FMCG	0.375	11	0.715

Appendix 5.11: Mean, median and quartile values of holding period (in days) of work-in-process inventory of constituent sectors of the sample companies over phase 3 (2007–2008) and phase 4 (2009–2011)

	Phase 3 (2007–2008)				Phase 4 (2009–2011)			
Sector	Mean	Median	Quartile 1	Quartile 3	Mean	Median	Quartile 1	Quartile 3
Housing	62.43	8.71	2.31	54.26	40.71	9.69	4.79	22.01
Diversified	36.46	2.62	–	6.03	5.53	3.48	0.65	7.85
Capital goods	31.81	22.90	9.72	35.80	33.83	23.67	9.99	46.61
Healthcare	18.65	16.39	10.50	24.41	22.31	17.09	9.46	27.47
Metals	10.85	4.46	0.69	10.07	14.84	5.90	1.92	15.65
Transport	6.35	1.54	–	8.43	8.27	3.32	0.38	9.10
Miscellaneous	5.21	0.16	–	8.21	4.56	1.90	0.25	6.80
FMCG	4.20	2.28	0.68	6.70	5.68	3.39	1.12	5.94
ICT	1.24	–	–	–	0.95	0.15	0.08	0.98
Oil and gas	0.89	–	–	1.69	2.66	1.50	0.99	3.38
Power	0.72	–	–	–	–	–	–	–

Sector	Phase 3 and Phase 4 *t*	*df*	Significance (2-tailed)
Metals	−1.772	17	0.094
Oil and gas	−1.494	13	0.159
Miscellaneous	1.273	15	0.222
Transport	−1.190	17	0.251
Power	1.001	10	0.341
ICT	0.939	17	0.361
Diversified	0.942	8	0.374
Healthcare	−0.718	13	0.486
FMCG	−0.668	11	0.518
Capital goods	−0.454	12	0.658
Housing	0.431	15	0.672

Appendix 5.12: ANOVA of the consolidated sample and the constituent sectors of the sample companies based on holding period (in days) of work-in-process inventory over phase 1 (2001–2006) and phase 2 (2007–2011) and phase 3 (2007–2008) and phase 4 (2009–2011)

	Phase 1 and Phase 2		Phase 3 and Phase 4	
Sector	*F*	Significance	*F*	Significance
Consolidated	6.745	0.000	7.277	0.000
Diversified	0.422	0.525	0.810	0.382
ICT	0.375	0.545	0.502	0.484
Transport	0.348	0.559	0.072	0.790
Capital goods	0.341	0.564	0.063	0.804
Oil and gas	0.304	0.586	0.657	0.425
Power	0.258	0.616	1.089	0.308
Miscellaneous	0.228	0.636	0.406	0.529
Healthcare	0.072	0.791	0.171	0.682
FMCG	0.027	0.872	0.142	0.710
Metals	0.013	0.909	0.259	0.614
Housing	2.335	–	0.452	0.506

Appendix 5.13: Mean, median and quartile values of holding period (in days) of finished goods inventory of constituent sectors of the sample companies over phase 1 (2001–2006) and phase 2 (2007–2011)

	Phase 1 (2001–2006)				Phase 2 (2007–2011)			
Sector	Mean	Median	Quartile 1	Quartile 3	Mean	Median	Quartile 1	Quartile 3
Miscellaneous	33.47	17.52	3.76	34.00	26.25	16.81	3.21	27.04
FMCG	28.56	20.84	17.07	29.95	31.37	19.92	15.32	27.08
Healthcare	21.99	22.12	9.53	31.94	18.65	19.11	9.31	28.88
Metals	19.34	14.85	7.16	25.01	19.03	13.95	5.47	20.54
Oil and gas	14.23	12.36	0.26	25.48	13.34	10.54	1.93	19.27
Diversified	12.58	13.50	3.41	17.02	11.88	10.74	2.38	16.25
Transport	11.13	4.24	0.78	20.00	8.89	4.69	0.82	15.28
Capital goods	8.73	7.30	4.06	10.54	8.06	4.06	1.16	7.87
Housing	8.15	4.16	–	8.87	4.26	2.25	0.38	4.24
ICT	5.67	–	–	0.28	5.37	1.22	0.31	3.56
Power	0.18	–	–	–	–	–	–	–

	Phase 1 and Phase 2		
Sector	*t*	*df*	Significance (2-tailed)
Oil and gas	2.107	13	0.055
Healthcare	1.740	13	0.106
Miscellaneous	1.540	15	0.144
Transport	1.419	16	0.175
Housing	1.292	16	0.215
Diversified	1.290	8	0.233
FMCG	−1.145	11	0.276
Capital goods	1.109	12	0.289
Power	1.000	10	0.341

(continued)

Appendix 5.13: (continued)

Sector	Phase 1 and Phase 2 *t*	*df*	Significance (2-tailed)
ICT	0.743	16	0.468
Metals	0.061	17	0.952

Appendix 5.14: Mean, median and quartile values of holding period (in days) of finished goods inventory of constituent sectors of the sample companies over phase 3 (2007–2008) and phase 4 (2009–2011)

	Phase 3 (2007–2008)				Phase 4 (2009–2011)			
Sector	Mean	Median	Quartile 1	Quartile 3	Mean	Median	Quartile 1	Quartile 3
Power	–	–	–	–	–	–	–	–
FMCG	31.42	20.12	14.82	29.41	31.34	19.79	15.65	25.53
Miscellaneous	25.50	17.94	–	30.13	26.75	16.06	5.35	24.98
Healthcare	18.16	18.53	6.64	30.11	18.97	19.49	11.08	28.07
Oil and gas	16.64	12.22	–	21.20	11.14	9.41	3.22	17.98
Metals	14.99	10.78	5.05	19.27	21.72	16.06	5.75	21.39
Diversified	12.25	11.27	1.74	18.80	11.63	10.39	2.80	14.54
Transport	8.81	3.87	–	16.56	8.94	5.24	1.36	14.42
Capital goods	6.77	4.00	0.50	6.11	8.92	4.09	1.60	9.05
ICT	3.21	–	–	0.41	6.82	2.04	0.52	5.66
Housing	2.55	1.59	–	3.65	5.40	2.70	0.64	4.63

Sector	Phase 3 and Phase 4 *t*	*df*	Significance (2-tailed)
Metals	−1.532	17	0.144
Transport	1.228	17	0.236
Oil and gas	1.159	13	0.267
Diversified	1.068	8	0.317
Housing	−0.921	17	0.370
ICT	−0.882	17	0.390
Capital goods	−0.415	12	0.686
FMCG	0.382	11	0.710
Healthcare	0.067	13	0.947
Miscellaneous	−0.041	15	0.968
Power	–	–	–

Appendix 5.15: ANOVA of the consolidated sample and the constituent sectors of the sample companies based on holding period (in days) of finished goods inventory over phase 1 (2001–2006) and phase 2 (2007–2011) and phase 3 (2007–2008) and phase 4 (2009–2011)

	Phase 1 and Phase 2		Phase 3 and Phase 4	
Sector	*F*	Significance	*F*	Significance
Consolidated	8.764	0.000	8.825	0.000
Housing	1.903	0.177	0.655	0.424
Power	1.192	0.287	–	–
Healthcare	0.456	0.506	0.000	0.987

(continued)

Appendix 5.15: (continued)

Sector	Phase 1 and Phase 2		Phase 3 and Phase 4	
	F	Significance	*F*	Significance
Transport	0.240	0.628	0.138	0.712
FMCG	0.219	0.644	0.002	0.966
Miscellaneous	0.213	0.647	0.000	0.995
Capital goods	0.122	0.730	0.060	0.808
ICT	0.115	0.736	0.056	0.814
Diversified	0.085	0.774	0.155	0.699
Metals	0.002	0.963	0.709	0.406
Oil and gas	0.000	0.997	1.303	0.264

Appendix 5.16: Mean, median and quartile values of debtors' collection period (in days) of constituent sectors of the sample companies over phase 1 (2001–2006) and phase 2 (2007–2011)

Sector	Phase 1 (2001–2006)				Phase 2 (2007–2011)			
	Mean	Median	Quartile 1	Quartile 3	Mean	Median	Quartile 1	Quartile 3
Capital goods	118.11	112.92	89.19	138.92	129.22	134.87	84.97	171.11
Power	110.16	100.92	54.12	159.75	78.67	57.57	35.03	108.81
ICT	106.03	86.31	60.91	126.18	87.18	72.32	58.56	99.18
Healthcare	91.65	86.73	55.53	114.62	93.42	88.86	65.56	118.88
Miscellaneous	63.48	48.50	25.07	84.27	65.88	60.73	25.00	99.02
Diversified	62.63	61.43	39.69	73.97	46.83	53.47	27.05	67.07
Housing	52.67	39.53	21.73	76.57	71.43	63.24	17.12	103.63
Metals	51.75	43.27	30.90	63.19	34.74	26.18	17.39	42.70
Transport	45.32	44.74	30.22	59.11	41.77	33.61	18.00	55.34
Oil and gas	35.56	22.68	11.98	40.98	29.67	22.54	14.97	34.88
FMCG	27.28	19.04	10.01	32.60	18.90	12.81	7.17	19.49

Sector	Phase 1 and Phase 2		
	t	*df*	Significance (2-tailed)
Housing	−2.306	16	0.035
Metals	2.193	17	0.042
Diversified	2.361	8	0.046
ICT	2.161	16	0.046
Power	1.947	10	0.080
FMCG	1.607	11	0.136
Capital goods	−1.027	12	0.325
Oil and gas	0.892	13	0.389
Healthcare	−0.692	13	0.501
Transport	0.467	16	0.647
Miscellaneous	0.149	15	0.884

Appendix 5.17: Mean, median and quartile values of debtors' collection period (in days) of constituent sectors of the sample companies over phase 3 (2007–2008) and phase 4 (2009–2011)

	Phase 3 (2007–2008)				Phase 4 (2009–2011)			
Sector	Mean	Median	Quartile 1	Quartile 3	Mean	Median	Quartile 1	Quartile 3
Capital goods	121.58	131.66	84.62	157.86	134.32	137.02	85.20	179.95
Healthcare	98.16	91.13	66.45	119.22	90.26	87.35	64.97	118.66
ICT	91.24	72.54	60.29	105.09	84.47	72.17	57.41	95.24
Miscellaneous	74.31	70.57	24.81	113.28	60.26	54.17	25.13	89.51
Power	74.17	50.70	21.83	92.75	81.67	62.14	43.83	119.52
Housing	65.78	54.64	14.00	94.70	75.19	68.98	19.19	109.59
Diversified	47.01	58.92	24.86	67.12	46.70	49.83	28.51	67.04
Transport	45.93	33.21	20.59	54.51	38.99	33.89	16.27	55.89
Metals	36.81	29.69	21.80	46.45	33.36	23.84	14.45	40.21
Oil and gas	32.32	23.33	15.27	40.70	27.90	22.01	14.77	31.01
FMCG	18.81	14.02	7.21	20.06	18.96	12.00	7.14	19.11

	Phase 3 and Phase 4		
Sector	*t*	*df*	Significance (2-tailed)
Miscellaneous	2.911	15	0.011
Capital goods	−1.698	12	0.115
ICT	1.165	17	0.260
Healthcare	1.143	13	0.274
Oil and gas	1.061	15	0.306
Metals	0.964	17	0.348
FMCG	−0.893	11	0.391
Transport	0.737	17	0.471
Housing	−0.518	17	0.611
Power	−0.275	10	0.789
Diversified	0.032	8	0.975

Appendix 5.18: ANOVA of the consolidated sample and the constituent sectors of the sample companies based on debtors' collection period (in days) over phase 1 (2001–2006) and phase 2 (2007–2011) and phase 3 (2007–2008) and phase 4 (2009–2011)

	Phase 1 and Phase 2		Phase 3 and Phase 4	
Sector	*F*	Significance	*F*	Significance
Consolidated	14.904	0.000	14.370	0.000
Metals	3.559	0.068	0.243	0.625
Housing	2.506	0.123	0.072	0.790
Diversified	2.416	0.140	0.000	0.984
Transport	1.265	0.270	0.465	0.500
ICT	0.735	0.398	0.139	0.712
FMCG	0.741	0.399	0.039	0.845
Power	0.627	0.437	0.094	0.762
Capital goods	0.303	0.587	0.276	0.604
Miscellaneous	0.124	0.727	0.299	0.588
Oil and gas	0.037	0.850	0.253	0.619
Healthcare	0.021	0.886	0.188	0.668

Appendix 5.19: Mean, median and quartile values of gross working capital cycle (in days) of constituent sectors of the sample companies over phase 1 (2001–2006) and phase 2 (2007–2011)

	Phase 1 (2001–2006)				Phase 2 (2007–2011)			
Sector	Mean	Median	Quartile 1	Quartile 3	Mean	Median	Quartile 1	Quartile 3
Capital goods	192.36	175.17	136.61	238.30	214.17	193.45	141.61	293.78
Healthcare	167.63	159.89	121.09	209.59	154.51	156.74	120.60	193.45
ICT	140.79	90.99	68.20	166.56	90.88	79.98	48.27	114.99
Housing	135.34	108.27	74.23	157.47	148.75	125.75	64.15	179.93
Miscellaneous	127.82	103.76	74.46	163.65	125.57	110.83	79.20	178.63
Metals	125.69	118.41	90.30	153.86	104.05	90.25	58.21	129.91
Diversified	123.11	112.77	94.88	133.54	134.69	98.80	75.02	114.84
Power	99.02	100.14	83.12	117.26	91.88	83.21	72.41	107.85
Transport	85.67	86.66	54.25	119.28	74.33	67.48	34.15	102.63
FMCG	83.98	79.74	52.35	109.09	79.43	76.20	49.52	111.77
Oil and gas	67.55	60.23	44.78	82.96	66.44	54.13	42.85	74.70

	Phase 1 and Phase 2		
Sector	*t*	*df*	Significance (2-tailed)
Metals	2.153	17	0.046
Capital goods	−1.447	12	0.173
ICT	1.254	8	0.245
Transport	0.940	16	0.361
Healthcare	−0.571	13	0.578
Diversified	−0.378	6	0.719
Housing	−0.309	15	0.761
FMCG	0.298	11	0.771
Miscellaneous	0.244	15	0.811
Oil and gas	0.144	13	0.888
Power	0.096	6	0.927

Appendix 5.20: Mean, median and quartile values of gross working capital cycle (in days) of constituent sectors of the sample companies over phase 3 (2007–2008) and phase 4 (2009–2011)

	Phase 3 (2007–2008)				Phase 4 (2009–2011)			
Sector	Mean	Median	Quartile 1	Quartile 3	Mean	Median	Quartile 1	Quartile 3
Capital goods	195.77	180.58	138.70	249.07	226.43	202.03	143.55	323.59
Healthcare	170.94	167.84	141.75	212.30	143.55	149.35	106.50	180.88
Housing	168.12	131.30	55.48	204.75	135.84	122.06	69.93	163.39
Diversified	138.59	108.47	75.44	120.91	132.09	92.35	74.73	110.78
Miscellaneous	131.54	129.36	89.85	172.01	121.59	98.47	72.09	183.04
Metals	97.16	87.71	60.47	122.57	108.64	91.93	56.70	134.80
ICT	92.93	80.64	42.39	128.21	89.52	79.53	52.18	106.17
Power	90.47	84.26	74.52	109.99	92.82	82.51	71.01	106.42
FMCG	78.63	75.54	49.79	107.91	79.97	76.63	49.34	114.34
Transport	77.04	76.14	38.10	105.80	72.52	61.70	31.52	100.51
Oil and gas	65.39	56.11	43.82	80.30	67.14	52.81	42.20	70.97

(continued)

Appendix 5.20: (continued)

	Phase 3 and Phase 4		
Sector	*t*	*df*	Significance (2-tailed)
Capital goods	−2.664	12	0.021
Miscellaneous	1.408	15	0.179
Metals	−1.155	17	0.264
Diversified	0.817	6	0.445
FMCG	−0.651	11	0.529
Oil and gas	−0.485	13	0.635
ICT	0.460	10	0.655
Transport	0.343	17	0.735
Healthcare	0.339	13	0.740
Power	0.341	6	0.745
Housing	0.251	13	0.806

Appendix 5.21: ANOVA of the consolidated sample and the constituent sectors of the sample companies based on gross working capital cycle (in days) over phase 1 (2001–2006) and phase 2 (2007–2011) and phase 3 (2007–2008) and phase 4 (2009–2011)

	Phase 1 and Phase 2		Phase 3 and Phase 4	
Sector	*F*	Significance	*F*	Significance
Consolidated	10.275	0.000	10.600	0.000
Metals	2.179	0.149	0.231	0.634
ICT	1.003	0.328	0.006	0.939
Capital goods	0.483	0.494	0.669	0.421
Transport	0.388	0.538	0.036	0.850
Power	0.311	0.586	0.098	0.759
Diversified	0.019	0.893	0.030	0.866
Miscellaneous	0.014	0.906	0.187	0.669
Healthcare	0.013	0.909	0.015	0.902
FMCG	0.004	0.950	0.035	0.853
Oil and gas	0.004	0.952	0.013	0.911
Housing	0.002	0.961	0.904	0.350

Appendix 5.22: Mean, median and quartile values of creditors' payment period (in days) of constituent sectors of the sample companies over phase 1 (2001–2006) and phase 2 (2007–2011)

	Phase 1 (2001–2006)				Phase 2 (2007–2011)			
Sector	Mean	Median	Quartile 1	Quartile 3	Mean	Median	Quartile 1	Quartile 3
Power	–	–	–	–	–	–	–	–
Housing	165.37	154.04	121.61	202.14	146.52	150.18	92.74	198.27
Capital goods	151.56	155.58	80.36	198.06	145.10	110.77	90.50	182.28
FMCG	135.02	122.02	104.39	156.98	112.47	118.97	83.58	150.18
Metals	132.02	104.53	77.85	180.13	116.83	94.36	50.30	167.55
Diversified	121.60	124.61	91.00	143.71	107.01	85.38	58.51	114.23
ICT	106.85	106.85	106.85	106.85	112.75	107.77	107.77	115.23

(continued)

Appendix 5.22: (continued)

	Phase 1 (2001–2006)				Phase 2 (2007–2011)			
Sector	Mean	Median	Quartile 1	Quartile 3	Mean	Median	Quartile 1	Quartile 3
Healthcare	102.26	102.18	76.45	124.75	117.07	109.92	86.15	143.61
Miscellaneous	92.67	81.39	56.51	114.90	96.01	90.78	46.05	136.27
Transport	77.35	76.42	48.40	95.92	69.43	68.26	43.83	88.28
Oil and gas	67.70	55.40	27.34	88.45	61.13	41.65	26.55	75.08

	Phase 1 and Phase 2		
Sector	*t*	d*f*	Significance (2-tailed)
Metals	2.061	14	0.058
Oil and gas	1.636	9	0.136
Healthcare	−1.539	13	0.148
FMCG	1.258	10	0.237
Transport	1.109	10	0.293
Diversified	0.938	6	0.385
ICT	−1.000	1	0.500
Miscellaneous	−0.076	11	0.941
Housing	0.073	5	0.945
Capital goods	0.049	12	0.962
Power	–	–	–

Appendix 5.23: Mean, median and quartile values of creditors' payment period (in days) of constituent sectors of the sample companies over phase 3 (2007–2008) and phase 4 (2009–2011)

	Phase 3 (2007–2008)				Phase 4 (2009–2011)			
Sector	Mean	Median	Quartile 1	Quartile 3	Mean	Median	Quartile 1	Quartile 3
Power	–	–	–	–	–	–	–	–
ICT	196.32	196.32	196.32	196.32	57.03	48.74	48.74	61.17
Capital goods	149.82	110.54	90.35	200.18	141.95	110.93	90.60	170.34
Housing	146.04	160.75	93.91	195.61	146.83	143.14	91.96	200.05
FMCG	114.79	127.41	92.62	152.75	110.93	113.34	77.56	148.46
Healthcare	110.71	112.71	85.41	138.34	121.32	108.06	86.64	147.12
Diversified	109.89	84.45	62.93	123.16	105.09	86.00	55.56	108.27
Metals	104.78	80.96	43.64	147.40	124.86	103.29	54.74	180.99
Miscellaneous	99.76	87.03	46.32	151.15	93.52	93.27	45.88	126.35
Transport	70.13	70.61	43.36	87.51	68.96	66.69	44.15	88.79
Oil and gas	64.93	42.47	25.64	71.55	58.60	41.10	27.15	77.44

	Phase 3 and Phase 4		
Sector	*t*	d*f*	Significance (2-tailed)
Oil and gas	−1.554	9	0.154
Metals	−1.238	13	0.238

(continued)

Appendix 5.23: (continued)

	Phase 3 and Phase 4		
Sector	*t*	*df*	Significance (2-tailed)
Healthcare	−1.119	13	0.283
FMCG	0.960	10	0.360
Capital goods	0.808	12	0.435
Housing	−0.859	3	0.453
ICT	1.000	1	0.500
Miscellaneous	0.566	11	0.583
Diversified	0.544	6	0.606
Transport	−0.243	11	0.813
Power	–	–	–

Appendix 5.24: ANOVA of the consolidated sample and the constituent sectors of the sample companies based on creditors' payment period (in days) over phase 1 (2001–2006) and phase 2 (2007–2011) and phase 3 (2007–2008) and phase 4 (2009–2011)

	Phase 1 and Phase 2		Phase 3 and phase 4	
Sector	*F*	Significance	*F*	Significance
Consolidated	4.358	0.000	4.509	0.000
Healthcare	0.730	0.401	0.258	0.616
Metals	0.718	0.404	0.140	0.711
Oil and gas	0.497	0.490	0.039	0.845
FMCG	0.452	0.509	0.090	0.767
ICT	0.636	0.509	13.672	0.066
Housing	0.259	0.618	0.026	0.874
Diversified	0.239	0.634	0.036	0.852
Transport	0.230	0.637	0.004	0.951
Miscellaneous	0.005	0.944	0.113	0.740
Capital goods	0	0.987	0.034	0.855
Power	–	–	–	–

Appendix 5.25: Mean, median and quartile values of net working capital cycle (in days) of constituent sectors of the sample companies over phase 1 (2001–2006) and phase 2 (2007–2011)

	Phase 1 (2001–2006)				Phase 2 (2007–2011)			
Sector	Mean	Median	Quartile 1	Quartile 3	Mean	Median	Quartile 1	Quartile 3
Power	–	–	–	–	–	–	–	–
Capital goods	110.19	98.45	43.06	169.90	119.57	108.53	39.24	189.00
ICT	95.38	95.38	95.38	95.38	47.24	47.24	47.24	47.24
Healthcare	87.67	88.77	35.62	118.98	96.78	78.70	40.21	129.74
Metals	65.23	52.66	34.91	95.00	74.41	64.84	33.18	108.67
FMCG	64.50	63.37	48.91	79.53	63.03	76.62	51.95	80.91
Miscellaneous	58.98	46.80	27.55	82.95	55.61	44.76	29.06	82.85
Transport	58.70	59.95	33.39	82.54	55.31	34.15	24.55	59.89
Diversified	57.14	47.54	32.57	74.01	33.09	27.76	19.51	41.94

(continued)

Appendix 5.25: (continued)

	Phase 1 (2001–2006)				Phase 2 (2007–2011)			
Sector	Mean	Median	Quartile 1	Quartile 3	Mean	Median	Quartile 1	Quartile 3
Oil and gas	24.29	24.85	16.97	30.88	14.65	14.67	9.52	20.84
Housing	22.38	22.38	21.92	22.84	62.53	62.53	56.25	68.81

	Phase 1 and Phase 2		
Sector	*t*	d*f*	Significance (2-tailed)
Oil and gas	1.982	5	0.104
FMCG	2.844	2	0.105
Transport	1.282	6	0.247
Miscellaneous	1.037	10	0.324
Diversified	1.084	4	0.339
Capital goods	–0.923	9	0.380
Metals	–0.398	10	0.699
Healthcare	–0.337	10	0.743
Housing	–	–	–
ICT	–	–	–
Power	–	–	–

Appendix 5.26: Mean, median and quartile values of net working capital cycle (in days) of constituent sectors of the sample companies over phase 3 (2007–2008) and phase 4 (2009–2011)

	Phase 3 (2007–2008)				Phase 4 (2009–2011)			
Sector	Mean	Median	Quartile 1	Quartile 3	Mean	Median	Quartile 1	Quartile 3
Power	–	–	–	–	–	–	–	–
Healthcare	98.22	76.82	37.30	140.39	95.82	79.96	42.15	122.64
Capital goods	91.84	71.20	35.20	147.77	138.06	133.42	41.94	216.49
FMCG	67.75	77.52	56.20	84.18	59.89	76.02	49.11	78.73
Metals	60.74	53.16	27.77	89.45	83.52	72.62	36.79	121.49
ICT	58.07	58.07	58.07	58.07	43.64	43.64	43.64	43.64
Housing	58.05	58.05	54.52	61.59	65.52	65.52	57.41	73.63
Transport	49.59	33.99	26.30	67.10	59.12	34.25	23.39	55.09
Miscellaneous	49.15	37.73	24.30	65.40	59.92	49.45	32.24	94.48
Diversified	39.92	34.15	22.89	52.68	28.53	23.49	17.25	34.78
Oil and gas	14.75	12.50	10.37	20.69	14.59	16.12	8.96	20.94

	Phase 3 and Phase 4		
Sector	*t*	d*f*	Significance (2-tailed)
Capital goods	–2.407	9	0.039
Diversified	2.000	3	0.139
Miscellaneous	–1.136	10	0.283
Metals	–0.956	8	0.367

(continued)

Appendix 5.26: (continued)

	Phase 3 and Phase 4		
Sector	*t*	*df*	Significance (2-tailed)
Transport	−0.779	5	0.471
FMCG	−0.827	2	0.495
Oil and gas	0.484	3	0.662
Housing	0.565	1	0.672
Healthcare	0.064	9	0.951
ICT	–	–	–
Power	–	–	–

Appendix 5.27: ANOVA of the consolidated sample and the constituent sectors of the sample companies based on net working capital cycle (in days) over phase 1 (2001–2006) and phase 2 (2007–2011) and phase 3 (2007–2008) and phase 4 (2009–2011)

	Phase 1 and Phase 2		Phase 3 and phase 4	
Sector	*F*	Significance	*F*	Significance
Consolidated	3.446	0.001	3.822	0.000
Housing	4.835	0.093	0.013	0.917
Oil and gas	3.389	0.093	0.107	0.751
Diversified	2.278	0.166	1.960	0.199
Miscellaneous	0.688	0.416	0.590	0.451
Healthcare	0.418	0.524	0.072	0.791
Transport	0.234	0.636	0.239	0.634
FMCG	0.113	0.748	0.128	0.735
Capital goods	0.079	0.782	0.043	0.838
Metals	0.009	0.927	0.738	0.401
ICT	–	–	–	–
Power	–	–	–	–

Appendix 5.28: Mean, median and quartile values of percentage of cash and bank to total current assets of constituent sectors of the sample companies over phase 1 (2001–2006) and phase 2 (2007–2011)

	Phase 1 (2001–2006)				Phase 2 (2007–2011)			
Sector	Mean	Median	Quartile 1	Quartile 3	Mean	Median	Quartile 1	Quartile 3
ICT	26.18	20.15	11.74	40.55	25.79	22.91	9.70	38.84
Transport	24.62	18.24	6.90	33.73	29.27	21.87	7.04	42.20
Power	24.50	17.66	10.27	28.49	34.02	35.09	14.71	49.31
Oil and gas	21.23	15.24	3.90	34.24	28.83	26.79	9.17	39.21
Miscellaneous	14.72	6.42	3.20	24.65	20.93	10.74	5.09	33.55
Capital goods	13.67	8.63	5.18	21.30	14.82	12.69	6.62	20.19
Metals	13.59	7.76	4.25	18.98	23.49	11.75	4.42	36.91
Housing	11.90	9.28	4.08	16.67	17.27	8.18	4.93	28.06
Diversified	10.41	8.07	4.00	11.70	13.65	4.50	3.11	16.63
Healthcare	9.04	3.85	1.91	7.79	13.28	5.68	1.73	16.50
FMCG	8.84	5.61	2.66	10.29	15.11	11.49	5.47	19.94

(continued)

Appendix 5.28: (continued)

Sector	Phase 1 and Phase 2 *t*	*df*	Significance (2-tailed)
FMCG	–3.313	11	0.007
Miscellaneous	–2.550	15	0.022
Metals	–2.327	17	0.033
Transport	–1.461	16	0.163
Housing	–1.276	16	0.220
Power	–1.257	12	0.233
Oil and gas	–1.039	14	0.317
Diversified	–0.764	8	0.467
Healthcare	–0.546	13	0.594
Capital goods	–0.513	12	0.617
ICT	–0.207	17	0.839

Appendix 5.29: Mean, median and quartile values of percentage of cash and bank to total current assets of constituent sectors of the sample companies over phase 3 (2007–2008) and phase 4 (2009–2011)

	Phase 3 (2007–2008)				Phase 4 (2009–2011)			
Sector	Mean	Median	Quartile 1	Quartile 3	Mean	Median	Quartile 1	Quartile 3
Power	32.84	32.42	13.58	47.04	34.80	36.88	15.47	50.82
Oil and gas	29.83	27.48	5.98	46.28	28.16	26.33	11.30	34.49
Transport	29.54	24.27	9.07	41.83	29.08	20.26	5.68	42.45
ICT	28.75	23.18	10.54	45.51	23.81	22.72	9.13	34.39
Metals	23.13	10.62	4.28	41.72	23.73	12.50	4.52	33.70
Housing	21.98	13.11	7.88	32.58	14.14	4.90	2.96	25.04
Miscellaneous	19.54	7.39	4.37	29.82	21.86	12.98	5.58	36.03
Capital goods	13.47	10.89	7.58	16.35	15.72	13.89	5.97	22.76
Diversified	12.02	5.91	4.73	12.26	14.73	3.57	2.03	19.54
Healthcare	11.34	5.59	2.16	18.30	14.57	5.74	1.44	15.30
FMCG	10.43	9.22	6.03	11.29	18.23	13.00	5.10	25.71

Sector	Phase 3 and Phase 4 *t*	*Df*	Significance (2-tailed)
Housing	2.893	17	0.010
FMCG	–2.497	11	0.030
ICT	1.193	17	0.249
Capital goods	–0.893	12	0.390
Miscellaneous	–0.802	15	0.435
Healthcare	–0.538	13	0.600
Diversified	–0.518	8	0.618
Oil and gas	0.478	15	0.640
Power	–0.377	13	0.712
Metals	–0.213	17	0.834
Transport	–0.088	17	0.931

Appendix 5.30: ANOVA of the consolidated sample and the constituent sectors of the sample companies based on percentage of cash and bank to total current assets over phase 1 (2001–2006) and phase 2 (2007–2011) and phase 3 (2007–2008) and phase 4 (2009–2011)

	Phase 1 and Phase 2		Phase 3 and Phase 4	
Sector	*F*	Significance	*F*	Significance
Consolidated	4.679	0.000	3.831	0.000
FMCG	2.126	0.159	2.237	0.149
Metals	1.934	0.173	0.006	0.940
Housing	1.618	0.212	1.856	0.182
Power	1.536	0.227	0.073	0.789
Oil and gas	1.271	0.269	0.061	0.806
Miscellaneous	0.593	0.447	0.056	0.814
Diversified	0.521	0.481	0.185	0.673
Healthcare	0.151	0.701	0.260	0.614
Transport	0.147	0.704	0.001	0.979
Capital goods	0.097	0.758	0.302	0.588
ICT	0.028	0.869	0.542	0.467

Appendix 5.31: Mean, median and quartile values of percentage of inventories to total current assets of constituent sectors of the sample companies over phase 1 (2001–2006) and phase 2 (2007–2011)

	Phase 1 (2001–2006)				Phase 2 (2007–2011)			
Sector	Mean	Median	Quartile 1	Quartile 3	Mean	Median	Quartile 1	Quartile 3
FMCG	36.40	39.84	23.34	47.97	41.52	42.42	22.98	56.24
Metals	35.85	35.35	25.51	47.86	29.95	29.54	17.03	43.45
Housing	34.08	29.29	17.58	44.78	30.01	28.71	11.00	44.06
Healthcare	29.66	29.21	19.84	36.56	26.03	25.14	17.29	33.30
Miscellaneous	28.98	28.40	9.29	42.10	23.71	21.31	8.55	34.88
Oil and gas	25.64	16.64	6.41	46.21	26.14	16.94	7.54	46.69
Transport	24.73	27.35	9.30	37.00	21.26	19.32	3.55	30.77
Capital goods	24.62	22.96	16.84	28.76	26.75	22.74	16.26	32.29
Diversified	23.38	23.29	8.03	37.83	26.16	27.54	9.05	36.30
Power	6.25	6.20	1.02	10.92	4.88	3.37	0.05	8.63
ICT	2.39	0.02	–	2.21	1.38	0.32	–	1.37

	Phase 1 and Phase 2		
Sector	*t*	*df*	Significance (2-tailed)
Miscellaneous	1.771	15	0.097
Metals	1.478	17	0.158
Healthcare	1.246	13	0.235
Transport	1.205	16	0.246
FMCG	−1.217	11	0.249
Housing	1.051	16	0.309
ICT	0.946	17	0.357
Oil and gas	−0.905	13	0.382

(continued)

Appendix 5.31: (continued)

	Phase 1 and Phase 2		
Sector	*t*	*df*	Significance (2-tailed)
Diversified	–0.834	8	0.429
Capital goods	–0.793	12	0.443
Power	0.540	12	0.599

Appendix 5.32: Mean, median and quartile values of percentage of inventories to total current assets of constituent sectors of the sample companies over phase 3 (2007–2008) and phase 4 (2009–2011)

	Phase 3 (2007–2008)				Phase 4 (2009–2011)			
Sector	Mean	Median	Quartile 1	Quartile 3	Mean	Median	Quartile 1	Quartile 3
FMCG	42.77	46.53	23.91	56.22	40.7	39.68	22.37	56.25
Metals	31.46	32.84	21.63	44.84	28.94	27.33	13.95	42.53
Housing	28.56	26.08	10.46	41.78	30.98	30.47	11.37	45.58
Oil and gas	27.94	14.17	6.96	54.90	24.93	18.79	7.93	41.22
Capital goods	27.33	22.81	18.49	32.36	26.36	22.69	14.78	32.25
Diversified	27.04	27.92	12.92	35.64	25.58	27.28	6.47	36.74
Healthcare	26.39	26.37	17.23	33.76	25.80	24.32	17.33	32.98
Miscellaneous	22.86	22.16	5.98	33.63	24.28	20.73	10.26	35.71
Transport	21.37	19.37	3.32	31.37	21.19	19.28	3.70	30.37
Power	5.94	4.65	–	9.99	4.18	2.52	0.08	7.72
ICT	1.33	0.32	–	1.35	1.41	0.32	0.01	1.38

	Phase 3 and Phase 4		
Sector	*t*	*df*	Significance (2-tailed)
Housing	–2.107	17	0.050
Oil and gas	1.695	14	0.112
Power	1.292	13	0.219
Miscellaneous	–1.154	15	0.267
Transport	0.932	17	0.364
Diversified	0.869	8	0.410
FMCG	0.815	11	0.432
Metals	0.778	17	0.447
Capital goods	0.435	12	0.672
ICT	–0.340	17	0.738
Healthcare	0.283	13	0.782

Appendix 5.33: ANOVA of the consolidated sample and the constituent sectors of the sample companies based on percentage of inventories to total current assets over phase 1 (2001–2006) and phase 2 (2007–2011) and phase 3 (2007–2008) and phase 4 (2009–2011)

	Phase 1 and Phase 2		Phase 3 and Phase 4	
Sector	*F*	Significance	*F*	Significance
Consolidated	14.755	0.000	14.101	0.000
Metals	1.323	0.258	0.175	0.679
ICT	0.452	0.506	0.009	0.926
Healthcare	0.389	0.538	0.019	0.891
FMCG	0.387	0.540	0.115	0.738
Miscellaneous	0.374	0.546	0.125	0.726
Housing	0.261	0.613	0.104	0.749
Capital goods	0.227	0.638	0.030	0.865
Power	0.182	0.673	0.598	0.446
Transport	0.159	0.693	0.010	0.919
Diversified	0.082	0.778	0.019	0.893
Oil and gas	0.059	0.810	0.212	0.649

Appendix 5.34: Mean, median and quartile values of percentage of debtors and bills receivables to total current assets of constituent sectors of the sample companies over phase 1 (2001–2006) and phase 2 (2007–2011)

	Phase 1 (2001–2006)				Phase 2 (2007–2011)			
Sector	Mean	Median	Quartile 1	Quartile 3	Mean	Median	Quartile 1	Quartile 3
Capital goods	41.43	41.52	30.50	50.26	40.71	40.37	31.46	52.69
Healthcare	35.87	35.34	27.90	43.82	30.85	32.75	24.24	38.00
ICT	34.41	32.30	18.82	47.11	31.74	31.64	16.91	44.41
Power	32.23	29.13	13.48	51.25	18.63	15.32	4.54	30.03
Diversified	29.93	29.10	23.03	32.45	20.25	22.92	11.84	30.54
Transport	26.25	26.17	17.11	35.15	21.57	18.63	11.80	28.39
Miscellaneous	24.50	22.48	14.85	32.84	22.76	22.34	14.38	29.52
Metals	23.13	22.03	14.86	31.42	14.12	12.45	5.91	19.39
Housing	16.93	13.88	5.70	22.28	13.42	12.05	3.58	19.62
FMCG	15.62	12.75	6.84	21.30	10.42	9.62	6.71	13.80
Oil and gas	14.67	12.46	7.80	19.12	13.80	11.26	7.67	16.70

	Phase 1 and Phase 2		
Sector	*t*	df	Significance (2-tailed)
Metals	4.434	17	0.000
Transport	3.044	16	0.008
Power	2.243	12	0.045
FMCG	2.075	11	0.062
Diversified	2.092	8	0.070
Healthcare	1.641	13	0.125
Miscellaneous	1.114	15	0.283

(continued)

Appendix 5.34: (continued)

	Phase 1 and Phase 2		
Sector	*t*	*df*	Significance (2-tailed)
Housing	1.017	16	0.324
ICT	0.760	17	0.457
Capital goods	0.194	12	0.849
Oil and gas	–0.161	14	0.875

Appendix 5.35: Mean, median and quartile values of percentage of debtors and bills receivables to total current assets of constituent sectors of the sample companies over phase 3 (2007–2008) and phase 4 (2009–2011)

	Phase 3 (2007–2008)				Phase 4 (2009–2011)			
Sector	Mean	Median	Quartile 1	Quartile 3	Mean	Median	Quartile 1	Quartile 3
Capital goods	42.68	43.64	35.90	56.00	39.39	38.19	28.49	50.48
ICT	34.42	36.61	18.60	47.58	29.95	28.33	15.78	42.30
Healthcare	33.83	33.74	28.31	38.57	28.86	32.10	21.53	37.62
Miscellaneous	24.11	22.38	17.33	32.61	21.87	22.32	12.41	27.47
Transport	23.99	20.34	13.22	32.15	19.95	17.49	10.86	25.89
Power	20.51	13.67	2.88	35.66	17.38	16.42	5.65	26.28
Diversified	20.44	21.90	14.07	30.58	20.12	23.61	10.36	30.52
Metals	18.11	16.80	7.36	25.16	11.46	9.55	4.94	15.54
Oil and gas	12.93	10.38	7.10	15.05	14.39	11.84	8.04	17.79
Housing	12.30	11.18	3.56	19.81	14.17	12.63	3.60	19.49
FMCG	11.26	10.44	7.92	14.68	9.85	9.07	5.90	13.22

	Phase 3 and Phase 4		
Sector	*t*	*df*	Significance (2-tailed)
Metals	2.867	17	0.011
Capital goods	2.044	12	0.064
ICT	1.609	17	0.126
Healthcare	1.622	13	0.129
Transport	1.525	17	0.146
Housing	−1.457	17	0.163
Miscellaneous	1.462	15	0.164
FMCG	1.384	11	0.194
Oil and gas	–0.806	15	0.433
Power	0.684	13	0.506
Diversified	0.212	8	0.837

Appendix 5.36: ANOVA of the consolidated sample and the constituent sectors of the sample companies based on percentage of debtors and bills receivables to total current assets over phase 1 (2001–2006) and phase 2 (2007–2011) and phase 3 (2007–2008) and phase 4 (2009–2011)

	Phase 1 and Phase 2		Phase 3 and Phase 4	
Sector	*F*	Significance	*F*	Significance
Consolidated	12.983	0.000	15.43	0.000
Metals	8.569	0.006	3.736	0.062
FMCG	3.458	0.076	0.228	0.638
Power	3.032	0.094	0.134	0.718
Diversified	2.129	0.164	0.003	0.961
Transport	1.591	0.216	0.757	0.390
Healthcare	0.653	0.426	1.142	0.295
Housing	0.508	0.481	0.284	0.597
Miscellaneous	0.250	0.621	0.413	0.525
ICT	0.088	0.768	0.512	0.479
Capital goods	0.020	0.888	0.326	0.573
Oil and gas	0.001	0.972	0.114	0.738

Appendix 5.37: Mean, median and quartile values of zero working capital ratio of constituent sectors of the sample companies over phase 1 (2001–2006) and phase 2 (2007–2011)

	Phase 1 (2001–2006)				Phase 2 (2007–2011)			
Sector	Mean	Median	Quartile 1	Quartile 3	Mean	Median	Quartile 1	Quartile 3
Diversified	2.22	1.80	1.50	2.14	1.53	1.55	1.29	1.98
Healthcare	2.21	2.29	1.99	2.44	2.11	2.36	1.98	2.42
Metals	1.89	1.87	1.47	2.39	1.73	1.69	1.28	2.18
Miscellaneous	1.80	1.88	1.32	2.34	1.76	1.83	1.19	2.34
Capital goods	1.76	1.73	1.45	2.05	1.96	1.81	1.68	2.24
Housing	1.73	1.78	1.46	2.13	1.44	1.31	0.97	1.87
Transport	1.41	1.39	0.86	1.87	1.38	1.18	0.77	1.98
Power	1.39	1.34	0.68	2.00	1.24	1.24	0.37	1.88
Oil and gas	1.25	1.15	0.79	1.7	1.22	1.18	0.83	1.58
FMCG	1.24	1.09	0.81	1.59	1.27	1.29	0.84	1.72
ICT	1.21	1.12	0.38	1.99	1.08	0.93	0.37	1.69

	Phase 1 and Phase 2		
Sector	*t*	*df*	Significance (2-tailed)
Metals	1.524	13	0.151
Capital goods	−1.437	6	0.201
Oil and gas	1.206	12	0.251
Diversified	1.227	7	0.259
Transport	0.946	14	0.360
FMCG	−0.957	9	0.363
Miscellaneous	0.886	13	0.392
Housing	−0.440	10	0.669
Power	−0.275	11	0.788
ICT	0.219	10	0.831
Healthcare	0.052	6	0.960

Appendix 5.38: Mean, median and quartile values of zero working capital ratio of constituent sectors of the sample companies over phase 3 (2007–2008) and phase 4 (2009–2011)

	Phase 3 (2007–2008)				Phase 4 (2009–2011)			
Sector	Mean	Median	Quartile 1	Quartile 3	Mean	Median	Quartile 1	Quartile 3
Healthcare	2.24	2.45	2.12	2.51	2.02	2.29	1.89	2.35
Capital goods	1.95	1.84	1.64	2.25	1.96	1.78	1.70	2.24
Miscellaneous	1.90	1.99	1.36	2.48	1.66	1.72	1.08	2.24
Metals	1.80	1.73	1.46	2.23	1.68	1.66	1.15	2.14
Housing	1.57	1.30	1.06	2.33	1.35	1.32	0.91	1.56
Transport	1.42	1.31	0.86	1.96	1.35	1.10	0.71	2.00
Diversified	1.35	1.44	1.26	1.83	1.66	1.62	1.30	2.08
Power	1.29	1.35	0.65	1.71	1.20	1.17	0.19	1.99
Oil and gas	1.28	1.27	0.92	1.67	1.18	1.12	0.78	1.53
FMCG	1.18	1.18	0.85	1.65	1.33	1.36	0.83	1.76
ICT	1.11	0.97	0.31	1.82	1.06	0.91	0.41	1.61

	Phase 3 and Phase 4		
Sector	*t*	*df*	Significance (2-tailed)
Housing	−2.326	8	0.048
FMCG	−1.925	9	0.086
Oil and gas	1.701	14	0.111
Metals	1.661	11	0.125
Healthcare	1.756	5	0.139
Diversified	−1.561	6	0.169
Miscellaneous	1.342	9	0.212
Power	−1.059	11	0.312
Capital goods	−0.608	7	0.563
Transport	0.351	15	0.731
ICT	0.048	10	0.963

Appendix 5.39: ANOVA of the consolidated sample and the constituent sectors of the sample companies based on zero working capital ratio over phase 1 (2001–2006) and phase 2 (2007–2011) and phase 3 (2007–2008) and phase 4 (2009–2011)

	Phase 1 and Phase 2		Phase 3 and Phase 4	
Sector	*F*	Significance	*F*	Significance
Consolidated	4.620	0.000	5.196	0.000
Diversified	1.016	0.329	0.939	0.349
Miscellaneous	0.895	0.352	1.561	0.225
Metals	0.832	0.369	0.454	0.506
Oil and gas	0.540	0.469	0.201	0.657
Transport	0.504	0.483	0.027	0.871
Capital goods	0.299	0.593	0.332	0.574
ICT	0.175	0.680	0.044	0.836
Power	0.074	0.788	0.029	0.865
Housing	0.040	0.843	0.275	0.606
FMCG	0.009	0.926	0.338	0.568
Healthcare	0.004	0.948	0.100	0.757

References

Afza T, Nazir MS (2009) Is it better to be aggressive or conservative in managing working capital? J Appl Finance 15(8):19–30

Ali A (1994) The incremental information content of earnings, working capital from operations and cash flows. J Account Res 32(1):61–74

Banomyong R (2005) Measuring the cash conversion cycle in an international supply chain. Annual Logistics Research Network (LRN) Conference Proceedings ISBN 1-904564-13-5, pp 7–9

Barth ME, Cram DP, Nelson KK (2001) Accruals and the prediction of future cash flows. Account Rev 76(1):27–58

Bates TW, Kahle KM, Stulz RM (2009) Why do U. S. firms hold so much more cash than they used to? J Finance LXIV(5):1985–2021

Cheng NS, Pike R (2003) The trade credit decision: evidence of UK firms. Manag Decis Econ 24:419–438

Chiou J-R, Cheng L (2006) The determinants of working capital management. J Am Acad Bus 10(1):149–155

Dechow PM (1994) Accounting earnings and cash flows as measures of firm performance: the role of accounting accruals. J Account Econ 18:3–42

Deloof M (2003) Does working capital management affect profitability of Belgian firms? J Bus Finance Account 30(3 and 4):573–587

Dong HP, Su J (2010) The relationship between working capital management and profitability: a Vietnam case. Int Res J Finance Econ 49:59–67

Fazzari SM, Petersen BC (1993) Working capital and fixed investment: new evidence on financing constraints. RAND J Econ 24(3):328–342

Filbeck G, Krueger T (2005) Industry related differences in working capital management. J Bus 20(2):11–18

Gentry JA, Vaidyanathan R, Lee HW (1990) A weighted cash conversion cycle. Financ Manage 19(1):90–99

Gill A, Biger N, Mathur N (2010) The relationship between working capital management and profitability: evidence from the United States. Bus Econ J BEJ-10:1–9

Gitman LJ, Moses EA, Thomas I (1979) An assessment of corporate cash management practices. Financ Manage 8(1):32–41

Hill MD, Kelly WG, Highfield MJ (2010) Net operating working capital behavior: a first look. Financ Manage 39(2):783–805

Jain PK, Kumar M (1997) Comparative financial management: practices of India and South East Asia. Hindustan Publishing Corporation, New Delhi, pp 43–44

Jain PK, Yadav SS (2000) Financial management practices in select private corporate enterprises – a comparative study of India. Hindustan Publishing Corporation, India/Thailand/Singapore

Jain PK, Yadav SS (2005) Financial management practices – a study of public sector enterprises in India. Hindustan Publishing Corporation, New Delhi

Kaur J (2010) Working capital management in Indian tyre industry. Int Res J Finance Econ 46:7–15

Kusnad Y, Wei KCJ (2011) The determinants of corporate cash management policies: evidence from around the world. J Corp Financ 17(3):725–740

Lamberson M (1995) Changes in working capital of small firms in relation to changes in economic activity. J Bus 10(2):45–50

Lazaridis I, Tryfonidis D (2006) Relationship between working capital management and profitability of listed companies in the Athens stock exchange. J Financ Manage Anal 19(1):26–35

Long MS, Malitz IB, Ravid SA (1993) Trade credit, quality guarantees, and product marketability. Financ Manage 22:117–127

Mramor D, Valentincic A (2003) Forecasting the liquidity of very small private companies. J Bus Ventur 18:745–771

Opler T, Pinkowitz L, Stulz RH, Williamson R (1999) Determinants and implications of corporate cash holdings. J Financ Econ 52:3–46

Raheman A, Qayyum A, Afza T, Bodla MA (2010) Sector-wise analysis of working capital management and firm performance in manufacturing sector of Pakistan. Interdiscip J Contemp Res Bus 2(7):412–437

Richards VD, Laughlin EJ (1980) A cash conversion cycle approach to liquidity analysis. Financ Manage 9(1):32–38

Saad N, Mohamad N (2010) Working capital management: the effect of market valuation and profitability in Malaysia. Int J Bus Manage 5(11):140–147

Sastry ASR (1970) The effect of credit on transactions demand for cash. J Finance 25(4):777–781

Smith KV (1973) State of the art of working capital management. Financ Manage 2(3):50–55

Sokoloff KL (1983) Investment in fixed and working capital during early industrialization: evidence from U.S. manufacturing firms. UCLA Department of Economics, Working Paper #311, pp 1–15

Sur D, Chakraborty K (2011) Evaluating relationship of working capital and profitability: a study of select multinational companies in the Indian pharmaceutical sector. IUP J Manage Res X(2):7–36

Teruel PJG, Solano PM (2007) Effects of working capital management on SME profitability. Int J Managerial Finance 3(2):164–177

Van Horne JC, Wachowicz JM (2004) Fundamentals of financial management, 12th edn. Prentice Hall, New York

Ward P (2004) Cash-to-cash is what counts. J Commerce 5(7):54

Part III
Corporate Governance, Risk Management and Professionalism

Chapter 6
Corporate Governance

Introduction

Weak corporate governance has been singled out as the leading cause for recent high profile cases of corporate fraud (Skaife et al. 2006). There is a growing demand for corporates to be more transparent and accountable in their dealings with their stakeholders and the community at large. In recent times, in particular after the liberalisation of the Indian economy in 1991, a large number of Indian companies have been raising capital overseas by getting listed on international stock exchanges. This is in tune with the efforts of Indian government to attract more foreign direct investment (FDI) into India. Given the fact that this trend of Indian companies to have more access to global capital markets (to raise financial resources) is likely to continue (in fact, may augment) in future, there is a growing realization that Indian companies would need to make their operations and financial results more transparent, that is, improve their standards of corporate governance (IndiaKnowledge@Wharton 2007).

The Securities and Exchange Board of India (SEBI), which regulates India's stock markets, had initially mandated the adherence of clause 49 of corporate governance (for all listed companies) from 1 April 2004. However, after wide public outcry against the provision (in its original form), SEBI had constituted a committee on corporate governance under the chairmanship of Mr. N.R. Narayana Murthy. Based on the recommendations of the committee and public comments received, certain amendments were made in Clause 49 of the Listing Agreement (http://www.sebi.gov.in/commreport/clause49.html). Clause 49 is basically a regulation that calls for an increase in the number of independent directors serving on the Boards of large Indian companies to ensure more transparency and better accountability. The modified clause 49 came into effect from 1 January 2006, and all listed companies were mandated to adhere to it with effect from 1 April 2006 (http://www.sebi.org/).

It is thus expected that all the sample companies would be following the corporate governance rules and regulations rigorously, indicating a high degree of professionalism, financial transparency and discipline in their management ethos. This may

P.K. Jain et al., *Financial Management Practices: An Empirical Study of Indian Corporates*, India Studies in Business and Economics, DOI 10.1007/978-81-322-0990-4_6, © Springer India 2013

also be naturally expected as the sample companies are amongst the largest companies in the country and are accountable to a vast number of stakeholders.

This aspect, thus, necessitates inquiry. This modest attempt (perhaps the first of its kind) aims at ascertaining the status of adherence to corporate governance regulations (based on primary data) amongst the sample companies.

For better exposition, this chapter has been divided into nine sections. Section I lays down the scope, data and methodology of the chapter. Section II contains a brief literature review concerning aspects of corporate governance. Section III presents the overall aspects of the corporate governance policy amongst the sample companies. Section IV looks at the management incentives provided. Requirements of financial reporting have been delineated in section V. Section VI is devoted to the separation/composition of the board of directors. Aspects relating to internal controls under corporate governance constitute the subject matter of section VII. Fulfillment of requirements under Clause 49 constitutes the subject matter of section VIII. Concluding observations are listed in section IX.

Section I Scope, Data and Methodology

Scope

Based on market capitalisation, the top 200 companies listed on the Bombay Stock Exchange constitute the BSE 200 index. Out of these 200 companies, 34 companies were engaged in the financial sector as on 1 April 2010, the sample selection date. Therefore, the scope of this study is limited to the 166 nonfinancial BSE 200 companies. The sample is representative in nature as the BSE 200 companies represent all industry groups. (Kindly refer to Appendix 1.1 for the complete list of BSE 200 companies and Appendix 1.2 for the 34 financial companies that have been excluded from the sample for the study). This apart, the selected sample comprised 84.32% of the total market capitalisation on the Bombay Stock Exchange, as on 1 April 2010. Clearly, the sample is representative of corporate sector enterprises in India.

Data and Methodology

The primary data on which the analysis is based consists of opinions/preferences of finance managers of the sample companies related to corporate governance. The research instrument for primary data consisted of a questionnaire (Appendix 1.3). Questions designed were simple and specific, relating to various aspects of corporate governance. Opinion-based and subjective information was kept to minimum in order to keep the study more objective and scientific. The questionnaire along with covering letter was sent by courier to the CFO/Finance Manager/Director Finance of each of the 166 companies. At the same time, an attachment file of the copy of the questionnaire was also emailed along with the covering letter so that, in case the respondent had a problem in the physical delivery of the questionnaire, he/she could download the questionnaire from the file attached. Subsequently, the questionnaire was re-mailed to the non-responding companies for follow-up in order to maximise the response rate. It was indicated to the CFOs that the individual responses would be kept strictly confidential and only aggregate generalisations would be published.

The initial response was very poor; only eight companies responded. Subsequently two reminders, both through post and email were sent to the remaining companies. Personal contacts were also established with the companies located in and around Delhi1.[1] This increased response level to 31. Thus, this part of the analysis is based on 31 responses received out of 166 (response rate being 18.67%).

Prima facie, the response rate may be seen as low. It should be borne in mind, however, that the number of respondents and the response rate are similar to previous studies using a similar method (Jain and Kumar 1997; Jain and Yadav 2000, 2005). Further, it is becoming difficult to encourage GPs (general practitioners) to participate in surveys (Templeton et al. 1997). Also, considering that the survey was addressed to time-constrained CFOs, this may be considered reasonably an adequate response.

Section II Literature Review

The literature review undertaken in this section highlights various philosophies behind corporate governance and lists evaluations of corporate governance practices across the world.

Corporate Governance: Different Aspects and Evaluations

Okpara (2011) revealed a number of constraints that hinder the implementation and promotion of corporate governance in Nigeria. These constraints included weak or non-existent law enforcement mechanisms, abuse of shareholders' rights, lack of commitment on the part of Board of Directors, lack of adherence to the regulatory framework, weak enforcement and monitoring systems and lack of transparency and disclosure. Mishra and Ratti (2011) examined corporate governance and foreign equity home bias in Chinese companies. They suggested that some institutions were effective monitors of firms they invested in. Foreign institutions were able to exert pressure because they had fewer business relations with the firm to jeopardise, unlike domestic institutions.

---

[1]Assistance was also sought from the Delhi Stock Exchange and Securities and Exchange Board of India, as a part of the primary data collection exercise.

Cheung et al. (2011) provided evidence in support of the notion that good corporate governance can predict future market valuation. Klai (2011) revealed that the governance mechanisms affected the financial information quality of the Tunisian companies. Particularly, the power of the foreigners, the families and the block-holders reduced the reporting quality, while the control by the State and the financial institutions was associated with a good quality of financial disclosure. Kocmanova et al. (2011) focused on the corporate governance and on economic, environmental and social issues relating to measurement of corporate performance. Neglecting such performance aspects by corporate management in the corporate sustainability reporting could lead to further and deeper problems.

Pergola and Joseph (2011) provided insight regarding the motivations and behaviour of Board Members and the impact of stock ownership on their actions. Monks (2011) found that a self-governing corporate structure was optimal if it could be made to work. The history of the last 30 years of supposed corporate 'self-restraint', coupled with the economic debacle of the last 2 years, offered compelling evidence that current efforts at corporate governance were not working. Mukweyi and Wiley (2010) made recommendations that may guide leaders in improving their corporate governance for the stakeholders.

Spitzeck (2009) developed insight into the structures which companies set up to deal with the corporate responsibility agenda. Li and Harrison (2008) showed that national culture had a dominant influence on corporate governance structure and its emphasis is recommended in future cross-national organisational research.

Garg (2007) studied whether the Board size and independence mattered in terms of influencing firm's performance. They found an inverse association between Board size and firm performance. Tuteja (2006) examined the Board size, composition and the professional experience as well as wisdom of its members that played a role of paramount importance in the sound management of a company. Gillan (2006) developed a corporate governance framework and provided a broad overview of recent corporate governance research.

Skaife et al. (2006) documented that firms' governance affects firms' credit ratings. Morck et al. (2005) stated that economic growth seemed related to the distribution of control over an economy's large corporate sector. Outside of the United States and United Kingdom, most large corporations had controlling owners, typically very wealthy families. Boubakri et al. (2005) found higher improvements in efficiency for firms in countries where stock markets were more developed and where property rights were better protected and enforced. Hermalin (2005) determined whether the replacement of a CEO was a costly option.

O'Sullivan (2000) argued that considerable change has indeed occurred recently in corporate governance systems. These changes cannot be understood, however, as the outcome of a market-driven, efficiency-enhancing process.

Corporate Governance in India

Sanan and Yadav (2011) evaluated the impact of corporate governance reforms initiated by Securities and Exchange Board of India (SEBI). The results of the study indicated that though corporate governance disclosures had improved in the post-reform period, yet the overall disclosures of the Indian companies were only moderate.

Godbole (2002) stated that Indian corporates needed to regard the issue of governance not as an irritant or impediment, but as an essential tool and mechanism for their very survival in the new economic environment.

Reed (2002) stated that India, like many developing countries, had been moving towards the adoption of an Anglo-American model of corporate governance in recent years. The impetus for this shift had been a combination of global political economy pressures and problems arising out of the previous business house model of governance.

Section III Corporate Governance Policy

In the effort to understand whether corporate governance was dealt with at the level of policymaking and adopted by companies, the managers were asked to respond to the questions relating to the institution of a corporate governance policy at the organisational level and its constituents.

From Table 6.1, it is evident that 89.65% of the respondent companies do have a corporate governance policy at the organisational level. On the other hand, it is pertinent to note that corporate governance regulations became mandatory for Indian listed companies from 1 April 2006, as per the SEBI guidelines. Keeping the same in mind, it is a matter of concern that 10.34% companies still do not have a corporate governance policy.

In terms of focus, bulk of the corporate governance policy addresses issues related to shareholders, management and the Board (88.46%). Regulatory authorities, the community at large and employees are next in order of priority (Table 6.2).

Of the companies that do adhere to corporate governance guidelines, more than 90% have an internal team primarily dedicated to corporate governance in the companies (Table 6.3). This is perhaps an indication of the professionalism and seriousness with which the sample companies are treating corporate governance regulations and their practice.

Table 6.1 Companies having corporate governance policy amongst the respondents

Options	Percentage
Yes	89.65
No	10.34

Table 6.2 Focus areas of the corporate governance policy for the respondent companies

Area of focus	Percentage
Shareholders	88.46
Management	88.46
Board of Directors	88.46
Regulatory authorities	69.23
Community at large	65.38
Employees	61.53
Customers	50.00
Creditors	46.15
Suppliers	42.30
Any other	7.69

Table 6.3 Presence of an internal team dedicated to corporate governance in the respondent companies

Options	Percentage
Yes	92.85
No	7.14

Table 6.4 Components of the internal corporate governance policy (if present) for the respondent companies

Components	Percentage
Monitoring by Board of Directors	100.00 (46.15)
Remuneration	50.00 (–)
Balance of power	34.61 (–)

Figures in brackets represent the opinion chosen exclusively. The same holds true for all tables

For better management and subsequent review and evaluation, a company needs to divide the overall corporate governance policy into two parts – one governing the internal policies and the other governing the company's interactions with the external stakeholders. It was desirable to understand the important components of both the internal and external corporate governance policies to be able to establish the focus areas.

According to Table 6.4, for the internal corporate governance policy, monitoring by the Board of Directors of the corporate governance regulations and their subsequent adherence is practised by all respondent companies. Remuneration forms the second important component followed by the balance of power.

For the external corporate governance policy, the primary focus behind the design and practice are the government regulations (85%) followed by the demand for and assessment of performance information, in particular, financial statements at 60% (Table 6.5).

Indian credit rating agencies like CRISIL (Credit Rating and Information Services of India Limited) and ICRA (Investment Information and Credit Rating Agency of India) have corporate governance ratings which assess corporate governance practices at a company with respect to their impact on all stakeholders (http://www.crisil.com/ratings/crisil-gvc-ratings.html).

Table 6.5 Components of the external corporate governance policy for the respondent companies

Components	Percentage
Government regulations	85.00 (30.00)
Demand for and assessment of performance information (especially financial statements)	60.00 (10.00)
Debt covenants	30.00 (–)
Competition	20.00 (–)
Media pressure	20.00
Managerial labour market	5.00
Takeovers	0.00

Table 6.6 Assessment of corporate governance practices by rating agency like CRISIL or ICRA for the respondent companies

Options	Percentage
Yes	11.53
No	88.46

CRISIL allots the GVC (governance and value creation) ratings while ICRA has the CGR (corporate governance ratings) (http://www.icra.in/rating.aspx).

On enquiring whether the sample companies get their corporate governance policies assessed/whetted by a rating agency like CRISIL or ICRA, only 11.53% companies responded in the affirmative (Table 6.6). The companies that did go in for the assessment of corporate governance practices were asked to disclose the rating they so secured. None of the companies responded.

This nonresponse reinforces the discouraging view that corporate India seems to be shying away from corporate governance ratings (http://www.financialexpress.com/news/few-takers-for-corporate-governance-ratings/103765/).

Section IV Management Incentives

This section briefly explores whether the sample companies incentivise the senior management for working towards increasing the corporate valuation.

As per Table 6.7, 78.27% of respondent companies have no incentive plans to motivate senior management to work towards a higher share price.

The CEO/MD of the respondent companies apparently holds less than 10% of the equity (Table 6.8).

An important aspect to note here is the presence of the dominant shareholder in corporate India in the form of three large categories: the public sector units (PSUs) where the government is the dominant (in fact, majority) shareholder, the multinational companies (MNCs) where the foreign parent is the dominant shareholder and the Indian business groups where the promoters, together with their friends and

Table 6.7 Incentives offered to senior management to work towards a higher share price in the respondent companies

Options	Percentage
Yes	21.42
No	78.57

Table 6.8 Percentage of equity holding of CEO/MD in the respondent companies

Percentage of equity holding (%)	Percentage
Below 10	90.90
10–25	0.00
25–50	9.09
Above 50	0.00

relatives, are the dominant shareholders (Varma 1997). The sample companies belong to one of these three categories. This, perhaps, could be the contributing factor towards the above findings.

Section V Financial Reporting

This section explores the extent to which various reporting regulations, as laid down in Clause 49 of Listing Agreement, are met by the sample companies.

On the financial reporting front, respondent companies have encouraging statistics where a large majority (90.32%) always publishes their annual report within stipulated time, that is, within 6 months of the end of the financial year and the remaining 9.67% submit the same (mostly) within the stipulated period. Similarly, in terms of the publishing of quarterly reports within the stipulated time of within 1 month from the end of the quarter, virtually all (96.42%) companies always do so. However, the statistics seem discouraging in the publishing of the semi-annual reports, with 10.71% of respondent companies never publishing the semi-annual reports within the stipulated time (Table 6.9).

As indicated in Table 6.10, 96.77% of respondent companies always disclose material-sensitive information to stakeholders. This is, perhaps, an indication of the growing professionalism in the sphere of material-sensitive disclosures and subsequent transparency in the dealings of the companies.

In accordance with clause 49, there should be a separate section on corporate governance in the annual report of a company with a detailed compliance report. Noncompliance of any mandatory requirement of this clause with reasons thereof should also be clearly stated (http://www.nseindia.com/getting_listed/content/clause_49.pdf). Evidently, all respondent companies adhere to this reporting regulation (Table 6.11).

Table 6.9 Publication schedule of annual, semi-annual and quarterly financial reports for the respondent companies

Objectives	Always	Mostly	Occasionally	Sometimes	Never
The company publishes its annual report within stipulated time (6 months) of the end of the financial year	90.32	9.67	0.00	0.00	0.00
The company publishes/announces semi-annual reports within 1 month of the end of the half-year	85.71	3.57	0.00	0.00	10.71
The company publishes/announces quarterly reports within 1 month of the end of the quarter	96.42	3.57	0.00	0.00	0.00

Table 6.10 Consistent disclosure of sensitive information to stakeholders by the respondent companies

Options	Percentage
Always	96.77
Sometimes	3.22
Never	0.00

Table 6.11 Inclusion of a separate section on corporate governance in the annual report in the respondent companies

Options	Percentage
Yes	100.00
No	0.00

Section VI Composition of Board

While understanding the corporate governance practice in a company, it is important to look at the composition of the Board as well as the important executive/management committees. Also, it is necessary to confirm whether separation exists amongst committees which may have conflicting interests to ensure that complete partiality is maintained in the practice and evaluation of corporate governance measures.

Majority of the sample companies (67.85%) have clear separation of Board and members of the executive/management committee (Table 6.12). However, the chairman-cum-managing director (in case of such a designation) would be a member of the Board in all cases.

As was expected, there is clear separation between statutory auditors and the top management of the company (Table 6.13). This is imperative to ensure that there

Table 6.12 Separation of Board Members and members of the executive/management committee in the respondent companies

Options	Percentage
Yes	67.85
No	32.14

Table 6.13 Separation between statutory auditors and the top management of the company in the respondent companies

Options	Percentage
Yes	100.00
No	0.00

Table 6.14 Inclusion of direct representatives of banks, financial/strategic investors and large creditors in the Board of the company in the respondent companies

Options	Percentage
Yes	29.03
No	70.96

Table 6.15 Appointment of an executive chairman in the company amongst respondents

Options	Percentage
Yes	41.37
No	58.62

is complete impartiality in the auditing of the financial information of the company by the auditors.

Initially, the Indian financial system allowed the provision/practice of having nominee directors from the lending financial institutions in the Board; clause 49 mandates that there shall be no nominee directors anymore (Khan 2011). If an institution wishes to appoint a director on the Board, such appointment would be made only by the shareholders.

From Table 6.14, it can be observed that currently 70.96% of respondent companies do not have any inclusion/direct representation from financial institutions like banks, strategic investors and large creditors in the Board. This could, perhaps, be an indication of more liberal and equity-oriented management practices without the interference of the other suppliers of corporate finance, namely, creditors.

Majority of the companies (58.62%) do not have an executive chairman in the company (Table 6.15). According to clause 49, in case where a non-executive chairman is the promoter of the company or is related to any promoter or person occupying management positions at the Board level or at one level below the Board, at least one-half of the Board of the company shall consist of independent directors (http://www.nseindia.com/getting_listed/content/clause_49.pdf).

Table 6.16 Presence of more than 50% independent directors on the Board in the respondent companies

Options	Percentage
Yes	75.00
No	25.00

Table 6.17 Presence of more than 33% independent directors on the Board in the respondent companies

Options	Percentage
Yes	86.36
No	13.63

Independent Directors and Composition of Board

As per clause 49, an independent director is one who, apart from receiving director's remuneration, does not have any material pecuniary relationships or transaction with the company, its promoters, its senior management or its holding company, its subsidiaries and associated companies, which, in the judgment of the Board, may affect independent judgment of the director (http://www.sebi.gov.in/commreport/clause49.html).

The Board of the company should have an optimum combination of executive and non-executive directors with not less than 50% of the Board comprising of non-executive directors. Where the chairman of the Board is a non-executive director, at least one-third of the Board should comprise of independent directors; in case the chairman is an executive director, at least half of the Board should comprise of independent directors (http://www.nseindia.com/getting_listed/content/clause_49.pdf).

From Table 6.16, it is evident that three-fourths of the respondent companies have more than 50% independent directors on the Board, suggesting perhaps that these companies have an executive director as the chairman of the Board.

Section VII Internal Controls Under Corporate Governance

As a non-mandatory requirement of clause 49, all companies are required to establish a mechanism called the whistle-blower policy for employees to report to the management concerns about unethical behaviour, actual or suspected fraud or violation of the company's code of conduct or ethics policy. The mechanism must provide for adequate safeguards against victimisation of employees who avail of the mechanism and must also provide where senior management is involved direct access to the chairman of the audit committee. The existence of the mechanism must be appropriately communicated within the organisation, and the audit committee must periodically

Table 6.18 Presence of a whistle-blower policy in the respondent companies

Options	Percentage
Yes	73.33
No	26.67

Table 6.19 Presence of an investors' grievance cell in the respondent companies

Options	Percentage
Yes	100.00
No	0.00

Table 6.20 Listing of companies on any exchange abroad

Options	Percentage
Yes	48.38
No	51.61

Table 6.21 Compliance requirement with Sarbanes–Oxley Act (SOX) for the respondent companies

Options	Percentage
Yes	13.79
No	86.20

review the existence and functioning of the mechanism (http://www.sebi.gov.in/commreport/clause49.html).

As per Table 6.18, nearly three-fourths (73.33%) of respondent companies have such a mechanism in place.

On a more encouraging note, all the respondent companies have an investors' grievance cell in the company to take up any investor grievance to its appropriate conclusion (Table 6.19).

Nearly half of the respondent companies (48.38%) are listed on an exchange abroad, an indication of the international face of the sample companies (Table 6.20). This also confirms the finding on risk management that Indian companies have increased operations abroad (Chap. 7). This would require such companies to comply with the corporate governance regulations of that particular country as well in addition to the Indian regulations.

Sarbanes–Oxley Act (SOX) of the United States of America is considered, in essence, to be the predecessor of clause 49 (KPMG 2012). Hence, it was desirable to know whether the sample companies are required to comply with SOX in case they are listed on an American stock exchange. Only 13.79% of respondent companies responded in the affirmative (Table 6.21). This is perhaps because the respondent companies are either not listed abroad at all or at least not in USA.

Table 6.22 Establishment and maintenance of internal controls and implementation of remediation and risk mitigation towards deficiencies in internal controls by the CEO and CFO in the respondent companies

Options	Percentage
Yes	100.00
No	0.00

Table 6.23 Certificate obtained from auditors/practising company secretaries regarding compliance of conditions as stipulated in clause 49 and annexing the same to the director's report by the respondent companies

Options	Percentage
Yes	96.77
No	3.22

As per clause 49, the chief executive officer (CEO) and the chief financial officer (CFO) should certify that they have reviewed financial statements and that, to the best of their knowledge and belief, these statements do not contain any materially untrue statement, omit any material fact or contain statements that might be misleading. They should also certify that there have been no transactions entered into by the company which are fraudulent, illegal or violative of the company's code of conduct or ethics policy (http://www.sebi.gov.in/commreport/clause49.html).

As per Table 6.22, all companies have established and maintained internal controls and have also implemented remediation and risk mitigation measures towards deficiencies in internal controls by the CEO and CFO.

Section VIII Fulfilment of Requirements Under Clause 49

As per clause 49, a company should obtain a certificate from either the auditors or practising company secretaries regarding compliance of regulations under corporate governance and annex the certificate with the directors' report, which is sent annually to all the shareholders of the company. Nearly all (96.77%) respondent companies have been obtaining the certificate (Table 6.23).

Further, the same certificate is also required to be filed at the stock exchanges where the company is listed along with the annual report (http://www.nseindia.com/getting_listed/content/clause_49.pdf). All companies are fulfilling this requirement (Table 6.24).

Despite it being mandatory under clause 49, one-fourth of respondent companies still do not have the mandatory/dedicated committee on corporate governance (Table 6.25).

Table 6.24 Submission of quarterly compliance report on corporate governance to the Stock exchange where it is listed in the prescribed form by the respondent companies

Options	Percentage
Yes	100.00
No	0.00

Table 6.25 Presence of the mandatory committee on corporate governance in the respondent companies

Options	Percentage
Yes	74.07
No	25.92

Table 6.26 Presence of the mandatory audit committee as per clause 49 in the respondent companies

Options	Percentage
Yes	100.00
No	0.00

Table 6.27 Presence of the remunerations committee as per clause 49 in the respondent companies

Options	Percentage
Yes	90.32
No	9.67

As per clause 49, a qualified and independent audit committee should be set up in the company with minimum three directors as members. Two-thirds of the members of audit committee are required to be independent directors and all members should be financially literate (http://www.nseindia.com/getting_listed/content/clause_49.pdf). All respondent companies do have the mandatory audit committee as per clause 49 (Table 6.26). It is an indication that respondent companies are perhaps serious about meeting the audit requirements.

Similarly, companies are required to have a remunerations committee responsible for detailing the remuneration of senior management and directors, as per clause 49. Ninety percent of the respondent companies have such a committee (Table 6.27).

Disclosure of contingent liabilities was already required in the past under Schedule VI to the Companies Act, 1956. However, during the revision of clause 49, it was decided that it was impractical for auditors to comment on management's views on contingent liabilities and any such view/comment may be construed as an admission

Table 6.28 Disclosure of contingent liabilities in the respondent companies

Options	Percentage
Yes	88.88
No	11.11

of the liability, which may be detrimental to the interests of the shareholders. It was, therefore, suggested that this clause be deleted in its entirety. However, it is interesting to note that such a disclosure is still adhered to by 88.88% companies (Table 6.28).

Section IX Conclusion

All in all, it appears that the sample companies do adhere to certain aspects of corporate governance but not in its entirety. This is an area of concern as the sample companies are amongst the largest companies in the country and, as such, are responsible to a large number of stakeholders. In that respect, they have a larger image to protect. These findings are similar to the findings of the recent study of Sanan and Yadav (2011) and Pande and Kaushik (2012).

At the time of writing this monograph, 6 years have passed since the date when clause 49 became mandatory. Companies have had adequate time to set up corporate governance structures and practices. The possible reasons for the continuing lacuna on certain aspects could be the finite supply of independent directors in the country and also the process of cultural change (Li and Harrison 2008; Pande and Kaushik 2012).

However, it is important that the Indian corporates need to regard the issue of governance not as an irritant or impediment but as an essential mechanism for their very survival in the new economic environment. This aspect draws support from the similar findings of Godbole (2002).

Also, good corporate governance is reported to indicate better valuations for the companies (Skaife et al. 2006; Cheung et al. 2011; Klai 2011; Kocmanova et al. 2011; Gurbuz et al. 2010). The sample companies, thus, would do well to be more serious and professional about adopting and practising good corporate governance.

References

Boubakri N, Cosset J-C, Guedhami O (2005) Liberalization corporate governance and the performance of privatized firms in developing countries. J Corp Finance 11:767–790

Cheung Y-L, Connelly JT, Jiang P, Limpaphayom P (2011) Does corporate governance predict future performance? Evidence from Hong Kong. Finance Manage 40(1):159–197

CRISIL (Credit Rating and Information Services of India Limited) website: http://www.crisil.com/ratings/crisil-gvc-ratings.html. Accessed 12 July 2012

Financial Express website: http://www.financialexpress.com/news/few-takers-for-corporate-governance-ratings/103765/. Accessed 12 July 2012
Garg AK (2007) Influence of board size and independence on firm performance: a study of Indian companies. Vikalpa 32(3):39–60
Gillan SL (2006) Recent developments in corporate governance: an overview. J Corp Finance 12(5):381–402
Godbole M (2002) Corporate governance: myth and reality. Econ Polit Wkly 37(30):3094–3102
Gurbuz AO, Aybars A, Kutlu O (2010) Corporate governance and financial performance with a perspective on institutional ownership: empirical evidence from Turkey. J Appl Manage Acc 8(2):21–37
Hermalin BE (2005) Trends in corporate governance. J Finance 60(5):2351–2384
ICRA (Investment Information and Credit Rating Agency of India) website: http://www.icra.in/rating.aspx. Accessed 12 July 2012
IndiaKnowledge@Wharton (2007) Corporate governance in India: has clause 49 made a difference? http://knowledge.wharton.upenn.edu/india/article.cfm?articleid=4152. Accessed 12 July 2012
Jain PK, Kumar M (1997) Comparative financial management: practices of India and South East Asia. Hindustan Publishing Corporation, New Delhi, pp 43–44
Jain PK, Yadav SS (2000) Financial management practices in select private corporate enterprises – a comparative study of India, Thailand and Singapore. Hindustan Publishing Corporation, New Delhi
Jain PK, Yadav SS (2005) Financial management practices – a study of public sector enterprises in India, Thailand and Singapore. Hindustan Publishing Corporation (India), New Delhi
Khan MY (2011) Indian financial system, 7th edn. Tata McGraw Hill, New Delhi
Klai N (2011) Corporate governance and financial reporting quality: the case of Tunisian firms. Int Bus Res 4(1):158–166
Kocmanova A, Hrebicek J, Docekalov M (2011) Corporate governance and sustainability. Econ Manage 16:543–550, ISSN 1822-6515
KPMG report (2012). http://www.in.kpmg.com/tl_files/pictures/cg%20survey%20report.pdf. Accessed 12 July 2012
Li J, Harrison JR (2008) Corporate governance and national culture: a multi-country study. Corp Gov 8(5):607–621, ISSN 1472-0701
Mishra AV, Ratti RA (2011) Governance, monitoring and foreign investment in Chinese companies. Emerg Mark Rev 12(3):171–188
Monks RAG (2011) Governance at crossroads: a personal perspective. Int J Discl Gov 8(1):62–76
Morck R, Wolfenzon D, Yeung B (2005) Corporate governance, economic entrenchment and growth. J Econ Lit 43(3):655–720
Mukweyi A, Wiley LC (2010) Managerial fraud and corporate governance in American corporations. Int J Bus Public Adm 7(1):57–70
NSE (National Stock Exchange) website: http://www.nseindia.com/getting_listed/content/clause_49.pdf. Accessed 12 July 2012
Okpara JO (2011) Corporate governance in a developing economy: barriers, issues and implications for firms. Corp Gov 11(2):184–199
O'Sullivan M (2000) Corporate governance and globalization. Ann Am Acad Pol Soc Sci 570 (1 – Dimensions of Globalization):153–172
Pande S, Kaushik KV (2012) Study on the state of corporate governance in India – evolution, issues and challenges for the future. http://www.iica.in/images/Evolution_of_Corporate_Governance_in_India.pdf. Accessed 12 July 2012
Pergola TM, Joseph GW (2011) Corporate governance and board equity ownership. Corp Gov 11(2):200–213, ISSN 1472-0701
Reed AM (2002) Corporate governance reforms in India. J Bus Ethics Corp Gov Ref Dev Ctries 37(3):249–268
Sanan N, Yadav S (2011) Corporate governance reforms and financial disclosures: a case of Indian companies. IUP J Corp Gov X(2):62–81
SEBI (Securities and Exchange Board of India) website: http://www.sebi.gov.in/commreport/clause49.html. Accessed 12 July 2012

Skaife HA, Collins DW, Ryan LF (2006) The effects of corporate governance on firms' credit ratings. J Account Econ 42(3):203–243

Spitzeck H (2009) The development of governance structures for corporate responsibility. Corp Gov 9(4):495–505, ISSN 1472-0701

Templeton L, Deehan A, Taylor C, Drummond C, Strang J (1997) Surveying general practitioners: does a low response rate matter? J Gen Pract 47(415):91–94

Tuteja SK (2006) Board structure in Indian companies: an empirical survey. J Manag Res 6(3):145–156

Varma JR (1997) Corporate governance in India: disciplining the dominant shareholder. IIMB Manage Rev 9(4):5–18

Chapter 7
Risk Management

Introduction

Risk management is the process of identification, assessment and prioritisation of risks followed by coordinated and economical application of resources to minimise, monitor and control the probability and/or impact of unfortunate events or to maximise the realisation of opportunities (Hubbard 2009).

The processes of liberalisation and globalisation have seeped into the economic fabric of all nations across the world. Even the countries which were largely closed to the external influence on their economic system have opened up in terms of trade and investment. It is a shared perception of economists and researchers that free market system and liberalisation of business bring about higher growth and wide spread development. In such a system, typically, business firms are able to raise resources at a global level as well as market their products across countries.

Before the year 1991, India remained a relatively closed economy, permitting only limited economic transactions with other countries. Domestic producers were sheltered from competition not only from abroad but also from within India itself (Lal and Clement 2005).

The macroeconomic policy of 1991 played a major role in India's economic progress in the 1990s and beyond. For example, Acharya (2001) concludes that India's devaluation of the rupee and its decision to increase the level of foreign investment helped it to make considerable economic progress. Joshi (2001) and Karunaratne (2001) state that India's policy of selective capital account liberalisation helped it to achieve important economic objectives. Gupta (1999) highlights the important role played by India's prudent management of exchange rate and monetary policy. Bhalla (2000) advocates the privatisation of the public sector enterprises in favour of market forces.

India's economy grew at an average rate of 6.3% from 1992–1993 to 2000–2001 (Acharya 2001). Further, its rate of inflation and fiscal deficit both decreased substantially (Bhalla 2000).

P.K. Jain et al., *Financial Management Practices: An Empirical Study of Indian Corporates*, India Studies in Business and Economics,
DOI 10.1007/978-81-322-0990-4_7, © Springer India 2013

In recent years too, the Indian economy has been showing the potential for continued growth (Economic Survey 2011).

But the questions arise: do the processes of liberalisation and globalisation/internationalisation create new risks? If they do, what are these risks? And, what is done or can be done to mitigate these risks? The answer to the first question is affirmative, meaning thereby, that international operations have all those risks that are inherent in purely domestic operations. In addition, they give rise to new risks such as country or political risk, exchange rate risk and interest rate risk.

These risks may be encountered more by companies in private sector as they are likely to have greater external orientation. The available literature does not indicate a comprehensive inquiry into globalisation and its resultant risk dynamics on a large corporate data set. This, then, constitutes the rationale to ascertain from the finance managers their current practices of risk management and also perceptions about the future practices in this regard. This is perhaps the first attempt, to the best of our knowledge, to delve into the manifestations of globalisation in terms of the nature and size of their international operations in a set of companies, and the resultant risks emanating therefrom and their management. Consequently, this chapter analyses and discusses the survey findings relating to the management of risks resulting from international operations.

For better exposition, the chapter is divided into ten sections. Section I outlines the scope and methodology. Section II contains a detailed literature review related to varying aspects of risk resulting from globalization. Attitude of the sample companies towards risk management is discussed in Section III. Section IV details the manifestations of internationalization in our the sample companies. Volatility and risk form the subject matter of Section V. Section VI addresses the management of political risk by the sample companies. Techniques used to manage foreign exchange rate risk constitute the subject matter of Section VII. Management of interest rate risk by the sample companies is presented in Section VIII. Section IX contains the concluding observations. Based on the findings and literature reviewed, suggestions have been made for practitioners to enable/facilitate them to manage risk better.

Section I Scope and Methodology

The companies constituting BSE 200 index form the sample of this study. Out of these 200 companies, 34 companies were affiliated to the financial sector as on 1 April 2010, that is, the date of the sample selection; the scope of this study is limited to the 166 nonfinancial BSE 200 companies engaged in manufacturing and service.

The research instrument for primary data consisted of a questionnaire (Appendix 1.3, Chap. 1). This was mailed to the chief financial officers (CFOs) of the sample companies. The initial response, in our case, was very poor; only eight companies responded. It is believed that follow-ups increase the response rate (Fox et al. 1988).

Subsequently two reminders (one through post and the other through email) were sent to the remaining companies. Personal contacts were also established with the companies located in and around Delhi.[1] This part of the analysis is based on 31 responses received out of 166 after 2 reminders. Thus, response rate works out to 18.67%.

Prima facie, the response rate may appear to be low; however, the number of respondents and the response rate are similar to previous studies using a similar questionnaire survey method (Jain and Kumar 1997; Jain and Yadav 2000, 2005). There is also evidence to suggest that it is becoming more difficult to encourage GPs (general practitioners) to participate in surveys (Templeton et al. 1997). Also, keeping in view that the survey was addressed to time-constrained CFOs, as well as the commercial sensitivity of some of the requested information, this may perhaps be considered a good and adequate response rate.

Section II Literature Review

Globalisation and International Finance

As economic/financial globalisation is a relatively recent phenomenon in most countries, there is dearth of extensive research into the different facets of the phenomenon and its impact.

Globalisation provides opportunity for expanding markets, the possibility of producing and marketing a larger range of goods, increasing chances for attracting capital and for accessing better technologies. The term 'globalisation' was first used in 1985 by Theodore Levitt to characterise the vast changes that have taken place over the last two to three decades in the international economy, that is, the rapid and pervasive changes that have taken place in production, consumption and investment globally as a result of both economic and financial liberalisation, structural adjustment programmes and dramatically diminishing the role of the state in the economy (Wahab 2003).

Tai and Iqbal (2011) found that both exchange rates and global industry shocks were statistically significant in explaining the performance of industries in relation to their domestic markets. Fratzscher (2009) found that negative US-specific macroeconomic shocks during the recent financial crisis had triggered a significant strengthening of the US dollar, rather than its weakening. Akdogu and MacKay (2008) examined the effect of industry structure on corporate investment patterns. Lane and Ferretti-Gian (2008) found that bilateral equity holdings were strongly correlated with bilateral trade in goods and services. Obadan (2006) stressed the need for sound macroeconomic policies, orderly liberalisation of capital accounts, adequate preparation of national financial systems and meeting other preconditions for countries to reap the benefits of financial globalisation at minimum costs.

[1] Assistance was also sought through the Delhi Stock Exchange and Securities and Exchange Board of India, as a part of the primary data collection exercise.

Malliaris (2002) examined the performance of global monetary arrangements. Magnus and Goran (2001) revealed that foreigners show a preference for large firms paying low dividends and firms with large cash positions on their balance sheets. Foster (2000) dealt with financial aspects of foreign direct investment (FDI). Lensik (1995) presented a model of developing countries featuring foreign exchange constraints. Chuppe et al. (1989) confirmed that the forces behind the trend toward global finance continue to operate around the world and international trade in financial services has been growing at a rapid pace.

In brief, the current dominant form of globalisation implies that decisions made in one part of the world have significant impact on nation states and local communities in other parts of the world. The world is said to be shrinking and globalisation is the new order that binds us all together (Wahab 2003).

Impact of Globalisation on India

India had the distinction of being the world's largest economy in the beginning of the Christian era, as it accounted for about 32.9% share of world GDP and about 32.5% of the world population. The goods produced in India had long been exported to far off destinations across the world. Therefore, the concept of globalisation, in terms of trade flows, is hardly new to India (Joshi 2009). But with the passage of time, many other countries/regions of the world marched ahead, leaving India far behind in its economic strength.

India accounted for 1.2% of world trade as of 2006 according to the World Trade Organization (WTO). Until the liberalisation of 1991, India was largely and intentionally isolated from the world markets, to protect its fledgling economy and to achieve self-reliance. International trade as a proportion of GDP reached 24% by 2006, up from 6% in 1985 and still relatively moderate (Economic Survey of India 2007; Srinivasan 2008).

As the fourth largest economy in the world in PPP terms, India is a preferred destination for FDI (Economic Survey of India 2007). The quantum of FDI inflows stood at US$143 billion in 2011 (RBI Bulleti 2011). Singh (2010) explored the emerging trends of FDI inflows into India against the backdrop of a series of liberalisation measures introduced in mid-1980s and further in 1991. The study indicated that the FDI inflows into India responded positively to the liberalisation measures introduced in the early 1990s.

Exchange Rate Forecasts

Nolte and Pohlmeier (2007) analysed the forecasting performance of survey methods using qualitative information from experts' forecasts and compared them with the performance of standard linear time series methods as well as with simple random walk forecasts. Baeka and Kwok (2002) examined the effects of foreign exchange (FX) rate and volatility on the corporate choice of foreign entry mode and shareholder wealth. Malik (2003) suggested a revaluation of the conclusions of studies on volatility persistence in exchange rates as they could overstate the degree to which shocks affect volatility.

Duru Bias and Reeb (2002) found that greater corporate international diversification is associated with less accurate and more optimistic forecasts. Oberlechner (2001) surveyed the perceived importance of chartist/technical and fundamental analysis amongst foreign exchange traders and financial journalists. MacDonald (2000) found that, in contrast to the literature based on the assumption of rational expectations, risk premium is present in the foreign exchange market.

Risk Management

In recent decades, the changing environment has posed a threat to the value maximisation process in organisations. Catastrophes and systemic shocks altered the way risk was managed in 1970s and 1980s. In fact, risk management has emerged as a separate discipline in the corporate world since the 1990s. The concept of risk management is not so new as risk management techniques like risk reduction through quality control, alternative risk financing and insurance have been in existence for a long time (Doherty 2000).

Risk management tasks have been conventionally confined to corporate treasurers, portfolio managers, insurers and the hedgers. Over the years, the risk management in organisations has undergone a paradigm shift. It has moved from being 'hazard type' to 'strategic type'. Risks are now not perceived as threats (adverse financial effects) but as potential opportunities. The focus of risk management has changed from all risks to critical risks (KPMG LLC 2001).

Recognition of risk management as a separate managerial function entails many advantages. Inclusion of risk management as a strategy in the general management function helps to enhance the value (Suryanarayana 2003).

More recently, the growth of derivative markets has enhanced the value of risk management in handling of market risks. Emerging markets globally have led the regional managers to diversify their risks in the developed markets (Alexander 1999). Every enterprise is subject to several types of risks and the focus varies across organisations. Risk has been defined, classified and interpreted from various perspectives (Lam 2001; BCBS 2003).

The risk management procedures, being currently followed by companies, tend to be reactive rather than proactive (Rekhi 2011). The role of the risk management team is not only to increase awareness of potential risk factors but also to bring a sense of urgency in taking actions to mitigate the impact of those risks (Ranganath 2011). Indian companies seem to follow a passive approach to risk management (Gupta 2011).

Section III Attitude Towards Risk Management

Kinds of Risks

It was considered important to understand the kinds of risks being faced by the sample companies under the broad categories of financial, business/operational and market risk (Table 7.1). Amongst financial risks, the most important one was the currency risk (92%) followed by interest rate risk (56%). Amongst business/operational risks, missed or ignored business opportunities was ranked at par with physical disasters (e.g. fire and explosions) with nearly 60% companies ranking them the most important manifestations of operational/business risk. Over reliance on key suppliers and customers (72.72%) was ranked the most important manifestation of market risk.

It is evident that market risk constitutes an important component of risk for the sample companies with international operations. This is similar to the findings of Rajkumar and Gupta (2010). Since the market risk cannot completely be foreseen and hence mitigated, an enquiry was made into the steps taken by the sample companies to mitigate the financial and business/operational risk.

An overwhelming majority of companies (96.42%) responds that risk is understood in its entirety by the company and measures are taken to mitigate it (Table 7.2). This is an indication of the sophisticated risk assessment and management practices being followed by the sample companies.

Table 7.1 Kinds of risks faced by the sample companies under separate categories

Risk type	Percentage of respondents facing the risk
Financial risk	
Currency risk	92.00
Interest risk	56.00
Credit risk	44.00
Liquidity risk	44.00
Higher cost of capital	16.00
Business/operational risk	
Missed or ignored business opportunities	59.25
Physical disasters (e.g. fire and explosion)	59.25
Stock-out of raw materials	44.44
Inability to reduce cost base	44.44
Failure to create and exploit intangible assets	14.81
Market risk	
Over reliance on key suppliers or customers	72.72
Failure of new products or services	40.90
Poor service levels	27.27
Any other	18.18

Table 7.2 Attitude of companies towards overall risk management and internal controls

Cases	Percentage
Risk is understood in its entirety and measures are taken to mitigate it	96.42
The Board thinks that risk management is 'not its problem'	3.57
Risk management is seen as the responsibility of one function, such as audit or insurance	3.57
The company is focused only on internal financial control rather than the wider scope of internal control	0.00
No key risk indicators have been determined	0.00
Employees have no training or experience in risk management	0.00
Any other	0.00

Table 7.3 Steps taken by the sample companies to mitigate the financial risk

Steps to mitigate financial risk	Percentage
Keep the debt–equity ratio close to the industrial benchmark	59.25 (14.81)
Have internal control ratios like cash flow return on investment	51.85 (3.70)
Make conscious efforts to keep the financial leverage as low as possible by reducing debt in the capital structure	44.44 (3.70)
Make conscious efforts to keep the interest coverage ratio as high as possible	44.44 (–)
Examine tax consequences of cross border activities and incorporate it in financial planning	22.22 (–)
Make extensive use of financial derivatives	14.81 (3.70)
Any other	0.00 (–)

As per Table 7.3, 'keeping the debt–equity ratio close to the industrial benchmark' was preferred by nearly 60% of the companies. The other important measures were to 'make conscious efforts to keep the financial leverage as low as possible by reducing debt in the capital structure' and 'make conscious efforts to keep the interest coverage ratio as high as possible', both at 44.44%.

'Regular monitoring and reallocation of budgets in line with revised risk/resource needs' is the most important measure to mitigate business/operational risk with more than nine-tenth of the respondent companies stating the same. 'Using adequate insurance coverage against fixed asset losses' was the second important measure with nearly three-fourth companies stating the same. The findings are indicative of strong and timely risk assessment in the sample companies, the foundation for effective risk management.

Liberalisation, in its wake, has not just brought enhanced risk; it has also heralded in new opportunities (Table 7.5). The sample companies have access to more lucrative investment opportunities (60.86%) and have been able to achieve economies of scale (52.17%). Thus, like any other significant economic phenomenon, liberalisation also continues to bring in both opportunities and threats for the underlying economic sectors.

Table 7.4 Steps taken by the sample companies to mitigate the business/operational risk

Steps to mitigate business/operational risk	Percentage
Budgets are regularly monitored and reallocated in line with revised risk/resource needs	92.85 (17.85)
Use adequate insurance coverage against fixed asset losses	71.42 (–)
Examine components like transfer pricing, excise duties, etc. as consequences of cross border activities and incorporate it in operational planning	39.28 (–)
There is a strong and conscious effort to focus on variable-costs-dominated ventures and strategies	35.71 (–)
Use leasing/hire-purchase arrangements to keep long-term investment as low as possible	21.42 (–)
Review acquisitions and handle disposal/liquidation of business components/ joint ventures	21.42 (–)
Any other	0.00 (–)

Table 7.5 Benefits to the sample companies due to increase in opportunities in the market, with the advent of liberalisation process, in the past decade

The way the company has benefited in the past decade due to increased opportunities	Percentage
More lucrative investment opportunities	60.86 (13.04)
Economies of scale	52.17 (8.69)
Lower input cost	30.43 (–)
Hedging of risk by diversification of investments	30.43 (–)
Any other	8.69 (–)

Section IV Manifestation of Globalisation

It is important to understand the dynamics through which globalisation manifests itself in our sample companies. It is with this intention that the following data as presented in Table 7.6 was sought from the sample companies.

The sample companies appear to have substantial and significant importing and exporting operations with other countries. Further, more than half of the sample companies have subsidiaries abroad, indicative of the increasingly global face of Indian companies. Nearly half of the sample companies are investing abroad, but the interesting feature is that less than one-fifth of the sample companies are receiving capital from abroad (Table 7.6). This perhaps indicates the major financing of their operations is from domestic sources. This could be due to the robust capital markets available in the Indian financial system and also the RBI restrictions on foreign capital inflows (Khan 2011; RBI Bulletin 2011). Our findings are supported by the existing findings of Morris (1987), Karunaratne (2001) and Jain and Yadav (2005).

From Table 7.7, it is evident that majority (83.33%) of the sample companies have more than INR 500 million worth of foreign exchange transactions per an.um,

Table 7.6 Forms of international transactions for the sample companies

Form of transaction	Percentage
Imports	82.75
Exports	79.31
Subsidiary abroad	62.06
Borrowing from abroad	55.17
Investing capital abroad	44.82
Receiving capital from abroad	17.24
Investing in foreign securities	10.34

Table 7.7 Size of yearly foreign exchange transactions for the sample companies

Amount (Rs. million)	Percentage
<10	0.00
10–50	4.16
50–100	0.00
100–500	8.33
500–1,000	20.83
Above 1,000	62.50

Table 7.8 Patterns of domestic/foreign holding and investment over the past decade for the sample companies

Patterns	In 2000	In 2010
Holding pattern		
Domestic holding	81.86	77.00
Foreign holding	18.14	23.00
Investment pattern		
Foreign portfolio investment vis-à-vis total investment	21.40	27.84
Foreign direct investment vis-à-vis total investment	12.00	13.67

with 62.50% of the sample companies having transactions of above INR 1,000 million per annum. This is indicative of the large and significant size of international operations for these companies and India in general. This is, perhaps, to be expected as India continues to be the second fastest growing economy in the world. Our findings are in tune with the data available in the Economic Survey of India (2007, 2011) and the RBI Bulletin (2011).

The holding pattern of the sample companies has changed marginally over the past decade (Table 7.8). The domestic holding has gone down by nearly 5 percentage points (from 81.86 to 77.00%) over the past decade. This is an indication of domestic holding being predominant in the sample companies and perhaps also of the restrictions imposed by India on foreign investment inflows (Khan 2011; RBI Bulletin 2011). In terms of risk management, this is perhaps indicative of the sample companies' financial risk being affected more by uncertainties in the Indian financial system than the international one. However, more than one-fifth of the holding of the sample companies is in foreign hands now, indicating growing exposure and higher risk from international operations and investment. Our findings are supported by the existing findings of Lane and Ferretti-Gian (2008) and Morris (1987).

Table 7.9 Ranking of sources of foreign currency in order of preference (1 being the most important) for the sample companies

Source preference	1	2	3	4
Foreign banks	60.86	13.04	4.34	4.34
Private banks	30.43	17.39	0.00	0.00
Any other[a]	17.39	0.00	0.00	0.00
Development financial institutions (DFIs)	13.04	4.34	8.69	0.00
GDRs/ADRs/Euro issues, etc.	13.04	8.69	4.34	4.34
Foreign collaborations/joint ventures	8.69	4.34	4.34	4.34

[a]Includes 'commercial papers' and 'Indian banks'

Table 7.10 Time span of exchange rate forecasts for the sample companies

Time period	Percentage
1 week	3.84
1 fortnight	3.84
1 month	3.84
2 months	7.69
3 months	30.76
Any other period[a]	26.92
No forecasts	46.15

[a]Includes 'one year', 'five years', 'medium term', 'deal-to-deal basis' and 'continuing exercise'

Table 7.11 Techniques/analysis for exchange rate forecasts used by the sample companies

Techniques	Percentage
Fundamental analysis	84.61
Technical analysis	53.84
Any other technique/model[a]	15.38

[a]Includes 'consensus amongst professionals'

Foreign banks are the major source of foreign currency followed by private banks. Hence, banks appear to dominate the financial system for foreign currency for the sample companies (Table 7.9). Our findings are in tune with the information available in Khan (2011) and RBI Bulletin (2011).

Nearly half of the sample companies do nothing to forecast exchange rates, preferring perhaps to react to exchange rate fluctuations as they happen. This could also perhaps be due to the inaccuracies in forecasting techniques (Duru Bias and Reeb 2002; MacDonald 2000). More than half of the companies forecast the rate for 3 months or more indicating a term greater than a quarter to make forecasts (Table 7.10).

An overwhelming majority (84.61%) of the sample companies use fundamental analysis to forecast exchange rates, while more than half use technical analysis (Table 7.11). This is indicative of the primary belief of the sample companies in the fundamentals of the economy in making forecasts. Our findings are supported by the findings of Oberlechner (2001).

Table 7.12 Fundamental factors considered for exchange rate forecasts by the sample companies

Factors	Percentage
Inflation rates	90.00
Interest rates	80.00
Structure of balance of payment	70.00
Foreign exchange reserves	60.00
Any other[a]	40.00

[a]Includes 'forward rate analysis' and 'research reports/group guidelines'

Table 7.13 Technical analysis methods considered for exchange rate forecasts by the sample companies

Methods	Percentage
Graph	83.33
Bar charts	33.33
Any other[a]	16.67

[a]There were no methods indicated

According to Table 7.12, the most important determinant of the fundamental factors for exchange rate forecasts is the inflation rates (90%) followed by the interest rates (80%) of the concerned companies. These are followed by the structure of the balance of payments (70%) and foreign exchange reserves (60%). Our findings are supported by the findings of Rajkumar and Gupta (2010).

Graphs dominate the methods used in technical analysis for our sample companies (Table 7.13). Possible reasons for the same could be the representation of a trend in the underlying values in a graph and the subsequent ease of comprehension.

Section V Volatility and Risk

The objective of this section is to enumerate in what ways the volatility manifests in the sample companies due to liberalisation. The aim is to understand the parameters to which the sample companies are vulnerable in terms of volatility and the resultant risk.

As indicated in Table 7.14, the largest number of responding companies has stated that the maximum volatility/uncertainty emanates from the fluctuations in input costs and exchange rates (each at 76%). 'Uncertainty about the product price' (40%) is the next aspect as regards the effect of liberalisation process on the volatility. If one looks at the overall impact, it has been observed that the highest impact comes in the form of exchange rate fluctuations and input costs which are interrelated. However, 'uncertainty about the product price' was identified as the main reason behind volatility by the sample of Indian public sector enterprises (Jain and Yadav 2005)

Table 7.15 indicates that the sample companies consider all the major kinds of risks, namely, financial, business/operational and market, with business/operational risk being the most important (96.42%), followed by financial (85.71%) and then market risk (82.14%). One-fourth of the sample companies also consider regulatory risk as an important specification under risk management.

Table 7.14 Manifestations of increased volatility in the market in the past decade, for the sample companies, with the advent of liberalisation process

The way volatility is getting manifested in the company	Percentage
Fluctuations in input cost	76.00 (4.00)
Fluctuations in exchange rates	76.00 (–)
Uncertainty about the product prices	40.00 (–)
Fluctuations in investments	8.00 (–)
Increased uncertainty about receivables	8.00 (–)
Any other	4.00 (–)

Figures in brackets represent the opinion chosen exclusively. The same holds true for all tables

Table 7.15 Types of risks considered under risk management specifications by the sample companies

Types of risk	Percentage
Business/operational risk	96.42
Financial risk (includes interest rate and foreign exchange rate risk)	85.71
Market risk	82.14
Any other[a]	25.00

[a]Includes 'regulatory risk'

Section VI Political Risk Management

Various precautions that the sample companies can take to minimise political/country risk are listed in Table 7.16. One of the ways that the sample companies follow for managing political/country risk is to incorporate a risk premium in the cost of capital. The question was posed whether the sample companies consider it a good technique to incorporate this risk in their cost of capital. Nearly half of the sample companies responded in the affirmative.

On making a composite score and ranking their measures, it is evident that the highest number of first preferences has been given to the measure 'creating joint venture with an enterprise of the host country' (50%). This has been considered the most suitable measure to reduce political/country risk. Normally, a foreign company would find it difficult to handle the complexities of the sociocultural and politico-economic milieu of the host country. On the other hand, the local partner from the host country would be able to get around these complexities better than their foreign counterpart. Thus, creating a joint venture with a local enterprise to reduce political risk appears to be a logically sound choice. The measure that obtained the next rank is 'incorporating a risk premium in the cost of capital'.

The other measures like 'integrating local products' (30%) and 'taking loans from local financial institutions' (12.50%) reduce political risk as they create interlocking relationship that cannot be easily broken. Thus, they deter the local authorities from taking hostile action against the foreign investment. The lowest importance has been accorded to 'increasing the number of employees from the host country' (10%) as a measure to reduce political risk. This measure, on the face of it, appears to be important because local employees can act as a pressure group against any

Table 7.16 Precautions to help minimise the political risk in international operations for the sample companies (1 means most preferred)

Precautions	1	2	3	4	5
Creating joint ventures with an enterprise of the host country	50.00	21.42	14.28	7.14	7.14
Incorporating a risk premium in the cost of capital	49.66	16.66	8.33	25.00	8.33
Integrating products of the host country in your business	30.00	20.00	20.00	10.00	20.00
Taking loans from the financial institutions of the host country	12.50	0.00	25.00	50.00	12.50
Increasing the number of the host country employees	10.00	30.00	50.00	0.00	10.00
Any other[a]	100.00	–	–	–	–

[a]Includes 'through corporate social responsibility (CSR) activities'

hostile action by local authorities. Yet, the responses of the sample companies indicate clearly that it is the least preferred measure out of the ones listed. Increasing the local employees may perhaps be effective to reduce political risk, but it may not always be possible to find local people having the skills and expertise required for a particular project.

It would be appropriate to mention here that the above findings are similar to those revealed by a survey done on private sector companies by Yadav and Jain (2000) and are also similar to the findings of Foster (2000), Jain and Yadav (2005) and Lane and Ferretti-Gian (2008).

Section VII Exchange Rate Risk Management

Exchange rate risk can arise from either trade or financial transactions or both. Trade transactions consist of exports and imports, whereas financial transactions can take the form of lending and borrowing or other investment activities.

To reduce exchange rate risk, business organisations are expected to use some hedging techniques. These techniques are classified into two categories as internal and external (Jain et al. 1997). The internal ones consist of (1) leads and lags, (2) netting, (3) back-to-back swaps, (4) re-invoicing through a centralised system, (5) risk sharing, etc. Netting and back-to-back swap (both at 47.05%) are the most popular techniques used by the sample companies to manage exchange rate risk. Nearly one-fifth of the respondent companies use back-to-back swaps exclusively for the same (Table 7.17).

External techniques of exchange risk management basically involve the use of instruments like forwards, options, futures and swaps. These are external simply because the organisations/institutions offering these instruments are external to the companies using them for hedging purposes. One of the important external techniques for covering foreign exchange risk is the use of forwards.

Table 7.17 Internal techniques[a] used by the sample companies for managing exchange rate risk

Technique	Yes	No
Leads and lags	29.41 (–)	70.58 (–)
Netting	47.05 (5.88)	52.94 (–)
Back-to-back swap	47.05 (17.64)	52.94 (–)
Re-invoicing through a centralised system	23.52 (–)	76.47 (–)
Risk sharing	23.52 (–)	76.47 (–)
Any other	29.41 (23.52)	70.58 (–)

[a]Internal techniques of exchange risk management, as the name implies, are the ones used by organisations internally either individually or in cooperation with another affiliate of the same MNC or another company with which it has dealings. Leads and lags consist of accelerating or delaying the receipt or payment in foreign currency as dictated by the expected depreciation/appreciation of that currency. Netting techniques consist of matching receivables and payables between two affiliates and making payment of the net balance amount. Back-to-back swap refers to an exchange of equivalent sum of two different currencies between two companies. Re-invoicing through a centralised system enables the routing of receipts and payments of foreign currencies in order to centralise exchange risk management. Risk sharing simply involves an agreement between the two transacting parties to decide in what proportion they would like to share the risk

Table 7.18 External techniques used by the sample companies to manage exchange rate risk

Instruments	Percentage
Currency forward contract	84.21 (42.10)
Currency options	52.63 (5.26)
Currency futures	26.31 (–)
Money market hedge	10.52 (–)

Table 7.18 indicates that, currency forward contract (84.21%) is the most popular technique followed by currency options (52.63%). More than 40% of the respondent companies resort exclusively to currency forwards to manage their exchange rate risk. This finding is supported by the Circular No. 5 issued by RBI[2] on the use of hedging opportunities – it is felt that wider hedging opportunities could enhance the flexibility for the companies to manage their currency risk dynamically.

Further, according to the same circular, international experiences have also established that the exchange traded currency futures contracts facilitate efficient price discovery, enable better counterparty credit risk management, wider participation, trading of standardised products, reduce transaction costs, etc. Accordingly, as a part of further developing the derivatives market in India and adding to the existing menu of foreign exchange hedging tools available to the residents, it has been decided to introduce currency futures in recognised stock exchanges or new exchanges recognised by the Securities and Exchange Board of India (SEBI) in the country.[3]

[2]Source: RBI/2008–2009/122 A.P. (DIR Series) Circular No. 05.

[3]Source: RBI/2008–2009/122 A.P. (DIR Series) Circular No. 05.

Table 7.19 Basic hedging strategies used by the sample companies against anticipated depreciation of local currency

Hedging strategies	Percentage
Buy foreign currency forward	78.94 (57.89)
Borrow locally	26.31 (10.52)
Invoice exports in foreign currency and imports in local currency	10.52 (5.26)
Reduce levels of local currency cash and marketable securities	5.26 (–)
Reduce local currency receivables	5.26 (–)
Delay collection of hard currency (appreciating currency) receivables	5.26 (–)
Speed up dividend and other remittances to parent	5.26 (–)
Delay payments of local currency payable	0.00 (–)

Table 7.20 Basic hedging strategies used by the sample companies against anticipated appreciation of local currency

Hedging strategies	Percentage
Sell foreign currency forward	68.42 (52.63)
Reduce local borrowing	26.31 (10.52)
Invoice exports in local currency and imports in foreign currency	15.78 (10.52)
Relax local currency credit terms (i.e. increase local currency receivables)	5.26 (–)
Speed up payments of local currency payable	5.26 (5.26)
Delay dividend and other remittances to parent	5.26 (–)
Speed up collection of soft currency (depreciating currency) receivables	0.00 (–)
Increase levels of local currency cash and marketable securities	0.00 (–)

However, according to our findings, currency futures are being used only by one-fourth of the respondent companies indicating, perhaps, the relatively low popularity of exchange traded futures vis-à-vis forward contracts.

As listed in Table 7.19, amongst the basic hedging strategies against anticipated depreciation of local currency, only three are used in any significant manner. 'Buying foreign currency forward' emerges as the main technique with nearly 80% respondent companies adopting this technique, and more than half (57.89%) adopting exclusively this technique to manage the risk arising out of depreciation of local currency. The strategy of 'borrowing locally' received the second position with more than one-fourth (26.31%) companies following this technique. The next important strategy is 'invoicing exports in foreign currency and imports in local currency' (10.52%). These findings are in contrast with the findings of an earlier study by Jain and Yadav 2005 on public sector undertakings in India. Other strategies are used sparingly.

Analysing the responses in relation to basic strategies to be adopted in the case of anticipated appreciation of the local currency (Table 7.20), it is evident that 'selling foreign currency forward' is the most preferred strategy (68.42%) followed by 'reducing

Table 7.21 Percentage of foreign exchange exposures covered by the sample companies

Percentage of foreign exchange exposures	Percentage
100	8.69
≥90	0.00
≥80	8.69
≥70	4.34
≥60	8.69
≥50	17.39
Any other[a]	52.17

[a]Includes '40%', '0%', '25–50%', '30%', 'varying', '80–100%' and 'depends on deal-to-deal'

Table 7.22 Source of advice for foreign risk management for the sample companies

Sources	Percentage
Internal team	77.27 (18.18)
Outside institutional consultancy services	45.45 (4.54)
Outside individual consultants	31.81 (9.09)
Any other	22.72 (0.00)

local currency borrowings' (26.31%). More than half of respondent companies use the strategy of selling foreign currency forward exclusively. It is worthwhile to note here that unlike the sample companies, the public sector undertakings studied by Jain and Yadav (2005) 'reduced local borrowings' as the main hedging strategy. It seems, then, that foreign currency forwards becoming popular is a recent phenomenon.

It is evident from the responses in the 'any other' category in Table 7.21 that the respondent companies have no specific foreign exchange exposure level covered by internal and external risk management techniques/strategies.

It would be appropriate to know what arrangements the companies have for managing exchange rate risk. With this in view, they were asked to indicate whether they have internal teams or external consultants to provide advice on this matter. Respondent companies rely heavily on their internal risk assessment/management team (77.27%) followed by outside institutional consultancy services (45.45%) as per Table 7.22.

In sum, it is evident that exchange rate risk is an important risk faced by companies with international operations. Our findings are in tune with those of Tai and Iqbal (2011).

Section VIII Interest Rate Risk Management

Interest rate risk arises from fluctuations in interest rates. For example, an enterprise has borrowed at floating rate and shortly, thereafter, interest rates start going up. Now this enterprise will have disadvantage vis-à-vis another enterprise that borrowed at a fixed rate initially. Or, say, another enterprise borrowed at 12% and soon, thereafter,

Table 7.23 Manifestations of interest rate risk for the sample companies

Manifestations	Percentage
Increase in financial charges	85.00 (50.00)
Increase in the value of debt	30.00 (5.00)
Decrease in financial income	25.00 (10.00)
Decrease in the value of credit	15.00 (–)
Any other	0.00 (–)

Table 7.24 Order of preference for the use of following instruments when available to cover interest rate risk for the sample companies

Instruments	1st	2nd	3rd	4th	5th	6th	7th	8th
Interest rate swaps	50.00	6.25	6.25	6.25	6.25	6.25	0.00	6.25
Forward interest rate agreements (FRA)	31.25	12.50	6.25	6.25	0.00	6.25	0.00	0.00
Interest rate caps	12.50	12.50	12.50	6.25	6.25	0.00	6.25	0.00
Forward to forward contracts	6.25	6.25	0.00	18.75	0.00	6.25	12.50	6.25
Interest rate futures	6.25	12.50	0.00	0.00	6.25	6.25	6.25	6.25
Interest rate options	0.00	6.25	18.75	0.00	12.50	6.25	0.00	0.00
Interest rate collar	0.00	12.50	0.00	0.00	6.25	6.25	12.50	6.25
Interest rate floors	0.00	0.00	6.25	6.25	6.25	6.25	0.00	6.25

borrowing rate came down to 11%. As a consequence, this enterprise would be at a disadvantage vis-a-vis its competitor who waited for a while and borrowed at a lower rate on a later date.

As per Table 7.23, 'increase in financial charges' is the most important manifestation of interest rate risk for the respondent companies (85%), with half the companies stating this exclusively. This is followed by 'increase in the value of debt' (30%) and 'decrease in financial income' (25%). The findings are supported by the findings of Jain and Yadav (2005). It is useful to note here that even though 'increase in financial charges' is the most important manifestation in both cases, its relative importance has gone up from 55.55% to 85% (Jain and Yadav 2005).

As more sophisticated instruments for covering interest rate risk are developing, it would be appropriate to know from companies whether they are/would be using these instruments and in what order of preference. The relative preferences are shown in Table 7.24.

At aggregate level, the highest performance (rank 1) has been shown for interest rate swaps followed by forward rate agreements (FRA), while the least preferred instruments would be interest rate collars and floors.

Section IX Concluding Observations

The sample companies are amongst the largest companies in India with substantial international exposure in terms of size of transactions. Yet their holding pattern still remains dominantly domestic. This is perhaps due to the restrictions imposed on

FDI by RBI. This factor could have been responsible in part for the relative insulation of the Indian economy in the aftermath of the financial crisis originating in the USA in the year 2008. Though the Indian economy has faced a slowdown, the profitability of the sample companies has not suffered considerable damage (for details, refer to Chap. 9 on 'Profitability Analysis').

The survey on risk management practices with regard to international operations in the sample companies elicited responses from practitioners on political risk, exchange rate risk and interest rate risk, respectively. The responses indicate that the sample companies are taking steps currently and also envisage using newer instruments/techniques in future.

The sample companies would like to reduce political or country risk by incorporating a risk premium in the cost of capital. Amongst other measures, creating a joint venture with an enterprise of the host country is the most preferred one.

As regards exchange risk management, certain techniques are suggested. In the case of anticipated depreciation, they are selling local currency forward, borrowing locally and invoicing exports in foreign currency and imports in local currency. In the case of anticipated appreciation, the most likely ways are to buy local currency forward and to reduce local currency borrowing.

From the survey, it is apparent that the sample companies are using only netting and back-to-back swap (internal techniques of exchange risk management) in any significant manner. As far as the use of external techniques is concerned, forwards are the most preferred, followed by currency swaps, currency options and currency futures. Exchange risk management is organised by internal teams as well as through the help of outside institutional consultants.

The survey revealed that the sample companies are faced with interest rate risk, and they would like to use newer instruments including derivatives such as interest rate options, swaps and futures, etc. in future.

An overwhelming majority (96.42%) of companies responds that risk is understood in its entirety by the company, and measures are taken to mitigate it.

Normative Framework

Guidelines for Practitioners

Given the interactions with managers and our research findings, the following aspects have been highlighted for business executives (as a ready reckoner) to help them manage risk better:

- There should be an *alignment of risk management with corporate strategy* (KPMG LLC 2001; Suryanarayana 2003; Alexander 1999; Chandra 2011).
- It is important to *classify risk specifically with corresponding mitigation routes* (Lam 2001; BCBS 2003).

- Set up a *proactive risk-assessment centre and methodology* rather than a reactive/passive one (Doherty 2000; Rekhi 2011; Gupta 2011).
- Do *not get lured by exotic derivative instruments*, in particular, when exposure is large. Use such instruments only for hedging and not for speculation.
- *Properly document risk management policy* and practice for the entire organisation.
- There should be an *urgency in the mitigation strategy* so that the risk can be contained immediately (Ranganath 2011).

References

Acharya S (2001) India's macroeconomic management in the nineties. Indian Council for Research on International Economic Relations, New Delhi

Akdogu E, MacKay P (2008) Investment and competition. J Finance Quant Anal 43(2):299–330

Alexander C (1999) Risk management and analysis, vol 2: New markets and procedures. Wiley, New York

Baeka HY, Kwok Chuck CY (2002) Foreign exchange rates and the corporate choice of foreign entry mode. Int Rev Econ Finance 11:207–227

BCBS (2003) Sound practices for the management and supervision of operational risk, bank for international settlements, Basel. J Risk Finance 12(2):136

Bhalla GS (2000) Political economy of Indian development in the 20th century: India's road to freedom and growth. Presidential address at the 83rd annual conference of the Indian Economic Association, University of Jammu, Jammu and Kashmir

Chandra P (2011) Financial management – theory and practice, 8th edn. Tata McGraw Hill, New Delhi

Chuppe TM, Haworth HR, Watkins MG (1989) Global finance: causes, consequences and prospects for the future. Global Finance J 1(1):1–20

Doherty NA (2000) Integrated risk management – technologies and strategies for managing corporate risk. McGraw-Hill, New York

Duru Bias A, Reeb DM (2002) International diversification and analysts' forecast accuracy and bias. Acc Rev 77(2):415–433

Economic Survey of India 2007: Policy brief. Available at http://indiabudget.nic.in/index.asp. Accessed 20 Apr 2012

Economic Survey of India 2011. Available at http://www.oecd.org/document/36/0,3746,en_2649_33733_48079140_1_1_1_1,00.html. Accessed 13 June 2012

Foster MJ (2000) Evaluating foreign direct investments: new challenges for strategic planners. J Oper Res Soc 51(1):45–52

Fox RJ, Crask MR, Kim J (1988) Mail survey response rate – a meta-analysis of selected techniques for inducing response. Public Opin Q 52(4):467–491

Fratzscher M (2009) What explains global exchange rate movements during the financial crisis? J Int Money Finance 28(8):1390–1407

Gupta SP (1999) Development experience of the nineties and search for a new paradigm. A.K. Dasgupta Memorial Lecture at the 82nd annual conference of the Indian Economic Association, Guru Nanak Dev University, Amritsar

Gupta PK (2011) Risk management in Indian companies: EWRM concerns and issues. J Risk Finance 12(2):121–139

Hubbard D (2009) The failure of risk management: why it's broken and how to fix it. Wiley, New York, p 46

Jain PK, Kumar M (1997) Comparative financial management: practices of India and South East Asia. Hindustan Publishing Corporation, New Delhi, pp 43–44

Jain PK, Yadav SS (2000) Financial management practices in select private corporate enterprises – a comparative study of India, Thailand and Singapore. Hindustan Publishing Corporation, New Delhi

Jain PK, Yadav SS (2005) Financial management practices – a study of public sector enterprises in India. Hindustan Publishing Corporation, New Delhi

Joshi V (2001) Capital controls and the national advantage: India in the 1990s and beyond. Oxf Dev Stud 29(3):305–320

Joshi RM (2009) International business. Oxford University Press, New Delhi/New York. ISBN 0195689097

Karunaratne ND (2001) Revisiting capital account convertibility in the aftermath of the currency crisis. Intereconomics 36(5):264–271

Khan MY (2011) Indian financial system, 7th edn. Tata McGraw Hill, New Delhi

KPMG LLC (2001) Understanding enterprise risk management – an emerging model for building shareholder value. KPMG. Available at: www.kpmg.ca. Accessed 10 Mar 2006

Lal AK, Clement RW (2005) Economic development in India: the role of individual enterprise (and entrepreneurial spirit). Asia Pac Dev J 12(2):81

Lam J (2001) Risk management – the CRO is here to stay. Prentice-Hall, New York

Lane PR, Ferretti-Gian MM (2008) International investment patterns. Rev Econ Stat 90(3):538–549

Lensik R (1995) Foreign exchange constraints and developing countries. Econ Model 12(2):179–191

MacDonald R (2000) Is the foreign exchange market 'risky'? Some new survey-based results. J Multinatl Finance Manage 10:1–14

Magnus D, Goran R (2001) Direct foreign ownership, institutional investors, and firm characteristics. J Finance Econ 59:413–440

Malik F (2003) Sudden changes in variance and volatility persistence in foreign exchange markets. J Multinatl Finance Manage 13:217–230

Malliaris AG (2002) Global monetary instability: the role of the IMF the EU and NAFTA. North Am J Econ Finance 13:72–92

Morris S (1987) Trends in foreign direct investment from India (1950–1982). Econ Pol Wkly 22(46):1963–1969

Nolte I, Pohlmeier W (2007) Using forecasts of forecasters to forecast. Int J Forecast 23:15–28

Obadan MI (2006) Globalization of finance and the challenge of national financial sector development. J Asian Econ 17:316–332

Oberlechner T (2001) Importance of technical and fundamental analysis in the European foreign exchange market. Int J Finance Econ 6:81–93

Rajkumar, Gupta H (2010) FII flows to India: economic indicators. SCMS J Indian Manage 7(1):104–116

Ranganath MD (2011) Risk management for competitive advantage. India Kellogg Wordpress. Available at http://indiakellogg.wordpress.com/2011/05/14/risk-management-for-competitive-advantage-m-d-ranganath-infosys-technologies-ltd/. Accessed 1 Apr 2012

RBI's Bulletin (2011) Table No. 44 – foreign investment inflows. Available at http://www.rbi.org.in/scripts/BS_PressReleaseDisplay.aspx?prid=23739. Accessed 1 Apr 2012

Rekhi (2011) Do our companies understand financial risk? The Hindustan Business Line. Available at: http://www.thehindubusinessline.com/todays-paper/tp-opinion/article1621246.ece. Accessed 1 Apr 2012

Singh J (2010) Economic reforms and foreign direct investment in India: policy, trends and patterns. IUP J Finance Econ VIII(4):59–69

Srinivasan G (2008) Rise in Indian services exports less than global average: WTO. The Hindu Business Line. Available at: http://www.thehindubusinessline.com/todays-paper/tp-economy/rise-in-indian-services-exports-less-than-global-average-wto/article1621926.ece?ref=archive. Retrieved 16 Nov 2008

Suryanarayana A (2003) Risk management models: a primer. ICFAI Reader. ICFAI Press, New Delhi

Tai C-S, Iqbal Z (2011) How important is global industry shock in explaining the relative performance of global industries? Manage Finance 37(5):474–481

Templeton L, Deehan A, Taylor C, Drummond C, Strang J (1997) Surveying general practitioners: does a low response rate matter? J Gen Pract 47(415):91–94

Wahab SBA (2003) Globalization and its implications on national security. J R Malays Police Sr Off Coll 27–36. Available at: http://rmpckl.rmp.gov.my/Journal/BI/globalisationnimplication.pdf. Accessed 1 Apr 2012

Yadav SS, Jain PK (2000) Corporate practices of risk management in international business operations in India – a survey. S Asian J Manage (SAJM) 7(1–2):1–14

Chapter 8
Index of Professionalism in Financial Decisions

Introduction

The financial performance of an organisation is generally measured by the following parameters: profit, cash flows, balance sheet strength, risk management, valuation and owners' net worth (Stern 2012). Apart from the numbers that the above parameters generate, human psychology and the merit/demerit associated with financial decision-making also play a vital role in determining eventual corporate success (De Bondt and Thaler 1995).

Keeping this in mind, the analysis of the sample companies has been carried out as presented in different chapters, based on their financial statements as well as financial policies. This chapter is based on the responses obtained from the questionnaire. The chapter sets out to rate the respondent companies based on the quality of their decision-making *vis-a-vis* sound finance theory. It attempts to understand the extent of professionalism behind the decisions.

Eric Hoyle (1980) defines professionalisation of any activity/decision-making as having the following aspects: long period of training, qualified membership, management control and continuous improvement of knowledge and the skills of the practitioners.

The decision-makers in the sample companies fulfil all the above criteria. It is obviously then expected that corporate performance would be better if activities are carried out in a professional manner, that is, by employing a systematic and sound knowledge in practice. This chapter makes an attempt to develop an index as a measure of professionalism in the area of financial management, as practised in the sample companies in India to understand if the same is true.

A corporate would be called professional if its management practices are consistent with the systematic body of knowledge and tools and techniques of sound theory. This means that the professional enterprises would not follow arbitrary/ad-hoc or rule-of-thumb approach in taking decisions.

P.K. Jain et al., *Financial Management Practices: An Empirical Study of Indian Corporates*, India Studies in Business and Economics,
DOI 10.1007/978-81-322-0990-4_8, © Springer India 2013

This chapter has been divided into three sections. Section I contains the detailed methodology used for the creation of the index. Section II lists the observations based on the scores obtained in each category of financial decision-making by the respondent companies and section III contains the concluding observations.

Section I Methodology

The basic methodology for preparation of this index has been taken from an earlier study on public sector enterprises in India (Jain and Yadav 2005). However, substantial modifications have been introduced in the questionnaire used for this study to reflect the emerging areas of research in financial management and evaluate them in terms of decision-making. Also, relatively recent aspects like corporate governance and risk management were included.

The questionnaire used in the survey was prepared with items pertaining to six practices of financial management. These were capital budgeting (CB), capital structure (CS), working capital management (WC), dividend policy (D), corporate governance (CG) and risk management (RM). The questionnaire was sent to 166 nonfinancial companies comprising the BSE 200 index. Final responses from 29 companies were taken for the preparation of the index.

The questionnaire (Appendix 1.3) was exploratory in nature with certain questions in each section directly enquiring about the practice followed in regard to that specific financial decision. Not all of these questions have responses that can directly be connected to sound decision-making. For instance, item 2, namely, 'In the past decade, the capital expenditure of your company has mainly constituted of outlays on', entails a choice dependent on the company's strategy. Similarly, questions that did not indicate directly a good/bad financial decision were not taken up for the creation of the index. This applies to all sections of the questionnaire comprising of 70 questions in all. As a result of this exercise, five out of nine items were picked up for the creation of the index from the capital budgeting section. For items in each category used for the development of index, refer to questionnaire provided as Appendix 8.8.

For each financial decision, a number of alternative practices is possible – each one of them varying in terms of theoretical soundness. For example, in working out cost of capital, weighted average cost of long-term finance is considered superior to other practices/methods. So maximum score is assigned to the item relating to the cost of capital if the response given by a particular enterprise shows that it uses the weighted average cost of capital. On the other hand, minimum score is assigned in case the enterprise responds that its cost of capital is decided by the top management in an ad-hoc manner. In this way, for each item, a maximum and minimum score are assigned. The scores awarded to each response was on a range of 0–5, with '5' being awarded to the response most in tune with sound financial theory and '0' being assigned to the response completely against sound theory.

Then, the total score obtained by that enterprise relating to a specific financial management category, say, capital structure decision, is divided by the maximum score that could be obtained if the company practised only the best methods under that category. The ratio thus obtained is multiplied by 100 in order to get an IPF (index of professionalism in financial management) for that company, in that category of financial management practice.

To illustrate further, there are four items in capital structure (CS) category. Suppose the score of a company on item 1 (1 varying from 1 to 4) is Si while maximum obtainable score on this item is Sim (maximum score). Then IPF (CS) for this enterprise:

$$\text{IPF(CS)} = \frac{\sum \text{Si}}{\sum \text{Sim}} \times 100$$

Thus, a set of six indices each has been constructed for each company. These are IPF (CB) for capital budgeting, IPF (CS) for capital structure, IPF (WC) for working capital, IPF (D) for dividend policy, IPF (CG) for corporate governance and IPF (RM) for risk management.

The detailed calculations of indices for each company are contained in Appendices 8.1, 8.2, 8.3, 8.4, 8.5 and 8.6.

Then an average value of IPF (CB), IPF (CS), IPF (WC), IPF (D), IPF (CG) and IPF (RM) is determined for all responding companies taken together (Table 8.1). Under each financial management practice, an average, as worked out, is given in the lowest row of the table. The average is based on the number of responding companies. For example, calculation of AvIPF (CB) is based on the responses of 29 companies. Abbreviations used in this chapter are all given in Appendix 8.7.

Table 8.1 also contains the average value of index for the sample companies as a whole under each category of financial management practices in the last row.

Finally, an overall aggregate single average index has been calculated as follows:

$$\text{AvIPF(AG)} = \frac{\begin{array}{c}\text{AvIPF(CB)} + \text{AvIPF(CS)} + \text{AvIPF(WC)} \\ + \text{AvIPF(D)} + \text{AvIPF(CG)} + \text{AvIPF(RM)}\end{array}}{6}$$

As per Table 8.1, the category aggregate scores (AvIPF (C)) are the highest for the dividend policy category (for the respondent companies) at 91.11%.

Finally, the AvIPF (AG) for all the respondent companies for all the categories taken together is 73.05%. This is encouraging as the majority of the respondent companies seem to be following sound financial management practices, based on financial theory, in all areas of financial management, undertaken in the study.

Section II Observations

As already pointed out, detailed calculations for the values of IPFs relating to different categories of financial management practices are given in Appendices 8.1, 8.2, 8.3, 8.4, 8.5 and 8.6. The summary of these is contained in Table 8.1.

Table 8.1 Professional index values for each sample company (in percentages)

Company	IPF (CB)	IPF (CS)	IPF (WC)	IPF (D)	IPF (CG)	IPF (RM)
1	65.00	32.00	64.00	60.00	87.50	22.86
2	100.00	64.00	80.00	100.00	87.50	51.43
3	60.00	64.00	100.00	20.00	93.75	31.43
4	100.00	84.00	92.00	100.00	75.00	28.57
5	70.00	48.00	76.00	100.00	76.25	60.00
6	75.00	80.00	100.00	60.00	93.75	31.43
7	100.00	80.00	64.00	100.00	88.75	48.57
8	95.00	48.00	100.00	100.00	87.50	54.29
9	55.00	68.00	100.00	100.00	93.75	40.00
10	100.00	44.00	100.00	100.00	83.75	51.43
11	65.00	64.00	100.00	100.00	93.75	57.14
12	55.00	68.00	64.00	100.00	100.00	57.14
13	70.00	60.00	60.00	100.00	87.50	40.00
14	60.00	64.00	100.00	100.00	81.25	48.57
15	90.00	64.00	80.00	100.00	81.25	51.43
16	75.00	64.00	64.00	100.00	87.50	–
17	100.00	80.00	92.00	100.00	87.50	51.43
18	80.00	–	44.00	100.00	87.50	–
19	–	48.00	100.00	60.00	81.25	51.43
20	–	60.00	52.00	100.00	87.50	34.29
21	100.00	60.00	56.00	60.00	87.50	25.71
22	45.00	68.00	72.00	100.00	68.75	51.43
23	80.00	68.00	80.00	–	68.75	25.71
24	75.00	80.00	80.00	100.00	93.75	42.83
25	75.00	44.00	44.00	–	95.00	31.43
26	–	44.00	–	100.00	81.25	–
27	100.00	48.00	100.00	100.00	93.75	37.14
28	75.00	64.00	72.00	100.00	57.50	20.00
29	100.00	44.00	84.00	100.00	75.00	62.86
AvIPF (C)	79.42	60.86	79.29	91.11	84.96	42.64
Range	45–100	32–80	44–100	20–100	57.50–100	20–62.86

In the calculation of AvIPF (C), only the companies that have responded to more than 50% of the questions in a particular category have been included in the calculation of the average
'–' denotes the companies not meeting the above criterion

It is observed that for the sample companies the IPF (CB) varies from as low as 45 to as high as 100. However, an average of 79.42 is quite high, signifying that, in nearly 80% companies, sound capital budgeting practices are in place. The average is higher than the IPF (CB) of 70.47 reported by Jain and Yadav (2000) in their study of private sector enterprises over the period 1991–1998 and that of 76.80 noted by Jain and Yadav (2005) in their study of Indian public sector undertakings, indicating growing professionalism amongst companies with regard to their capital budgeting decisions. Similar observations can be made for different categories of financial management practices.

Further, it is observable that average index values are generally above 75 for all categories except for capital structure decisions (60.86) and risk management (42.64). This is surprising as the sample companies are amongst the largest and well-established companies in the country and have access to various sources of finance enabling them to follow sound capital structure practices and also employ more risk management tools and techniques. Further, Jain and Yadav (2000) reported an IPF (CS) of 76.54 for private sector enterprises, and the public sector undertakings studied by Jain and Yadav (2005) reported an IPF (CS) of 74.57. The sample companies report a dismal performance comparatively. Similarly, the IPF (WC) of 79.29 is lower than the IPF (WC) of 84.96 reported by the sample private sector companies over 1991–1998 (Jain and Yadav 2000) and the IPF (WC) of 88.32 reported for the public sector undertakings (Jain and Yadav 2005).

However, it is pertinent to note that the two indices and their valuations are not entirely comparable as the questions and their numbers varied for each category in all the three questionnaires. Also, the additional categories of corporate governance and risk management and the overall methodology in the creation of this index had minor modifications from the ones used by Yadav and Jain (2000, 2005). Hence, any comparisons, in this regard, should be viewed in the light of the aforementioned.

By and large, the index values are generally high for capital budgeting, working capital, dividend policy and corporate governance. The averages are above 75. This indicates the sample companies are paying close attention to aspects like investments, liquidity, inventory, receivables, investors and corporate legislations. Of course, this and other results have to be taken with a pinch of salt since the calculations are based on a small number of enterprises, that is, 29.

The aggregate professional index value (73.05) indicates that the sample companies, in particular, those that have responded to the questionnaire, are following sound financial management practices.

Section III Concluding Observations

What has been described and discussed above is an attempt to develop an index of professional practices relating to financial management. The index has been developed on the basis of the responses received to a questionnaire sent to all the 166 the sample companies. Though the number of responses received and used, being 29, was not very high, it can be considered a fairly good representation of the sample. In conclusion, it can be said that the sample companies are using sound financial management practices in a great measure. Needless to say, there is a greater scope for improving professionalism in some categories (capital structure and risk management) of financial management practices than others.

Appendices

Appendix 8.1: Calculations for professional index values of each sample company relating to capital budgeting (CB) practices

Company	Item 1	Item 2	Item 3	Item 4	ΣSi / ΣSim	IPF (CB)
1	2/5	5/5	1/5	5/5	13/20	65.00
2	5/5	5/5	5/5	5/5	20/20	100.00
3	1/5	5/5	1/5	5/5	12/20	60.00
4	5/5	5/5	5/5	5/5	20/20	100.00
5	3/5	5/5	1/5	5/5	14/20	70.00
6	5/5	5/5	–	5/5	15/20	75.00
7	5/5	5/5	5/5	5/5	20/20	100.00
8	4/5	5/5	5/5	5/5	19/20	95.00
9	1/5	5/5	–	5/5	11/20	55.00
10	5/5	5/5	5/5	5/5	20/20	100.00
11	5/5	2/5	1/5	5/5	13/20	65.00
12	3/5	2/5	1/5	5/5	11/20	55.00
13	4/5	5/5	–	5/5	14/20	70.00
14	1/5	5/5	1/5	5/5	12/20	60.00
15	3/5	5/5	5/5	5/5	18/20	90.00
16	5/5	5/5	–	5/5	15/20	75.00
17	5/5	5/5	5/5	5/5	20/20	100.00
18	5/5	5/5	1/5	5/5	16/20	80.00
19	5/5	5/5	5/5	5/5	20/20	100.00
20	5/5	2/5	1/5	1/5	9/20	45.00
21	5/5	5/5	1/5	5/5	16/20	80.00
22	5/5	5/5	–	5/5	15/20	75.00
23	5/5	5/5	–	5/5	15/20	75.00
24	5/5	5/5	5/5	5/5	20/20	100.00
25	5/5	5/5	–	5/5	15/20	75.00
26	5/5	5/5	5/5	5/5	20/20	100.00
AvIPF (CB)						79.42

*Questions 5 (item 2), 6 (item 3), 7 (item 4) and 9 (item 5) are the four questions picked up from the capital budgeting section (Section B) from Appendix 1.3 and their scores are shown under item 1–4, respectively, in the table

**The scores of 26 companies (out of 31) that responded to more than 50% of the questions in this category have been shown here

Appendix 8.2: Calculations for professional index values of each sample company relating to capital structure (CS) decisions

Company	Item 1	Item 2	Item 3	Item 4	Item 5	ΣSi / ΣSim	IPF (CS)
1	5/5	1/5	1/5	1/5	–	8/25	32.00
2	5/5	0/5	5/5	1/5	5/5	16/25	64.00
3	5/5	5/5	–	1/5	5/5	16/25	64.00
4	5/5	5/5	5/5	1/5	5/5	21/25	84.00
5	5/5	5/5	1/5	1/5	0/5	12/25	48.00
6	5/5	5/5	5/5	–	5/5	20/25	80.00
7	5/5	5/5	5/5	–	5/5	20/25	80.00
8	5/5	5/5	1/5	1/5	0/5	12/25	48.00
9	5/5	5/5	1/5	1/5	5/5	17/25	68.00
10	5/5	5/5	1/5	–	0/5	11/25	44.00
11	5/5	5/5	1/5	–	5/5	16/25	64.00
12	5/5	5/5	1/5	1/5	5/5	17/25	68.00
13	5/5	5/5	5/5	–	0/5	15/25	60.00
14	5/5	5/5	1/5	–	5/5	16/25	64.00
15	5/5	0/5	5/5	1/5	5/5	16/25	64.00
16	5/5	5/5	–	1/5	5/5	16/25	64.00
17	5/5	5/5	5/5	–	5/5	20/25	80.00
18	5/5	1/5	1/5	–	5/5	12/25	48.00
19	5/5	5/5	5/5	–	0/5	15/25	60.00
20	5/5	5/5	5/5	–	0/5	15/25	60.00
21	5/5	1/5	5/5	1/5	5/5	17/25	68.00
22	5/5	5/5	1/5	1/5	5/5	17/25	68.00
23	5/5	5/5	5/5	–	5/5	20/25	80.00
24	5/5	5/5	1/5	–	0/5	11/25	44.00
25	5/5	5/5	1/5	–	0/5	11/25	44.00
26	5/5	0/5	1/5	1/5	5/5	12/25	48.00
27	5/5	5/5	1/5	–	5/5	16/25	64.00
28	5/5	5/5	1/5	–	0/5	11/25	44.00
AvIPF (CS)							60.86

*Questions 3 (item 1), 11 (item 2), 13(B) (item 3), 14 (item 4) and 16 (item 5) are the five questions picked up from the capital structure section (Section C) from Appendix 1.3, and their scores are shown under item 1–5, respectively, in the table

**The scores of 28 companies (out of 31) that responded to more than 50% of the questions in this category have been shown here

Appendix 8.3: Calculations for professional index values of each sample company relating to working capital (WC) decisions

Company	Item 1	Item 2	Item 3	Item 4	Item 5	ΣSi / ΣSim	IPF (WC)
1	5/5	0/5	1/5	5/5	5/5	16/25	64.00
2	5/5	0/5	5/5	5/5	5/5	20/25	80.00
3	5/5	5/5	5/5	5/5	5/5	25/25	100.00
4	5/5	3/5	5/5	5/5	5/5	23/25	92.00
5	5/5	3/5	1/5	5/5	5/5	19/25	76.00
6	5/5	5/5	5/5	5/5	5/5	25/25	100.00
7	5/5	0/5	1/5	5/5	5/5	16/25	64.00
8	5/5	5/5	5/5	5/5	5/5	25/25	100.00
9	5/5	5/5	5/5	5/5	5/5	25/25	100.00
10	5/5	5/5	5/5	5/5	5/5	25/25	100.00
11	5/5	5/5	5/5	5/5	5/5	25/25	100.00
12	5/5	0/5	1/5	5/5	5/5	16/25	64.00
13	5/5	5/5	5/5	–	–	15/25	60.00
14	5/5	5/5	5/5	5/5	5/5	25/25	100.00
15	0/5	5/5	5/5	5/5	5/5	20/25	80.00
16	5/5	5/5	1/5	–	5/5	16/25	64.00
17	5/5	3/5	5/5	5/5	5/5	23/25	92.00
18	–	0/5	1/5	5/5	5/5	11/25	44.00
19	5/5	5/5	5/5	5/5	5/5	25/25	100.00
20	5/5	3/5	5/5	–	–	13/25	52.00
21	0/5	3/5	1/5	5/5	5/5	14/25	56.00
22	0/5	3/5	5/5	5/5	5/5	18/25	72.00
23	5/5	0/5	5/5	5/5	5/5	20/25	80.00
24	5/5	0/5	5/5	5/5	5/5	20/25	80.00
25	5/5	5/5	1/5	–	–	11/25	44.00
26	5/5	5/5	5/5	5/5	5/5	25/25	100.00
27	5/5	3/5	5/5	–	5/5	18/25	72.00
28	5/5	5/5	1/5	5/5	5/5	21/25	84.00
AvIPF (WC)							77.38

*Questions 19 (item 1), 20 (item 2), 23 (item 3), 25 (B) (item 4) and 25 (C) (item 5) are the five questions picked up from the working capital section (Section D) from Appendix 1.3, and their scores are shown under item 1–5, respectively, in the table

**The scores of 28 companies (out of 31) that responded to more than 50% of the questions in this category have been shown here

Appendix 8.4: Calculations for professional index values of each sample company relating to dividend (D) policy

Company	Item 1	Item 2	ΣSi / ΣSim	IPF (D)
1	1/5	5/5	6/10	60.00
2	5/5	5/5	10/10	100.00
3	1/5	1/5	2/10	20.00
4	5/5	5/5	10/10	100.00
5	5/5	5/5	10/10	100.00
6	5/5	1/5	6/10	60.00
7	5/5	5/5	10/10	100.00
8	5/5	5/5	10/10	100.00
9	5/5	5/5	10/10	100.00
10	5/5	5/5	10/10	100.00
11	5/5	5/5	10/10	100.00
12	5/5	5/5	10/10	100.00
13	5/5	5/5	10/10	100.00
14	5/5	5/5	10/10	100.00
15	5/5	5/5	10/10	100.00
16	5/5	5/5	10/10	100.00
17	5/5	5/5	10/10	100.00
18	5/5	5/5	10/10	100.00
19	5/5	1/5	6/10	60.00
20	5/5	5/5	10/10	100.00
21	5/5	1/5	6/10	60.00
22	5/5	5/5	10/10	100.00
23	5/5	5/5	10/10	100.00
24	5/5	5/5	10/10	100.00
25	5/5	5/5	10/10	100.00
26	5/5	5/5	10/10	100.00
27	5/5	5/5	10/10	100.00
AvIPD (D)				91.11

*Questions 27 (A) (item 1) and 27 (B) (item 2) are the two questions picked up from the dividend policy section (Section E) from Appendix 1.3, and their scores are shown under item 1–2, respectively, in the table

**The scores of 27 companies (out of 31) that responded to more than 50% of the questions in this category have been shown here

Appendix 8.5: Calculations for professional index values of each sample company relating to corporate governance (CG)

Company	Item 1	Item 2	Item 3	Item 4	Item 5	Item 6	Item 7	Item 8	Item 9	Item 10	Item 11	Item 12	Item 13	Item 14	Item 15	Item 16	ΣSi/ΣSim	IPF (CG)
1	5/5	0/5	5/5	5/5	5/5	5/5	5/5	5/5	5/5	5/5	5/5	5/5	5/5	0/5	5/5	5/5	70/80	87.50
2	5/5	–	5/5	5/5	5/5	5/5	5/5	–	5/5	5/5	5/5	5/5	5/5	5/5	5/5	5/5	70/80	87.50
3	5/5	0/5	5/5	5/5	5/5	5/5	5/5	5/5	5/5	5/5	5/5	5/5	5/5	5/5	5/5	5/5	75/80	93.75
4	–	0/5	5/5	0/5	5/5	5/5	5/5	0/5	5/5	5/5	5/5	5/5	5/5	5/5	5/5	5/5	60/80	75.00
5	5/5	0/5	5/5	0/5	5/5	1/5	5/5	5/5	5/5	5/5	5/5	–	5/5	5/5	5/5	5/5	61/80	76.25
6	5/5	0/5	5/5	5/5	5/5	5/5	5/5	5/5	5/5	5/5	5/5	5/5	5/5	5/5	5/5	5/5	75/80	93.75
7	5/5	0/5	1/5	5/5	5/5	5/5	5/5	5/5	5/5	5/5	5/5	5/5	5/5	5/5	5/5	5/5	71/80	88.75
8	5/5	5/5	5/5	5/5	5/5	5/5	5/5	0/5	5/5	5/5	5/5	5/5	5/5	0/5	5/5	5/5	70/80	87.50
9	5/5	0/5	5/5	5/5	5/5	5/5	5/5	5/5	5/5	5/5	5/5	5/5	5/5	5/5	5/5	5/5	75/80	93.75
10	5/5	0/5	5/5	1/5	1/5	5/5	5/5	5/5	5/5	5/5	5/5	5/5	5/5	5/5	5/5	5/5	67/80	83.75
11	5/5	0/5	5/5	5/5	5/5	5/5	5/5	5/5	5/5	5/5	5/5	5/5	5/5	5/5	5/5	5/5	75/80	93.75
12	5/5	5/5	5/5	5/5	5/5	5/5	5/5	5/5	5/5	5/5	5/5	5/5	5/5	5/5	5/5	5/5	80/80	100.00
13	5/5	0/5	5/5	5/5	5/5	5/5	5/5	5/5	5/5	5/5	5/5	5/5	0/5	5/5	5/5	5/5	70/80	87.50
14	5/5	0/5	5/5	5/5	5/5	5/5	5/5	5/5	5/5	5/5	5/5	5/5	5/5	–	5/5	0/5	65/80	81.25
15	5/5	0/5	5/5	5/5	5/5	5/5	5/5	0/5	5/5	5/5	5/5	5/5	5/5	–	5/5	5/5	65/80	81.25
16	5/5	0/5	5/5	5/5	5/5	5/5	5/5	5/5	5/5	5/5	5/5	5/5	5/5	–	5/5	5/5	70/80	87.50
17	–	–	5/5	5/5	5/5	5/5	5/5	5/5	5/5	5/5	5/5	5/5	5/5	5/5	5/5	5/5	70/80	87.50
18	5/5	0/5	5/5	5/5	5/5	5/5	5/5	5/5	5/5	5/5	5/5	5/5	5/5	0/5	5/5	5/5	70/80	87.50
19	5/5	0/5	5/5	–	–	5/5	5/5	5/5	5/5	5/5	5/5	5/5	5/5	5/5	5/5	5/5	65/80	81.25
20	5/5	0/5	5/5	5/5	5/5	5/5	5/5	0/5	5/5	5/5	5/5	5/5	5/5	5/5	5/5	5/5	70/80	87.50

21	5/5	0/5	5/5	5/5	5/5	5/5	5/5	5/5	5/5	5/5	5/5	5/5	5/5	0/5	5/5	5/5	70/80	87.50
22	0/5	0/5	5/5	5/5	5/5	5/5	5/5	0/5	5/5	5/5	5/5	5/5	5/5	0/5	5/5	0/5	55/80	68.75
23	0/5	0/5	5/5	–	–	5/5	5/5	5/5	5/5	5/5	5/5	5/5	5/5	–	5/5	5/5	55/80	68.75
24	5/5	–	5/5	5/5	5/5	5/5	5/5	5/5	5/5	5/5	5/5	5/5	5/5	5/5	5/5	5/5	75/80	93.75
25	5/5	5/5	1/5	5/5	5/5	5/5	5/5	5/5	5/5	5/5	5/5	5/5	5/5	5/5	5/5	5/5	76/80	95.00
26	5/5	–	5/5	5/5	5/5	5/5	5/5	0/5	5/5	5/5	–	5/5	5/5	5/5	5/5	5/5	65/80	81.25
27	5/5	–	5/5	5/5	5/5	5/5	5/5	5/5	5/5	5/5	5/5	5/5	5/5	5/5	5/5	5/5	75/80	93.75
28	5/5	0/5	1/5	–	–	5/5	5/5	0/5	5/5	5/5	5/5	5/5	5/5	0/5	5/5	0/5	46/80	57.50
29	5/5	0/5	–	5/5	5/5	5/5	–	5/5	–	5/5	5/5	5/5	5/5	5/5	5/5	5/5	60/80	75.00
AvIPF (CG)																		84.96

*Questions 32 (A) (item 1), 33 (A) (item 2), 36 (A) (item 3), 36 (B) (item 4), 36 (C) (item 5), 37 (item 6), 39 (item 7), 41 (A) (item 8), 41 (B) (item 9), 45 (item 10), 46 (item 11), 47 (item 12), 48 (item 13), 49 (A) (item 14), 49 (B) (item 15) and 49 (C) (item 16) are the 16 questions picked up from the corporate governance section (Section F) from Appendix 1.3, and their scores are shown under item 1–16, respectively, in the table

**All 31 companies had responded to this (corporate governance) section's questions. However, two of them had responded to questions of this section only. Hence, they have not been included in the calculation of the index

Appendix 8.6: Calculations for professional index values of each sample company relating to risk management (RM)

Company	Item 1	Item 2	Item 3	Item 4	Item 5	Item 6	Item 7	ΣSi / ΣSim	IPF (RM)
1	1/5	1/5	5/5	1/5	–	–	–	8/35	22.86
2	4/5	3/5	5/5	5/5	1/5	–	–	18/35	51.43
3	1/5	3/5	5/5	–	–	1/5	1/5	11/35	31.43
4	1/5	1/5	5/5	1/5	–	1/5	1/5	10/35	28.57
5	4/5	4/5	5/5	5/5	1/5	1/5	1/5	21/35	60.00
6	1/5	2/5	5/5	–	1/5	1/5	1/5	11/35	31.43
7	3/5	3/5	5/5	5/5	1/5	–	–	17/35	48.57
8	3/5	3/5	5/5	1/5	2/5	3/5	2/5	19/35	54.29
9	3/5	3/5	0/5	4/5	2/5	1/5	1/5	14/35	40.00
10	2/5	2/5	5/5	3/5	4/5	1/5	1/5	18/35	51.43
11	2/5	3/5	5/5	5/5	1/5	2/5	2/5	20/35	57.14
12	2/5	4/5	5/5	1/5	2/5	3/5	3/5	20/35	57.14
13	3/5	4/5	5/5	–	–	1/5	1/5	14/35	40.00
14	4/5	4/5	5/5	–	2/5	1/5	1/5	17/35	48.57
15	2/5	4/5	5/5	2/5	3/5	1/5	1/5	18/35	51.43
16	2/5	4/5	5/5	5/5	–	1/5	1/5	18/35	51.43
17	4/5	4/5	5/5	–	2/5	1/5	2/5	18/35	51.43
18	2/5	2/5	5/5	3/5	–	–	–	12/35	34.29
19	1/5	2/5	5/5	1/5	–	–	–	9/35	25.71
20	3/5	3/5	5/5	–	4/5	2/5	1/5	18/35	51.43
21	1/5	2/5	5/5	–	1/5	–	–	9/35	25.71
22	2/5	4/5	5/5	2/5	–	1/5	1/5	15/35	42.83
23	–	3/5	5/5	–	1/5	1/5	1/5	11/35	31.43
24	2/5	1/5	5/5	1/5	1/5	2/5	1/5	13/35	37.14
25	1/5	1/5	0/5	5/5	–	–	–	7/35	20.00
26	5/5	5/5	5/5	–	5/5	1/5	1/5	22/35	62.86
AvIPF (RM)									39.90

*Questions 59 (item 1), 60 (item 2), 61 (item 3), 64 (item 4), 65 (A) (item 5), 65 (B) (item 6) and 65 (C) (item 7) are the seven questions picked up from the risk management section (Section H) from Appendix 1.3, and their scores are shown under item 1–7, respectively, in the table

**The scores of 26 companies (out of 31) that responded to more than 50% of the questions in this category have been shown here

Appendix 8.7: Abbreviations with their expansions

IPF (CB): Index of professionalism with regard to capital budgeting (*CB*) practices in the sample company

AvIPF (CB): Average index of professionalism with regard to capital budgeting (CB) practices for the sample as a whole

IPF (CS): Index of professionalism with regard to capital structure (CS) practices in the sample company

AvIPF (CS): Average index of professionalism with regard to capital structure (CS) practices for the sample as a whole

IPF (WC):	Index of professionalism with regard to working capital (WC) practices in the sample company
AvIPF (WC):	Average index of professionalism with regard to working capital (WC) practices for the sample as a whole
IPF (D):	Index of professionalism with regard to dividend (D) practices in the sample company
AvIPF (D):	Average index of professionalism with regard to dividend (D) practices for the sample as a whole
IPF (CG):	Index of professionalism with regard to corporate governance (CG) practices in the sample company
AvIPF (CG):	Average index of professionalism with regard to corporate governance (CG) practices for the sample as a whole
IPF (RM):	Index of professionalism with regard to risk management (RM) practices in the sample company
AvIPF (RM):	Average index of professionalism with regard to risk management (RM) practices for the sample as a whole
IPF (C):	Aggregate value of the index of professionalism for all companies for one category of financial management practice
IPF (AG):	Aggregate value of the index of professionalism for all companies and all financial management practices combined

Appendix 8.8: Questionnaire for the calculation of index

I – Items Related to Capital Budgeting (CB) Practices

1. How many year(s) ahead do you plan for capital expenditure?

   (a) [ ] For next 1 year only
   (b) [ ] For next 5 years
   (c) [ ] For next 10 years
   (d) [ ] As and when the opportunity takes place
   (e) [ ] Any other (please specify) ________________

2. Does your company ever forego any expected profitable investment opportunity because of paucity of financial resources? Yes [ ] No [ ]
3. (A) Please identify capital expenditure evaluation technique(s) used in your company

   (a) [ ] Accounting rate of return on investment
   (b) [ ] Payback period
   (c) [ ] Discounted cash flow techniques

      (i) [ ] Net present value
      (ii) [ ] Internal rate of return
      (iii) [ ] Profitability index/present value index

   (d) [ ] Any other (please specify) ________________

(B) Is your company using the following techniques?

(a) [ ] Real options Yes [ ] No [ ]

4. Please state method(s) followed to incorporate project risk into your investment decision

(a) [ ] Shorter payback period for risky projects
(b) [ ] Higher cut-off rate for risky projects
(c) [ ] Sensitivity analysis
(d) [ ] Any other (please specify) _______________

II – Items Related to Capital Structure Decisions

1. During the course of capital expenditure projects, does your company opt for sound capital structure to ensure a low cost of capital for the project?
   Yes [ ] No [ ]
2. Which method do you use to determine cost of capital?

   (a) [ ] Weighted average cost of long-term sources of finance
   (b) [ ] Marginal cost of additional funds raised to finance new asset
   (c) [ ] Decided by the top management
   (d) [ ] Any other (please specify) _________________

3. In your opinion the ratio of debt to equity should be maintained less than 1, 1:1, 2:1, 3:1 or greater than 3.
4. If your firm prefers to have predominantly more equity, the reason(s) could be

   (a) [ ] Firm is not under obligations to pay dividends.
   (b) [ ] There is flexibility in paying dividends.
   (c) [ ] Equity is easy to raise.
   (d) [ ] Any other (please specify) ________________

5. Cost of retained earnings in your company is equivalent to

   (a) [ ] Cost of equity capital
   (b) [ ] Opportunity cost of using these funds by company
   (c) [ ] Opportunity cost of using these funds by equity-holders
   (d) [ ] No cost is considered
   (e) [ ] Any other (please specify) _______________

III – Items Related to Working Capital Management

1. Which of the following forms the basis for working capital determination?

   (a) [ ] Percentage of budgeted production
   (b) [ ] Percentage of budgeted sales

(c) [ ] Length of operating cycle
(d) [ ] Determination of individual components of current assets and current liabilities (based on raw material holding period, debtors collection period, creditors payment period and so on)
(e) [ ] Any other (please specify) _______________

2. Please state your company's policy regarding financing of working capital

(a) [ ] Mainly from long-term sources
(b) [ ] Mainly from short-term sources
(c) [ ] Temporary/seasonal needs from short-term sources and only for period needed
(d) [ ] Permanent needs from long-term sources and temporary/seasonal needs from short-term sources
(e) [ ] Any other (please specify) _________________

3. How do you manage emergency requirements of cash? (Arising due to unexpected events or to exploit an opportunity)

(a) [ ] Always maintain minimum cash balance over and above the required amount
(b) [ ] Bank overdraft
(c) [ ] Utilisation of cash credit limit from bank
(d) [ ] Discount bill receivables
(e) [ ] Have special arrangements with some lending agency for such purposes
(f) [ ] Sell marketable securities
(g) [ ] Raise loan against warehouse receipt
(h) [ ] Any other (please specify) ______________

4. Is risk analysis of customers made before granting credit? Yes [ ] No [ ]
5. Is the ageing schedule of debtors prepared? Yes [ ] No [ ]

IV – Items Related to Dividend Policy

1. Does your company follow a stable dividend policy? Yes [ ] No [ ]
2. Does your company follow a constant payout ratio? Yes [ ] No [ ]

V – Items Related to Corporate Governance

1. Does your company have an internal team dedicated to corporate governance? Yes [ ] No [ ]
2. Has the company been assessed for its corporate governance practices by any rating agency like CRISIL or ICRA etc. Yes [ ] No [ ]
3. Does the company publish its annual report within stipulated time of 6 months after the end of the financial year?

Always [ ] Mostly [ ] Occasionally [ ] Sometimes [ ] Never [ ]

4. Does the company publish/announce semi-annual reports within 1 month of the end of the half-year?

   Always [ ] Mostly [ ] Occasionally [ ] Sometimes [ ] Never [ ]

5. Does the company publish/announce quarterly reports within 1 month of the end of the quarter?

   Always [ ] Mostly [ ] Occasionally [ ] Sometimes [ ] Never [ ]

6. Does the company consistently disclose material sensitive information to stakeholders?

   Always [ ] Sometimes [ ] Never [ ]

7. Are the statutory auditors of the company unrelated to the top management of company? Yes [ ] No [ ]
8. Is there a whistle-blower policy in your company? Yes [ ] No [ ]
9. Is there an investors' grievance cell in your company? Yes [ ] No [ ]
10. Do the CEO and CFO of your company establish and maintain internal controls and implement remediation and risk mitigation towards deficiencies in internal controls? Yes [ ] No [ ]
11. Does your company submit a quarterly compliance report on corporate governance to the stock exchange where it is listed in the prescribed form? Yes [ ] No [ ]
12. Does your annual report contain a separate section on corporate governance with a detailed compliance report? Yes [ ] No [ ]
13. Does your company obtain a certificate either from auditors or practising company secretaries regarding compliance of conditions as stipulated in clause 49 and annex the same to the director's report? Yes [ ] No [ ]
14. Does your company have a committee on corporate governance as per clause 49? Yes [ ] No [ ]
15. Does your company have the mandatory audit committee as per clause 49? Yes [ ] No [ ]
16. Does your company have the remunerations committee as per clause 49? Yes [ ] No [ ]

VI – Items Related to Risk Management

1. What are some of the steps your company takes to mitigate its financial risk?

   (a) [ ] Keep the debt/equity ratio close to the industrial benchmark.
   (b) [ ] Make conscious efforts to keep the financial leverage as low as possible by reducing debt in the capital structure.
   (c) [ ] Have internal control ratios like cash flow return on investment.
   (d) [ ] Make conscious efforts to keep the interest coverage ratio as high as possible.
   (e) [ ] Make extensive use of financial derivatives.

(f) [ ] Examine tax consequences of cross border activities and incorporate it in financial planning.
(g) [ ] Any other (please specify) ____________

2. What are some of the steps your company takes to mitigate its business/operational risk?

(a) [ ] Use adequate insurance coverage against fixed asset loss.
(b) [ ] Use leasing/hire-purchase arrangements to keep long-term investment as low as possible.
(c) [ ] Examine components like transfer pricing, excise duties etc as consequences of cross border activities and incorporate it in operational planning.
(d) [ ] Review acquisitions and handle disposal/liquidation of business components/joint ventures.
(e) [ ] Budgets are regularly monitored and reallocated in line with revised risk/ resource needs.
(f) [ ] There is a strong and conscious effort to focus on variable-cost-dominated ventures and strategies.
(g) [ ] Any other (please specify) ____________

3. If operating risk is high, does your company make a strong effort to reduce financial risk (or vice versa) in order to keep the overall risk low? Yes [ ] No [ ]
4. Indicate the order of preference as to which of the following precautions could help in minimising the political risk in international operations. (1 for most important, 2 for next preference and so on)

(a) [ ] Incorporating a risk premium in the cost of capital
(b) [ ] Integrating products of the host country in your business
(c) [ ] Taking loans from the financial institutions of the host country
(d) [ ] Increasing the number of the host country employees.
(e) [ ] Creating joint ventures with an enterprise of the host country
(f) [ ] Any other (please specify) ______________

5. For managing exchange rate risk, do you use the following technique(s)?

	Yes	No
(a) Leads and lags	[ ]	[ ]
(b) Netting	[ ]	[ ]
(c) Back to back swap	[ ]	[ ]
(d) Re-invoicing through a centralised system	[ ]	[ ]
(e) Risk sharing	[ ]	[ ]
(f) Any other (please specify) ______________	[ ]	[ ]

6. In the case of anticipated depreciation of local currency, which of the basic hedging strategies are used by your company? (Please tick mark.)

(a) [ ] Buy foreign currency forward.
(b) [ ] Reduce levels of local currency cash and marketable securities.
(c) [ ] Reduce local currency receivables.

(d) [ ] Delay collection of hard currency (appreciating currency) receivables.
(e) [ ] Borrow locally.
(f) [ ] Delay payments of local currency payable.
(g) [ ] Speed up dividend and other remittances to parent.
(h) [ ] Invoice exports in foreign currency and imports in loc.l currency.

7. In the case of anticipated appreciation of local currency which of the basic hedging strategies used by your company? (Please tick mark.)

(a) [ ] Sell foreign currency forward.
(b) [ ] Increase levels of local currency cash and marketable securities.
(c) [ ] Relax local currency credit terms (i.e. increase local currency receivables)
(d) [ ] Speed up collection of soft currency (depreciating currency) receivables.
(e) [ ] Reduce local borrowing.
(f) [ ] Speed up payments of local currency payable.
(g) [ ] Delay dividend and other remittances to parent.
(h) [ ] Invoice exports in local currency and imports in foreign currency.

References

De Bondt WFM, Thaler RH (1995) Financial decision-making in markets and firms: a behavioral perspective. In: Jarrow R et al (eds) Chapter 13: Handbook in OR and MS, vol 9. Elsevier Science B.V., North Holland

Hoyle E (1980) Professionalization and deprofessionalization in education, world year book of education. Kogan Page Ltd., London, p. 42

Jain PK, Yadav SS (2000) Financial management practices in select private corporate enterprises – a comparative study of India, Thailand and Singapore. Hindustan Publishing Corporation, New Delhi

Jain PK, Yadav SS (2005) Financial management practices – a study of public sector enterprises in India. Hindustan Publishing Corporation, New Delhi

Stern D (2012) 7 ways to measure financial performance. http://davidsterncfo.wordpress.com/learning/7-ways-to-measure-financial-performance/. Accessed 19 July 2012

Yadav SS, Jain PK (2000) Professionalism in financial management: construct of an index. Manage Change 4(2):287–308

Yadav SS, Jain PK (2005) Financial management practices in public enterprises: development of an index of professionalism. Manage Change 9(1):1–34

Part IV
Summary and Conclusions

Chapter 9
Profitability Analysis

Introduction

The profit test is more than a conventional test of economic efficiency, that is, whether the resources are gainfully employed or not and whether the business enterprise is operating competitively or not. It has a direct bearing on the company's ability to function as a successful business firm. Further, the company's ability to tap capital markets and/or other sources of finance (for its growth and additional requirements) would depend on its commercial profitability.

Given the significance of financial viability of business operations, the objective of this chapter is to assess the financial performance of the sample companies primarily in terms of profitability with a special focus on the pre- and post-recession period. Expectedly, financial management of resources in terms of profitability constitutes, by far, the most important element of operational efficiency and hence the significance to study this aspect. Further, to the best of the authors' knowledge, an analysis of the impact (if any) of the recent recession on such a large sample has not been undertaken. Analysis that follows seeks to answer such basic questions with respect to the sample companies as the following: (a) Are their profits adequate? (b) What rates of return do they earn? and (c) Are their returns to equity owners satisfactory?

It is in this context that profitability of the sample companies has been analysed in this chapter. Analysis is based on profit margins on sales as well as rates of return earned on total assets, capital employed and shareholders' funds. To begin with, the basic components of profits, namely, gross profit and net profit are determined for the sample companies for the entire 11-year period of the study (sub-divided into four phases). Then three sets of rates of return (RoR) have been computed. These are (a) return on total assets (ROTA), (b) return on capital employed (ROCE) and (c) return on ordinary shareholders' equity (ROSE). The first two rates of return highlight how efficiently financial resources are deployed by the sample companies; the RoR on the common shareholders' equity indicates the return provided to their equity owners.

P.K. Jain et al., *Financial Management Practices: An Empirical Study of Indian Corporates*, India Studies in Business and Economics,
DOI 10.1007/978-81-322-0990-4_9, © Springer India 2013

The first two types of RoRs have been determined on the basis of operating profits, that is, earnings before interest and taxes. By precluding effect of financial structure and taxes, these rates focus directly on operational efficiency. The rationale of inclusion of interest is that the RoRs (related to total assets and capital employed) exclusively based on pre-tax profits would be an underestimate as the interest paid to lenders is excluded from the net profits (in numerator), whereas total capital employed as well as total assets (as a part of denominator) includes borrowed funds. Therefore, a better and reliable indicator of the true/real return on assets/capital employed is the pre-tax profits inclusive of interest.

Given the positive nexus between the effective utilisation of assets and profitability, the analysis has been extended to compute major efficiency ratios, namely, total assets turnover, fixed assets turnover and current assets turnover of the sample companies.

As far as the scope, methodology and sources of data on which the analysis is based, they are the same as mentioned in Chap. 1 of the study. Section I contains a brief literature review covering profitability and the impact (if any) of the recent recession on India. Section II presents the profitability of the sample companies (in terms of gross profit and net profit margins) with a special emphasis on pre-recession and post-recession analysis (phases 3 and 4). While section III attempts to present profitability analysis in terms of the ROTA and ROCE, the ROSE constitutes the subject matter of section IV. The major efficiency ratios showing the efficiency levels of current assets, fixed assets and total assets have been examined in section V. Industry analysis of the constituent sectors of the sample companies forms the subject matter of Section VI. Concluding observations are contained in section VII.

Section I Literature Review

This section enumerates a brief literature review on (a) profitability as a measure of financial performance and (b) the impact (if any) of the recent financial crisis and the resultant recession on Indian companies.

Profitability as a Measure of Financial Performance

Fukui and Ushijima (2011) decomposed the business-level profit rate of Japanese multi-business corporations by performing a variance components analysis on a large sample of publicly traded non-financial firms in 1998–2003. Kaymaz and Kaymaz (2010) identified the firm-level determinants underlying the profitability in brokerage institutions operating in Turkey. Zeli and Mariani (2009) analysed profitability and productivity for large Italian companies (operating in industrial sectors) for the years 1998–2002.

Monea (2009) presented a picture about company's profitability, its financial position and use of its assets' efficiency through profitability ratios. Karacaer and Kapusuzoğlu (2008) made evaluations on 30 ratios listed under the title of liquidity, leverage, activity and profitability ratios on the financial positions of enterprises (profit/loss) of 61 enterprises traded on the Istanbul Stock Exchange. Niu et al. (2008) determined that in case a company wants to increase shareholders' wealth, return on equity (ROE) must be improved on the basis of the size of shareholders' equity, and shareholders' equity will grow on the premise that ROE is greater than cost of equity capital.

Rajan et al. (2006) examined empirically how a firm's return on investment (ROI) is impacted by two central variables: accounting conservatism and growth. Holz (2002) found that liability–asset ratio of China's industrial state-owned enterprises (SOEs) had increased dramatically in the course of the economic reform period. They, however, perceive that low profitability SOEs tend to have a high liability–asset ratio, perhaps due to government-ordained support through bank loans.

Zhang et al. (2002) assessed the reform of state-owned enterprises (SOEs) by examining the effect of ownership on the profitability and productivity of Chinese industrial firms. The subsequent analysis, based on revised profitability measurements, suggested that the effects of capital structure, taxes and welfare burdens were significant in determining firm performance. Claver et al. (2002) used return on assets (ROA) as the profitability measure in their research.

Nissim and Penman (2001) used financial statement analysis for equity valuation. Standard profitability analysis was incorporated, extended and was complemented with an analysis of growth.

Impact of Recent Financial Crisis on India

Brazil, the Russian Federation, India and China (the so-called BRIC economies) are four of the top five destinations preferred by the world's largest multinational companies according to the *world investment prospects survey* undertaken by the United Nations Council on Trade and Development (UNCTAD) in 2009. Interestingly, all these economies are estimated to have experienced a rise in inward foreign direct investment (FDI) in 2008 over 2007. Difficulties and uncertainties in their economies have increased substantially, however, after the sudden worsening of the global financial crisis in September and October 2008. Coupled with the reduced availability of capital worldwide, this has led to a reversal of a growth cycle of inflows to these economies by the end of the year 2008 (Source: UNCTAD website. http://www.unctad.org/en/docs/webdiaeia20095_en.pdf. Accessed 17 Nov 2011).

According to the remarks prepared for the International Monetary Fund (IMF)–Financial Stability Forum (FSF), on the recent financial turmoil and policy responses for India, Reserve Bank of India (RBI, India's central bank) in October 2008 stated that India had (at that time) not been seriously affected by the recent financial crisis. The reasons for the relative resilience shown by the Indian economy, the impact and likely implications have been summarised below (Source: RBI website. http://rbidocs.rbi.org.in/rdocs/Speeches/PDFs/87784.pdf; Economic Surveys of India).

India has been following a rather calibrated and cautious approach to the opening up of the capital account and the financial sector. Evidence suggests that the greatest gains for an economy are obtained from the opening to foreign direct investment followed by portfolio equity investment.

Therefore, while encouraging foreign investment flows (in particular, direct investment flows), a cautious approach has been adopted related to debt flows. Debt flows are subject to ceilings and some end-use restrictions (modulated from time to time), taking into account evolving macroeconomic and monetary conditions. Similarly, portfolio investment in government securities and corporate bonds are also subject to macro ceilings, which are also moderated from time to time. These prudential policies have attempted to prevent excessive recourse to borrowings and dollarisation of the economy. As far as capital outflows are concerned, the policy framework has been progressively liberalised to enable the corporate sector to invest abroad.

As a result, investments have been predominantly financed by domestic savings in India. The government's fiscal deficit has been high by international standards but is also largely internally financed through a vibrant and well-developed government securities market, and thus, despite large fiscal deficits, macroeconomic and financial stability has been maintained.

However, with the increasing integration of the Indian economy and its financial markets with the rest of the world, there is recognition that the country does face some downside risks from these international developments. The risks arise mainly from the potential reversal of capital flows on a sustained medium-term basis. As might be expected, the main impact of the global financial turmoil in India has emanated from the significant change experienced in the capital account. Total net capital flows fell from US$17.3 billion in April–June 2007 to US$13.2 billion in April–June 2008.

On the positive side, however, the characteristics of India's external and financial sector management coupled with ample foreign exchange reserves and the growing underlying strength of the Indian economy reduce the susceptibility of the Indian economy to global turbulence (Source: Reserve Bank of India website. http://www.rbi.org.in/scripts/WSSViewDetail.aspx?TYPE=Section&PARAM1=2. Accessed 4 Dec 2011).

The financial crisis in the advanced economies and the likely slowdown in these economies could, however, have some impact on the IT sector. According to the latest assessment by the NASSCOM (the software trade association), the current developments with respect to the US financial markets are very eventful; these developments may have a direct impact on the IT industry and are likely to create a downstream impact on other sectors of the US economy and worldwide markets. About 15–18%

of the business coming to Indian outsourcers includes projects from banking, insurance and the financial services sector which is now uncertain (Source: Reserve Bank of India website. http://rbidocs.rbi.org.in/rdocs/Speeches/PDFs/87784.pdf).

As per the Economic Survey of India of 2010–2011, the Indian economy has emerged with remarkable rapidity from the slowdown caused by the global financial crisis of 2007–2009. With the growth in 2009–2010 estimated at 8% by the Quick Estimates released on 31 January 2011 and 8.6% in 2010–2011 as per the Advance Estimates of the Central Statistics Office (CSO) released on 7 February 2011, the turnaround has been fast and strong. Much of the economic stress (if any) in 2011 can be attributed to continued food inflation and a temporary slowdown in industrial growth (Source: http://indiabudget.nic.in/. Accessed 17 Nov 2011).

Section II Profitability Ratios

This section examines the gross profit and the net profit of the sample companies for the entire 11-year period of the study as well as through the pre-recession and post-recession periods (phases 3 and 4). The impact of recession (if any) has been tested through the paired *t*-test statistic (amongst others).

Gross Profit

The sample companies recorded an increase in the gross profit percentage in a statistically significant manner in phase 2 over phase 1. It showed a dip in the post-recession period (statistically significant) even though the difference in mean was of one percentage point. This could perhaps be due to the varied nature of the constituent sectors making up the sample and the impact of recession on each one of them. This aspect is better supported by high positive skewness and kurtosis in phase 4 which indicates that there were only few companies that recorded a high gross profit percentage in the post-recession period (Table 9.1). This aspect is further supported by the frequency distribution (Table 9.2) which shows a decline in the percentage of companies recording a gross profit between 10 and 20% in phase 2 over phase 1. At the same time, there is, however, an increase in the percentage of companies achieving a gross profit in the higher range of 20–30% in phase 4 compared to phase 3, indicating that some sectors were able to increase profitability in spite of the recession. The sector analysis would perhaps be able to offer further explanations.

Standard deviation and coefficient of variation were moderately high, perhaps due to the different constituent sectors (making up the sample) and their respective profit situations (Fig. 9.1).

Table 9.1 Mean, standard deviation, coefficient of variation, skewness, kurtosis, median and quartile values related to gross profit percentage of the sample companies, 2001–2011 (Figures are in percentages)

Year ending[a]	Number	Mean	Standard deviation	Coefficient of variation (%)	Skewness	Kurtosis	Median	Quartile 1	Quartile 3
2001	115	21.00	19.00	87.21	1.78	4.96	15.00	8.00	31.00
2002	134	19.00	19.00	101.83	−1.74	16.59	15.00	9.00	26.00
2003	139	20.00	14.00	69.74	1.32	1.66	16.00	10.00	27.00
2004	143	23.00	16.00	67.93	1.22	1.43	18.00	12.00	31.00
2005	153	23.00	17.00	71.81	1.06	0.89	19.00	10.00	33.00
2006	153	26.00	19.00	75.23	1.45	2.16	20.00	13.00	32.00
2007	157	27.00	20.00	74.38	1.68	3.55	22.00	14.00	35.00
2008	157	29.00	20.00	68.76	1.24	1.42	22.00	14.00	37.00
2009	158	28.00	24.00	86.23	1.97	4.94	20.00	12.00	34.00
2010	158	28.00	22.00	78.43	2.06	6.26	22.00	14.00	34.00
2011	156	26.00	19.00	73.31	1.33	1.88	22.00	12.00	36.00
2001–2011	137	25.00	19.00	77.72	1.21	4.16	19.00	12.00	32.00
Phase 1 (2000–2001 to 2005–2006)	134	22.00	17.00	78.96	0.85	4.62	17.00	10.00	30.00
Phase 2 (2006–2007 to 2010–2011)	157	28.00	21.00	76.22	1.66	3.61	22.00	13.00	35.00

Phase 3 (2006–2007 to 2007–2008)	157	28.00	20.00	71.57	1.46	2.49	22.00	14.00	36.00
Phase 4 (2008–2009 to 2010–2011)	157	27.00	22.00	79.32	1.79	4.36	21.00	13.00	35.00

[a](1) The Indian financial year begins on April 1 and ends on March 31 of the following year. The same holds true for all subsequent tables and notations
(2) Extreme values of 150% or more and negative values are excluded

		Paired differences							
					95% confidence interval of the difference				
		Mean	Standard deviation	Standard error mean	Lower	Upper	*t*	*df*	Significance (2-tailed)
Pair 1	Phase 1–Phase 2	–0.05169	0.12971	0.01032	–0.07207	–0.03130	–5.009	157	0.000
Pair 2	Phase 3–Phase 4	0.01812	0.09411	0.00749	0.00333	0.03290	2.420	157	0.017

Table 9.2 Frequency distribution related to gross profit percentage of the sample companies, 2001–2011 (Figures are in percentages)

Gross profit (%)	2001	2002	2003	2004	2005	2006	2007	2008	2009	2010	2011
Less than 10	8.73	7.04	4.14	3.38	1.30	1.91	1.23	0.61	2.45	1.23	2.45
10–20	56.35	59.86	60.00	54.05	51.95	48.41	45.68	40.49	48.47	38.27	44.79
20–30	11.11	11.27	16.55	17.57	19.48	21.02	18.52	19.63	17.79	29.63	20.25
30–40	6.35	10.56	9.66	11.49	9.09	11.46	15.43	14.11	11.04	9.26	12.27
40–60	13.49	8.45	7.59	10.81	14.94	7.64	9.88	14.11	9.20	12.35	11.66
Above 60	3.96	2.82	2.07	2.71	3.25	9.55	9.26	11.04	11.03	9.26	8.58
Total	100	100	100	100	100	100	100	100	100	100	100

Total (100) may not tally due to rounding off. The same holds true for other frequency distribution tables

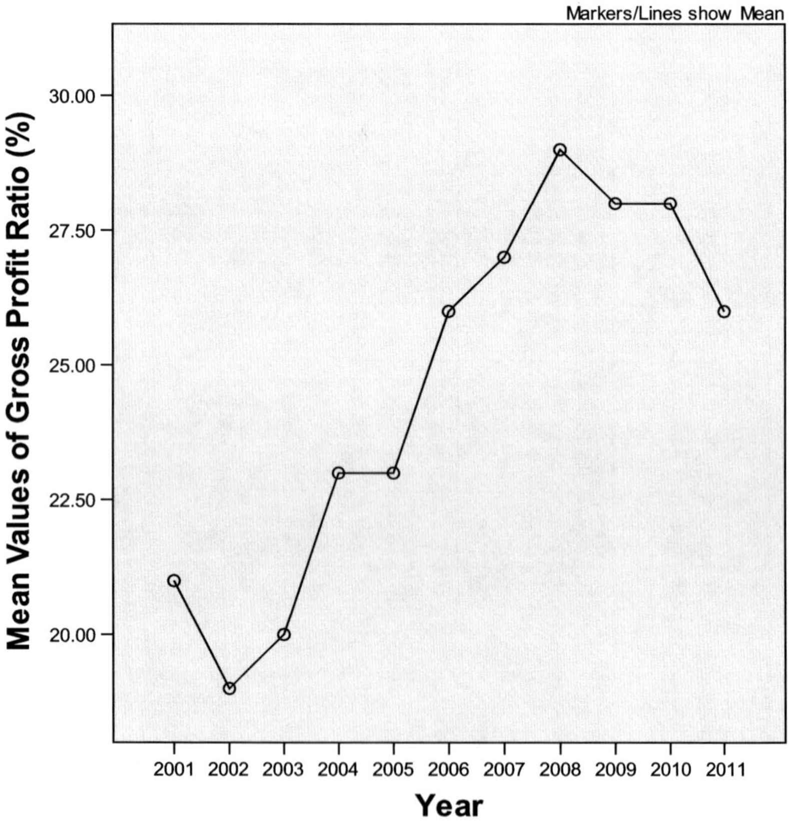

Fig. 9.1 Mean values of gross profit percentage for the sample companies, 2001–2011

Net Profit

Net profit percentages also mirror the trend of gross profit percentages. The sample companies recorded an increase in the net profit percentage (statistically significant) in phase 2 over phase 1. The mean net profit margin of the sample companies over the entire period of the study has been 15%. The net profit recorded a dip in the post-recession period (statistically significant) albeit the difference of one and a half percentage point only (Table 9.3). This aspect is further supported by the frequency distribution (Table 9.4) which shows a decline in the percentage of companies recording a net profit between 10 and 20% in phase 2 over phase 1. At the same time, there is, however, an increase in the percentage of companies achieving a net profit in the higher interval of above 40%. In sum, the decrease in net profit margin, prima facie, during post-recession period seems to be marginal (Fig. 9.2).

Even though phase 4 does indicate a statistically significant decline in profitability (albeit marginal), all in all, the sample exhibits stable earnings and profits. While, there appears to be an impact of recession on the sample, it does not appear to merit concern in terms of very marginal decline in profit margins. The sample continued to record a rather robust/healthy profit throughout the entire period of the study, indicative of the sound fundamentals of the companies.

Section III Rates of Return on Total Assets and Total Capital Employed

The objective of this section is to measure profitability of the sample companies in terms of ROTA and ROCE.

Rate of Return on Total Assets (ROTA)

ROTA has been calculated based on (earnings after tax (EAT) + interest − tax advantage on interest) / average total assets, where total assets denote total assets less (revaluation reserves + miscellaneous expenses not written off + advance tax).

Relevant data related to ROTA of the sample companies (Table 9.5) indicate that the mean has been 14% during the aggregate period (2001–2011) and 15% and 13% during the pre-recession and post-recession period, respectively. In general, these rates appear to be adequate, indicating satisfactory performance of the sample companies. This is in sharp contrast to the findings of an earlier study conducted by the authors on the public sector undertakings (PSUs) in India (Jain and Yadav 2005) where the average ROTA was at an unsatisfactory level of 1.96% from 1991 to 2003.

ROTA statistics are similar to the trend reported through the profitability ratios discussed in section II. The sample companies recorded an increase in the ROTA in

Table 9.3 Mean, standard deviation, coefficient of variation, skewness, kurtosis, median and quartile values related to net profit percentage of the sample companies, 2001–2011 (Figures are in percentages)

Year ending	Number	Mean	Standard deviation	Coefficient of variation (%)	Skewness	Kurtosis	Median	Quartile 1	Quartile 3
2001	108	14.00	15.00	105.49	3.14	16.34	9.00	5.00	22.00
2002	127	12.00	11.00	94.69	1.15	1.45	8.00	4.00	19.00
2003	137	12.00	10.00	86.54	1.56	3.20	9.00	4.00	17.00
2004	140	14.00	12.00	85.50	1.74	3.90	10.00	6.00	18.00
2005	150	14.00	11.00	77.61	1.31	2.10	11.00	6.00	20.00
2006	155	16.00	15.00	99.30	2.73	11.20	11.00	7.00	21.00
2007	155	18.00	18.00	97.37	3.33	15.84	14.00	8.00	23.00
2008	156	19.00	15.00	80.18	2.08	6.24	15.00	8.00	24.00
2009	155	18.00	16.00	88.88	1.79	3.54	13.00	7.00	23.00
2010	153	17.00	14.00	81.67	1.68	3.52	13.00	8.00	22.00
2011	155	16.00	13.00	80.85	1.21	1.14	13.00	6.00	23.00
2001–2011	132	15.00	14.00	88.92	1.98	6.22	11.00	6.00	21.00
Phase 1 (2000–2001 to 2005–2006)	132	14.00	12.00	91.52	1.94	6.36	10.00	5.00	19.00
Phase 2 (2006–2007 to 2010–2011)	155	18.00	15.00	85.79	2.02	6.05	14.00	8.00	23.00

Phase 3 (2006–2007 to 2007–2008)	156	18.50	16.50	88.78	2.71	11.04	14.50	8.00	23.50
Phase 4 (2008–2009 to 2010–2011)	154	17.00	14.00	83.80	1.56	2.73	13.00	7.00	23.00

Extreme values of 150% or more and negative values are excluded

		Paired differences							
					95% confidence interval of the difference				
		Mean	Standard deviation	Standard error mean	Lower	Upper	*t*	*df*	Significance (2-tailed)
Pair 1	Phase 1–Phase 2	−0.03724	0.09611	0.00767	−0.05239	−0.02209	−4.855	156	0.000
Pair 2	Phase 3–Phase 4	0.01698	0.10798	0.00851	0.00017	0.03379	1.995	160	0.048

Table 9.4 Frequency distribution related to net profit percentage of the sample companies, 2001–2011 (Figures are in percentages)

Net profit (%)	2001	2002	2003	2004	2005	2006	2007	2008	2009	2010	2011
Less than 0	14.29	11.27	6.21	5.41	3.23	2.55	3.70	3.07	4.32	4.32	4.27
10–20	62.70	68.31	76.55	72.97	72.26	71.97	65.43	61.96	66.67	65.43	66.46
20–30	15.87	11.97	10.34	13.51	16.13	15.29	17.90	20.25	13.58	14.81	14.63
30–40	4.76	7.04	4.14	4.73	5.16	4.46	5.56	6.13	7.41	6.17	4.88
Above 40	2.38	1.41	2.76	3.38	3.23	5.73	7.41	8.59	8.03	9.25	9.76
Total	100	100	100	100	100	100	100	100	100	100	100

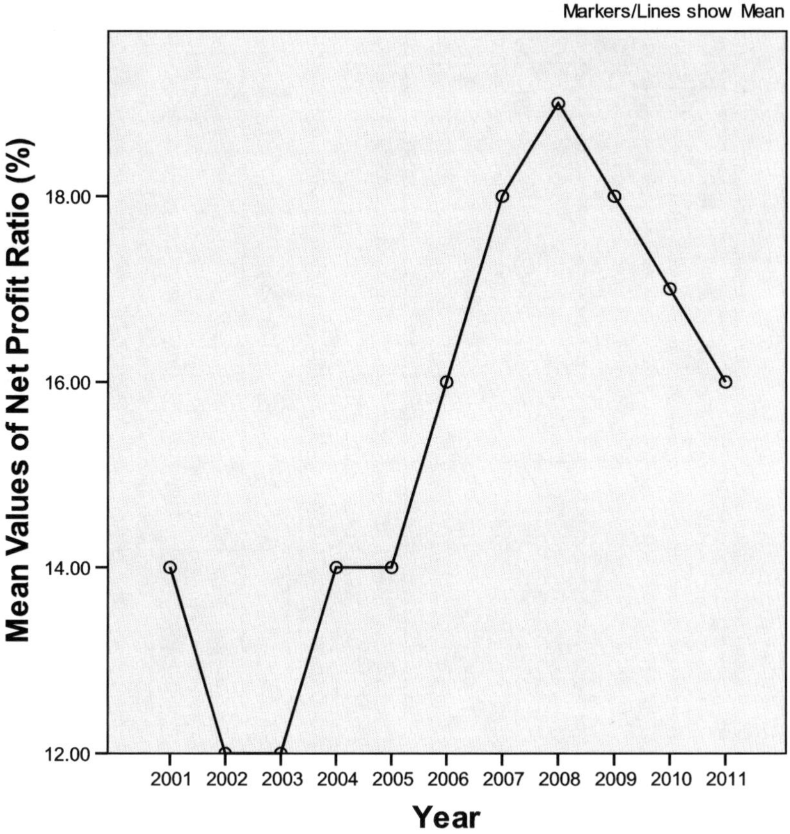

Fig. 9.2 Mean values of net profit percentage for the sample companies, 2001–2011

a statistically significant manner in phase 2 over phase 1. The mean ROTA dipped in the post-recession period (statistically significant) as is evident from Table 9.5. This aspect is further supported by the frequency distribution (Table 9.6).

Further, as per trend, it has been noted that ROTA for the sample remained stable at 15% from 2004 to 2008, reporting a dip in the post-recession period (Fig. 9.3).

Rate of Return on Capital Employed (ROCE)

The ROCE is another variant of rate of return on investments. It is similar to ROTA except in one respect, that is, the denominator is related to average capital employed instead of average total assets. Since the sum of capital employed (shareholders'

Table 9.5 Mean, standard deviation, coefficient of variation, skewness, kurtosis, median and quartile values related to return on total assets (*ROTA*) of the sample companies, 2001–2011

Year ending	Number	Mean	Standard deviation	Coefficient of variation (%)	Skewness	Kurtosis	Median	Quartile 1	Quartile 3
2001	139	10.00	11.00	104.70	0.67	1.65	9.00	4.00	15.00
2002	145	12.00	11.00	97.75	−0.02	3.43	10.00	6.00	15.00
2003	147	12.00	11.00	88.52	0.14	4.64	11.00	7.00	18.00
2004	147	15.00	12.00	77.30	1.57	6.56	14.00	8.00	22.00
2005	154	15.00	12.00	78.27	0.11	2.43	13.00	7.00	20.00
2006	152	15.00	12.00	76.78	0.77	1.14	12.00	7.00	22.00
2007	152	15.00	11.00	72.14	0.67	0.00	12.00	8.00	22.00
2008	158	15.00	11.00	69.34	0.93	0.63	13.00	7.00	22.00
2009	159	13.00	10.00	73.98	0.78	0.58	11.00	7.00	19.00
2010	155	13.00	11.00	82.31	0.21	3.36	10.00	6.00	19.00
2011	159	12.00	10.00	84.49	0.84	1.72	9.00	6.00	18.00
2001–2011	149	14.00	11.00	82.33	0.61	2.38	11.00	7.00	19.00
Phase 1 (2000–2001 to 2005–2006)	147	13.00	11.00	87.22	0.54	3.31	11.00	6.00	19.00
Phase 2 (2006–2007 to 2010–2011)	156	14.00	10.00	76.45	0.69	1.26	11.00	7.00	20.00
Phase 3 (2006–2007 to 2007–2008)	155	15.00	11.00	70.74	0.80	0.32	13.00	8.00	22.00
Phase 4 (2008–2009 to 2010–2011)	157	13.00	10.00	80.26	0.61	1.89	10.00	6.00	18.00

Extreme values of ±50% are excluded

		Paired differences							
					95% confidence interval of the difference				
		Mean	Std. deviation	Std. error mean	Lower	Upper	*t*	*df*	Significance (2-tailed)
Pair 1	Phase 1–Phase 2	−0.01775	0.08951	0.00710	−0.03177	−0.00373	−2.501	158	0.013
Pair 2	Phase 3–Phase 4	0.02613	0.06931	0.00551	0.01523	0.03702	4.738	157	0.000

Table 9.6 Frequency distribution related to return on total assets (*ROTA*) of the sample companies, 2001–2011 (Figures are in percentages)

ROTA (%)	2001	2002	2003	2004	2005	2006	2007	2008	2009	2010	2011
Less than 0	9.09	6.71	5.19	6.45	2.50	3.11	4.29	3.01	3.01	3.07	3.03
0–5	19.58	12.08	12.34	9.03	12.50	7.45	9.20	10.84	11.45	12.27	16.36
5–10	22.38	29.53	27.92	20.00	20.63	27.95	21.47	21.69	27.11	31.29	32.73
10–15	23.08	23.49	22.08	18.71	18.75	21.12	21.47	20.48	22.89	15.34	13.94
15–50	23.08	25.50	28.57	42.58	42.50	35.40	37.42	39.16	31.33	33.13	30.30
Above 50	2.80	2.68	3.90	3.23	3.13	4.97	6.13	4.82	4.22	4.91	3.64
Total	100	100	100	100	100	100	100	100	100	100	100

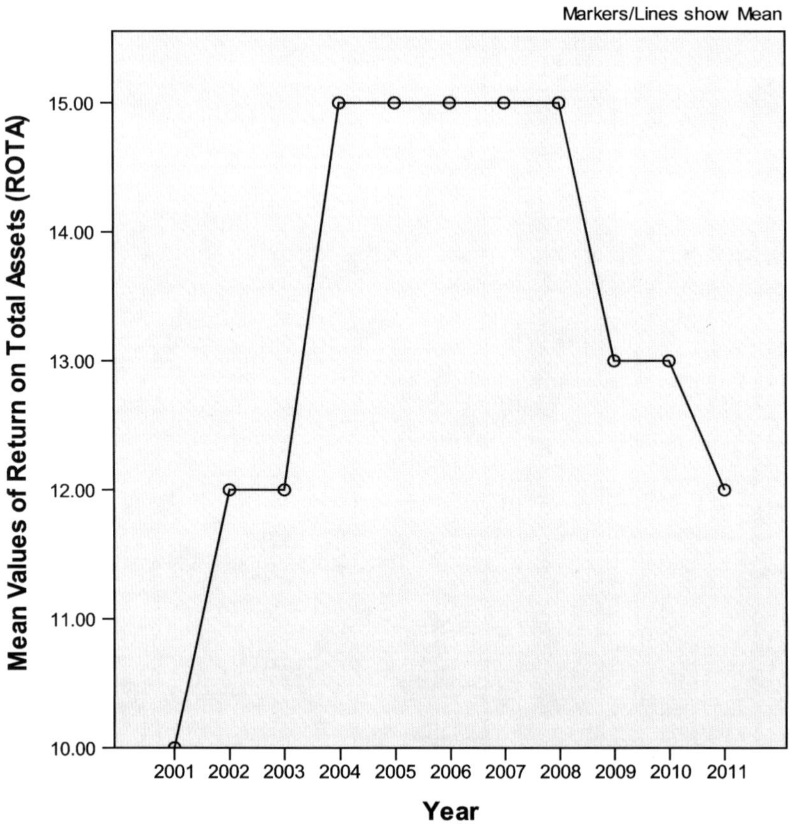

Fig. 9.3 Mean values of return on total assets (*ROTA*) for the sample companies, 2001–2011

equity + borrowings) is lower than total assets, the ROCE, perforce, would be higher than ROTA. The ROCE indicates how efficiently the long-term funds of owners and lenders are being used. The higher the ratio, the more efficient is the use of capital employed.

As expected, the analysis indicates that the ROCE is higher than the ROTA. For instance, the average ROCE is 16% compared to a ROTA of 14% for the entire period of the study. Similar conclusions follow in the basis of median and quartiles. The increase in ROCE in phase 2 over phase 1 (17 and 16%, respectively) has not been statistically significant but the decline in phase 4 ROCE (16%) when compared to phase 3 (18%) is statistically significant as per the paired *t*-test. Skewness and kurtosis figures are high, indicating that only few companies record a very high ROCE when compared to the sample, perhaps due to their unique corporate financing practices. The varying capital structure practices followed by the sample are also supported by the high coefficient of variation (Table 9.7).

As per trend also, increase (albeit marginal) in ROCE has been noted in 2010–2011 after the dip in the beginning of phase 4 (Fig. 9.4).

Table 9.7 Mean, standard deviation, coefficient of variation, skewness, kurtosis, median and quartile values related to return on capital employed (*ROCE*) of the sample companies, 2001–2011

Year ending	Number	Mean	Standard deviation	Coefficient of variation (%)	Skewness	Kurtosis	Median	Quartile 1	Quartile 3
2001	143	13.00	17.00	131.82	3.19	16.50	11.00	4.00	16.00
2002	149	14.00	17.00	124.11	3.71	27.26	10.00	6.00	17.00
2003	154	16.00	24.00	148.83	5.90	48.55	11.00	7.00	20.00
2004	153	17.00	15.00	89.08	2.33	10.23	14.00	8.00	23.00
2005	160	17.00	18.00	105.94	3.84	28.36	14.00	8.00	21.00
2006	161	19.00	21.00	111.46	3.66	19.28	13.00	8.00	23.00
2007	163	18.00	15.00	83.65	1.53	3.17	14.00	8.00	26.00
2008	166	18.00	18.00	99.27	3.52	17.79	14.00	8.00	24.00
2009	166	16.00	18.00	108.57	3.70	19.04	12.00	7.00	21.00
2010	164	16.00	18.00	111.69	3.37	16.81	12.00	7.00	19.00
2011	165	17.00	17.00	100.11	2.14	8.31	14.00	7.00	23.00
2001–2011	155	16.00	18.00	110.41	3.35	19.57	13.00	7.00	21.00
Phase 1 (2000–2001 to 2005–2006)	152	16.00	19.00	118.54	3.77	25.03	12.00	7.00	20.00
Phase 2 (2006–2007 to 2010–2011)	165	17.00	17.00	100.66	2.85	13.02	13.00	7.00	22.00

(continued)

Table 9.7 (continued)

Year ending	Number	Mean	Standard deviation	Coefficient of variation (%)	Skewness	Kurtosis	Median	Quartile 1	Quartile 3
Phase 3 (2006–2007 to 2007–2008)	165	18.00	17.00	91.46	2.53	10.48	14.00	8.00	25.00
Phase 4 (2008–2009 to 2010–2011)	165	16.00	17.00	106.79	3.07	14.72	13.00	7.00	21.00

Extreme values of ±50% are excluded

		Paired differences							
					95% confidence interval of the difference				
		Mean	Standard deviation	Standard error mean	Lower	Upper	*t*	*df*	Significance (2-tailed)
Pair 1	Phase 1–Phase 2	−0.01417	0.14459	0.01136	−0.03660	0.00827	−1.247	161	0.214
Pair 2	Phase 3–Phase 4	0.01803	0.09009	0.00699	0.00422	0.03184	2.578	165	0.011

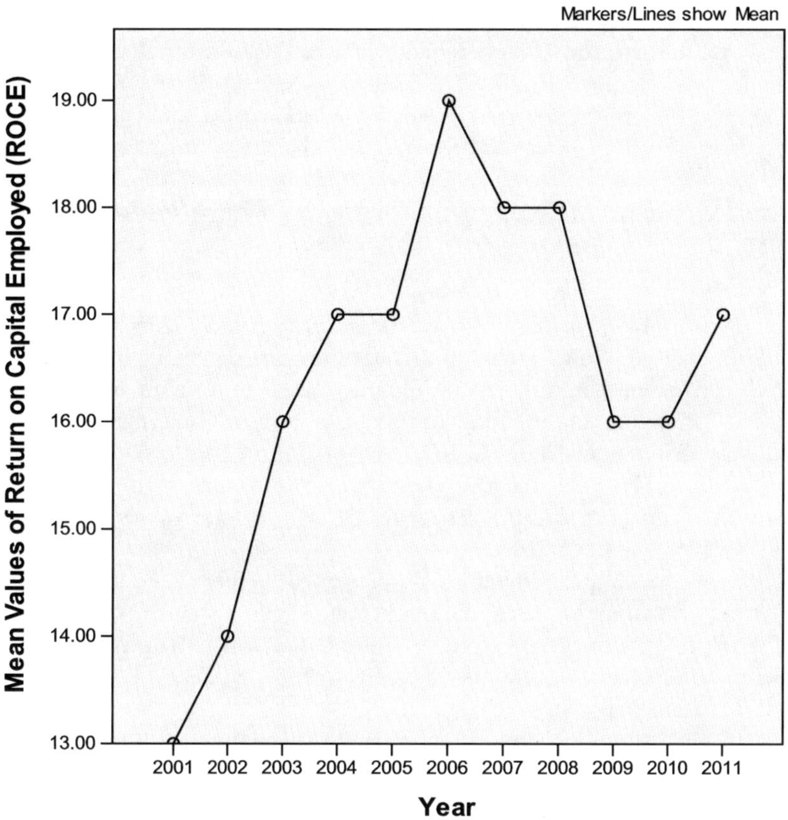

Fig. 9.4 Mean values of return on capital employed (*ROCE*) for the sample companies, 2001–2011

Table 9.8 Frequency distribution related to return on capital employed (*ROCE*) of the sample companies, 2001–2011 (Figures are in percentages)

ROCE (%)	2001	2002	2003	2004	2005	2006	2007	2008	2009	2010	2011
Less than 0	9.09	6.71	4.55	5.81	1.88	2.48	3.68	2.41	3.01	3.07	3.64
0–10	39.86	42.28	38.96	26.45	32.50	36.65	30.06	31.93	38.55	42.94	35.15
10–20	34.27	30.20	31.82	36.77	37.50	29.19	31.90	33.13	31.93	31.29	29.70
20–30	8.39	12.75	15.58	20.65	16.25	14.91	19.02	18.67	13.25	13.50	16.36
Above 30	8.39	8.06	9.09	10.33	11.88	16.77	15.34	13.86	13.25	9.20	15.15
Total	100	100	100	100	100	100	100	100	100	100	100

Equally important finding is that the sample companies' profitability record in terms of ROCE seems to be fairly satisfactory. In fact, one fourth of the sample companies have earned ROCE of more than 21% (as shown by upper quartile). Similar conclusions follow on the basis of frequency distribution tables (Table 9.8). ROCE of the sample companies is also significantly higher than the average ROCE (11.68%) reported by the PSUs in India (Jain and Yadav 2005).

In sum, it can safely be concluded that the sample companies are deploying their finances well and are providing adequate returns on the capital employed to the providers.

Section IV Rate of Return on Ordinary Shareholders Equity (ROSE)

The real owners of the business firm are the ordinary shareholders who bear all the risk and are entitled to all residual profits after all outside claims including preference dividends are met in full. The profitability of a firm from the owners' point of view should, therefore, in the fitness of things, be assessed in terms of the return to the ordinary shareholders' equity (ROSE). This ratio under reference serves this purpose. The ROSE is calculated dividing profits after taxes and preference dividends by the average equity funds/net worth. The extreme values (having ROSE more than ±50%) are excluded.

The data of the sample companies are presented in Table 9.9. Given the current interest rates prevailing in the capital market and social responsibilities the companies have to perform, the average rate of return (ROSE) of 17%, prima facie, can be considered satisfactory. The decline in ROSE to 15% in phase 4 compared to 19% of phase 3 is statistically significant.

Frequency distribution data further reinforce the above contention (Table 9.10). The percentage of companies having negative ROSE is 4.24% in 2011. This is again in contrast to the findings of an earlier study conducted by the authors on PSUs (Jain and Yadav 2005) where 20% of such companies had negative ROSE (Fig. 9.5).

From the above, it is reasonable to conclude that the sample companies appear to be providing adequate returns to their owners, adhering to the primary objective of maximising the wealth of its shareholders.

Based on the findings of sections III and IV, it may be safely concluded that even though the sample companies reported a decline in returns on total assets, capital employed and shareholders' equity in phase 4, the overall returns continue to be satisfactory/adequate, bearing witness to the growing/expansionary Indian economy. The reason for such a contention is that the lower values (15%) of post-recession phase do not seem to be indicative of unsatisfactory financial performance.

Section V Efficiency Ratios

Efficiency ratios are concerned with measuring the efficiency with which assets are used in a business enterprise by its management. For this reason, they are aptly referred to as *assets utilisation ratios*. Obviously, such ratios will have a marked

Table 9.9 Mean, standard deviation, coefficient of variation, skewness, kurtosis, median and quartile values related to return on shareholders' equity (*ROSE*) of the sample companies, 2001–2011

Year ending	Number	Mean	Standard deviation	Coefficient of variation (%)	Skewness	Kurtosis	Median	Quartile 1	Quartile 3
2001	136	10.00	16.00	151.57	−1.00	3.25	12.00	2.00	19.00
2002	136	12.00	13.00	105.58	−0.81	3.73	12.00	6.00	19.00
2003	146	14.00	14.00	98.16	−0.57	3.02	13.00	6.00	22.00
2004	144	18.00	17.00	94.63	2.95	27.32	17.00	9.00	25.00
2005	151	26.00	98.00	377.53	11.99	146.10	17.00	10.00	26.00
2006	150	19.00	12.00	61.70	0.55	−0.13	18.00	10.00	26.00
2007	150	19.00	12.00	61.43	0.12	−0.50	20.00	10.00	27.00
2008	157	19.00	12.00	61.51	0.24	−0.47	19.00	10.00	25.00
2009	160	16.00	11.00	69.97	−0.15	1.49	15.00	9.00	24.00
2010	154	15.00	10.00	69.17	−0.29	1.28	16.00	7.00	22.00
2011	160	14.00	12.00	84.25	−0.02	4.03	13.00	6.00	22.00
2001–2011	148	17.00	21.00	112.32	1.18	17.19	16.00	8.00	23.00
Phase 1 (2000–2001 to 2005–2006)	143	17.00	28.00	148.20	2.18	30.55	15.00	7.00	23.00
Phase 2 (2006–2007 to 2010–2011)	155	17.00	11.00	69.27	−0.02	1.17	16.00	9.00	24.00

(continued)

Table 9.9 (continued)

Year ending	Number	Mean	Standard deviation	Coefficient of variation (%)	Skewness	Kurtosis	Median	Quartile 1	Quartile 3
Phase 3 (2006–2007 to 2007–2008)	154	19.00	12.00	61.47	0.18	−0.49	20.00	10.00	26.00
Phase 4 (2008–2009 to 2010–2011)	157	15.00	11.00	74.47	−0.15	2.27	15.00	8.00	22.00

		Paired differences							
					95% confidence interval of the difference				
		Mean	Standard deviation	Standard error mean	Lower	Upper	t	df	Significance (2-tailed)
Pair 1	Phase 1–Phase 2	−0.00055	0.24166	0.01917	−0.03841	0.03730	−0.029	158	0.977
Pair 2	Phase 3–Phase 4	0.04515	0.08644	0.00688	0.03157	0.05874	6.566	157	0.000

Table 9.10 Frequency distribution related to return on shareholders' equity (*ROSE*) of the sample companies, 2001–2011 (Figures are in percentages)

ROSE (%)	2001	2002	2003	2004	2005	2006	2007	2008	2009	2010	2011
Less than 0	10.49	10.74	5.84	5.81	6.10	1.86	3.68	3.01	3.61	3.07	4.24
0–5	17.48	12.08	12.34	5.81	9.15	8.70	7.98	9.64	10.24	14.11	15.76
5–10	15.38	17.45	18.18	14.84	10.98	12.42	10.43	11.45	15.06	14.11	20.00
10–15	18.18	20.13	17.53	10.97	10.98	13.04	9.82	13.25	19.28	14.72	15.15
15–25	20.98	19.46	25.32	31.61	33.54	31.68	31.90	30.72	27.11	32.52	29.09
25–50	12.59	14.77	16.23	24.52	23.78	26.09	28.22	26.51	21.69	15.95	12.12
Above 50	4.90	5.37	4.55	6.45	5.49	6.21	7.98	5.42	3.01	5.52	3.64
Total	100	100	100	100	100	100	100	100	100	100	100

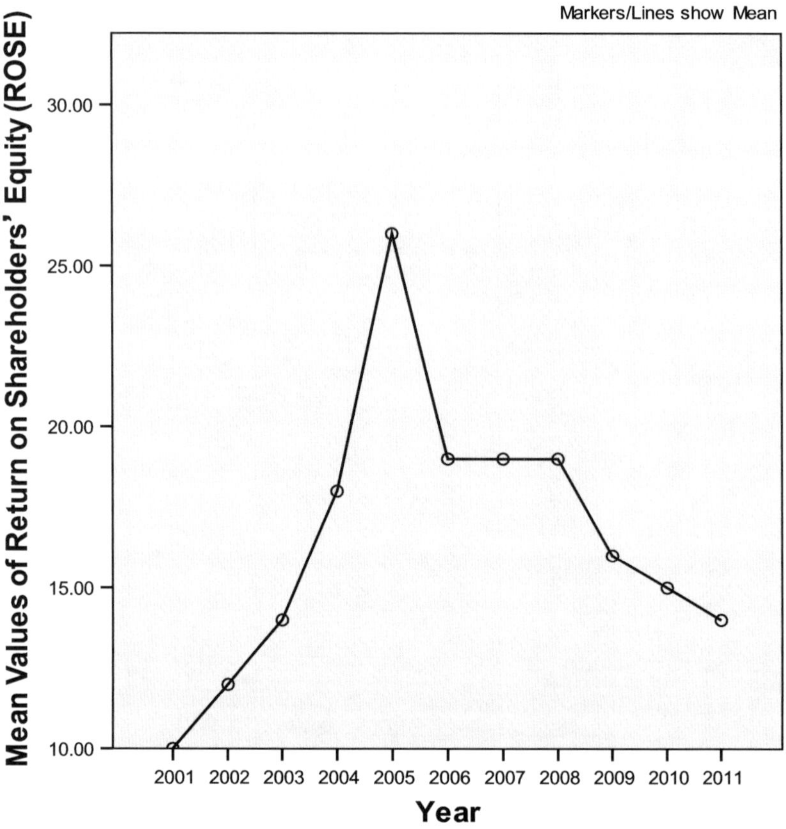

Fig. 9.5 Mean values of return on shareholders' equity (*ROSE*) for the sample companies, 2001–2011

bearing on profitability of the sample companies. Other things being equal, the more efficient is the utilisation of assets, the higher/better is the profitability of the companies.

Turnover is the primary mode of measuring the extent of efficient employment of assets by relating them to sales (more appropriately with cost of sales/cost of production) as denominator is also at cost price. The greater is the rate of turnover or conversion, the more efficient is the utilisation of assets.

In contrast, low turnover ratios are indicative of under-utilisation of available resources and presence of idle capacity. The objective of this section is to describe the major efficiency ratios, namely, total assets turnover ratio, fixed assets turnover ratio and current assets turnover ratio of the sample companies. In computing the first two ratios, the total assets are net of depreciation and exclusive of fictitious assets like debit balance of profit and loss account, deferred expenses and so on.

Total Assets Turnover Ratio (TATR)

TATR measures the relationship between the cost of sales and average total assets of a the sample company. Relevant data pertaining to TATR indicate that the sample companies, prima facie, seem to have efficient operations (Table 9.11). The average TATR for the period is 1.4. Similar conclusions follow on the basis of frequency distribution table (Table 9.12).

Paired *t*-test denotes that the decline in TATR (albeit marginal) in phase 4 over phase 3 was statistically significant, indicating that recession did impact the efficiency of the sample companies. High coefficient of variation figures is possibly due to the varying natures of business of the constituent sectors and the different levels of utilisation of total assets. High skewness and kurtosis also indicate that only few companies in the sample had very high TATR and hence were significantly more efficient than their peers. This could also be due to the industry characteristics of which they are a part (Fig. 9.6).

It may be useful to note that the average TATR (1.44) reported by the sample companies is nearly double of the TATR (0.83) reported by the PSUs in an earlier study conducted by the authors (Jain and Yadav 2005) for the period 1991–2003.

Fixed Assets (Net) Turnover Ratio (FATR)

In contrast, FATR (measured on the basis of relationship between cost of production and average net fixed assets) presents a better picture of utilisation of fixed assets by the sample companies. For instance, the average FATR for the period is more than twice the TATR at 3.25%. Better utilisation of fixed assets seems to be a pan sample phenomenon as is supported by the moderate skewness and kurtosis and also the median value of 2.27 (Table 9.13).

Another significant finding is that FATR has recorded a statistically significant increase in phase 2 over phase 1, and even though there is a marginal decline in FATR in the post-recession period, the paired *t*-test indicates that it is not statistically significant (Fig. 9.7 and Table 9.14).

Interestingly, the average FATR (3.25) reported by the sample companies is nearly identical to the average FATR (3.24) reported by the Indian PSUs for the period 1991–2003 (Jain and Yadav 2005). It is useful to point out here that the sample companies include a significant number of public sector undertakings as well.

Current Assets Turnover Ratio (CATR)

A priori, it is hypothesised that the CATR of the sample companies is likely to be high as these companies are amongst the large companies in India and would be able to manage current assets efficiently.

Table 9.11 Mean, standard deviation, coefficient of variation, skewness, kurtosis, median and quartile values related to total assets turnover ratio (*TATR*) of the sample companies, 2001–2011

Year ending	Number	Mean	Standard deviation	Coefficient of variation (%)	Skewness	Kurtosis	Median	Quartile 1	Quartile 3
2001	125	1.31	1.19	91.06	2.08	4.51	0.93	0.57	1.51
2002	141	1.39	1.25	89.86	2.33	7.36	1.08	0.60	1.70
2003	141	1.47	1.35	91.99	2.51	7.82	1.14	0.65	1.67
2004	145	1.59	1.48	93.19	2.36	6.95	1.12	0.71	1.96
2005	151	1.50	1.44	96.20	2.42	7.67	1.06	0.64	1.89
2006	154	1.53	1.56	101.73	2.21	5.50	1.00	0.57	1.72
2007	158	1.38	1.38	100.59	1.75	2.86	0.88	0.47	1.61
2008	162	1.40	1.62	115.23	2.56	7.83	0.79	0.51	1.54
2009	163	1.35	1.54	114.02	2.60	8.06	0.83	0.50	1.50
2010	162	1.28	1.48	115.33	2.47	7.09	0.83	0.44	1.47
2011	164	1.24	1.52	122.33	2.65	8.43	0.74	0.39	1.33
2001–2011	145	1.40	1.44	102.87	2.36	6.73	0.95	0.55	1.63
Phase 1 (2000–2001 to 2005–2006)	140	1.47	1.38	94.01	2.32	6.63	1.06	0.62	1.74
Phase 2 (2006–2007 to 2010–2011)	161	1.33	1.51	113.50	2.41	6.85	0.81	0.46	1.49
Phase 3 (2006–2007 to 2007–2008)	160	1.39	1.50	107.91	2.16	5.35	0.84	0.49	1.58
Phase 4 (2008–2009 to 2010–2011)	163	1.29	1.51	117.22	2.58	7.86	0.80	0.44	1.44

Extreme values of 10 or more are excluded

		Paired differences							
					95% confidence interval of the difference				
		Mean	Standard deviation	Standard error mean	Lower	Upper	*t*	*df*	Significance (2-tailed)
Pair 1	Phase 1–phase 2	0.10319	0.90286	0.07183	–0.03868	0.24506	1.437	157	0.153
Pair 2	Phase 3–phase 4	0.12508	0.56072	0.04392	0.03836	0.21181	2.848	162	0.005

Table 9.12 Frequency distribution related to total assets turnover ratio (*TATR*) of the sample companies, 2001–2011 (Figures are in percentages)

TATR (%)	2001	2002	2003	2004	2005	2006	2007	2008	2009	2010	2011
Less than 0.5	18.40	19.86	17.02	16.55	21.71	16.88	27.22	24.69	25.15	30.86	31.10
0.5–1.0	37.60	22.70	25.53	27.59	23.68	33.12	26.58	33.33	30.06	29.63	33.54
1.0–1.5	17.60	27.66	26.24	18.62	19.08	20.78	19.62	15.43	19.63	14.81	12.20
1.5–2.0	9.60	10.64	12.06	13.79	10.53	6.49	6.33	6.17	6.75	7.41	4.27
Above 2.0	16.80	19.15	19.15	23.45	25.00	22.73	20.25	20.37	18.40	17.28	18.90
Total	100	100	100	100	100	100	100	100	100	100	100

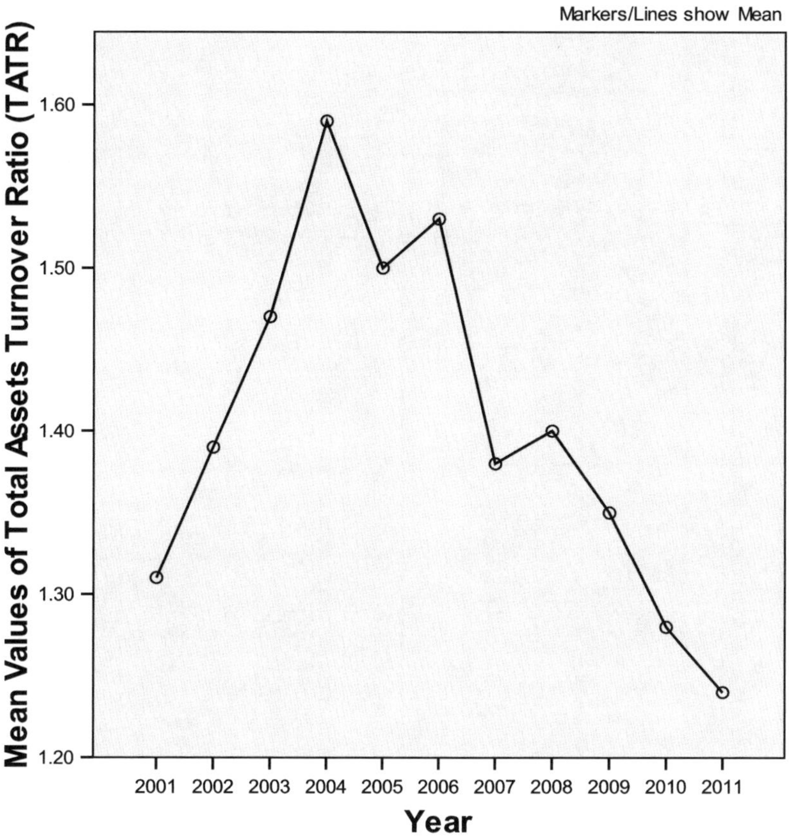

Fig. 9.6 Mean values of total assets turnover ratio (*TATR*) for the sample companies, 2001–2011

The CATR has reported a decline in phase 2 over phase 1 and phase 4 over phase 3 respectively; however, both are statistically insignificant (Table 9.15). High skewness and kurtosis indicate that only few companies are able to manage their current assets aggressively and hence would report better profitability when compared to their competitors. Similar conclusions are supported by the frequency distribution where nearly one fourth of companies have a CATR of more than 2.5 (Table 9.16). This is also supported by the quartile 3 value of 2.42 for the period.

The average CATR (1.87) reported by the sample companies is significantly higher than the average CATR (1.31) reported by the PSUs in India (Jain and Yadav 2005). Better efficiency in managing current assets could perhaps be the reason behind the sample companies having a much higher TATR (as well) when compared to the PSUs.

Expectedly, the conclusions drawn from the findings of this section are also similar to the findings of the chapter on working capital management.

Table 9.13 Mean, standard deviation, coefficient of variation, skewness, kurtosis, median and quartile values related to fixed assets turnover ratio (*FATR*) of the sample companies, 2001–2011

Year ending	Number	Mean	Standard deviation	Coefficient of variation (%)	Skewness	Kurtosis	Median	Quartile 1	Quartile 3
2001	119	2.76	2.29	82.84	1.21	0.79	1.92	1.04	3.90
2002	131	2.84	2.25	79.29	1.01	0.20	1.95	1.14	4.42
2003	132	3.04	2.42	79.65	1.27	1.70	2.19	1.21	4.47
2004	135	3.34	2.66	79.61	1.01	0.05	2.46	1.32	4.99
2005	129	3.18	2.54	79.89	1.08	0.37	2.20	1.35	4.83
2006	132	3.56	2.89	81.23	0.94	0.02	2.35	1.32	5.78
2007	133	3.23	2.63	81.65	0.79	−0.62	2.34	1.10	5.53
2008	139	3.66	3.08	84.14	0.86	−0.61	2.36	1.26	5.82
2009	136	3.51	3.08	87.78	1.32	1.97	2.28	1.24	5.64
2010	141	3.46	2.85	82.23	0.75	−0.71	2.66	1.13	5.79
2011	133	3.16	2.68	84.69	0.85	−0.49	2.26	0.96	5.05
2001–2011	130	3.25	2.67	82.09	1.01	0.24	2.27	1.19	5.11
Phase 1 (2000–2001 to 2005–2006)	127	3.12	2.51	80.42	1.09	0.52	2.18	1.23	4.73
Phase 2 (2006–2007 to 2010–2011)	137	3.40	2.86	84.10	0.91	−0.09	2.38	1.14	5.56
Phase 3 (2006–2007 to 2007–2008)	136	3.45	2.86	82.90	0.83	−0.62	2.35	1.18	5.68
Phase 4 (2008–2009 to 2010–2011)	137	3.38	2.87	84.90	0.97	0.26	2.40	1.11	5.49

Extreme values of 10 or more are excluded

		Paired differences							
					95% confidence interval of the difference				
		Mean	Standard deviation	Standard error mean	Lower	Upper	*t*	*df*	Significance (2-tailed)
Pair 1	Phase 1–Phase 2	−0.75429	1.78499	0.14773	−1.04626	−0.46231	−5.106	145	0.000
Pair 2	Phase 3–Phase 4	0.16237	1.29712	0.11082	−0.05678	0.38152	1.465	136	0.145

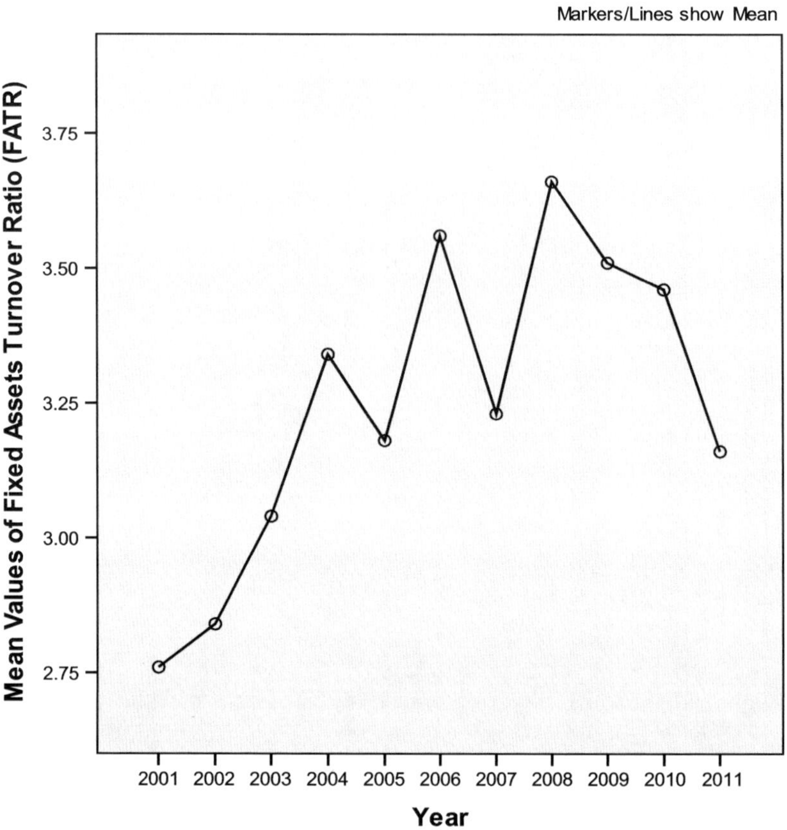

Fig. 9.7 Mean values of fixed assets turnover ratio (*FATR*) for the sample companies, 2001–2011

Section VI Sectoral Analysis

Gross Profit

The gross profit of the constituent sectors (for details refer to Table 1.2, Chap. 1) of the sample showed fluctuations during the phases underlying the period of the study. The housing sector nearly doubled its gross profit from 16.91% in phase 1 to 31.49% in phase 2 (Appendix 9.1). While the power sector reported the highest gross profit figures at 38.23% in phase 1 which increased further to 41.36% in phase 2, the metals sector had a decline in gross profits in phase 4 (29.72%) from 36.07% in phase 3 (Appendix 9.2). The changes in mean values of gross profit percentages were statistically significant for the power sector in both phases 1 and 2 and phases 3 and 4, metals sector for phases 3 and 4, capital goods, FMCG, health and miscellaneous sectors for phases 1 and 2. The ANOVA test (Appendix 9.3) indicates statistically

Table 9.14 Frequency distribution related to fixed assets turnover ratio (*FATR*) of the sample companies, 2001–2011 (Figures are in percentages)

FATR (%)	2001	2002	2003	2004	2005	2006	2007	2008	2009	2010	2011
Less than 0.5	7.20	6.34	6.25	5.44	5.19	6.41	7.45	4.94	5.59	8.81	9.32
0.5–1.0	16.00	14.79	7.64	10.20	8.44	7.69	12.42	10.49	12.42	10.69	13.66
1.0–1.5	15.20	15.49	15.28	10.20	9.74	10.26	8.07	12.35	11.18	9.43	7.45
1.5–3.0	25.60	22.54	28.47	27.89	29.22	25.00	22.36	24.07	21.12	20.75	18.63
3.0–5.0	13.60	16.20	13.89	14.97	11.04	8.97	8.07	6.79	8.07	11.32	12.42
5.0–10.0	17.60	16.90	19.44	22.45	19.48	25.64	24.22	25.31	24.22	26.42	21.12
Above 10	4.80	7.75	9.03	8.84	16.88	16.03	17.39	16.05	17.39	12.58	17.39
Total	100	100	100	100	100	100	100	100	100	100	100

Table 9.15 Mean, standard deviation, coefficient of variation, skewness, kurtosis, median and quartile values related to current assets turnover ratio (*CATR*) of the sample companies, 2001–2011

Year ending	Number	Mean	Standard deviation	Coefficient of variation (%)	Skewness	Kurtosis	Median	Quartile 1	Quartile 3
2001	125	1.83	1.22	66.34	2.32	8.40	1.69	1.11	2.24
2002	142	1.89	1.30	69.03	2.10	6.09	1.62	1.15	2.17
2003	143	1.90	1.13	59.69	1.56	3.35	1.68	1.15	2.31
2004	146	1.99	1.25	62.87	1.35	2.76	1.74	1.21	2.58
2005	152	1.96	1.23	62.75	1.17	1.63	1.70	1.07	2.53
2006	155	1.90	1.32	69.71	1.45	2.28	1.53	1.00	2.43
2007	160	1.88	1.48	78.91	1.53	2.88	1.57	0.82	2.55
2008	161	1.83	1.37	75.21	1.30	1.96	1.45	0.76	2.54
2009	162	1.84	1.52	82.76	1.88	4.57	1.46	0.85	2.45
2010	162	1.85	1.54	83.41	1.63	3.34	1.31	0.77	2.47
2011	164	1.75	1.50	85.72	1.75	4.36	1.27	0.75	2.39
2001–2011	145	1.87	1.35	72.40	1.64	3.78	1.55	0.97	2.42
Phase 1 (2000–2001 to 2005–2006)	140	1.91	1.24	65.07	1.66	4.08	1.66	1.12	2.38
Phase 2 (2006–2007 to 2010–2011)	162	1.83	1.48	81.20	1.62	3.42	1.41	0.79	2.48
Phase 3 (2006–2007 to 2007–2008)	161	1.86	1.43	77.06	1.42	2.42	1.51	0.79	2.55
Phase 4 (2008–2009 to 2010–2011)	163	1.81	1.52	83.96	1.75	4.09	1.34	0.79	2.44

Extreme values of 10 or more are excluded

		Paired differences							
					95% confidence interval of the difference				
		Mean	Standard deviation	Standard error mean	Lower	Upper	*t*	df	Significance (2-tailed)
Pair 1	Phase 1–Phase 2	0.06666	0.80992	0.06443	–0.06061	0.19393	1.034	157	0.303
Pair 2	Phase 3–Phase 4	0.07274	0.63182	0.04964	–0.02529	0.17077	1.465	161	0.145

Table 9.16 Frequency distribution related to current assets turnover ratio (*CATR*) of the sample companies, 2001–2011 (Figures are in percentages)

CATR (%)	2001	2002	2003	2004	2005	2006	2007	2008	2009	2010	2011
Less than 0.5	6.40	6.34	5.56	5.41	7.14	6.37	11.73	10.43	11.04	9.88	12.73
0.5–1.0	13.60	14.08	13.89	14.19	15.58	18.47	22.22	22.70	19.02	24.07	22.42
1.0–1.5	24.00	24.65	19.44	21.62	18.18	23.57	12.35	18.40	20.86	24.07	21.82
1.5–2.0	20.80	22.54	23.61	16.89	16.23	14.01	17.28	14.11	15.34	6.17	10.91
2.0–2.5	17.60	15.49	15.28	12.16	15.58	12.74	9.88	7.36	9.20	11.73	7.88
Above 2.5	17.60	16.90	22.22	29.73	27.27	24.84	26.54	27.00	24.54	24.07	24.25
Total	100	100	100	100	100	100	100	100	100	100	100

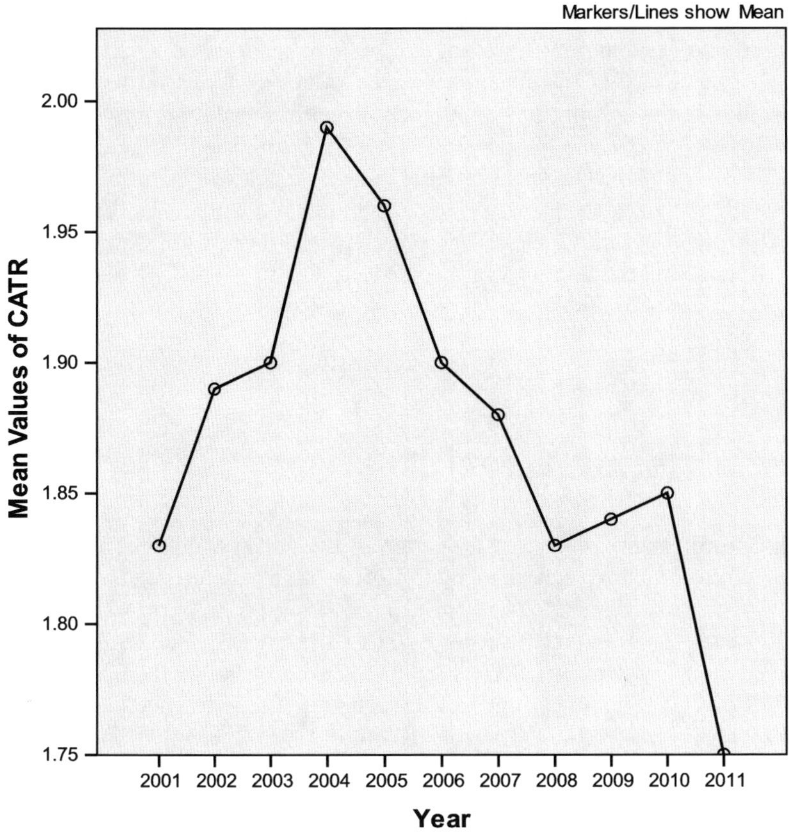

Fig. 9.8 Mean values of current assets turnover ratio (*CATR*) for the sample companies, 2001–2011

significant difference amongst the variances for the consolidated sample as a whole over the period of the study (phases 1 and 2 as well as phases 3 and 4) and the power sector amongst the constituent sectors or the sample.

Thus, it is evident that some sectors (like power and housing) have actually increased profitability in the post-recession period while some sectors like metals have reduced profits. The ICT sector, expectedly, has shown fluctuations in the gross profits reported, but the changes are not statistically significant.

Net Profit

All constituent sectors of the sample companies recorded an increase in their net profits in phase 2 over phase 1 of the study. Notable amongst them was the housing sector that grew from 6.71 to 21.41% (Appendix 9.4). Expectedly, most sectors reported a decline in net profits in phase 4 over phase 3 except for the FMCG, health, oil and gas and power sectors that, in fact, reported an increase in their net profits (Appendix 9.5). The changes in mean values of net profit percentages were statistically significant for the capital goods, health, metals and miscellaneous sectors in phases 1 and 2 and the housing sector for both phases 1 and 2 and phases 3 and 4. The ANOVA test (Appendix 9.6) indicates statistically significant difference amongst the variances for the consolidated sample as a whole over the period of the study (for phases 1 and 2 as well as phases 3 and 4) and the housing sector for phases 1 and 2. In brief, the sectors (like FMCG, health, oil and gas and power) have actually increased profitability in the post-recession period while others report reduced profits.

Return on Total Assets (ROTA)

In phase 4 all sectors registered a decline in their ROTA save the FMCG sector. Sectors with notable decrease in their ROTA were capital goods decreasing to 19.85% in phase 4 from 25.22% in phase 3, diversified from 9.91 to 7.90%, housing from 13.88 to 9.31% and metals from 18.31 to 13.50% (Appendix 9.8). The sample registered an increase in their ROTA in phase 2 over phase 1 except for the diversified, FMCG, ICT, oil and gas and power sectors that reported declines. The capital goods sector increased its ROTA from 16.68 to 22% (Appendix 9.7). The changes in mean values of ROTA were statistically significant for the capital goods sector in both phases 1 and 2 and phases 3 and 4 and diversified, housing and metals sectors for phases 3 and 4. Variances were statistically significant only for the consolidated sample as a whole (Appendix 9.9).

Return on Capital Employed (ROCE)

As far as ROCE is concerned, it increased for the sample in phase 2 over phase 1 except for the oil and gas sector that fell from 13.60 to 11.59% and the power sector that dipped to 6.61 from 8.24% (Appendix 9.10). In phase 4, all sectors save the FMCG, power and miscellaneous registered a decline in their ROCE over phase 3. FMCG actually posted an increase in its ROCE from 14.49% in phase 3 to 20.23% in phase 4; the power sector increased from 6 to 7.02% and miscellaneous sector increased from 13.11 to 15.31% (Appendix 9.11). The changes in mean values of ROCE were statistically significant for the FMCG sector in phases 1 and 2 and for the capital goods, diversified and metals sectors for phases 3 and 4. Statistically significant variances were reported for the consolidated sample as a whole throughout the period of the study and the capital goods sector for phases 3 and 4 (Appendix 9.12).

Return on Shareholders' Equity (ROSE)

All sectors except FMCG, ICT, oil and gas, health and power were able to increase the ROSE in phase 2 over phase 1 (Appendix 9.13). In phase 4, out of 11 sectors of the study, the 2 sectors, namely, the FMCG and miscellaneous registered a decline in their ROSE (Appendix 9.14). None of the changes in mean values of ROSE were statistically significant for phases 1 and 2 but were significant for the decrease in ROSE in phase 4 over phase 3 for the capital goods, healthcare, housing, metals and transport sectors. The sample as a whole showed significant variances throughout the period of the study and the capital goods, metals and housing sector for phases 3 and 4 (Appendix 9.15).

Total Assets Turnover Ratio (TATR)

Surprisingly, all constituent sectors of the sample reported a decrease in their TATR in phase 2 over phase 1 (Appendix 9.16). However, this decrease was statistically significant only for the healthcare and housing sectors. Expectedly, all sectors registered a decline in their TATR in phase 4 over phase 1 except for the oil and gas sector that went up from 1.84 in phase 3 to 1.92 in phase 4, power which increased from 0.40 to 0.59 in the same period and the miscellaneous sector from 0.61 in phase 3 to 0.71 in phase 4 (Appendix 9.17). Healthcare and housing sectors' changes were statistically significant for both phases 1 and 2 and phases 3 and 4. Capital goods, ICT and miscellaneous sectors' changes were significant only for phases 4 over 3. The sample showed significant variances for the entire period of the study and the capital goods for phases 3 and 4 (Appendix 9.18).

Fixed Assets Turnover Ratio (FATR)

On a more positive note, all constituent sectors of the sample reported better utilisation of their fixed assets in phase 2 over phase 1 (Appendix 9.19). Statistically significant improvements were recorded for diversified, FMCG, metals and the oil and gas sectors. The trend continued in phases 3 and 4 for most of the sectors save the metals, power, transport and miscellaneous sectors which registered a decline in their FATR in phase 4 over phase 3 (Appendix 9.20) though none of these were statistically significant. The sample showed significant variances in FATR for the entire period of the study (Appendix 9.21).

Current Assets Turnover Ratio (CATR)

The cause for decreasing TATR for most of the constituent sectors appears to be the CATR. In phases 1 and 2, the CATR for six constituent sectors registered a decrease

(Appendix 9.22); FMCG dipped marginally from 2.96 to 2.80, healthcare from 1.53 to 1.29, housing from 1.59 to 1.24, metals from 1.88 to 1.69, power from 1.38 to 1.19 and miscellaneous from 2.04 to 1.81. Out of these, however, only healthcare changes were statistically significant. The trend continued in phases 3 and 4 except for the diversified, oil and gas, power, transport and miscellaneous sectors which registered an increase in their CATR in phase 4 over phase 3 (Appendix 9.23), though only the increase in the CATR for the metals sector from 1.75 to 1.85 was statistically significant. Like TATR and FATR, the sample showed significant variances in CATR also for the entire period of the study (Appendix 9.24).

All in all, it is evident from the above discussion that certain sectors witnessed declines in some ratios while others posted gains, in spite of the recessionary situation in phase 4, thereby aiding the sample as a whole to remain fairly stable.

Section VII Concluding Observations

The profitability of the sample companies (measured through gross profit and net profit), prima facie, appears to be stable and attractive (as an investment choice). Though the recession in phase 4 did witness some fluctuations in the profitability of certain constituent sectors, overall, the sample seems to have emerged unscathed from the impact of the recession, perhaps due to its strong financial fundamentals.

Also, the Indian economy is more domestically driven (source: RBI website. http://rbidocs.rbi.org.in/rdocs/Speeches/PDFs/87784.pdf; Economic Surveys of India), and the scattered effect of recession that is evident is due to the increased exposure of the sample companies to the world market and economy. The impact appears to be more on those sectors which are either internationally exposed or those whose revenues are in dollars. Government control on capital flows is perhaps another reason for the successful handling of recession.

The other aspects of profitability, namely, return on total assets (ROTA), return on capital employed (ROCE) and earnings for equity owners (reflected in ROSE) appear to be equally satisfactory. All in all, not only are the sample companies deploying funds efficiently and providing adequate returns to the capital providers, they are working towards generating better returns for their shareholders. These findings are notable as well as they support the RBI's views on the resilience of the Indian economy.

In terms of efficiency, the sample companies appear to be doing a commendable job as well. However, there appears to be some scope for improvement in the TATR figures. The sample companies, being amongst the largest in the country, can afford to manage assets better with improved processes and technology.

Appendices

Appendix 9.1: Mean, median and quartile values of gross profit percentage of constituent sectors of the sample companies over phase 1 (2001–2006) and phase 2 (2007–2011)

	Phase 1 (2001–2006)				Phase 2 (2007–2011)			
Sector	Mean	Median	Quartile 1	Quartile 3	Mean	Median	Quartile 1	Quartile 3
Power	38.23	30.97	18.79	61.59	41.36	32.38	22.13	57.34
Internet and communications technology (ICT)	33.14	35.00	28.51	39.18	33.30	29.09	22.03	36.52
Metals	26.65	22.46	12.60	37.47	32.26	26.28	15.70	42.03
Oil and gas	25.06	20.24	8.23	38.95	28.01	18.95	6.37	45.22
Transport	21.58	19.53	12.26	27.55	24.89	20.67	14.66	31.14
Healthcare	20.40	18.54	15.52	25.13	28.46	26.07	20.35	36.09
Diversified	17.78	13.69	6.00	20.93	15.10	13.16	8.29	17.40
Miscellaneous[a]	17.13	13.91	9.70	20.00	23.00	15.91	11.35	30.00
Housing	16.91	12.80	8.52	17.59	31.49	26.98	14.17	42.85
Fast-moving consumer goods (FMCG)	15.65	15.98	6.99	18.94	18.69	18.23	13.45	22.71
Capital goods	11.43	10.27	6.81	13.86	14.93	13.66	11.33	18.29

[a]Miscellaneous sectors comprises of the media and publishing sector, agriculture, chemicals and petro-chemicals, tourism, textiles and miscellaneous sectors

Paired samples t-test of constituent sectors of the sample companies based on gross profit percentage over phase 1 (2001–2006) and phase 2 (2007–2011).

	Phase 1 and Phase 2		
Sector	*t*	*df*	Significance (2-tailed)
Healthcare	–4.535	13	0.001
Power	–5.306	8	0.001
Capital goods	–3.195	12	0.008
Housing	–2.913	16	0.010
Miscellaneous	–2.307	15	0.036
FMCG	–2.359	11	0.038
Metals	–1.812	17	0.088
Transport	–1.562	16	0.138
Oil and gas	–0.778	13	0.451
ICT	–0.712	16	0.487
Diversified	–0.678	8	0.517

Appendix 9.2: Mean, median and quartile values of gross profit percentage of constituent sectors of the sample companies over phase 3 (2007–2008) and phase 4 (2009–2011)

	Phase 3 (2007–2008)				Phase 4 (2009–2011)			
Sector	Mean	Median	Quartile 1	Quartile 3	Mean	Median	Quartile 1	Quartile 3
Power	41.06	27.90	19.04	61.10	41.56	35.37	24.19	54.83
Metals	36.07	30.75	18.76	48.31	29.72	23.30	13.65	37.83
Housing	33.23	29.58	17.67	44.46	30.33	25.25	11.84	41.79
ICT	31.25	28.64	22.12	34.69	34.66	29.40	21.97	37.74
Healthcare	28.70	24.69	20.19	35.00	28.30	26.99	20.46	36.82
Oil and gas	26.44	18.21	7.86	44.39	29.06	19.45	5.39	45.78
Transport	26.39	22.12	14.34	34.36	23.88	19.71	14.87	28.99
Miscellaneous	24.05	16.29	11.97	34.92	22.29	15.66	10.94	26.58
Diversified	20.14	18.83	11.67	25.26	11.74	9.38	6.05	12.17
FMCG	19.28	18.96	15.25	21.19	18.29	17.74	12.24	23.72
Capital goods	16.11	13.95	12.63	19.50	14.13	13.47	10.46	17.48

Paired samples *t*-test of constituent sectors of the sample companies based on gross profit percentage over phase 3 (2007–2008) and phase 4 (2009–2011)

	Phase 3 and Phase 4		
Sector	*t*	*df*	Significance (2-tailed)
Power	–4.995	10	0.001
Metals	3.665	17	0.002
Housing	2.900	15	0.011
Diversified	1.761	7	0.122
Capital goods	1.626	11	0.132
Miscellaneous	1.386	15	0.186
Transport	1.366	17	0.190
Oil and gas	–1.131	14	0.277
FMCG	0.576	11	0.576
ICT	–0.315	17	0.757
Healthcare	0.285	13	0.780

Appendix 9.3: ANOVA of the consolidated sample and the constituent sectors of the sample companies based on gross profit percentage over phase 1 (2001–2006) and phase 2 (2007–2011) and phase 3 (2007–2008) and phase 4 (2009–2011)

	Phase 1 and Phase 2		Phase 3 and Phase 4	
Sector	*F*	Significance	*F*	Significance
Consolidated	21.310	0.000	18.466	0.000
Power	19.894	0.000	26.525	0.000
Healthcare	5.116	0.032	0.024	0.877
Housing	4.987	0.032	0.122	0.729
Capital goods	4.317	0.049	0.717	0.406
Metals	1.145	0.292	0.756	0.391
FMCG	1.060	0.314	0.116	0.737
Miscellaneous	0.842	0.366	0.105	0.748

(continued)

Appendix 9.3: (continued)

Sector	Phase 1 and Phase 2		Phase 3 and Phase 4	
	F	Significance	*F*	Significance
ICT	0.431	0.516	0.007	0.936
Oil and gas	0.312	0.581	0.177	0.677
Transport	0.190	0.665	0.204	0.655
Diversified	0.053	0.822	2.993	0.104

Appendix 9.4: Mean, median and quartile values of net profit percentage of constituent sectors of the sample companies over phase 1 (2001–2006) and phase 2 (2007–2011)

Sector	Phase 1 (2001–2006)				Phase 2 (2007–2011)			
	Mean	Median	Quartile 1	Quartile 3	Mean	Median	Quartile 1	Quartile 3
ICT	21.55	23.38	18.13	28.45	22.40	21.21	13.66	26.88
Power	21.13	18.87	8.33	32.74	24.68	20.38	12.05	36.35
Metals	14.52	11.87	6.36	23.24	20.87	15.93	10.16	24.50
Healthcare	14.32	13.29	9.46	18.82	20.31	17.33	13.77	27.62
Transport	11.53	9.66	5.96	15.34	13.63	10.32	7.07	18.24
Oil and gas	11.22	10.13	3.42	17.80	16.00	11.87	3.70	24.84
FMCG	10.07	10.03	4.89	12.34	12.13	12.32	7.97	17.02
Miscellaneous	9.70	7.34	4.31	12.22	13.60	8.67	5.84	19.06
Capital goods	7.05	6.07	4.07	8.50	9.84	8.62	7.09	12.34
Housing	6.71	5.74	4.07	7.67	21.41	15.14	8.62	27.46
Diversified	5.49	3.24	1.41	7.70	7.29	6.85	4.71	9.69

Paired samples *t*-test of constituent sectors of the sample companies based on net profit percentage over phase 1 (2001–2006) and phase 2 (2007–2011).

Sector	Phase 1 and Phase 2		
	t	*df*	Significance (2-tailed)
Healthcare	−3.610	13	0.003
Capital goods	−3.158	12	0.008
Housing	−3.053	16	0.008
Metals	−2.576	17	0.020
Miscellaneous	−2.572	15	0.021
FMCG	−1.769	11	0.105
Oil and gas	−1.039	13	0.318
Diversified	−0.945	8	0.372
Transport	−0.692	16	0.499
ICT	−0.511	15	0.617
Power	−0.356	10	0.730

Appendix 9.5: Mean, median and quartile values of net profit percentage of constituent sectors of the sample companies over phase 3 (2007–2008) and phase 4 (2009–2011)

Sector	Phase 3 (2007–2008)				Phase 4 (2009–2011)			
	Mean	Median	Quartile 1	Quartile 3	Mean	Median	Quartile 1	Quartile 3
Housing	27.09	18.90	12.02	35.83	17.63	12.63	6.35	21.87
Power	23.89	18.78	10.79	36.92	25.20	21.45	12.89	35.96

(continued)

Appendix 9.5: (continued)

	Phase 3 (2007–2008)				Phase 4 (2009–2011)			
Sector	Mean	Median	Quartile 1	Quartile 3	Mean	Median	Quartile 1	Quartile 3
ICT	22.73	19.98	13.88	25.72	22.18	22.04	13.52	27.66
Metals	21.52	16.81	10.72	25.96	20.44	15.35	9.79	23.52
Healthcare	19.72	17.30	12.99	26.47	20.70	17.36	14.30	28.39
Miscellaneous	14.68	8.32	6.62	22.34	12.89	8.91	5.33	16.87
Transport	14.65	11.22	7.92	21.71	12.95	9.72	6.49	15.94
Oil and gas	14.28	11.98	3.79	22.79	17.13	11.79	3.65	26.21
FMCG	11.89	12.30	8.88	15.62	12.29	12.33	7.37	17.96
Capital goods	10.74	8.51	7.44	14.30	9.24	8.70	6.86	11.04
Diversified	8.78	7.42	5.26	13.09	6.29	6.47	4.35	7.42

Paired samples *t*-test of constituent sectors of the sample companies based on net profit percentage over phase 3 (2007–2008) and phase 4 (2009–2011).

	Phase 3 and Phase 4		
Sector	*t*	*df*	Significance (2-tailed)
Housing	2.138	16	0.048
Diversified	1.718	8	0.124
Miscellaneous	1.429	15	0.173
Capital goods	1.326	12	0.210
Metals	0.980	16	0.342
Transport	0.961	17	0.350
Oil and gas	−0.932	13	0.368
Healthcare	−0.812	13	0.432
ICT	0.755	16	0.461
Power	−0.067	10	0.948
FMCG	−0.054	11	0.958

Appendix 9.6: ANOVA of the consolidated sample and the constituent sectors of the sample companies based on net profit percentage over phase 1 (2001–2006) and phase 2 (2007–2011) and phase 3 (2007–2008) and phase 4 (2009–2011)

	Phase 1 and Phase 2		Phase 3 and Phase 4	
Sector	*F*	Significance	*F*	Significance
Consolidated	3.510	0.000	5.260	0.000
Housing	5.091	0.031	1.567	0.219
Healthcare	3.520	0.072	0.077	0.783
Capital goods	3.037	0.094	0.773	0.388
Metals	2.352	0.134	0.001	0.975
Oil and gas	1.564	0.221	0.277	0.603
FMCG	0.881	0.358	0.001	0.974
Miscellaneous	0.830	0.370	0.168	0.685
Diversified	0.273	0.609	0.936	0.348
Transport	0.198	0.659	0.274	0.604
ICT	0.036	0.850	0.251	0.620
Power	0.003	0.960	0.103	0.752

Appendix 9.7: Mean, median and quartile values of return on total assets (*ROTA*) of constituent sectors of the sample companies over phase 1 (2001–2006) and phase 2 (2007–2011)

	Phase 1 (2001–2006)				Phase 2 (2007–2011)			
Sector	Mean	Median	Quartile 1	Quartile 3	Mean	Median	Quartile 1	Quartile 3
FMCG	17.86	10.98	8.00	25.63	16.80	15.42	8.02	24.15
Healthcare	16.76	16.52	10.47	21.02	17.00	15.98	11.83	21.72
Capital goods	16.68	17.16	12.07	21.43	22.00	22.62	16.02	30.53
ICT	15.42	15.47	5.73	26.46	15.02	14.15	7.43	22.45
Oil and gas	14.65	13.74	6.30	20.88	11.70	9.63	5.85	17.28
Transport	13.95	13.46	9.94	17.47	14.93	14.10	8.33	19.89
Metals	12.45	10.99	7.01	19.82	15.43	11.87	7.89	20.64
Miscellaneous	11.45	9.52	5.89	14.82	12.61	9.56	6.45	14.98
Housing	9.41	8.60	6.45	11.87	11.14	9.53	7.23	14.73
Diversified	9.14	9.68	7.11	12.65	8.71	10.29	4.21	13.30
Power	7.31	7.34	4.44	10.42	6.45	6.41	4.04	8.48

Paired samples *t*-test of constituent sectors of the sample companies based on Return on Total Assets (*ROTA*) over phase 1 (2001–2006) and phase 2 (2007–2011).

	Phase 1 and Phase 2		
Sector	*t*	d*f*	Significance (2-tailed)
Capital goods	−2.372	12	0.035
FMCG	−2.036	7	0.081
Metals	−1.375	17	0.187
Housing	−1.062	16	0.304
Miscellaneous	−0.714	15	0.486
Diversified	−0.578	8	0.579
Healthcare	−0.399	13	0.697
Power	−0.148	12	0.885
Transport	−0.110	16	0.914
Oil and gas	0.066	14	0.948
ICT	−0.038	17	0.970

Appendix 9.8: Mean, median and quartile values of return on total assets (*ROTA*) of constituent sectors of the sample companies over phase 3 (2007–2008) and phase 4 (2009–2011)

	Phase 3 (2007–2008)				Phase 4 (2009–2011)			
Sector	Mean	Median	Quartile 1	Quartile 3	Mean	Median	Quartile 1	Quartile 3
Capital goods	25.22	25.90	18.30	33.63	19.85	20.43	14.50	28.47
Metals	18.31	13.59	9.67	26.53	13.50	10.71	6.71	16.72
Healthcare	18.14	16.57	11.63	22.81	16.24	15.59	11.95	21.00
Transport	16.76	16.47	12.06	20.30	13.71	12.53	5.85	19.61
ICT	16.43	13.15	8.66	24.35	14.08	14.82	6.62	21.18
Housing	13.88	11.01	7.76	21.32	9.31	8.54	6.87	10.33
FMCG	13.45	9.37	7.78	18.69	19.03	19.45	8.17	27.79
Oil and gas	13.17	10.52	5.63	18.95	10.72	9.04	6.00	16.16
Miscellaneous	11.62	10.00	5.98	14.11	13.26	9.28	6.77	15.56
Diversified	9.91	11.75	5.09	16.49	7.90	9.32	3.63	11.17
Power	6.63	6.44	4.00	9.32	6.32	6.39	4.06	7.93

(continued)

Appendix 9.8: (continued)

Paired samples *t*-test of constituent sectors of the sample companies based on Return on Total Assets (*ROTA*) over phase 3 (2007–2008) and phase 4 (2009–2011).

	Phase 3 and Phase 4		
Sector	*t*	d*f*	Significance (2-tailed)
Housing	4.098	17	0.001
Capital goods	3.095	11	0.010
Diversified	3.172	8	0.013
Metals	2.493	17	0.023
Transport	2.076	17	0.053
Healthcare	1.867	12	0.087
Miscellaneous	−1.305	15	0.212
ICT	1.220	16	0.240
FMCG	−0.749	6	0.482
Oil and gas	0.506	14	0.621
Power	−0.163	12	0.873

Appendix 9.9: ANOVA of the consolidated sample and the constituent sectors of the sample companies based on return on total assets (*ROTA*) over phase 1 (2001–2006) and phase 2 (2007–2011) and phase 3 (2007–2008) and phase 4 (2009–2011)

	Phase 1 and Phase 2		Phase 3 and Phase 4	
Sector	*F*	Significance	*F*	Significance
Consolidated	5.181	0.000	5.843	0.000
Capital goods	3.592	0.070	3.109	0.091
Metals	1.158	0.289	1.740	0.196
Housing	0.624	0.435	4.107	0.051
Miscellaneous	0.202	0.656	0.354	0.556
Healthcare	0.140	0.712	0.459	0.504
Transport	0.115	0.737	0.749	0.393
Diversified	0.095	0.761	0.386	0.543
Oil and gas	0.054	0.818	0.566	0.458
FMCG	0.015	0.903	1.233	0.285
Power	0.008	0.929	0.018	0.893
ICT	0.001	0.979	0.282	0.599

Appendix 9.10: Mean, median and quartile values of return on capital employed (*ROCE*) of constituent sectors of the sample companies over phase 1 (2001–2006) and phase 2 (2007–2011)

	Phase 1 (2001–2006)				Phase 2 (2007–2011)			
Sector	Mean	Median	Quartile 1	Quartile 3	Mean	Median	Quartile 1	Quartile 3
Healthcare	18.49	18.04	11.77	23.48	18.69	17.69	12.60	24.98
Capital goods	18.35	17.04	12.49	23.67	21.74	21.36	16.22	28.82
FMCG	16.64	10.65	7.73	22.99	17.94	17.24	8.92	25.41
ICT	14.86	14.05	5.61	25.44	14.95	14.82	7.62	22.61
Transport	14.32	13.57	10.16	18.03	15.08	14.79	8.97	20.19
Oil and gas	13.60	14.39	6.28	19.04	11.59	10.74	6.32	17.18

(continued)

Appendix 9.10: (continued)

	Phase 1 (2001–2006)				Phase 2 (2007–2011)			
Sector	Mean	Median	Quartile 1	Quartile 3	Mean	Median	Quartile 1	Quartile 3
Metals	12.70	11.38	7.32	19.66	15.53	13.03	8.38	21.10
Miscellaneous	12.58	10.38	6.77	17.46	14.43	11.93	6.85	19.51
Diversified	9.90	9.79	7.20	13.57	10.55	8.73	3.03	14.33
Housing	9.89	8.99	6.57	12.23	12.89	11.02	7.48	17.44
Power	8.24	7.25	4.06	10.18	6.61	6.52	4.20	9.27

Paired samples *t*-test of constituent sectors of the sample companies based on Return on Capital Employed (*ROCE*) over phase 1 (2001–2006) and phase 2 (2007–2011).

	Phase 1 and Phase 2		
Sector	*t*	*df*	Significance (2-tailed)
FMCG	−2.352	8	0.047
Housing	−1.951	16	0.069
Metals	−1.324	17	0.203
Capital goods	−1.034	12	0.322
Miscellaneous	−0.868	15	0.399
Power	0.686	12	0.506
Oil and gas	−0.581	14	0.571
Diversified	−0.579	8	0.578
ICT	−0.158	17	0.877
Healthcare	−0.144	13	0.887
Transport	−0.047	16	0.963

Appendix 9.11: Mean, median and quartile values of return on capital employed (*ROCE*) of constituent sectors of the sample companies over phase 3 (2007–2008) and phase 4 (2009–2011)

	Phase 3 (2007–2008)				Phase 4 (2009–2011)			
Sector	Mean	Median	Quartile 1	Quartile 3	Mean	Median	Quartile 1	Quartile 3
Capital goods	26.60	26.38	20.67	33.99	18.50	18.02	13.25	25.36
Healthcare	20.10	18.31	13.36	26.26	17.75	17.28	12.10	24.12
Metals	17.70	13.88	9.34	24.36	14.09	12.46	7.74	18.94
Transport	16.79	17.48	12.04	21.16	13.95	13.00	6.93	19.54
ICT	15.74	13.11	7.37	23.39	14.43	15.96	7.79	22.09
Housing	14.58	12.84	8.10	22.58	11.77	9.80	7.07	14.02
FMCG	14.49	9.86	8.47	20.26	20.23	22.15	9.22	28.84
Miscellaneous	13.11	12.82	6.45	15.76	15.31	11.35	7.11	22.01
Diversified	12.05	10.05	4.74	17.37	9.54	7.85	1.89	12.30
Oil and gas	11.13	9.66	5.20	17.02	11.89	11.46	7.06	17.29
Power	6.00	5.91	3.37	9.21	7.02	6.92	4.76	9.30

(continued)

Appendix 9.11: (continued)

Paired samples *t*-test of constituent sectors of the sample companies based on Return on Capital Employed (*ROCE*) over phase 3 (2007–2008) and phase 4 (2009–2011).

	Phase 3 and Phase 4		
Sector	*t*	*df*	Significance (2-tailed)
Capital goods	3.872	12	0.002
Metals	2.889	17	0.010
Diversified	2.518	8	0.036
Transport	1.798	17	0.090
Healthcare	1.737	13	0.106
Housing	1.593	17	0.130
Power	−1.554	13	0.144
Miscellaneous	−1.378	15	0.188
Oil and gas	−1.235	14	0.237
ICT	0.692	16	0.499
FMCG	−0.718	6	0.500

Appendix 9.12: ANOVA of the consolidated sample and the constituent sectors of the sample companies based on return on capital employed (*ROCE*) over phase 1 (2001–2006) and phase 2 (2007–2011) and phase 3 (2007–2008) and phase 4 (2009–2011)

	Phase 1 and Phase 2		Phase 3 and Phase 4	
Sector	*F*	Significance	*F*	Significance
Consolidated	5.152	0.000	5.979	0.000
Housing	2.256	0.143	1.405	0.244
Capital goods	1.155	0.293	6.406	0.018
Metals	0.973	0.331	2.184	0.149
Power	0.726	0.402	0.747	0.395
FMCG	0.412	0.529	0.472	0.503
Miscellaneous	0.378	0.544	0.360	0.553
Transport	0.106	0.746	0.648	0.427
Diversified	0.088	0.771	0.293	0.596
ICT	0.009	0.924	0.094	0.761
Healthcare	0.009	0.926	0.582	0.453
Oil and gas	0.001	0.976	0.002	0.969

Appendix 9.13: Mean, median and quartile values of return on shareholders' equity (*ROSE*) of constituent sectors of the sample companies over phase 1 (2001–2006) and phase 2 (2007–2011)

	Phase 1 (2001–2006)				Phase 2 (2007–2011)			
Sector	Mean	Median	Quartile 1	Quartile 3	Mean	Median	Quartile 1	Quartile 3
ICT	26.87	16.72	7.70	27.51	19.31	19.97	9.95	27.77
FMCG	21.85	15.25	9.57	28.74	20.31	18.59	8.60	28.80
Healthcare	21.21	21.26	14.70	26.97	21.14	21.39	16.04	27.53
Oil and gas	20.42	20.73	15.21	24.72	16.03	16.07	12.00	21.31
Capital goods	18.12	17.01	11.98	24.26	22.02	23.13	17.23	28.67
Transport	16.28	16.66	12.23	21.34	17.67	18.93	10.89	23.15

(continued)

Appendix 9.13: (continued)

	Phase 1 (2001–2006)				Phase 2 (2007–2011)			
Sector	Mean	Median	Quartile 1	Quartile 3	Mean	Median	Quartile 1	Quartile 3
Metals	14.78	15.42	11.27	18.70	18.94	19.44	12.83	24.30
Miscellaneous	14.09	14.89	8.49	21.04	15.69	16.99	10.58	21.04
Housing	12.10	12.37	7.65	17.50	15.30	12.89	8.63	22.12
Diversified	10.70	10.23	6.89	15.57	13.43	12.40	3.10	20.83
Power	10.12	10.45	8.07	12.58	9.18	9.81	6.28	12.26

Paired samples *t*-test of constituent sectors of the sample companies based on Return on Shareholders' Equity (*ROSE*) over phase 1 (2001–2006) and phase 2 (2007–2011).

	Phase 1 and Phase 2		
Sector	*t*	*df*	Significance (2-tailed)
Housing	−1.425	16	0.173
Capital goods	−1.008	12	0.334
Miscellaneous	−0.768	15	0.454
ICT	0.743	17	0.468
Metals	−0.671	17	0.512
Power	0.660	10	0.524
Oil and gas	−0.622	14	0.544
Diversified	−0.622	8	0.551
Healthcare	0.470	13	0.646
FMCG	−0.364	9	0.724
Transport	0.114	16	0.911

Appendix 9.14: Mean, median and quartile values of return on shareholders' equity (*ROSE*) of constituent sectors of the sample companies over phase 3 (2007–2008) and phase 4 (2009–2011)

	Phase 3 (2007–2008)				Phase 4 (2009–2011)			
Sector	Mean	Median	Quartile 1	Quartile 3	Mean	Median	Quartile 1	Quartile 3
Capital goods	27.31	26.81	24.27	33.99	18.50	20.69	12.54	25.12
Healthcare	24.33	23.98	19.48	29.05	19.01	19.66	13.75	26.51
Metals	23.13	23.82	17.55	28.98	16.15	16.53	9.68	21.18
Transport	21.36	22.73	16.82	24.95	15.21	16.40	6.93	21.95
ICT	21.10	20.29	10.82	29.39	18.12	19.76	9.37	26.70
Housing	20.49	16.15	9.83	31.90	11.84	10.73	7.82	15.60
Oil and gas	18.38	19.32	14.94	23.26	13.84	14.53	10.04	20.02
FMCG	16.91	14.57	8.96	22.20	22.58	21.27	8.36	33.21
Diversified	16.07	14.61	4.81	24.13	11.67	10.93	1.96	18.63
Miscellaneous	15.66	16.57	11.75	21.00	15.71	17.27	9.81	21.07
Power	9.66	10.31	6.39	12.81	8.86	9.48	6.20	11.90

(continued)

Appendix 9.14: (continued)

Paired samples *t*-test of constituent sectors of the sample companies based on return on rhareholders' equity (*ROSE*) over phase 3 (2007–2008) and phase 4 (2009–2011).

	Phase 3 and Phase 4		
Sector	*t*	df	Significance (2-tailed)
Housing	3.852	17	0.001
Metals	4.229	17	0.001
Capital goods	3.760	12	0.003
Transport	2.919	17	0.010
Healthcare	2.514	13	0.026
ICT	1.912	15	0.075
Diversified	1.842	8	0.103
Oil and gas	1.103	14	0.289
FMCG	0.540	6	0.609
Miscellaneous	–0.286	15	0.779
Power	0.276	10	0.788

Appendix 9.15: ANOVA of the consolidated sample and the constituent sectors of the sample companies based on return on shareholders' equity (*ROSE*) over phase 1 (2001–2006) and phase 2 (2007–2011) and phase 3 (2007–2008) and phase 4 (2009–2011)

	Phase 1 and Phase 2		Phase 3 and Phase 4	
Sector	*F*	Significance	*F*	Significance
Consolidated	2.194	0.018	3.333	0.000
Housing	1.377	0.249	7.073	0.012
Capital goods	1.255	0.274	6.465	0.018
Power	0.541	0.470	0.158	0.695
ICT	0.445	0.509	0.242	0.626
Miscellaneous	0.306	0.584	0.021	0.885
Metals	0.277	0.602	4.796	0.035
Diversified	0.242	0.630	0.626	0.441
Transport	0.151	0.700	2.122	0.154
Healthcare	0.096	0.759	3.037	0.093
Oil and gas	0.027	0.870	0.641	0.430
FMCG	0.000	0.998	0.944	0.347

Appendix 9.16: Mean, median and quartile values of total assets turnover ratio (*TATR*) of constituent sectors of the sample companies over phase 1 (2001–2006) and phase 2 (2007–2011)

	Phase 1 (2001–2006)				Phase 2 (2007–2011)			
Sector	Mean	Median	Quartile 1	Quartile 3	Mean	Median	Quartile 1	Quartile 3
Capital goods	2.51	2.47	1.94	2.88	2.24	2.23	1.39	3.16
FMCG	2.03	1.57	0.97	3.01	1.62	1.14	0.77	2.01
Oil and gas	1.96	1.19	0.60	3.31	1.89	1.38	0.29	3.43
Transport	1.56	1.52	0.83	1.94	1.48	1.44	0.39	2.15
Diversified	1.40	0.94	0.51	1.38	1.39	0.90	0.45	1.64
Healthcare	1.10	1.04	0.87	1.28	0.83	0.82	0.68	0.99
Housing	1.08	0.93	0.67	1.35	0.70	0.71	0.23	1.10

(continued)

Appendix 9.16: (continued)

	Phase 1 (2001–2006)				Phase 2 (2007–2011)			
Sector	Mean	Median	Quartile 1	Quartile 3	Mean	Median	Quartile 1	Quartile 3
Metals	0.97	0.88	0.62	1.22	0.83	0.70	0.56	1.06
Miscellaneous	0.92	0.93	0.59	1.23	0.67	0.62	0.50	0.82
ICT	0.87	0.74	0.46	1.26	0.87	0.73	0.50	1.12
Power	0.53	0.41	0.23	0.56	0.51	0.32	0.11	0.49

Paired samples *t*-test of constituent sectors of the sample companies based on Total Assets Turnover Ratio (*TATR*) over phase 1 (2001–2006) and phase 2 (2007–2011).

	Phase 1 and Phase 2		
Sector	*t*	*df*	Significance (2-tailed)
Healthcare	3.967	13	0.002
Housing	2.956	16	0.009
Diversified	1.685	8	0.130
FMCG	−1.518	9	0.163
Power	1.494	10	0.166
Metals	1.423	17	0.173
Miscellaneous	1.338	15	0.201
Transport	0.977	16	0.343
Capital goods	0.929	12	0.371
Oil and gas	−0.783	13	0.448
ICT	0.258	16	0.799

Appendix 9.17: Mean, median and quartile values of total assets turnover ratio (*TATR*) of constituent sectors of the sample companies over phase 3 (2007–2008) and phase 4 (2009–2011)

	Phase 3 (2007–2008)				Phase 4 (2009–2011)			
Sector	Mean	Median	Quartile 1	Quartile 3	Mean	Median	Quartile 1	Quartile 3
Capital goods	2.82	2.80	1.73	3.96	1.85	1.85	1.16	2.62
FMCG	2.01	1.26	0.76	2.89	1.36	1.06	0.78	1.43
Oil and gas	1.84	1.14	0.20	3.65	1.92	1.53	0.34	3.28
Transport	1.53	1.64	0.43	2.23	1.44	1.31	0.36	2.10
Diversified	1.51	0.93	0.46	1.83	1.30	0.88	0.44	1.51
ICT	0.98	0.79	0.53	1.24	0.79	0.69	0.48	1.04
Metals	0.93	0.80	0.66	1.15	0.76	0.63	0.49	1.00
Healthcare	0.89	0.85	0.74	1.06	0.79	0.79	0.63	0.95
Housing	0.78	0.81	0.34	1.23	0.65	0.65	0.15	1.01
Miscellaneous	0.61	0.58	0.43	0.66	0.71	0.65	0.54	0.92
Power	0.40	0.31	0.12	0.49	0.59	0.32	0.10	0.49

Paired samples *t*-test of constituent sectors of the sample companies based on Total Assets Turnover Ratio (*TATR*) over phase 3 (2007–2008) and phase 4 (2009–2011).

	Phase 3 and Phase 4		
Sector	*t*	*df*	Significance (2-tailed)
Capital goods	5.809	12	0.000
ICT	2.506	17	0.023

(continued)

Appendix 9.17: (continued)

	Phase 3 and Phase 4		
Sector	*t*	*df*	Significance (2-tailed)
Healthcare	2.461	12	0.030
Housing	2.323	17	0.033
Miscellaneous	−2.189	15	0.045
Metals	1.843	17	0.083
Diversified	1.647	8	0.138
Transport	1.557	17	0.138
FMCG	1.563	7	0.162
Power	−1.080	11	0.303
Oil and gas	−0.248	15	0.807

Appendix 9.18: ANOVA of the consolidated sample and the constituent sectors of the sample companies based on total assets turnover ratio (*TATR*) over phase 1 (2001–2006) and phase 2 (2007–2011) and phase 3 (2007–2008) and phase 4 (2009–2011)

	Phase 1 and Phase 2		Phase 3 and Phase 4	
Sector	*F*	Significance	*F*	Significance
Consolidated	6.771	0.000	7.428	0.000
Healthcare	7.276	0.012	1.681	0.207
Housing	3.745	0.062	0.600	0.444
Metals	1.711	0.200	1.947	0.172
Power	0.704	0.410	0.015	0.902
Diversified	0.461	0.507	0.064	0.804
Capital goods	0.309	0.583	4.596	0.042
ICT	0.133	0.718	1.050	0.313
FMCG	0.080	0.781	2.359	0.143
Miscellaneous	0.050	0.824	0.249	0.621
Transport	0.003	0.957	0.138	0.713
Oil and gas	0.001	0.976	0.005	0.946

Appendix 9.19: Mean, median and quartile values of fixed assets turnover ratio (*FATR*) of constituent sectors of the sample companies over phase 1 (2001–2006) and phase 2 (2007–2011)

	Phase 1 (2001–2006)				Phase 2 (2007–2011)			
Sector	Mean	Median	Quartile 1	Quartile 3	Mean	Median	Quartile 1	Quartile 3
Capital goods	6.52	6.81	5.42	8.27	6.89	7.12	5.44	8.23
FMCG	4.48	4.70	2.75	5.64	5.17	5.52	3.41	7.14
Oil and gas	3.67	2.42	1.30	6.34	3.78	2.70	1.37	6.57
Transport	3.05	2.33	1.20	4.29	3.50	2.95	0.70	5.65
ICT	3.03	2.50	1.05	4.84	3.53	2.54	0.87	5.97
Healthcare	2.94	2.64	2.00	3.39	3.01	2.78	2.08	3.17
Housing	2.76	1.60	1.01	3.74	2.93	1.71	1.07	3.72
Miscellaneous	2.47	1.91	1.36	3.23	2.76	1.91	1.25	2.89
Diversified	2.30	1.75	1.60	2.32	2.95	2.72	1.95	3.38
Metals	2.09	1.85	1.08	2.73	2.78	2.02	1.25	3.10
Power	0.82	0.76	0.30	1.14	1.19	0.73	0.24	1.34

(continued)

Appendix 9.19: (continued)

Paired samples *t*-test of constituent sectors of the sample companies based on Fixed Assets Turnover Ratio (*FATR*) over phase 1 (2001–2006) and phase 2 (2007–2011).

	Phase 1 and Phase 2		
Sector	*t*	*df*	Significance (2-tailed)
FMCG	−3.471	11	0.005
Oil and gas	−2.611	12	0.023
Metals	−2.230	17	0.040
Diversified	−2.652	5	0.045
Transport	−2.007	16	0.062
ICT	−1.543	15	0.144
Capital goods	−1.438	11	0.178
Healthcare	−1.063	12	0.309
Power	0.938	9	0.373
Housing	−0.881	14	0.393
Miscellaneous	−0.845	13	0.413

Appendix 9.20: Mean, median and quartile values of fixed assets turnover ratio (*FATR*) of constituent sectors of the sample companies over phase 3 (2007–2008) and phase 4 (2009–2011)

	Phase 3 (2007–2008)				Phase 4 (2009–2011)			
Sector	Mean	Median	Quartile 1	Quartile 3	Mean	Median	Quartile 1	Quartile 3
Capital goods	6.89	7.63	6.01	8.19	6.89	6.77	5.06	8.27
FMCG	5.14	5.47	3.33	7.12	5.19	5.55	3.46	7.15
Transport	3.79	4.21	0.79	6.00	3.31	2.10	0.63	5.42
Oil and gas	3.68	2.16	1.08	7.14	3.85	3.05	1.56	6.19
ICT	3.44	2.03	0.98	5.94	3.59	2.87	0.80	6.00
Metals	3.30	2.24	1.33	3.63	2.43	1.87	1.20	2.74
Miscellaneous	2.92	2.04	1.23	2.96	2.66	1.82	1.27	2.84
Healthcare	2.86	2.60	2.02	2.98	3.11	2.91	2.12	3.30
Housing	2.80	2.02	1.16	3.50	3.02	1.51	1.01	3.87
Diversified	2.31	2.54	1.94	2.77	3.38	2.85	1.95	3.78
Power	1.58	0.75	0.25	1.63	0.93	0.71	0.24	1.16

Paired samples *t*-test of constituent sectors of the sample companies based on Fixed Assets Turnover Ratio (*FATR*) over phase 3 (2007–2008) and phase 4 (2009–2011).

	Phase 3 and Phase 4		
Sector	*t*	*df*	Significance (2-tailed)
Transport	2.047	16	0.057
Metals	1.741	16	0.101
Diversified	−2.005	4	0.115
FMCG	−1.108	9	0.297
Healthcare	−1.058	12	0.311
Capital goods	1.109	5	0.318
Power	0.986	10	0.347
Miscellaneous	0.907	13	0.381
Oil and gas	−0.662	14	0.519
ICT	0.289	15	0.777
Housing	0.134	12	0.896

Appendix 9.21: ANOVA of the consolidated sample and the constituent sectors of the sample companies based on fixed assets turnover ratio (*FATR*) over phase 1 (2001–2006) and phase 2 (2007–2011) and phase 3 (2007–2008) and phase 4 (2009–2011)

	Phase 1 and Phase 2		Phase 3 and Phase 4	
Sector	*F*	Significance	*F*	Significance
Consolidated	7.064	0.000	7.302	0.000
Metals	2.676	0.111	0.832	0.368
Capital goods	1.121	0.301	0.063	0.805
FMCG	0.985	0.332	0.002	0.969
Power	0.892	0.356	0.883	0.358
Transport	0.574	0.454	0.030	0.863
ICT	0.426	0.518	0.017	0.897
Oil and gas	0.323	0.574	0.070	0.793
Miscellaneous	0.256	0.617	0.029	0.866
Diversified	0.097	0.762	1.547	0.245
Housing	0.001	0.978	0.158	0.694
Healthcare	0.000	0.988	0.126	0.725

Appendix 9.22: Mean, median and quartile values of current assets turnover ratio (*CATR*) of constituent sectors of the sample companies over phase 1 (2001–2006) and phase 2 *(2007–2011)*

	Phase 1 (2001–2006)				Phase 2 (2007–2011)			
Sector	Mean	Median	Quartile 1	Quartile 3	Mean	Median	Quartile 1	Quartile 3
FMCG	2.96	2.61	1.94	3.53	2.80	2.72	1.98	3.45
Oil and gas	2.69	2.36	1.05	3.84	2.88	2.09	0.82	4.90
Transport	2.32	2.12	1.75	2.61	2.37	2.13	1.31	2.99
Miscellaneous	2.04	1.73	1.02	2.91	1.81	1.46	0.85	2.41
Metals	1.88	1.86	1.41	2.26	1.69	1.50	0.97	2.22
Diversified	1.87	1.79	1.24	2.53	1.69	1.93	0.60	2.34
Housing	1.59	1.40	0.86	2.00	1.24	0.83	0.26	1.33
Healthcare	1.53	1.42	1.14	1.92	1.29	1.26	0.97	1.59
ICT	1.44	1.35	0.89	1.95	1.64	1.42	0.74	2.32
Capital goods	1.39	1.44	1.08	1.63	1.54	1.31	0.85	1.71
Power	1.38	1.16	0.77	1.56	1.13	0.81	0.44	1.33

Paired samples *t*-test of constituent sectors of the sample companies based on Current Assets Turnover Ratio (*CATR*) over phase 1 (2001–2006) and phase 2 (2007–2011).

	Phase 1 and Phase 2		
Sector	*t*	d*f*	Significance (2-tailed)
Healthcare	2.199	13	0.047
Housing	1.818	16	0.088
Oil and gas	−1.845	13	0.088
Miscellaneous	0.964	15	0.350
Metals	0.850	17	0.407
Power	0.840	10	0.421
Capital goods	−0.830	12	0.423
Diversified	0.605	8	0.562
FMCG	0.552	11	0.592
ICT	−0.497	16	0.626
Transport	0.362	16	0.722

Appendix 9.23: Mean, median and quartile values of current assets turnover ratio (*CATR*) of constituent sectors of the sample companies over phase 3 (2007–2008) and phase 4 (2009–2011)

	Phase 3 (2007–2008)				Phase 4 (2009–2011)			
Sector	Mean	Median	Quartile 1	Quartile 3	Mean	Median	Quartile 1	Quartile 3
FMCG	2.89	2.81	1.89	3.76	2.75	2.67	2.04	3.23
Oil and gas	2.65	1.60	0.60	4.84	3.04	2.41	0.96	4.95
Transport	2.25	2.18	1.33	2.70	2.45	2.10	1.30	3.17
Metals	2.01	1.77	1.08	2.72	1.48	1.32	0.89	1.90
Miscellaneous	1.75	1.48	0.73	2.43	1.85	1.45	0.93	2.40
ICT	1.71	1.60	0.70	2.41	1.59	1.30	0.76	2.26
Diversified	1.66	1.91	0.80	2.36	1.71	1.95	0.47	2.33
Capital goods	1.60	1.49	1.00	1.93	1.50	1.20	0.75	1.56
Healthcare	1.37	1.30	0.97	1.75	1.24	1.23	0.97	1.48
Housing	1.34	0.85	0.41	1.38	1.17	0.81	0.17	1.30
Power	0.95	0.83	0.50	1.33	1.25	0.79	0.40	1.32

Paired samples *t*-test of constituent sectors of the sample companies based on Current Assets Turnover Ratio (*CATR*) over phase 3 (2007–2008) and phase 4 (2009–2011).

	Phase 3 and Phase 4		
Sector	*t*	*df*	Significance (2-tailed)
Metals	2.506	17	0.023
Housing	1.878	17	0.078
ICT	1.782	17	0.093
Healthcare	1.393	13	0.187
FMCG	1.264	11	0.232
Oil and gas	−1.011	14	0.329
Capital goods	0.886	12	0.393
Miscellaneous	−0.850	15	0.409
Transport	−0.423	16	0.678
Diversified	−0.371	8	0.720
Power	0.313	10	0.760

Appendix 9.24: ANOVA of the consolidated sample and the constituent sectors of the sample companies based on current assets turnover ratio (*CATR*) over phase 1 (2001–2006) and phase 2 (2007–2011) and phase 3 (2007–2008)and phase 4 (2009–2011)

	Phase 1 and Phase 2		Phase 3 and Phase 4	
Sector	*F*	Significance	*F*	Significance
Consolidated	6.319	0.000	6.179	0.000
Healthcare	1.295	0.265	0.680	0.417
Power	0.803	0.379	0.205	0.655
Housing	0.745	0.394	0.150	0.701
Metals	0.389	0.537	2.566	0.118
Capital goods	0.261	0.614	0.076	0.784
Miscellaneous	0.203	0.656	0.368	0.549
Oil and gas	0.107	0.746	0.149	0.702
Diversified	0.107	0.748	0.009	0.925
FMCG	0.081	0.779	0.152	0.701
ICT	0.010	0.921	0.128	0.723
Transport	0.002	0.964	0.226	0.638

References

Claver E, Molina J, Tari J (2002) Firm and industry effects on firm profitability: a Spanish empirical analysis. Eur Manage J 20(3):321–328
Economic Surveys of India. http://indiabudget.nic.in/. Accessed 17 Nov 2011
Fukui Y, Ushijima T (2011) What drives the profitability of Japanese multi-business corporations? A variance components analysis. J Jpn Int Econ 25:1–11
Holz CA (2002) The impact of the liability–asset ratio on profitability in China's industrial state-owned enterprises. China Econ Rev 13(1):1–26
Jain PK, Yadav SS (2005) Financial management practices – a study of public sector enterprises in India. Hindustan Publishing Corporation, New Delhi
Niu J, Yue H, Jiang G (2008) Profitability analysis of Chinese listed firms: 1992–2004. Front Bus Res China 2(4):497–517. doi:10.1007/s11782-008-0029-0
Karacaer S, Kapusuzoğlu A (2008) An analysis of the effect of financial ratios on financial situation of Turkish enterprises resulting from their annual operations. Int Res J Finance Econ 19:139–149, ISSN 1450-2887
Kaymaz Ö, Kaymaz Ö (2010) The firm-level determinants underlying the profitability in brokerage institutions: some evidence from Turkey. Afr J Bus Manage 4(2):172–190
Monea M (2009) Financial ratios – reveal how a business is doing? Ann Univ Petroşani Econ 9(2):137–144
Nissim D, Penman SH (2001) Analysis and equity valuation: from research to practice. Rev Acc Stud 6(1):109–154
Rajan MV, Reichelstein S, Soliman MT (2006) Conservatism, growth, and return on investment. Research Paper No. 1956, Research paper series. Stanford Graduate School of Business, Stanford
Reserve Bank of India's Database on Indian Economy. http://dbie.rbi.org.in/InfoViewApp/listing/main.do?appKind=InfoView&service=%2FInfoViewApp%2Fcommon%2FappService.do. Accessed 19 Oct 2011
Reserve Bank of India's website. http://rbidocs.rbi.org.in/rdocs/Speeches/PDFs/87784.pdf. Accessed 17 Nov 2011
United Nations Council on Trade and Development (UNCTAD) website. http://www.unctad.org/en/docs/webdiaeia20095_en.pdf. Accessed 17 Nov 2011
Zeli A, Mariani P (2009) Productivity and profitability analysis of large Italian companies: 1998–2002. Int Rev Econ 56(2):175–188
Zhang A, Zhang Y, Zhao R (2002) Profitability and productivity of Chinese industrial firms: measurement and ownership implications. China Econ Rev 13(1):65–88

Chapter 10
Concluding Observations

The objective of this concluding chapter is to provide a bird's eye view of financial management practices followed by the sample companies and their implications. This study has examined financial management practices amongst the 166 nonfinancial companies (segregated into 11 constituent sectors) comprising the BSE-200 index. The analysis is based on secondary as well as primary data. The secondary data is related to the 11-year period with effect from 2000–2001 to 2010–2011. The primary data takes into account the survey responses from 31 companies (amongst the 166 companies) on various aspects of financial decision-making. The study has dwelt upon the following specific dimensions of financial management of the sample companies:

- Capital budgeting practices.
- Capital structure decisions.
- Management of working capital.
- Dividend policy decisions.
- Risk management practices (especially related to international transactions).
- Corporate governance practices.
- Profitability analysis.

In the light of financial management practices followed, an attempt has been made to devise/develop an index of professionalism in financial management (IPF), based on normative framework/sound tenets to be used for such financial decisions.

The important conclusions emerging out of the study may now be underlined.

Capital budgeting practices in India, at least amongst the sample companies, appear to have improved over the past two decades with an increasing number of companies using more sophisticated DCF techniques. A striking finding of the survey is that internal rate of return (IRR) is preferred over the net present value (NPV) method by most of the sample companies, in spite of the superiority of the NPV method. The theory–practice gap is a recurrent theme in the capital budgeting literature, in particular with regard to NPV. Despite the recommendations of the financial

P.K. Jain et al., *Financial Management Practices: An Empirical Study of Indian Corporates*, India Studies in Business and Economics,
DOI 10.1007/978-81-322-0990-4_10, © Springer India 2013

literature on using NPV as the primary technique, this research too found that respondent firms indicated a preference for IRR compared to NPV.

As far as the capital expenditure activity is concerned, the sample companies have made substantial investments in acquisition of new fixed assets. It is pertinent as well as satisfactory to note that paucity of funds is not an inhibiting factor in undertaking capital projects by the sample companies. While it is true that the post-liberalisation period has witnessed a salubrious effect on their investment activity, the rate of investment in new fixed assets (measured on a year-to-year basis) has been impressive in that it has been at a rate of 18.06% during the 11-year period of the study. This is in contrast to the modest figure of less than 5% recorded for the public sector enterprises (PSEs) over a 13-year period (1991–2003) in a separate study conducted by the authors (Jain and Yadav 2005). Above all, the global recession has not impacted the sample companies (representing vital segment of Indian economy) significantly.

As far as the financing pattern of long-term investment projects is concerned, it is satisfying to note that the sample companies are following sound policies in this regard – their fixed assets have been financed from long-term sources. In fact, more commendable is the aspect that their permanent working capital needs have also been financed through long-term sources of finance. This is in conformity with the sound principles of financial management.

Cost of capital constitutes an integral part of capital budgeting proposals. It is encouraging to note that the vast majority of the sample companies follow theoretically sound and conceptually correct basis of computing cost of capital, that is, weighted average cost of capital (WACC). More than two-thirds (67.85%) of the firms have been following the appropriate WACC basis compared to other methods, suggesting a reduction in the theory–practice gap compared to the past studies. Also, consistent with finance theory, the survey reveals that the sample companies are risk-averse. Sensitivity analysis is the most popular approach used by these companies to incorporate risk in their capital budgeting decisions, followed by shorter payback period method and higher cut-off rate for more risky projects.

Another notable finding is the emergence of new techniques of real options and abandonment options as a part of practice by the sample companies, while evaluating capital budgeting proposals. This perhaps signals the adoption of emerging techniques by our the sample companies, an encouraging indication of growing professionalism amongst them. Half of the respondent firms (50%) used real options while evaluating their investment projects. The results are in sharp contrast with other international studies reporting low usages.

Very high fixed-cost components of capital projects and the irregularities in prediction of future cash flows due to decrease in sales and increased competition seem to be the major factors leading to failures of capital budgeting decisions for the sample companies. This is perhaps a reflection of the growing challenges of a volatile global marketplace.

As far as designing of *capital structure* is concerned, the study brings to fore that debt (which was the most important constituent of corporate financing during pre-economic liberalisation period) is steadily being replaced by equity by the majority of the sample companies in India. This is an aspect that is corroborated as well, from the steadily declining debt–equity ratios over the past two decades brought forth by the earlier studies.

Another notable finding of the study is that there seems to be a significant portion of short-term debt in the total debt. Reliance on short-term debt to such a marked extent in preference to long-term debt is not in conformity with sound tenets of finance theory as it causes grave risk, at least, in terms of non-renewal and interest rate fluctuations. Therefore, there is need for substitution of short-term debt with long-term sources, in particular, when the requirements are permanent in nature.

It is also pertinent to revisit here that the development/public financial institutions (DFIs/PFIs) constituted the backbone of the Indian financial system until 2000; however, their relative significance in the emerging financial scenario had been declining, indicating a shift in corporate financing in India, in terms of greater reliance of industry on non-institutional sources of finance and greater recourse to the capital market.

Another important aspect that may be favouring equity financing (even though it is a more expensive source of finance vis-à-vis debt) is the growing impression that credits publicly traded (listed) companies with greater transparency and enhanced goodwill and more professional operations (when compared to their debt dominated counterparts). After clause 49 of corporate governance becoming mandatory in India (from 1 April 2006), companies that disclose material information (as a part of being publicly traded) are assumed to have better financial discipline, diversified/pedigree ownership, better corporate governance and management and corporate social responsibility. It is our contention that these aspects (now and in the future) will perhaps increasingly affect the valuations of companies. This could be the possible future indication of our findings and the road ahead for corporate financing.

Yet another notable finding of the study is that the sample companies seem to be comfortable with the servicing of debt in terms of both payment of interest and repayment of principal. It is pertinent to note here that this level of comfort could also be brought about by the steadily declining proportion of debt in the capital structure of such companies (over the past two decades). Further, companies are even able to meet their total external obligations comfortably indicating sound earning capacity. Given the fact that the companies raise funds (externally) to meet their financial needs, they are perforce to have sound fundamentals in terms of reasonable/low risk and so on. It is satisfying to note, then, that they have low operating and financial risk (as per operating and financial leverage).

A matter of concern is the finding of a low component of secured loans to total borrowings. These large the sample companies with substantial assets base should be able to raise finance from secured loans as it will relatively (probably) be the cheaper source of finance compared to other borrowings. Hence, there is untapped opportunity of lowering cost of capital by having the relatively lower cost of debt.

Another important finding is that the sample companies show non-adherence to the pecking order hypothesis (in its entirety). This could perhaps be due to the robust capital markets in the country making it easier for the companies to raise equity. This further strengthens our contention that equity for aspects like signalling theory and reduction in agency costs is finding favour with the sample companies over the traditional model of debt being utilised first and equity finance only being raised as the last resort (under the pecking order hypothesis).

Majority of the sample companies follow stable *dividend policy* (they seem to follow an approach similar to Lintner's model). The survey findings on the preference to adopt stable dividend policy were in fact more encouraging. This practice is in tune with the sound principles of financial management. In terms of amount, however, the companies have paid out less than one-quarter of their net profits after taxes as dividends during the 11-year period of the study. The low dividend payout ratio signifies that retained earnings constitute an important source of finance for the sample companies and also that the companies have growth opportunities necessitating the ploughing back of earnings.

It is satisfying to note that the sample companies have comfortable short-term liquidity/financial position (reflected in mean current ratio and acid-test ratio for the 11-year period) and, therefore, are not likely to encounter any major difficulty in paying/discharging their short-term obligations in time. As far as cash management is concerned, it is encouraging to note that the sample companies are following sound cash management practices. While cash credit limit (from the banks) constitutes the major source of dealing with cash deficit situations, deposit with banks for short term has been identified as the important method of deploying cash by majority of the sample companies. Further, cash credit facility from the banks appears to be an enabling factor for the sample companies to operate at lower cash balances.

Likewise, it is a matter of satisfaction to note that the sample companies have reasonably low holding period for raw materials, work-in-process and finished goods inventory. Given the fact that carrying inventory involves substantial financial costs, this is sound inventory management. Debtors and creditors form other significant constituents of *working capital* cycle. It is common practice amongst the sample companies to assess the financial health of customers before granting credit and to prepare ageing schedule of debtors for monitoring purposes.

Another notable finding is that the sample companies use the professional method of 'determination of individual components of current assets and current liabilities (based on raw material holding period, debtors' collection period, creditors' payment period and so on)' as the basis of working capital determination. As far as the policy towards financing working capital is concerned, 'permanent needs from long-term sources and temporary/seasonal needs from short-term sources' (the 'matching' approach) seem to be favoured by the majority. These findings are in conformity with sound theory of financial management.

Although extraordinary situations involving shortage and surplus of working capital (including cash) cannot be completely eliminated, their frequency can be minimised through rationalisation and standardisation of working capital management practices. It is encouraging to note that the majority of the sample companies have not experienced working capital shortage and if they do, they face it only occasionally. Poor collections from debtors and accumulation of excess inventory have been cited as the two major reasons for working capital deficiency by such companies. In surplus working capital situation, it is equally satisfying to note that funds are not kept idle. They have been temporarily parked in banks in the form of special deposits or utilised to retire short-term debt by most of the sample companies.

It appears that the components of cash and bank, inventory and debtors and bills receivables account for more than 60% of the total current assets for the sample companies indicating a high degree of advance payments and/or prepaid expenses in the balance sheets of the companies.

Perhaps for the first time, the concept of zero working capital (inventory + debtors – payables) and its practice amongst the sample companies was studied. It is encouraging to note that one-fourth of the sample companies are operating on zero working capital. Even though the statistics supporting zero working capital seem modest, the trend does support growing aggressiveness/professionalism in the management of working capital by the sample companies.

The constituent sectors exhibit variations amongst all aspects of working capital management. Some sectors (FMCG, housing, metals and power) appear to have been impacted from the recession, but most of the sectors seem to have withered the post-recession period with little/no alterations in their working capital management.

In brief, the importance of liquidity is not lost on the sample companies. However, the sample companies could do well to be more aggressive with their working capital management as they are large and stable companies and may attempt a better trade-off between risk and profitability.

In spite of the sample companies being amongst the largest companies in India (with substantial international exposure in terms of size of transactions), their holding pattern still remains dominantly domestic. This is perhaps due to the restrictions imposed on FDI by RBI. This factor could have been responsible in part for the relative insulation of the Indian economy in the aftermath of the financial crisis originating in the USA in the later part of 2007. Though the Indian economy has faced a recession, the profitability of the sample companies has not suffered any considerable damage.

The survey on *risk management* practices with regard to international operations in the sample companies elicited responses from practitioners on political risk, exchange rate risk and interest rate risk, respectively. The responses revealed that the sample companies are taking steps to mitigate such risks currently and also envisage using newer risk management instruments/techniques in future.

The sample companies would like to reduce political or country risk by incorporating a risk premium in the cost of capital. Amongst other measures, creating a joint venture with an enterprise of the host country is the most preferred one. As regards exchange risk management, in case of anticipated depreciation, companies are selling local currency forward, borrowing locally and invoicing exports in foreign currency and imports in local currency. In the case of anticipated appreciation, the most likely ways are to buy local currency forward and to reduce local currency borrowing. From the survey, it is apparent that the sample companies are only using netting and back-to-back swap (internal techniques of exchange risk management) in any significant manner. As regards the use of external techniques, forwards are the most preferred, followed by currency swaps, currency options and currency futures. Exchange risk management is organised by internal teams as well as with the help of outside institutional consultants. The survey revealed that the sample companies are faced with interest rate risk and they would like to use newer instruments including derivatives such as interest rate options, swaps and futures as they become more and more prevalent in the market.

An overwhelming majority of companies (96.42%) respond that risk is understood in its entirety by the company and measures are taken to mitigate it. This is an indication of the sophisticated risk assessment and management practices being followed by the sample companies.

Profitability of the sample companies (measured through gross profit and net profit), prima facie, appears to be stable and attractive (as an investment choice). Though the recession in phase four did witness some fluctuations in the profitability of certain constituent sectors like the metals sector, sectors like housing and power increased profits in a statistically significant manner, overall, the sample seems to have emerged unscathed from the impact of the recession, perhaps due to its strong management fundamentals. The other aspects of profitability, namely, return on total assets (ROTA), return on capital employed (ROCE) and earnings for equity owners (reflected in ROSE) appear to be equally satisfactory. All in all, not only are the sample companies deploying funds efficiently and providing adequate returns to the capital providers, they are working towards generating better returns for their shareholders. These findings are notable as well as they support the RBI's views on the resilience of the Indian economy.

It appears that the sample companies do adhere to certain aspects of *corporate governance* but not in its entirety. This is an area of concern as the sample companies are amongst the largest companies in the country (and as such have a large number of stakeholders they are responsible to). In that regard, they have a larger image to protect. At the time of writing this monograph, 6 years have passed since the date when clause 49 became mandatory. The companies have had adequate time to set up corporate governance structures and practices (in the meanwhile). It is important that the Indian corporates need to regard the issue of governance not as an irritant or impediment but as an essential tool and mechanism for their very survival in the new economic environment. The sample companies, thus, can do well to be more serious and professional about adopting and practising good corporate governance.

Finally, what has been described and discussed above was included in the development of an *index of professional practices* relating to financial management. The index has been developed in the basis of the responses received to a questionnaire sent to all the 166 the sample companies. Though the number of responses received, being 31, was not very high, it can be considered a fairly good representation of the sample. In conclusion, it can be said that the sample companies are using sound financial management practices in a great measure. However, there is a greater scope for improving professionalism in some categories of financial management practices (like capital structure and risk management) than others.

In conclusion, it appears safe to summarise that the sample companies seem to be following sound financial management practices. Needless to say, there are several areas where more emphasis in training and practice could further enhance financial decision-making (this has been highlighted in the form of a normative framework at the end of the chapters). Nonetheless, this research adds to the body of knowledge on financial decision-making by showing where Indian companies stand in this decade and identifying specific areas for improvement. There are surprising (rather positive) findings like use of WACC, extensive use of DCF methods, prevalence of use real options, easy financing of assets, aggressive working capital management, adequate coverage of total external obligations, stable dividend policies and encouraging profitability and efficiency levels, indicating the growing sophistication in financial decision-making.

Reference

Jain PK, Yadav SS (2005) Financial management practices – a study of public sector enterprises in India. Hindustan Publishing Corporation, New Delhi

Authors' Profiles

P.K. Jain is a Professor of Finance and the Modi Chair Professor at the Department of Management Studies, Indian Institute of Technology (IIT Delhi), India. He has been the Dalmia Chair Professor as well. Recently, he has been awarded with 'Best Faculty Award' at IIT Delhi. He has more than 40 years of teaching experience in subjects related to Management Accounting, Financial Management, Financial Analysis, Cost Analysis and Cost Control. He has been a visiting faculty at the AIT Bangkok; University of Paris; Howe School of Technology Management at Stevens Institute of Technology, New Jersey; and ICPE, Ljubljana. He has authored three well-known text books published by TMH and more than ten research monographs. He has contributed more than 150 research papers in journals of national and international repute. Email: pkjain@dms.iitd.ac.in

Shveta Singh is an Assistant Professor of finance at the Department of Management Studies, Indian Institute of Technology (IIT Delhi), India. She teaches Managerial Accounting and Financial Management, Indian Financial System and Security Analysis and Portfolio Management. Overall, she has more than a decade of professional experience, having spent three years in the corporate sector prior to joining academics. She has published research papers in journals of national and international repute. Email: shvetasingh@dms.iitd.ac.in

Surendra S. Yadav is a Professor of Finance at the Department of Management Studies, Indian Institute of Technology (IIT Delhi), India. He teaches Corporate Finance, International Finance, International Business and Security Analysis and Portfolio Management. He has been a visiting professor at the University of Paris, Paris School of Management, INSEEC Paris, and the University of Tampa, USA. He has published nine books and contributed more than 150 papers to research journals and conferences. He has also contributed more than 30 papers to financial/economic newspapers. He is the editor-in-chief of the *Journal of Advances in Management Research* (JAMR) published by Emerald Publishing, UK. Email: ssyadav@dms.iitd.ac.in

P.K. Jain et al., *Financial Management Practices: An Empirical Study of Indian Corporates*, India Studies in Business and Economics,
DOI 10.1007/978-81-322-0990-4, © Springer India 2013

Index

P.K. Jain et al., *Financial Management Practices: An Empirical Study of Indian Corporates*, India Studies in Business and Economics,
DOI 10.1007/978-81-322-0990-4,

D

E

Printed by Printforce, the Netherlands